ANGLO-SAXON ORAL POETRY

ANGLO-SAXON ORAL POETRY

POETRY

A Study of the Traditions

JEFF OPLAND

YALE UNIVERSITY PRESS
NEW HAVEN AND LONDON
1980

Designed by James J. Johnson
and set in Monotype Bembo type.
Printed in the United States of America by
Edwards Brothers Inc., Ann Arbor, Michigan.

Library of Congress Cataloging in Publication Data

Opland, Jeff, 1943–
   Anglo-Saxon oral poetry.

   Bibliography: p.
   Includes index.
   1.   Anglo-Saxon poetry—History and criticism.
2.   Folk poetry, Anglo-Saxon—History and criticism.
3.   Oral tradition—England.   I.   Title.
PR203.06   829′.1   79–24202
ISBN 0–300–02426–6

10   9   8   7   6   5   4   3   2   1

Contents

For Cynthia

Preface

This book attempts to describe an essentially ephemeral phenomenon that disappeared at least 900 years ago: the poetry that was diffused orally by the Anglo-Saxons. It attempts to do this through a study of all the available sources of evidence extant from Anglo-Saxon England. Where such evidence is confusing or lacking, reference is made to information derived from the study of other oral poetic traditions, living or dead.

Oral poetry concerned students of Anglo-Saxon literature long before Francis Magoun took up Albert Lord's comparative studies thirty years ago and applied some of Lord's theories to the evidence of some Old English texts. The debate that ensued in Anglo-Saxon studies (see Watts) produced much information about the style and diction of the extant literature, but I am not primarily concerned with that extant literature. The reader will search in vain here for any contribution to the debate on the formula (see most recently Miletich; Whitman); this book is not a survey of the extant literature, for which the reader is directed to the standard works of such scholars as G. K. Anderson, Greenfield, Malone, Shippey, or Wrenn. I seek, rather, to characterise the Anglo-Saxon traditions of oral poetry, to study the role of oral poetry in early English society, and to try to understand how poetry lived and operated among the people. My work is related to the attempts of R. M. Wilson and C. E. Wright to provide an account of what has not survived from Anglo-Saxon times, to supplement the extant literature by placing it in the context of English tradition. In many ways it is an extension of the work of scholars such as Heusler, Norman (1938), Padelford, Werlich, and Wissmann, who have surveyed extant references to the Germanic poet in an attempt to characterise the role of the poet or of poetry in society.

The approach to the subject of Anglo-Saxon oral poetry adopted in this book differs in three respects from other studies of the same subject: it accepts only the evidence in Old English or Anglo-Latin extant from Anglo-Saxon England as primary; it surveys that evidence chronologically; and for supplementary evidence it draws to a large extent on the living traditions of Africa. I have tried to assemble as much primary information as I could find that is relevant to our understanding of Anglo-Saxon oral poetry, and have tried to separate that evidence quite clearly from all other evidence, which I consider to be secondary. Scholars may well adduce other secondary evidence, or find fault with my interpretation of the primary evidence; certainly the conclusions I arrive at are often hypothetical, tentative, or based on limited data. Any alternative interpretations or conclusions, however, must not be based on a convenient selection of evidence; they must provide a reasonable explanation of *all* the primary evidence available to us. My conclusions attempt to do no more than that.

Two scholarly idiosyncracies call for explanation. Since this book is intended to be a confrontation with the primary evidence, I avoid the opportunity either to summarise the conclusions of other scholars who have analysed the same evidence or to set out my points of agreement or disagreement with them. My documentation accordingly is solely bibliographical. At points in the text chosen to provide least distraction to the reader, I have inserted references to the bibliography at the end of the book. In this way I have eschewed footnotes and have, I hope, maintained a sound and happy relationship with the publishers while doing my bit to stem the tide of rampant scholarly annotation. My second idiosyncracy has to do with the vexed question of Anglo-Saxon names, especially the Ethels and the Alfs. After due deliberation, I have decided on the grounds of consistency to use an *A* for all names commencing with *Æ*, as we usually do for Alfred (Old English *Ælfred*). There is no difference in pronunciation. Thus Anglo-Saxon scholars might well take exception to my *Alfric*, but should consider the noninitiate who might be puzzled by the pronunciation of *Ælfric* or *Aelfric*; after all, we do make concessions by writing *th* for *þ*. So I choose *Athelred* rather than *Æthelræd*, *Ethelred*, or any of the other orthographical permutations.

My debt to colleagues and friends is great. In my own ideas I have been more influenced by the research of Albert Lord than by that of any other scholar; the immense respect I feel for his work is unimpaired by any disagreement I may presume to have with him on points of detail. A number of colleagues who encouraged me in my work have helped me more than they can imagine: I am deeply indebted to Larry Benson, Thomas Cable, Angus Cameron, Colin Chase, Trevor Cope, T. R. H. Davenport, Joseph Duggan, Robert T. Farrell, Derek Fivaz, Roberta Frank, Donald K. Fry, Joseph Harris, Thomas D. Hill, R. E. Kaske, Albert Lord, Wallace McLeod, Herbert Pahl, Alain Renoir, Michael Roberts, Fr. Michael Sheehan, Fr. Laurence K. Shook, Rudy Spraycar, and especially Jess Bessinger, who generously sustained me through many years in the wilderness. I profited greatly from discussions with my students at the Pontifical Institute of Mediaeval Studies and the Centre for Medieval Studies at the University of Toronto in 1975; I am particularly indebted to those whose research produced material for chapter 9, Alison Kingsmill, Lance Reemtsma, and especially Bill Stoneman and Mary Jo Calarco. I owe a special debt of gratitude to John Leyerle, who did so much more for me than offer advice and criticism based on his experiences with me in the field, and above all to Morton Bloomfield and Fred Robinson, who joined me on memorable field trips and who read and commented on a draft of this book. The book is mine, circumscribed by my scholarly limitations, but I have profited personally by my association with these scholars, and with many others besides. I am grateful to the Human Sciences Research Council of South Africa for the award of a Senior Bursary in 1975, which contributed to the cost of research for this book. Parts of chapters 1 and 8 have appeared in articles in *Mediaeval Studies* and *Acta Germanica*; I am grateful to the editors of those journals for permission to reprint the material. I am also deeply indebted to Renee Vroom and Vera Ochtman for producing a coherent manuscript from the bits and pieces I handed to them for typing, and to Ellen Graham and Barbara Folsom for their courteous and efficient editorial assistance. My final acknowledgement of immeasurable gratitude must go to my wife Cynthia, who tolerates more than it is fair of me to expect.

J. O.

Institute of Social and Economic Research
Rhodes University
Grahamstown, South Africa
April 1979

I

Materials and Methodology

In the late 'twenties of this century, Milman Parry's study of the diction of the Homeric poems had led him to the conviction that the *Iliad* and the *Odyssey* had been composed orally, and he sought to confirm this theory by investigating at first hand the tradition of oral narrative song surviving in Yugoslavia. In 1934 and 1935, therefore, Parry worked in Yugoslavia, assembling on phonograph discs and in manuscript the 12,500 texts that now make up the Parry Collection at Harvard University. In 1935 he defined the aim of his field work in these terms:

> The aim of the study was to fix with exactness the *form* of oral story poetry, to see wherein it differs from the *form* of written story poetry. Its method was to observe singers working in a thriving tradition of unlettered song and see how the form of their songs hangs upon their having to learn and practice their art without reading and writing. The principles of *oral form* thus gotten would be useful in two ways. They would be a starting point for a comparative study of oral poetry which sought to see how the way of life of a people gives rise to a poetry of a given kind and a given degree of excellence. Secondly, they would be useful in the study of the great poems which have come down to us as lonely relics of a dim past: we would know how to work backwards from their form so as to learn how they must have been made. [Parry, 469]

The main object of Parry's research was thus the *form* of the poetry, and Albert Lord, who accompanied Parry to Yugoslavia and continued his work after his death in 1935, has largely adopted the same emphasis in his work (see Lord: 1960). Basing his conclusions on his study of the Southslavic tradition of narrative song, Lord proposed that oral narratives were composed of formulas, formulaic expressions, and themes; he argued that Homer was an oral poet because the formulaic techniques, the thematic structure, and the relatively low incidence of enjambment in the Homeric poems were characteristics of the oral narrative tradition that he had studied in the Balkans. Parry's assumption that there was a dichotomy between "oral story poetry" and "written story poetry" was adopted and argued for by Lord, who wrote in terms of the oral mentality and the written mentality of poets, thereby in effect seeming to deny the possibility of "transitional" texts, poems written by a poet who had grown up in a flourishing oral tradition, poems that exhibited certain of the observed characteristics of oral poetry even though they were literate productions. The thrust of Lord's work has been almost entirely along the lines suggested by Parry as the second application of his research: the conclusions derived from the study of a living tradition about the form of oral poetry should be of use in the study of dead traditions. Little attention has been paid to Parry's expressed interest in the way in which the social structure of a people determines the kind of literature they produce (see Finnegan: 1977, chap. 8).

Lord's work has come in for heavy criticism by scholars who felt uncomfortable with the rigidity of his categories, or with the methodology of his comparative studies. Francis Magoun, who learnt of Parry's research through Lord, exaggerated and distorted a number of the hypotheses of Parry and Lord when he applied the tentative conclusions about the Yugoslavian tradition to Old English poetry (see Magoun: 1953; and Watts). The excesses of Magoun and his supporters, as well as the weaknesses in some of Lord's arguments, have tended to bring the whole "oral theory" into disrepute, so that a charged atmosphere now exists in medieval or classical studies in which it is difficult to discuss any aspect of the oral origins of the western European literatures with objectivity. There is much that can be learnt about dead poetic traditions from a study of living traditions if a proper concern for methodology is observed. There is much in the writings of Parry and Lord to criticise, but there is much of abiding value.

Many critics of Parry and Lord have denied this theory a sympathetic hearing. Parry hardly had time to absorb his material: he died almost immediately on his return from Yugoslavia. Lord waited until 1960 before he published his major statement, *The Singer of Tales*, but many of the theories contained in it were simply theories: critics and supporters alike unfortunately tended to treat the pronouncements as dogmatic. While scholars persist in taking *The Singer of Tales* as the text for their critical homilies, Lord has continued to develop his theories. He is as aware as many of his critics are of the weaknesses of some of the theories he proposed. Recently Lord produced a constructive survey of the research that his work has spawned (Lord: 1975). He comments critically on his own work and on that of other scholars, pointing to new areas of research that he considers would prove fruitful. Many of the axioms and dogmas of the debate on the oral theory are revealed to be far from rigid. For example, on formulaic analysis he writes, "I have long been acutely aware that to date my formulaic analysis of a few of Salih Ugljanin's verses in *The Singer of Tales* is the main one on which we base our knowledge of oral traditional formulas in Serbo-Croatian." Later, "It is certain that at the moment our knowledge of the facts is incomplete" (19). On transitional poetry:

> The fact of the matter is that the oral traditional style is easy to imitate by those who have heard much of it. Or, to put it another way, a person who has been brought up in an area, or lived long in one, in which he has listened to the singing and found an interest in it, can write verse using the general style and some of the formulas of the tradition. After all, the style was devised for rapid composition. If one wishes to compose rapidly in writing and comes from or has had much contact with an oral traditional poetry one not only can write in formulas, or something very like them, but normally does so. The style is natural to him. When the ideas are traditional the formulas may be those of the oral traditional poetry; when the ideas are not traditional, they will not. [Lord: 1975, 18]

Not only is our knowledge of the facts of oral style incomplete, however, our current approach to the origins of classical and medieval literature has been shaped almost exclusively by the research of Parry and Lord into Southslavic narrative song. There are other descriptions of oral poetic traditions:

> Generally speaking, while comparatively little work has been done on analysis of living oral tradition, much has been written on applying oral theory to ancient and medieval texts. The application has outdistanced the new presentation of an exact description of an oral traditional poetry. I say new, because we tend to forget that before Parry's time at least three oral poetries had been well described. [Lord: 1975, 1; he refers to Radloff's description of Turkish epic, Comparetti's book on the *Kalevala*, and the work on the Russian tradition by various scholars]

There are also emphases in the study of oral poetic traditions other than those that concerned Lord (and here Lord seems to be inviting a return to the first application that Parry envisaged for his research): "The texts must be viewed from all aspects, not only of stylistics but also of sociology, religion, and history, so that a concept of oral literature's place in the whole society may be properly understood" (5); and Lord concludes, "Finally, although I have spoken almost exclusively of stylistic matters, because it is through style that we have tried to identify and characterize oral literature, one should not forget the many other aspects of oral literature, above all its function and its meaning" (24).

It would be indeed a pity if Anglo-Saxonists—understandably annoyed at the veritable explosion of often vacuous writing that Magoun initiated—were to consider the oral theory a closed issue. Since there is no doubt that literature of some kind or another existed among the pre-Christian Germanic peoples, it is highly likely that the migrating Anglo-Saxons brought with them to England a tradition of poetic composition and performance. It is likely, too, that this tradition informed the vernacular poetry that came to be written after the introduction of writing for literary purposes by the Christian missionaries. We can choose to draw a curtain over this period, convinced that nothing can be said of it with any degree of certainty; but if we prefer to speculate on the possible character of this tradition, conscious that our speculations are never susceptible of proof, it is clearly better to do so with regard to those materials and methods we have at our disposal than to speculate without regard to any controls at all. A reasoned hypothesis based on the evidence and techniques available to us may well be only a little better than a decision not to speculate at all, but it *is* a little better.

For the period from the origins to about A.D. 600, we have no firsthand account of poetic activity—indeed we have no poetry—from any Anglo-Saxon; we must rely on the evidence of historians who observed the Germanic peoples on the Continent. We can postulate something about a common Indo-European poetic tradition through a study of the most archaic of the Indo-European literatures, the Celtic and the Indic, and we can piece together some evidence about the status of poetry from comparative Indo-European philology. The classical historians, however, are often less than reliable, and even if one could accept their testimony, one would have to concede that none of them writes about the ancestors of the Anglo-Saxons; our acceptance of their testimony as valid for the Anglo-Saxons would depend on an assumption that there was a common Germanic poetic tradition identical in all respects among all the Germanic peoples. Comparative Indo-European research yields some fascinating data, but it is based on a study of dead texts and is limited to those relevant references that chance to survive. There remain many questions we would like to ask an Anglo-Saxon poet if only we could interview one, questions that would reveal to us aspects of his art and the function of his poetry in society. It is for information in this area, information on the mechanics of the tradition as it lived and operated among the people, that we are compelled to turn to poets living today who practise an oral art analogous to that of the Anglo-Saxons and who live in a society similar to theirs.

The idea that a study of modern phenomena can inform us about past ages is not new: the great school of British folklorists, a group of scholars that included Alfred Nutt, Andrew Lang, and E. B. Tylor, perceived the potential value of a study of analogous phenomena and made it an integral part of their methodology of folklore (selections from their writings can be found conveniently in Dorson: 1968b). In 1871 Tylor wrote in *Primitive Culture*:

> Look at the modern European peasant using his hatchet and his hoe, see his food boiling or roasting over the log-fire, observe the exact place which beer holds in his calculation of happiness, hear his tale of the ghost in the nearest haunted house, and of the farmer's niece who was bewitched with knots in her inside till she fell into fits and died. If we choose out in this way things which have altered little in a long course of centuries, we may draw a picture where there shall be scarce a hand's breadth of difference between an English ploughman and a negro of central Africa. [Dorson: 1968a, 193f.]

In *Custom and Myth* Lang wrote in 1884, "Now, with regard to all these strange usages, what is the method of folklore? The method is, when an apparently irrational and anomalous custom is found in any country, to look for a country where . . . the practice is . . . in harmony with the manners and ideas of the people among whom it prevails" (Dorson: 1968a, 210). Commenting on Nutt's attitude toward this creed, Richard Dorson writes, "What was the orthodoxy which Lang administered as high priest? Nutt restated the dogmas succinctly: The belief and fancy of the relatively uncultured European peasant and the absolutely uncultured savage are substantially the same, and observations made in the one case may be used to supplement and control observations in the other" (236). Of course, quoting the views of Tylor, Lang, or Nutt does not prove that comparative studies of oral literatures are methodologically sound, but it does show that the method enjoys scholarly precedent. Nor is quoting these British folklorists intended to imply that their views are accepted by contemporary folklorists or that their ideas are couched in a language acceptable to contemporary anthropologists; nonetheless, it is clear that a methodological analogue for the comparative study of oral literatures can be found in related disciplines.

In fact, a methodological analogue for such comparative arguments exists in Anglo-Saxon studies. In his reconstruction of the helmet from the many fragments found on the site at Sutton Hoo, Herbert Maryon found he had insufficient surviving fragments to complete one panel.

> So the surviving fragments were mounted on the helmet in what was felt might be their correct position. This was done so that by publication the attention of scholars might be directed to them, and the existence of any parallel examples might be reported.
>
> Now it happened that Mr Bruce-Mitford, on a visit to Sweden, observed at Uppsala on a hitherto unpublished helmet from Valsgärde, a recently reconstructed panel. On this are the figures of two warriors, similar to those on the Sutton Hoo panel, standing side by side. Their outer hands hold spears, and their nearer hands hold swords above crossed spears, as on a fragment from Sutton Hoo. As a result of this valuable discovery the reconstruction of the panel itself and the consequent rearrangement of the panels on the helmet now becomes possible. [Maryon, 139]

The examination of the Valsgärde helmet permitted a coherent reconstruction of the fragments surviving from Sutton Hoo.

One of the criticisms levelled at the comparative work of Parry and Lord, especially as applied to Anglo-Saxon studies, was that contemporary Yugoslavia has no connection with Anglo-Saxon England; accordingly, a study of contemporary Southslavic oral poetry could be of but little relevance to the study of Anglo-Saxon poetry. This attitude is partly unjustified and partly justified. It is correct in that Lord erred in seeking a general definition of oral poetry based on his Yugoslavian experiences; Magoun and his followers claimed to adopt from Parry a definition of an oral poet which apparently held good for all oral poets and hence for Anglo-Saxon poets, and forced this definition onto the facts of the Anglo-Saxon tradition (see, for example, Creed: 1958 and 1959; Magoun: 1955; cf. Watts, 195). To attempt to derive a definition of oral poets in general from an observation of only one oral tradition is statistically and methodologically unsound. Although the debate aroused by Magoun's articles has brought to light much valuable information about the diction of Old English poetry, by and large Anglo-Saxonists were correct to resist the presentation of the Yugoslavian *guslar* (Lord's "singer of tales") as in effect an exclusive model for the Anglo-Saxon poet. There were many obstacles. The guslar entertained an exclusively male audience with narrative songs; the Old English poets do not seem to have performed before restricted audiences, their poems are not always designed for entertainment, nor are the poems always purely narrative. Then again, the two societies, Anglo-Saxon and Yugoslavian, were quite different in structure.

These objections are valid up to a point, but the guslar can serve as a model for useful comparison with the Anglo-Saxon poet if the proper methodology is observed. If we are aware that what we are studying in the two cultures is an *analogous* phenomenon, then it is not necessary that the cultures be either similar or contemporaneous. A collation of the information we have about the guslar as well as a host of other poets from various cultures alive and performing today might yield a theory of oral poetry that is universally applicable; but even if that were possible, the definition would probably then be so general as to have limited value, so diverse are the oral poetic traditions that have so far been defined (see Finnegan: 1977). A study of the craft of the guslar, however, of his method of poetic composition and other elements of significance in his tradition, should produce a set of observations that might or might not be helpful in understanding other oral poets. The student of any one living tradition ought to find relevance in the study of any other living tradition: he will probably find some points of agreement and other points on which the two traditions differ; the earlier definition might well help him to arrive at a coherent definition of the phenomena he is observing. The student of a dead oral tradition can similarly find relevance in the study of living oral traditions. Some observations on the contemporary traditions will fit the extant facts of his dead tradition, others will not; he must pick and choose what seem to him to be illuminating points of comparison. He must never assume a one-to-one correspondence between any two traditions, an assumption that would lead him to force the facts of a living tradition onto those of a dead one. The information extant about the tradition he is studying—after due assessment of its reliability—can provide the only primary data: all else (including the facts about any analogous living tradition) is secondary. Nutt believed that observations of the living phenomena ought to be used to *supplement* and *control* observations of the other, never to supersede them. The fragments of the Sutton Hoo helmet remain the only primary evidence from Sutton Hoo, however illuminating a study of the Valsgärde reconstruction might be.

It may be, however, that the extant information about the dead tradition does not afford evidence on areas that the scholar needs to discuss. It is all very well to permit data culled from the study of surviving traditions to supplement the facts of a dead tradition, but what are we to do if the dead tradition does not furnish us with any facts to supplement? Here again the student of surviving oral traditions might be able to help. Sir Leonard Woolley once stressed the necessity for a field archaeologist not only to publish his material scientifically, but also to draw his own conclusions from it. Publication of the bare artifacts was not enough: he must provide an interpretation of the artifacts as well. However, Woolley continues,

> It might be urged that the man who is admirably equipped to observe and record does not necessarily possess the powers of synthesis and interpretation, the creative spirit and the literary gift which will make of him a historian. But no record can ever be exhaustive. As his work in the field goes on, the excavator is constantly exposed to impressions too subjective and too intangible to be communicated, and out of these, by no exact logical process, there arise theories which he can state, can perhaps support, but cannot prove: their proof will ultimately depend on his own calibre, but in any case they have their value as a summing up of experiences which no student of his objects and his notes can ever share. [Woolley, 118 f.]

It is precisely these "experiences" of a scholar working in a thriving oral tradition that enables him to make reasonable assumptions about classical or medieval oral literatures. This much Parry and Lord had going for them: few of their critics could claim to have had the firsthand experience of an oral tradition that enabled Parry and Lord to make the kind of hypothetical claims for Homer that had never been made before. The proof of these claims ultimately depends on their calibre as scholars, but they have their value as statements made by classical scholars with an intimate understanding of the mechanics of an analogous living tradition. Students of surviving traditions today are starting to develop a sociologically oriented theory of oral literature that may help classicists and medievalists to breathe life into the sparse extant references to poetic activity (see, for example, Ben-Amos: 1971, the first three chapters of Finnegan: 1970, Finnegan: 1977, and the extracts from Biebuyck and from Jackson quoted in chapter 4 below); if the correct methodology is observed, and if the primary facts are clearly identified, the dry and sometimes imperfect skeleton may be animated by reasoned hypothesis.

In Anglo-Saxon studies, Francis Magoun and his followers took the first halting steps towards such a reconstruction of the poetic tradition, but they were unfortunately too much bound by the figure of the Yugoslavian guslar as the exclusive model of an oral poet: thus the Anglo-Saxon oral poet had to be, like the guslar, an illiterate male who underwent a long period of apprenticeship and training to acquire the skill to entertain his audience with narrative songs that he composed in performance to the accompaniment of a musical instrument. This was a severely limited view of the Anglo-Saxon oral poet and obviously did not allow for the patently complex character of his tradition. Earlier scholars, like Stopford Brooke or L. F. Anderson, who worked on the extant texts without the model of the guslar to distract them, did testify to the different kinds of poets and the different kinds of poetry current in Anglo-Saxon times, and were thus closer to a rounded description of the tradition as revealed by the extant texts than Magoun and his followers were.

The difference was this: where there were gaps in the extant evidence and the scholars had recourse to hypothesis, Brooke and Anderson, positing a common Germanic tradition, relied on information from other Germanic traditions (notably the Old Norse), whereas Magoun relied on the Southslavic tradition. The earlier descriptions of the Anglo-Saxon poetic tradition are on the whole more complete and more convincing. Nonetheless, for the first time in Anglo-Saxon studies, Magoun sought to define the mechanics of the poetic tradition by comparing it to an observable, living tradition: comparative studies within the ancient Germanic traditions or even between a Germanic and a medieval Celtic tradition are necessarily limited by the evidence that happens to survive. Apart from a few notable exceptions (like Cædmon or Cynewulf), the Anglo-Saxon poets are all anonymous; the guslar that Magoun presented to Anglo-Saxonists was at least an individual. Unfortunately, Magoun himself had never met a guslar, and his knowledge of the Southslavic tradition was limited by Parry and Lord's description of it (see Curschmann). Yet a new dimension was added to our potential understanding of the nature of the Anglo-Saxon poetic tradition by the bold use of the living Southslavic tradition as an analogue.

In Anglo-Saxon studies to date, only two other living analogues have been proposed as alternatives to the Southslavic tradition for the purpose of comparative study. Alan Jabbour argued convincingly that the Southslavic tradition was unsatisfactory as an exclusive model of the Anglo-Saxon, and suggested that the later British ballad tradition provided a more satisfactory alternative. Jabbour's objection to the Southslavic tradition was that it was primarily improvisational, whereas he produced evidence from a study of those Old Eng-

lish poems (or sections of poems) that exist in more than one text, that the
Anglo-Saxon tradition was primarily memorial. He defined these two terms
as follows:

> If we discover that in a certain oral poetical tradition the variants of a song
> are related only in subject-matter and have no discernible history of word-
> for-word or phrase-by-phrase transmission, we may conclude that the
> tradition is improvisational. It would, however, be more than likely that
> passages would crop up here and there with a considerable number of
> verbal parallels, especially in separate renditions by the same singer, rendi-
> tions from father and son or teacher and pupil, and renditions from the
> same locality. Such cases would require us to qualify our description, using
> the term "primarily improvisational" to show our recognition that memo-
> rial transmission is also taking place. If, on the other hand, we discover that
> in a certain tradition the variants of a song show a history of word-for-
> word or phrase-by-phrase oral transmission from a known or presumed
> archetype, we may describe the tradition as memorial. But considerable
> variation would almost certainly appear in the several texts, such as omis-
> sion, addition, interpolation from other songs, stylizing, formulizing, or
> the like. These improvisational traits would compel us to call the tradition
> "primarily memorial." [Jabbour: 1969, 178]

Jabbour is unfortunately just as extreme as Magoun: both assume that the
Anglo-Saxon poetic tradition can be reduced to a simple monolithic definition.
Both produce evidence that is convincing in varying degrees, but both fail to
appreciate that there might have been both improvisers and memorisers among
the ranks of Anglo-Saxon poets, that the tradition might have been complex
and not simple.

The role of improvisation in an oral poetic tradition was fully explored by
Lord, and it proved to be one of the most illuminating aspects of his description
of the Southslavic tradition. It is perhaps unfortunate for the purpose of comparative studies that he chose to emphasise only the improvising guslar, exclud-
ing from his definition of an oral poet the memoriser: the memorising guslar
certainly does exist in Yugoslavia, as do lyric poets (see Lord: 1960, 279, and
Coote), and their exclusion from consideration by Lord created the unfortunate
impression that "the Southslavic poetic tradition" was represented by the
guslar alone and was accordingly "primarily improvisational." Magoun and
Jabbour, following Parry and Lord, work within the same restricted view of
oral poetic traditions; Brooke and Anderson present us with a picture of com-

plexity. Both the Southslavic and the later British ballad traditions provide illuminating analogues for *aspects* of the Anglo-Saxon traditions; neither should be used as an exclusive model on the assumption of a one-to-one correspondence between them.

Apart from the Southslavic and the British ballad traditions, the only other living tradition that has been proposed as a potentially useful analogue for the Anglo-Saxon is that of the Bantu-speaking peoples in southern Africa. I have argued on a number of occasions that the oral traditions of Africa furnish examples of phenomena analogous to those that must have been current throughout the Middle Ages: students of medieval history and literature could find in contemporary Africa a living laboratory for experiments in the process of oral transmission (see Opland: 1969; 1970; 1971; 1973; 1976a; see also Mafeje: 1967; Kesteloot; and Carter). I commenced my own field work amongst the Xhosa- and Zulu-speaking peoples in South Africa in 1969 in search of an alternative analogue for the Anglo-Saxon tradition, and was immediately struck by the apparent similarities between Anglo-Saxon and southeastern Bantu society: both are tribal societies with warrior ethics in which individuals owe loyalty to the chiefs they choose to follow and to their kin. For the purposes of the comparative study of their literatures, it may be of minimal relevance that Bantu social structure seems to be more similar to that of the Anglo-Saxons than the Southslavic is, but this may well be a factor worthy of consideration by any scholars who care to pursue the lines of research, indicated by Parry, into "how the way of life of a people gives rise to a poetry of a given kind and a given degree of excellence": a corollary of such a thesis, if it can be proven, would be that human societies similar in structure tend to produce similar literatures.

It might be argued that the southeastern Bantu analogue is less relevant than the Southslavic, since at least the Serbocroatian and the Anglo-Saxon are Indo-European cultures. Perhaps the fullest use that has been made so far of the similarities between Anglo-Saxon and southeastern Bantu society is to be found in A. S. Diamond's *Primitive Law, Past and Present*. Diamond divides his book into two sections, "one examining the evidence afforded only by the legal remains of the past, and the other the legal usages of present and recent peoples and the light they throw on past laws and legal systems" (vii f.). The underlying thesis is that "we can see in history a correlation between the economic development and the legal" (4). Diamond proceeds to examine the legal development of societies according to certain established strata in socio-economic development. He labels the period in Anglo-Saxon England from

A.D. 600 to 900 the period of early codes (chap. 5), corresponding to a stage of development in which "peoples live by agriculture and cattle-keeping with subsidiary hunting" (271). In the second section of his book, when Diamond studies "Recent Peoples of the Early Codes" (chaps. 19–21), the recent society that he cites most extensively for the purpose of comparison with Anglo-Saxon society is that of the southeastern Bantu, especially the Zulu- and the Xhosa-speaking peoples (274–87). It is evident from the information Diamond produces that the Anglo-Saxon and contemporary southeastern Bantu societies bear closer resemblances than do the Anglo-Saxon and contemporary South-slavic societies.

More important, however, than these resemblances in socioeconomic development is the fact that poetry among the Zulu- and Xhosa-speaking peoples in southern Africa is eulogistic. The Southslavic tradition defined by Lord and the British ballad tradition cited by Jabbour were both narrative traditions and as such provide useful analogues for much of the narrative poetry that survives in Anglo-Saxon manuscripts. Some of that extant poetry, however, is not narrative at all, but eulogistic; it is probable that eulogy was a prominent feature of the native oral traditions. The traditions of southeastern Bantu eulogy have been affected considerably by contact with Western society over the past two centuries, but the alteration in these traditions seems to have been less radical than anywhere else in Africa. The Zulu- and Xhosa-speaking peoples afford us much information about the operation and significance of eulogy in their societies, and this information complements that derived from a study of contemporary narrative traditions like the Southslavic. A study of contemporary traditions of eulogy (as distinct from narrative) is particularly relevant to an attempt to understand the operation and significance of poetry in primitive Indo-European society.

The study of living poetic traditions can teach us much about how oral poetry lived and operated in societies remote in time. The classicist or medievalist who has before him the text of a poem can at best have only one facet of an oral performance. An oral poet performing before an audience enjoys a unique relation with them at the time of the performance. He is there and the audience can see him, they can hear his voice and the rhythmical cadences of his delivery. He moves before them with facial expressions and gestures. If his poem is occasional, relevant to that particular moment in time and a product of that particular set of circumstances, there will exist a common experience shared by poet and audience that informs that particular performance. The words he utters are only one aspect of the poet's performance: the impact on the audience is aural, visual, and emotional. They experience a totality of performance, a unique sequence that can never be repeated. All these facets of the performance are necessarily lost when an oral poem is committed to paper; a modern tape recording preserves the aural aspects, a sound film would recapture the visual aspects as well, but nothing can replace the unique bond that existed at the moment of performance between poet and audience (see Clark). For the textual critic, such considerations are perhaps of minimal relevance, but if one wishes to reconstruct the tradition of poetry as it lived and operated among the Anglo-Saxons, such considerations—hypothetical as they may be—must be entertained.

And perhaps such considerations might be of help to the textual critic. *The Wife's Lament*, for example, has long been one of the most puzzling of Old English texts; it presents the critic with problems shared by *Wulf and Eadwacer* and *The Husband's Message*. Although there are clearly narrative passages or narrative matrices for each of these works, they are not explicitly narrative in the way that, say, *Beowulf* or *The Battle of Maldon* are. Even though they are commonly called elegies, scholars still tend to insist on the narrative element as the key to interpretation. I. L. Gordon, quoting Nora Kershaw, once urged that the narrative element was not significant, that the elegies were studies in emotion (I. L. Gordon: 1960, 15), but this suggestion has in no way deterred scholars from producing new interpretations of *The Wife's Lament*—most of them centring on an explication of the narrative situation. Perhaps these texts were more happily termed lyrics; in an article whose implications seem to have been largely overlooked, Kemp Malone classified *The Wife's Lament* as a *frauenlied* (Malone: 1963; see also Clifford Davidson). Anglo-Saxonists have assumed that those extant texts that can be conveniently divided into alliterative lines are all poems; perhaps some of them were songs.

Among the Xhosa-speaking peoples, poems are *izibongo* and songs are *amaculo*: there is a clear distinction in the techniques of performance as well as in social function and the traditional diction and styles associated with each genre. The text itself may not necessarily reveal its origins; the distinction manifests itself in performance. (For example, the text of the well-known Xhosa hymn composed by Ntsikana and quoted in chapter 5 below is indistinguishable from the text of a Xhosa oral poem, but the hymn is now invariably sung; an extract from a performance by the Zwelitsha choir led by S. T. Bokwe can be found on *Music of Africa Series No. 18: Music from the Roadside No. 1: South Africa*, Gallo GALP 1110.) Poems have been set to music and sung, the lyric of a song transcribed might be read as a poem; but we would have no hesitation in differentiating generically between a Schubert *lied* or a Rodgers and Hammerstein song and a poem read by Dylan Thomas or Yevtushenko if we attended the recital or show. If *The Wife's Lament* is the text of a song originally sung by a woman, its technique may be a factor of its genre: the audience might have been content with the plaintive melody and the phrases connotative of isolation, they might have shared with the performer the emotion of sadness and not in any way have felt the urge to learn the reasons for the emotion. As among the Xhosa, songs might have had a function in Anglo-Saxon society different from that of poems. The function of the texts Parry and Lord collected was primarily entertainment and, strictly speaking, the guslari produced songs not poems: as Harry Levin says in his introduction to *The Singer of Tales*, "The poem is . . . a song," and Lord himself says that "oral epic song is narrative poetry" (Lord: 1960, 4). As far as possible, I shall try to differentiate between the two terms.

Recourse to the comparative study of oral poetic traditions might be necessary for a hypothetical reconstruction of the pre-Christian Anglo-Saxon oral tradition since no primary evidence produced by an Anglo-Saxon exists, but for the Christian period we do have a fairly extensive body of writing on which to base our conclusions. It should go without saying that any treatment of the subject must take account of *all* the extant evidence, giving due weight to chronology. But the extant evidence ought to be exploited with care; although they constitute primary data for the study of the Anglo-Saxon oral poet, these extant texts vary widely in reliability. For example, perhaps the most commonly cited source of information is *Beowulf*. The evidence provided by this single source is frequently allowed to weigh more heavily than conflicting evidence from other sources; the current conception of the Anglo-Saxon oral poet as a performer entertaining the company feasting in his lord's hall with narrative songs accompanied by a harp—a picture satisfactorily in harmony with Lord's description of the guslar in a Bosnian coffeehouse—is derived largely from the scenes depicting the joy in Heorot in *Beowulf*. Yet allowance might have to be made for the poetic medium through which this information is transmitted; for a number of reasons, poetry might be less reliable than prose as evidence of social activity (see Opland: 1976a). First, our interpretation of Old English poetry is often influenced by the editor's treatment of the text or by the lexicographer's glossing of words in the text, both of which in turn occasionally depend on their interpretation of what the text means. In an article indispensable for the study of Old English literature, Fred Robinson (1970) wrote that sometimes when a lexicographer is assessing the meaning of a word in a given occurrence, he slips unawares into the role of literary interpreter, recording a meaning for a word not on the basis of lexicographical evidence but purely because his particular critical interpretation of the passage requires such a meaning. Scholars who then encounter his judgments in the dictionary often fail to distinguish between what is lexicographical fact and what is the dictionary-maker's momentary indulgence in literary criticism. In some instances, these unsubstantiated *ad hoc* meanings can fix the critical interpretation of a passage in a permanent course of error; for, so long as they remain unchallenged, the dictionary definitions of words are necessarily the starting point for any critical explication of the literature which uses those words. [99 f.]

Old English manuscripts do not contain a system of punctuation such as we commonly use today. Hence, the editor's punctuation of a text frequently—indeed necessarily—derives from his interpretation of the text, but that punctuation may well serve to hinder the search for an alternative interpretation. For example, consider the passage in *Beowulf* that introduces the Finn episode:

> Þær wæs sang ond sweg   samod ætgædere
> fore Healfdenes   hildewisan,
> gomenwudu greted,   gid oft wrecen,
> ðonne healgamen   Hroþgares scop
> æfter medobence   mænan scolde
> be Finnes eaferum . . .
>
> [ASPR, IV, 1063-68]

I shall have occasion later to discuss in detail the interpretation of this passage, but it is usually taken to mean that in the presence of Hrothgar there was song and music, the harp was touched, a poem often recited, when for the sake of hall entertainment Hrothgar's bard had to tell the story of Finn's sons. As punctuated, then, the passage implies that there was singing and music, and the harp was often played; one example of this harp song was the court poet's performance of the Finn episode. This interpretation is valid if *ðonne* (l. 1066) is taken to be a temporal subordinating conjunction. But the editorial punctuation depends on the editor's acceptance of this interpretation. If, for example, the editor had external evidence to indicate that the Anglo-Saxon *scop* did not play a harp, he could equally well have a full stop at the end of line 1065 and start a new sentence with *Ðonne*, which then becomes an adverb, and frees the Finn episode from harp accompaniment.

There are other reasons why Old English poetry might be less reliable as evidence of social activity than prose. The poetic style often renders the meaning ambiguous. For example, when the *Beowulf* poet mentions the revelry in the hall that enraged Grendel, he says, "þær wæs hearpan sweg, swutol sang scopes" (89f.), "the sound of the harp was there, the clear song of the scop." The Old English poetic technique of variation confuses the interpretation of this clause: it could mean that the sound of the harp and the sound of the scop were simultaneous if the second half-line is taken as a notional variation of the first; or it could mean that there were in the hall two separate things, the sound of the harp and the sound of the scop, if the second half-line is merely a second complement to "wæs," syntactically parallel with "hearpan sweg." The passage could mean that Grendel was disturbed by the sound of the scop singing to the accompaniment of his harp, or it could equally well mean that both a harper and a poet were performing in Heorot and that these were two different men.

Again, as a result of the metrical or alliterative demands of his tradition, the poet might on occasion have had to choose a less precise word than the writer of prose could choose. For example, there are many verbs in *Beowulf* that are used to refer to the performance of a poem or song, verbs like *mænan, wrecan, sprecan, cwiðan, secgan, singan, reccan*. In prose, these words are usually distinguishable, but because of the alliterative demands of his metre, it is not possible to say whether the poet implies a musical context for the verb *singan* or a non-musical context for *cwiðan* or *sprecan*. The prose translator of Boethius's *Consolation of Philosophy*, however, frequently preferred two verbs in combination to translate one Latin word, producing phrases like *giddode and cwæð*, or *singende cwæð*; this may indicate that he conceived of the poetic performance neither as a song nor as a speech, but as something in between, a chant or recitative (see chap. 9 below). One can expect more precision from a writer of prose; the poet may be limited by his need to preserve a set of synonyms or near-synonyms that are for his purposes interchangeable and differentiated only by the initial sounds of their stressed syllables.

In assessing the evidence of Old English poetry about poetic activity one might have to make allowances for the conventional diction of the tradition. It has been argued, for example, that Homer composed the *Iliad* at a time when chariots were no longer used in battle, but since he had inherited through the tradition a set of poetic phrases referring to chariots, he found occasion to use

these in his poem because they were traditional, even though he seems not to
have conceived of any function for chariots other than transport to and from a
battle. A traditional poetry might retain descriptions of objects or practices long
after they have ceased to be current. A traditional poetry, too, seems to exploit
the suggestive quality of its words and phrases, so that one cannot always demand precise meaning from traditional formulas or themes. Lord writes of
oral poetic style:

> It is certainly possible that a formula that entered the poetry because its
> acoustic patterns emphasized by repetition a potent word or idea was kept
> after the peculiar potency which it symbolized and which one might say it
> even was intended to make effective was lost—kept because the fragrance of
> its past importance still clung vaguely to it and kept also because it was now
> useful in composition. It is *then* that the repeated phrases, hitherto a driving
> force in the direction of accomplishment of those blessings to be conferred
> on the story by song, began to lose their precision through frequent use.
> Meaning in them became vestigial, connotative rather than denotative.
> [Lord: 1960, 65]

Before *The Singer of Tales* appeared, in one of the finest articles to emerge from
the debate on the oral theory in Anglo-Saxon studies, Stanley Greenfield (1955)
wrote of the suggestive quality of traditional diction:

> A highly stylized poetry like Anglo-Saxon, with its many formulas and
> presumably many verbal conventions, has certain advantages in comparison
> with a less traditional type of poetry. The most notable advantage is that
> the very traditions it employs lend extra-emotional meaning to individual
> words and phrases. That is, the associations with other contexts using a sim-
> ilar formula will inevitably color a particular instance of a formula so that a
> whole host of overtones springs into action to support the aesthetic response.
> . . . The chief disadvantage of a conventional poetry is that its very virtue,
> the extra-emotional meanings, may supplant the denotation that should
> inhere in a specific situation, and the words and phrases become "conven-
> tional" in the pejorative sense of the word. [206]

The passages describing poetic activity in extant Old English poems might well
be "conventional" in this sense, highly suggestive and imbued with an "aura of
meaning" rather than accurate descriptions of practices current in the poet's day.
   All these considerations are complicated by the fact that most Old English

poetry is neither dated nor datable, so that a literary chronology cannot be established. Furthermore, most of the poetry as it survives was almost certainly transcribed by clerics and quite possibly was composed by clerics, and as such participates in a tradition significantly different from the pre-Christian oral tradition. It might be argued, however, that no one is better informed about the poetic tradition than the poet himself, but students of oral literatures have often noted that the poets frequently lack an objective knowledge of their own traditions, or that collectors analyse the poetry in terms of concepts quite foreign to the poets. This is not surprising, since one could not expect a precise knowledge of the grammatical structure of English from an Englishman, for example, simply because he speaks the language; few of us are objectively aware of the customs and oral traditions that frequently mould our lives. One might accept as accurate a poet's description of an occasion on which poetry is performed, for example, since he is a member of the community, but one might have to be more cautious with passages that refer to the process of composition. Yugoslavian singers or Xhosa poets often believe that every performance of a song or poem on the same subject will be verbally identical—whereas the collector can often test this assertion and demonstrate it to be false—and the poets believe this either because they really think that they do produce identical poems on the same subjects or because they have a concept of identity that differs from that of the collector (thematic identity, in the case of the guslar, as opposed to verbal: see Lord: 1960, chap. 5).

And so, however attractive poems like *Beowulf* might be as a source of information about poets and poetry, their evidence should not simply be accepted uncritically. The testimony furnished by poetic sources like *Beowulf* must be assessed within the context of what can be learned from all extant Old English and Anglo-Latin sources, from a comparative study of Germanic and Indo-European literatures, and from a comparative study of analogous traditions surviving today. When all these sources of information are taken into account with due respect for a proper methodology, it might be possible to write the history of the oral poet in Anglo-Saxon society—the story of the changes that the poet and his tradition underwent as the continental warrior-bands became chiefdoms, as the chiefdoms became kingdoms and the kingdoms became England, as the Anglo-Saxons were converted to Christianity and their poetry for the first time came to be transcribed and preserved for posterity. The following chapters of this book attempt to assemble the material evidence relevant to that history and to reconstruct it, however hypothetical the result.

EXCURSUS: XHOSA AND ZULU POETRY

The southeastern Bantu peoples of southern Africa can be divided into a number of linguistic units, such as the Sotho and the Nguni. Sotho and Nguni languages are not mutually intelligible, although the trained linguist readily appreciates that the languages are closely related in structure and vocabulary. The
different Nguni languages, however, languages like Swazi, Xhosa and Zulu, are
mutually intelligible and some of them are in turn subject to dialectal variation.
It is primarily with the Xhosa-speaking peoples, who live in the areas known as
Transkei and the Ciskei in the Cape Province, and to a lesser extent with the
Zulus, who live in Natal, that I have worked. To establish a parallel with the
Germanic languages, the various dialects of the Xhosa language (Thembu,
Mpondo, Bhaca, etc.) are analogous to the dialects of Old English (Northumbrian, Mercian, West Saxon, or Kentish); the relation between Xhosa and Zulu
(both Nguni languages) is analogous to that between Old English and Old
Norse in Anglo-Saxon times (both Germanic languages and apparently mutually intelligible); and Old Irish and Old English, both Indo-European languages
though from different groups (Celtic and Germanic), both spoken in contigu-
ous areas though presumably mutually unintelligible, shared a relationship analogous to that of Tswana and Xhosa, both Bantu languages though from
different groups (Sotho and Nguni). With regard to the Nguni tradition of oral
poetry as propagated by the tribal poets, it should be noted immediately that the
Zulu tradition is primarily memorial whereas the Xhosa is primarily improvisational (see Opland: 1974), a fact that should serve to caution scholars against
assuming too readily that there was absolute uniformity within the various
Germanic poetic traditons.

The Xhosa tradition of poetry (*izibongo*) is complex: there are different
kinds of poets and different kinds of poetry. In traditional society, a number of
memorial poetic traditions are current. Most people know the poems about
their clans, poems which are transmitted in fixed form from generation to generation (see Kuse; Mzolo; and Rycroft: 1976). These poems may be produced as
an expression of greeting, pride, encouragement, or congratulation directed at a
member of the clan, often by his wife. Heads of households also know the poems
treating their departed ancestors, which are recited on ritual or ceremonial occasions in order to initiate communication between the living and the dead (see
Callaway). These poems are fixed in form, memorised, and passed on to succeeding generations, though they tend to have a shorter currency than the clan

poems: most men seem to know the poems about their father and grandfather, but not much further back in their lineage. The clan poems treat physical characteristics and historical events in the life of the clan, and knowledge of them is not confined to members of the clan; personal poems treat the physical and moral characteristics of an individual and the major events he participated in during his life, and tend to be known only to members of a family.

These personal poems pass into a memorial tradition that is fixed by virtue of its ritual connotation but arise from a tradition that is primarily memorial. From an early age, boys compose poems about themselves or their friends. These poems consist of a collection of verses either composed by the subject or by others, and are added to as the subject passes through significant experiences. The subject himself utters his autobiographical poem as an expression of pride, or his familiars may recite his poem in order to encourage him in some activity such as fighting or dancing. A boy will hear his father's autobiographical poem often, and will use that poem as a ritual medium of communication with his father after his father's death. Thus autobiographical poems that participate in a primarily memorial tradition during the lifespan of the performer pass into a memorial biographical tradition upon his death. These poems tend to be composed in large part, and assembled, by the subject of the poem; they will be transmitted by his associates and especially by his eldest son on his death.

Other poems are composed by individuals and participate in a memorial or primarily memorial tradition, though their currency tends to be limited to the composers. Boys compose poems about their dogs or animals while herding livestock; girls compose poems about the cows or goats they milk; men compose poems about their favourite horses or oxen. These poems are usually uttered as an encouragement to the subject, to the cows during milking or the oxen during ploughing.

In addition to these memorial and primarily memorial traditions of poetry, poems are also composed within a primarily improvisational tradition. In a moment of inspiration or excitement, Xhosa-speaking men or women are wont to burst into poetry, poetry that might quote lines from memorial clan or biographical poems, but that is essentially the unique response to a particular set of circumstances, and as such cannot subsequently be repeated in the same form. Such poetic outbursts are a common feature of traditional dances, faction fights, and ceremonial occasions, but also occur nowadays at political meetings and sports matches.

Xhosa-speaking people living in a rural environment, and even some in an urban environment, grow up with traditions of oral poetry—traditions that bind together persons in society as a whole, members of a clan, members of a family, and people to the animals that form a significant part of rural existence.

Just as the head of a family is expected to recite the poems about his ancestors on ceremonial occasions, so too the tribal poet is expected to produce poems about his chief or important visitors on festive occasions. This significant figure, the *imbongi* (plural *iimbongi* in Xhosa, *izimbongi* in Zulu), is socially the most prominent of many poets in the community, and his activities ought to be viewed within the context of all poetic productions, and as being dependent on the traditions that generate those poetic productions. Unlike the Yugoslavian guslar, the imbongi does not serve a period of conscious apprenticeship during which he acquires the skill and confidence to perform in public. This is something he has always been potentially able to do, like any other member of his society. An imbongi is a man with a particular talent, so he performs more often and at a higher level of sophistication than other poets in the community. Socially, the guslar performed before mainly masculine audiences in Bosnian coffeehouses; the imbongi's audience is the whole chiefdom. Parry and Lord described a guslar whose function was primarily entertainment; the imbongi performs a social function more serious than entertainment. He functions as herald, historian, genealogist, custodian of lore, political commentator, prophet, moulder of public opinion, mediator between people and chief, propagandist, inciter (see further Mafeje: 1963; 1967). He performs on official occasions such as the installation of chiefs, weddings, or court hearings whenever his chief attends. There is no figure in Xhosa society to compare with the wandering minstrel: an imbongi generally forms an attachment to one chief or royal line only. His poetry is primarily eulogistic: it deals with the characters of his subjects and their deeds. The izibongo may contain explicitly narrative passages, but their general attitude is analytical: they are addressed to people, and they comment on people known to their audiences or ancestors of people known to their audiences.

All the different kinds of poetry among the Xhosas are solo performances unaccompanied by music. For entertainment or instruction the Xhosa do narrate stories about animals or legends about heroes; they often sing songs while working or dancing (see Jordan: 1973a; Kirby; Scheub: 1975; and Theal). The songs may be solo performances accompanied by a musical instrument or hand-clapping, or they may be choral or antiphonal, but songs are quite distinct from poems in performance as well as in function. The izibongo may on occasion be amusing, but they are never performed primarily for entertainment.

There exists in the oral tradition no epic as such, although epics are now being written. The poems of the imbongi are commonly eulogistic: they are about people and their involvement in current or historical events. They are allusive and elliptical rather than explicitly narrative, and they tend to be short— about five to ten minutes in length. (Longer performances would tax the imbongi physically, since izibongo are shouted out in a characteristically guttural voice.)

Lord set out to collect the full corpus of Southslavic narratives, but this would not be possible in the Xhosa tradition, since each poem is unique: there is no one version of the izibongo of contemporary chiefs, for each imbongi is an individual commentator and different iimbongi would assess the character of any one chief differently. In range, the imbongi is not limited to topics he has prepared beforehand: a good imbongi can produce a spontaneous poem on demand about virtually any suitable topic, so the number of poems one can collect from an imbongi is not a factor of his repertoire. The quality of improvisation is thus significantly different from that of the guslar. The ability to compose poetry spontaneously on unpremeditated subjects is essential to the imbongi if he is to fulfil his social function properly. He has the ability to comment on events as they are happening: he may, for example, try to sway the opinions of his audience about a debate during the very course of that debate.

> Few of the Xhosa *iimbongi* I have met prepare a poem in advance, and few of them consciously memorise their poetry. Most of them draw a clear distinction between poets like themselves who are never at a loss for words, and those who are limited in scope. The former are free to refer in their poetry to anything or anyone they see or know about, the latter can go no further than the poems they have learnt by heart. [Opland: 1974, 8]

A memoriser would have to remain silent in a moment of unexpected crisis. On first hearing, a poet who has to compose and memorise a poem in advance (say about a personage he knows will be present at a forthcoming function) might be indistinguishable in performance from the improvising poet, but his social function and influence is restricted since he is not free to comment on events as and when they happen.

The poetry of the Nguni peoples (Xhosa, Zulu, Swazi, etc.) in southern Africa which is produced by the imbongi or tribal poet is eulogistic: the poems almost invariably contain the praise-names of the subject and place him in the context of his genealogy, they record his deeds and achievements and assess his character, they describe significant features of his physical appearance (on Nguni eulogy, in addition to works by Mafeje and Opland, see Cook; Cope;

Finnegan: 1970; Jordan: 1973b; Kuse; Lestrade: 1935, 1937; Ndabanda; Nyembezi: 1948; Vilakazi: 1945). The subject is usually a chief or king, a distinguished warrior, or a visiting dignitary; most frequently the poet eulogises the chief he serves. An intimate bond exists between chief and poet: the imbongi of the great Zulu king Shaka is said to have asked to be put to death on the body of his murdered patron, and his request was promptly granted. The imbongi invariably forms part of the chief's entourage when he travels to neighbouring chiefdoms; on such visits, the chief's arrival is announced by the imbongi declaiming his izibongo, presenting to the people his ancestry and his achievements. In this way the imbongi acts as a herald for the touring chief. At home, the imbongi always performs at official functions attended by his chief, at dances, court cases, or weddings. He has the licence to use obscene words in public, and he may choose to be witty or sly, but his function is never primarily to entertain. He is a solo performer whose performance is attended to keenly. Generally there is no other competing noise when the imbongi performs, though he may encourage people to greater efforts by declaiming his poetry while they are dancing or fighting.

The imbongi exerts a powerful influence on the emotions of his audience: one old Xhosa told me that the imbongi was a bad personage since if my informant started quarrelling with a fellow at a beer party, and the imbongi stood up and declaimed his praises, he would hit his opponent whether he wished to or not. It is this power to incite that made the imbongi an important figure during a battle, when he would praise his own troops and heap abuse on the enemy. At such times he was a protected person—one informant told me he then had the status of a woman—since it was considered shameful to kill an imbongi during a battle.

The imbongi has the licence to use ribald language, but he is also permitted to criticise the chief publicly with impunity: he is accorded the liberty to speak his mind freely in public, for he has a responsibility to chief and people to tell the truth as he sees it. (If he lacks honesty he will not gain acceptance as an imbongi.) Thus his eulogistic poetry contains not only praise but also blame (see Jordan: 1973b, 26; Mafeje: 1967, 193; Ntantala; on poetic criticism, see Elliott). His poetry is designed to inspire the people to loyalty for the chief, but he reserves the right to criticise the chief's actions if necessary. This last is never done with the motive of stirring the tribe to civil disobedience but is intended, rather, to express openly before the chief what tribesmen might be afraid to say: the chief is too harsh in judgement, perhaps, or he favours the wives of too many of his warriors. Praise and blame are twin aspects of the imbongi's soothsaying.

The criticism is not intended to undermine the social order; above all else the imbongi upholds the social norm. He presents to the people an ideal of conduct and decries any acts that are excessive or diverge from the norm.

The imbongi's function is supported by a number of unexpressed privileges, and many of these—his licence to criticise with impunity, his freedom to use whatever words come to mind free of social approbation—seem to be consequences of his obligation to tell the truth as he sees it and acknowledgement of the fact that in some way he has no control over what he says and cannot be held responsible for it. In other words, these privileges seem to support the belief that he is utterly inspired, that he communes with the spirits while performing. The Zulu imbongi utters his izibongo in a rapid rhythmical style that can be described as incantatory (see Rycroft: 1960; 1962). The Xhosa imbongi in performance actively moves about gesticulating and thrusting emphatically with his spears, declaiming his izibongo in a strained, guttural voice at the level of a shout. This is how one early missionary recorded a Sotho performance:

> In a large gathering, sitting round waiting to hear a royal message, a man seems suddenly seized by an irresistible devil. He leaps forward, parades in front of his friends, his head held high, his eyes large and staring, his face contorted, his voice raised in pitch, making violent gestures; he declaims his praises but without varying the intonation of his voice, and with such a stream of words that it is difficult to understand the words. He goes on and on as if deluded, possessed and mad, and when he reaches the end of his long poem, he engages in several wild capers, his feet kicking up the dust around him, sketching with his hand the gesture of a warrior hitting his enemy or stabbing him with a spear. Then his features relax, a contented smile takes the place of the ferocious expression of a moment ago and he goes calmly back to his place by his friends, to listen to and admire the grimaces of him who has replaced him in this strange exercise. The white man laughs, finding this infantile, ridiculous and grotesque. As for the black man, he admires, he exults at this spectacle which for him is worthy of heroes and which responds to his most intimate ideas and to all that is virile in him. [quoted in Kunene: 1971, xii; cf. Kunene: 1967, 1–8]

It would have been easy for a Christian missionary in the nineteenth century to believe that the poet was possessed by a devil.

There are other indications that the poet in performance is spiritually inspired. An eminent ethnographer, N. J. van Warmelo, notes that the Zulu imbongi always smoked marijuana before performing (van Warmelo, 7; cf.

Webb and Wright, 169). I can quote at least one clear example from my own field experience to support the view that the poet in performance functions not on the conscious but on the preconscious level. I once returned to a Xhosa poet a few months after recording his poetry in order to check the transcription and translation of the earlier performances. Before we started I played him a tape recording of a poem produced by another imbongi and asked his opinion of it. He replied that it was a good poem, but he felt that the criticism of the early missionaries contained in the poem ought not to have been expressed since a white audience would not understand and a black audience would be aroused. Later, when we were working through the poem that he had produced some months earlier, we came upon a passage that expressed precisely the same anti-missionary sentiment (see Opland: 1975, 198 and 202). Consciously the poet felt that it was not politic for such feelings to be voiced in public, yet he had himself done just that in performance. Modern Xhosa iimbongi still wear a cloak and hat of animal skins when they perform, though they are at a loss to explain why they do so; the anthropologist might note that a connection with the animal world is one of the universal characteristics of the shaman. (On shamans see, for example, Brodzky; Eliade; Hatto: 1970.)

All of the above comments about Xhosa and Zulu izibongo must be placed within a religiomagical context. Not only does the imbongi have the power to incite, the izibongo itself has power. One old, illiterate Xhosa once produced an izibongo that he had composed about myself and my car; he claimed that recitation of this izibongo would ensure that I had a safe journey home. He maintained that this same effect would be secured even if he went off on his own and recited the izibongo with neither ourselves nor anyone else to hear him.

Both Zulus and Xhosas venerate their ancestors. In times of trouble, male members of a family will enter the cattle enclosure (an area restricted to males) to slaughter an animal and in so doing will recite the izibongo of their ancestors. This recitation conjures the presence of the spirits of the ancestors, so that they may be importuned to intercede with the Great Spirit on behalf of the troubled tribesmen. I once asked an old Zulu if he knew any izibongo; he replied that he did, but declined to recite them for us on the grounds that he was a Christian. His non-Christian brother, however, did not share his reluctance, and produced for us a number of izibongo of chiefs past and present. Yet when we asked him to recite the izibongo of his own father and grandfather, he was hesitant, and when he finally did so, he turned his head to one side and spoke in a reverent undertone. The imbongi's official function of reciting the izibongo of his chief and his chief's ancestors must be viewed in this religiomagical context.

While we were recording the izibongo of two Zulu izimbongi, both uncles of the chief, Trevor Cope noticed that they referred to the poems in a curious way, not as poems but as the subjects of the poems. "Do you know the praises of Dingana?" we would ask; "Yes, I know him" was the reply (not "it"). If they stumbled in reciting these memorised poems they said "I have forgotten him" not "I have forgotten it [the poem]." A few minutes later we asked the poets' chief, Mangosuthu Gatsha Buthelezi, who is currently chief minister of Kwa-Zulu, about this. He replied that the izibongo of a person *is* the person, that the recitation of an izibongo is a form of praying.

Opland: Now this is interesting: when you say that it's a form of prayer, that praising is a form of prayer—Every Zulu knows the praises of his father . . . and he will *bonga* [recite the eulogies of] his ancestors when he needs help (*Buthelezi*: Yes, quite so) in order to commune with them.

Buthelezi: Quite. It is true.

O: Now the imbongi will bonga your ancestors: does this have the same kind of function, as communing with your ancestors? Every time he bongas the chief he refers to his father and the chief's grandfather. Would it have a, really a *ritual* significance?

B: It always has a ritual significance.

O: Always?

B: Always, yes. . . .

O: So the imbongi, in saying the praises of your father and your grandfather, is in a sense praying, communing with your ancestors?

B: Oh yes . . . because he sees me as the—as actually the living—that I'm the living symbol of all of them.

O: Of all the Zulus? Or all the tribe?

B: No, no, of this line, you see, because I'm the embodiment of them now. . . . They say to me "You are uNdaba," you see, "UnguMnyamana wena," you know ["You are Mnyamana, Ndaba"—ancestors of the chief]. They say this to me quite often, because they regard me as the reincarnation of all my ancestors.

Douglas Mzolo: Also, it means to seal up that link, to seal up the link, you see, between your ancestors and yourself.

B: Yes, but I think it's even more than that. It's really—It has also a religious connotation, because [my uncle] believes that at one time he was very seriously ill and in his dreams some people said "Shenge!" you know, saluting one of our chiefs, and then he turned and he said he saw me, you see. So he said, you know, actually "Uyidlozilami" ["You are my ancestor"], that means that as I am now even not dead I'm one of his—some kind of a live and social spirit as I am. I mean these people believe sincerely that—in that. Even yesterday some people shook hands with me to wish me well, but some people said openly that they were taking luck from me. You know, it's a priestly sort of thing, you see, like a blessing and so on. [Item 348 in Opland Collection]

The izibongo relate the subject to his line of descent, they chronicle his deeds and assess his character; after his death, the izibongo *is* the subject. As a traditional poem in praise of the king Dingana (d. 1840) puts it,

> People will die, but their izibongo remain;
> These will remain to weep for them in their deserted homes.
>
> [Cope, 67]

The subject's memory lives on—*he* lives on—in the poem that defines him. Recitation of the poem by his descendants, naming him in effect, invokes his presence and ensures his protective sympathy; recitation of the izibongo of a dead chief by an imbongi ensures the protective sympathy of that chief for his ruling descendant, in whom resides the well-being of the people. Thus the tribal poet is intimately involved with the very life of the people: his poetry serves to establish and maintain the social order, it confirms the sacral king in his rule. As a noted Zulu playwright, H. I. E. Dhlomo, put it, "the tribal man will tell you that the izibongo are the wealth of our country, the soul of our state, the dignity and meaning of the Race—are God himself" (Dhlomo: 1948, 47; see also Dhlomo: 1939).

2

The Pre-Christian Period to A.D. 100

The pre-Christian period presents more problems than any other. It is in extent by far the longest period that we shall consider; the conclusions will necessarily be the most hypothetical; and what little evidence is available to us for a study of poetry in this period will be subject to the most restrictive constraints. As a result of recent archaeological research, the history of man in northern Europe has been taken back far beyond ca. 300 B.C., the date of the earliest extant written observations of these early Germanic peoples; this history now stretches back not for thousands but for tens of thousands of years. We are not concerned, however, with the origins of poetry among the Indo-European peoples (as were many nineteenth-century scholars: see the summary of opinion in Gummere: 1970); we are concerned only with the period of their literary history that is relevant to an understanding of the later poetic tradition in Anglo-Saxon England. Nonetheless, a major difficulty presents itself in the discussion of the period of time ending in about A.D. 100. This is the vagueness of the chronology: although the period under consideration may extend for many centuries, we can never be sure exactly what point in time we are considering. Whereas a historical work in Latin or Greek can be reasonably dated, an argument from etymology or comparative Indo-European religion yields evidence that is less precisely fixed in time.

Our evidence for the period prior to the extant Greek or Latin descriptions of Germanic people is drawn from the study of etymology and comparative Indo-European culture; the period from ca. 100 to ca. 600, during which the ancestors of the English were still pagan, is set apart from the preceding period by virtue of the evidence available to us, and will be considered in the next chapter. In spite of the nature of the evidence on the earlier period, a tentative hypothesis can be advanced. It seems reasonable that the Germanic poetic tradi-tion—if one may use the term meaningfully—before the second century was complex and that there were different forms of poetry and song; it seems likely that poetry performed a serious function in society; it is possible that the most elevated form of early Germanic poetry was eulogy, and that the poets who propagated this tradition were intimately connected with the kingship.

Much of the work produced by scholars in the broad field of comparative Indo-European culture derives from an appreciation of the fact that the early Celtic and Indian writings preserve details of archaic traditions that are closest to the postulated common Indo-European tradition. The geographically ex-treme cultures—the far east and the far west of the Indo-European linguistic family—are in many ways the most conservative. The Sanskrit and Celtic writings thus hold the key to any reconstruction of the way of life of the early Indo-Europeans. In an article entitled "Indo-European Metrics and Archaic Irish Verse," Calvert Watkins devotes some attention to the words referring to poets and poetry in the Indo-European languages. The Celtic languages, especially Old Irish, "represent an extraordinarily archaic and conservative lin-guistic tradition within the Indo-European tradition" (212) reflected in linguis-tic structure and vocabulary. "Not only the vocabulary, but the institutions themselves, the whole social structure of early Ireland, represent a remarkably faithful reflex of what we know of 'Indo-European' tribal society" (213). The Old Irish poet, the *fili*, enjoyed special privileges in his society; the *filid* were highly respected and sometimes feared personages, who performed their function invested with an aura of magic. They composed poems in praise of the kings they served and elegies on their deaths; they were the custodians of the legal and traditional lore of the people; they were genealogists and his-torians. A study of the vocabulary suggests a connection between poetry and magic: "The verb *canid*, together with its compounds *ar-cain*, *do-cain*, 'sings, chants, recites,' is applied to poetry, to charms and magical formulas, and to legal pronouncements and maxims as well. It is identical with Latin *canere*, with its derivatives *carmen*, *uāti-cinium*, *in-cantāre*, etc." (214). Watkins similarly argues for an association between poetry and music, prophecy, and inspiration (drawing this last back to roots literally signifying "breath" or "wind").

The Celtic words that Watkins cites are placed in their fuller Indo-European context in a recent article by H. Wagner, who arranges the cognates as follows:

(a) Ir. *fáth* "prophecy, cause"; W. *gwawd* "poem"; O. Icel. *óðr* "poetry," O. Engl. *wóþ* "singing, sound, voice, poetry."

(b) Goth. *wods*, O. Icel. *óðr*, O. Engl. *wód*, OHG. *wuot* "mad," German *Wut* "madness," *wuten* "to rage" etc.

(c) O. Icel. *Óðinn*, O. Engl. *Wóden*, OHG. *Wuotan*, the Germanic god *Wotan*.

(d) Ir. *fáith* "seer, prophet," Lat. *vātēs*, Gaulish οὐάτεις (pl.). *id.*

(e) Sanskrit (and Avestic) *api-vat-*, originally meaning "to blow at, to inspire." [46]

Wagner does not agree on all points with Watkins, but for the moment I wish simply to draw attention to the work of those Indo-European etymologists who have established a semantic context for some words associated with poetry that are suggestive of magic and prophetic frenzy associated with the gods (see Watkins: 1970). (I shall have occasion to return to Old English *wop* and *wod* later, in chapter 9.) This etymological and generally linguistic research would seem to suggest that the primitive Indo-European poet was a figure set apart from ordinary men, a man who in uttering his poetry lost possession of himself as he communed with the gods, somewhat like a shaman.

The research of other scholars in related areas suggests that this common Indo-European tradition was eulogistic in character (see Dumézil: 1943; Nagy; and Ward). J. E. Caerwyn Williams establishes the Indo-European context for his study of "The Court Poet in Medieval Ireland." Williams cites other scholars on the poet in medieval Ireland, scholars such as O. J. Bergin, who writes of the Irish poet:

> He was, in fact, a professor of literature and a man of letters, highly trained in the use of a polished literary medium, belonging to a hereditary caste in an aristocratic society, holding an official position by virtue of his train-ing, his learning, his knowledge of the history and traditions of his country and his clan. He discharged . . . the functions of the modern journalist. He was not a song writer. He was often a public official, a chronicler, a political essayist, a keen and satirical observer of his fellow-countrymen. [85]

Williams also cites James Carney, who claims that the poet was "the shadow of a high-ranking pagan priest or druid" (86), and Eleanor Knott, who says that "the bardic profession was built upon the ruins of—or perhaps we might say was a protective metamorphosis of—the ancient druidic order, and was always a craft with its own dues, privileges, and prerogatives, decided by itself" (86).

These figures of considerable stature and importance in early Irish society, the *ollavs* or *filid*, have their counterparts in other European societies, and Williams briefly characterises the Welsh *pencerdd* and *bardd teulu*, the Scandinavian *skald*, and (drawing on the work of Heusler, L. F. Anderson, and Chadwick and referring to *Beowulf, Widsith* and *Deor*) the Anglo-Saxon scop. The scop unfortunately does not quite fit the pattern Williams proceeds to establish, largely because—as I hope to show in this book—his sources of information have certain limitations. But he does make a number of general statements about the western European (Celtic and Germanic) poetic traditions which provide a context within which I believe the tradition of the scop should also be placed. First,

> most of the verse composed by skald, *pencerdd*, and ollav is praise or celebration-poetry and its underlying assumption is that fame and honour are the supreme values. . . . Secondly, these poems are essentially aristocratic. They celebrate a hero before an audience of heroes, and they are composed by heroes. . . . Thirdly, these poems originally had a social and religious significance . . . originally they were declaimed before an assembled audience, and the intricacy of their metres, the richness of their diction, the wealth of their allusion, and the comparative simplicity of their themes, all show that their composers were well aware that part at least of their function was to demonstrate that they were Lords of the Word in a world in which words had not yet lost their magic power. [93 f.]

Drawing on evidence from classical writings on the early Celts and Germans, arguing from etymology, and citing the conclusions of students of comparative Indo-European culture (notably Dumézil), Williams proceeds to demonstrate the intimate bond between the early poet and his royal patron. The poetry eulogised the sacral ruler and confirmed the subject's status: the poetry was designed to uphold the social order. Both king and poet derive their power from the gods. Williams concludes:

> Every primitive poet was to some extent a shaman or magician, in other words he claimed the ability to exercise power over things, and his poetry was the means to that end. The early court poet practised his poetry to instil into men those qualities which they prized above all others. Of course, *menos, kudos, timē*, etc., were the gifts of the gods but the poet in declaring that his patron had them was in a way forcing the hands of the gods: he made these qualities exist, or if they already existed, he made them stronger. In a sense then by affirming the courage and honour of his patron he gave

and confirmed courage, he gave and confirmed honour, and in so doing he ensured his fame. [109 f.]

The poems strengthened or created in the subject "qualities of mind and body which would produce the actions of which everyone would soon be talking" (110).

Williams next turns to examine the Irish tradition in detail, and in so doing makes many points which might well be relevant to an understanding of early Germanic poetry as well. For example, in discussing the Celtic elegies, Williams writes:

> In the beginning the lament or the dirge served the same purpose as the panegyric. It belongs to the same world of ideas as that which gave rise to hero-cults. In this world the dead are still powerful. That is why the possession of the hero's remains and his grave is a matter of great importance. That is why the hero's goodwill has to be retained and secured by sacrifices at his tomb. In this world, too, the family is a living corporate entity. The solidarity of the primitive family is a fact too well known to call for emphasis here, but it should be remembered that it included not only the living but also the dead members, and that the living felt that they needed the help of the dead and especially of those who could contribute greatly to their well-being and that of their descendants. . . . If, as we believe, the early praise-song was designed to strengthen the living, it could also strengthen the dead. [112]

Williams thus traces the court poet in medieval Ireland back to a common Indo-European tradition of eulogy performed by a shamanistic poet in praise of a sacral king. Recently scholars have turned their attention to the concept of sacral kingship in early Germanic society (see Binchy; De Vries: 1956; Hauck; Höfler). J. M. Wallace-Hadrill, for example, states that kings "could link the gods with those they ruled; they could appease and placate the gods and be deposed in sacrificial propitiation when things went wrong. The kings of the migrating Germans, like those of the Scandinavians, were sacral, by which we mean that they were cult-kings, representing the moral lives and domestic ideals of their people, incapsulating good luck" (8). This sacral kingship is often associated with the god Woden, from whom most of the Anglo-Saxon dynasties later traced their descent. The king links the people with the gods and if blessed brings to the people the luck that will ensure victory in battle, success in the harvest, and continued rule by the Woden-descended family of kings. Conversely, failure in battle or of the crops may lead to deposition of the king and his sacrificial slaughter to propitiate the gods.

William A. Chaney's *The Cult of Kingship in Anglo-Saxon England* attempts to demonstrate the continuity of these beliefs from the continental period through the conversion to Christianity, and in doing so provides a context within which to place, for example, Alcuin's statement in his letter to Athelred in 793: "In the king's righteousness is the prosperity of the whole folk, victory of the army, mildness of the seasons, abundance of the land, the blessing of sons, the health of the people." Chaney often strains his evidence to make his points; Wallace-Hadrill seems at times to admit later Scandinavian beliefs as valid for the continental Germans, or generalises about the Germans from Gothic or Lombardic evidence. Nonetheless, both depict a concept of kingship that is in harmony with that postulated for early Indo-European kings by Dumézil, De Vries, and other scholars. The poet is one of the functionaries associated with such a royal cult figure. (On this relationship in the Indo-European context, see especially Dumézil: 1943, chap. 1, and in the context of ancient Israel, see Johnson: 1962 and 1979.)

The structure that has emerged from the foregoing summary of the conclusions of other scholars is admittedly hypothetical, since there are patently no primary data extant from Indo-European times. It is based on the assumption that the Indic and Celtic tradition are of great antiquity and preserve to a significant degree elements of the postulated common Indo-European tradition, elements capable of extrapolation by scholars. It is based, too, on a study of elements common to later Indo-European traditions and preserved in the Indo-European vocabularies. And it is based on a comparative study of Indo-European social and religious beliefs. These studies necessarily reinforce and depend on each other, but the hypothetical conclusions that can be derived about the context of poetry draw a measure of confirmation from a study of contemporary analogous traditions; indeed, such studies might succeed to a certain extent in animating the Indo-European construct.

Caerwyn Williams refers to a sentiment common to Indo-European poetic traditions, the hero's concern for his enduring reputation, and quotes the Welsh proverb "Wealth vanishes, praise [fame] does not" and the Irish stanza "If the wealth of the world were to be assessed—this is the sum total of the matter— nothing in the world is other than futile except only eulogy" (93 f.). In an ode in praise of an athletic victor, Pindar says:

> If a man be fortunate and win, he casts the delight
> of his cause in the Muses' stream; even high strength,

lacking song, goes down into the great darkness.
There are means to but one glass that mirrors
   deeds of splendour:
by the shining waters of Memory
is found recompense for strain in poetry that
   rings far.

[Nemean Odes, VII, trans. Lattimore]

In Germanic literature, one reads in the Heliand the exhortation "Let us all follow him on this journey: our lives lose nothing of value in this, but in his following, together with him, we die with our lord. Then our glory lives after us, the good reputation of men" (Heliand, 3998–4002, in Andersson: 1974, 591); in Hávamál:

> Cattle die,   kinsmen die,
>   one day you die yourself;
> but the words of praise   will not perish
>   when a man wins fair fame.
> Cattle die,   kinsmen die,
>   one day you die yourself;
> I know one thing   that never dies—
>   the dead man's reputation

[76–77, trans. Terry]

and Beowulf tells Hrothgar:

> Ure æghwylc   sceal ende gebidan
> worolde lifes;   wyrce se þe mote
> domes ær deaþe;   þæt bið drihtguman
> unlifgendum   æfter selest.

[ASPR, IV, 1386–89]

[Each of us must experience an end to life in this world; let him who can achieve fame before death; that is the best thing for a retainer after his passing.]

With these Indo-European sentiments, compare the Zulu lines

> People will die, but their praises [izibongo] remain;
> These will remain to weep for them in their deserted homes.

[Cope, 67]

Much of the preceding discussion about Indo-European eulogy and sacral king-ship applies just as well to the southeastern Bantu; a description of the function and privileges of the medieval Celtic poet holds almost without change for the contemporary Xhosa poet (see Mafeje: 1967).

It is quite possible that before the Christian era Germanic tribal poetry par-ticipated in a system such as that of the contemporary Xhosa- or Zulu-speaking peoples in South Africa, so that the observable facts of the living modern tradi-tion might suggest a hypothetical reconstruction of the dead ancient one. In the absence of primary data, it is reasonable to suppose from the evidence of etymology, of the comparative study of Indo-European culture, and from the comparative study of analogous living traditions, that the primitive Germanic tribal poet was a eulogiser intimately connected with a sacral king (on Nguni sacral kingship, see the unsatisfactory Pettersson; on Anglo-Saxon ancestor veneration, see Hilda Davidson: 1950; Gummere: 1930, 364ff.; cf. Hilda Da-vidson: 1967, 37; and Ellis). In other words, as Caerwyn Williams noted, this court poet produced praise or celebration poetry that had a social and religious significance.

Williams also made the point that the poems were essentially aristocratic, composed by heroes celebrating heroes before an audience of heroes. Certainly not all Germanic men were aristocratic or heroic: in considering what the full tradition might have been like, we must allow for variations within this tradi-tion, for other forms of poetry and other kinds of poets. Strictly speaking, of course, one cannot talk of a poetic tradition at all except in the most general of terms. However much he participates in a common tradition, each poet per-ceives reality through his own eyes and cultivates his own creative talent: as Albert Lord puts it, "the singing bard is never a type but an individual" (1960, 31). The Xhosa imbongi wears his cloak and hat of animal skins and performs on ceremonial occasions in the presence of his chief, but each individual imbongi exhibits personal traits in performance—one punctuates his delivery with dra-matic gestures or strikes studied poses, another restlessly paces back and forth—as well as personal interests and talent—one favours historical allusions, another is more concerned with contemporary politics. This means that although it is true that the imbongi operates within a eulogistic tradition, the manifestations of this tradition in individual izibongo may vary.

In content an izibongo usually includes a genealogy of the subject, an enu-meration of significant events in which he participated, and a characterisation of the subject from both a physical and a moral point of view, but this does not mean that every izibongo contains all these elements in the same proportion. A recitation of the genealogy of a chief, for example, may take the imbongi into a recitation of the deeds and qualities of his ancestors. Although essentially allusive and elliptical rather than explicitly narrative, the izibongo is nevertheless potentially narrative: a recitation of the deeds of a chief, for example, may take the imbongi into an extended account of one particular exploit. The eulogy is thus subject to considerable variation in content: a poet may praise past chiefs to demonstrate the inadequacies of their descendants, or he may recount heroic exploits in order to incite his audience to acts of bravery. (Lord talks of "the analogical thinking or associative thinking of oral poets everywhere," 1960, 159.) The purpose is never entertainment, however much the audience might enjoy seeing and hearing the imbongi perform: the poet is a political cartoonist rather than a stand-up comic. (The characteristics alluded to in this paragraph are exemplified by the poems printed in Opland: 1977a; on Latin panegyric, see Riggio, chap. 1; on Welsh panegyric, see Matonis; and for a psychological approach to Anglo-Saxon eulogy, see Grosz.)

One element is common to all variations, however: the eulogy concerns people. It refers to people past or present who lived in the public domain. The izibongo is public: it may express the poet's feelings, but these are feelings of public concern about events or personalities within the common experience. In other words, the imbongi is not a lyric poet. The distinction is implicit in A. C. Jordan's assessment of the greatest Xhosa imbongi, S. E. K. Mqhayi, who wrote many poems in addition to performing as a traditional imbongi on ceremonial occasions, "Essentially a poet of the traditional type, for theme he is almost wholly confined to concrete subjects, usually human beings" (Jordan: 1973b, 111), and again, " 'Nature for Nature's sake' hardly has a place in the izibongo of the old type, and Mqhayi's nature poems are on the whole disappointing" (115). The eulogy is concerned with public personalities rather than private emotions. Even the poet's association with his chief, however personal, is ultimately public, for he is the tribal poet: as Jordan sensitively put it, "one of the essential qualities of *ubumbongi* ["being a poet"] was true patriotism, not blind loyalty to the person of the chief, but loyalty to the principles that the chieftainship does or ought to stand for" (112).

Although he dominates, the imbongi is not the only poet in the community. Young boys often amuse themselves while herding cattle by composing and memorising poems about themselves, their peers, or their fathers' cattle. Most men have learnt poems about themselves (which they may utter while dancing or fighting as an expression of pride), about their cattle (which they may shout out while ploughing to encourage the team), or about their ancestors (which they recite on ritual occasions to conjure their presence and request their aid). Women are especially knowledgeable about the traditional poems of their own and their husband's clan, appropriate snatches of which they utter as an expression of thanks or acknowledgement of achievement. All these will be memorised poems that either the performer or someone else has composed, and each of them has a clear role to play in social life. However, among the Xhosa at any rate, everyone is potentially a spontaneous poet, and men and women are likely to give poetic expression to strong feelings on the inspiration of the moment with no premeditation: I have seen this happen or heard of its happening while men are dancing or playing sport, while boys are preparing to fight against a neighbouring faction, or at a funeral or a political meeting. These spontaneous poems are produced not by an imbongi but by amateurs who could not subsequently repeat the words, since the particular moment that prompted the reaction could not be repeated. Finally, though not much is known about it, there are likely to be poems used professionally by diviners and herbalists, poetic spells and incantations used for divining and influencing the present (on such poems among the Sotho, see Guma, 148–51, and Laydevant; on Nguni diviners, see Callaway; Kohler). All these different and varied forms of poetry would be called "izibongo" by Nguni peoples like the Zulu and the Xhosa.

A study of the function of Nguni poetry can certainly serve to explain the evidence produced by etymologists and comparativists on the social significance of Indo-European poetry. If eulogy functioned in a similar way in Indo-European society, it served, like Xhosa and Zulu poetry, as a medium of communication between man and the gods or ancestors. Just as a man recites the eulogy of his departed ancestor to enter into communication with him, so too the tribal poet's recitation of the eulogy of the chief ensures the sympathetic attention of the chief's ancestors to the well-being of the chief, thereby ensuring the well-being of the chiefdom. The Nguni imbongi operates today within a living tradition of eulogy, providing us with a model of the way in which eulogy might have operated in early Indo-European times.

One cannot stop at this point in surveying the tradition, however, for one must include a consideration of song and its relation to poetry. The distinction between a poem and a song might not be apparent from a scrutiny of the text; the distinction manifests itself in performance and perhaps in social function. Poems may be set to music, and if sung they are songs; if read in a book they are poems. Texts of songs—such as the British ballads, for example—may be read and appreciated as poems with no knowledge of their original musical setting. The difference is not in the words but in the performance: presented with a text one might not be able to say whether it was a poem or a song, but confronted by a performance one would have no hesitation in deciding. A song is produced to the accompaniment of a musical tune either vocal or instrumental; a poem is recited or declaimed with no such integral accompaniment. The Bantu-speaking peoples in South Africa know many different kinds of songs, choral or antiphonal or solo, accompanied by instruments or unaccompanied. Songs are sung in the course of work, dance, or play, at weddings or funerals or initiations, in the fields or on the battleground. Songs may be personal expressions of emotion uttered in isolation or communal performances produced in unison by throngs. In Xhosa, to perform a song is *ukucula*, to perform a poem is *ukubonga*; the two activities are quite distinct. (In English, to produce a song is to sing, but there is no comparable verb for the oral production of a poem: declaim? utter? produce? perform? chant?) In all subsequent discussions, I shall try where possible to maintain a distinction between poetry and song on the basis of the presence or absence of musical accompaniment whether vocal or instrumental.

It would be surprising indeed if the early Germanic peoples did not share similar practices. It is extremely unlikely that the eulogistic poems of the court or tribal poet were the only form of poetry known to them: it is reasonable to suppose that, in common with other primitive communities right down to the present time, the Germanic people knew different forms of poetry and different kinds of song. Although one cannot argue that there was identity in all respects, there is likely to be a general agreement in structure between the Nguni and the Germanic traditions of poetry, especially in view of the similarities in the social structures of the two societies (see Diamond). In all probability, Germanic warriors knew autobiographical poems which they uttered individually, like the Zulu and the Xhosa, on engaging in battle, just as it is probable that, like the Zulu and the Xhosa, they sang war songs in unison on entering into battle. There are likely to have been charms and spells, genealogies and lists committed to memory in poetic form. There are also likely to have been other forms of verbal play, such as riddles and proverbs—perhaps in poetic form—legends and folktales. Sometimes the folktales might incorporate songs, or the legends explain a line or two from a traditional eulogy (for an example of the latter with remarkably Germanic characteristics, see van Warmelo). Traditions of verbal art among all primitive peoples are complex, and there is often considerable exchange and interplay between the various forms.

Confirmation of some of these suppositions about early Germanic poetry will come from an examination of the documents of later times. The outline of the hypothetical structure proposed above starts to emerge in the very earliest references in Greek and Latin to poetic practices among the Germanic people, which we shall examine in the next chapter.

3

The Pre-Christian Period: A.D. 100–600

From about A.D. 100 to 600 the ancestors of the English remained unconverted to Christianity as in the preceding centuries, but a number of factors encourage us to view this period separately. For the first time we have descriptions of the way of life of the Germanic peoples in their homelands: we move out of the realm of hypothesis towards more definite conclusions. This is the period of the Germanic migrations in which the Germanic peoples act and interact with other cultures, notably that of Rome. The ancestors of the English cross the Channel and in Britain become the Anglo-Saxons; from this point on they are separated from the common Germanic tradition and their history takes on a personal character and individuality. In the preceding chapter we were obliged to work on the assumption that, as far as poetry was concerned, there was such a thing as a common Germanic culture; now, as each section of the Germanic people comes into contact with various alien cultures—Greek or Roman, Arabic, Slavic, or Celtic—the likelihood that generalisations about Germanic poetry are accurate lessens considerably. Sixth-century Anglo-Saxons already have a distinct historical background that separates them clearly from, say, their sixth-century Gothic cousins.

There are two broad spheres of evidence for this period. A number of authors who wrote in Greek or Latin have given us descriptions of practices among the Germanic people that might be considered to be poetic. The reliability of these sources varies, as does the value of their testimony. None of the statements, however, refers specifically to the ancestors of the English, the Angles, Saxons, Jutes, or Frisians (see Morris; Myres). Individual members of these nations may well have come within the ambit of Roman cultural influence by serving in the Roman army or trading with Roman merchants; however much influenced these individuals might have been by Roman literary practices, though, it is unlikely that they would have affected traditional customs and tastes on their return to their homelands. Throughout this period the ancestors of the English on the Continent and later in England remained effectively non-Christian and accordingly preliterate; their chiefs and kings did not participate in the life of Rome. The same cannot be said of the Germanic peoples living to the south or east of them, and the Roman historians supply evidence of the influence of Rome on the musical and poetic tastes of the Gothic peoples especially. From the time when the English crossed the Channel to settle in England, we are afforded more particular and intimate information about them, for they then enter historical times: their movements and some of their customs can be reconstructed by archaeological research, as well as from the reports of them in extant British histories.

First, then, let us consider the continental Greek and Latin writings. We could treat this material either by category, as Andreas Heusler has done (1911; 1957), or chronologically, as I propose to do. Heusler conceived of the common Germanic tradition as multiform, consisting of different kinds of poetry and song—magical (whether religious or ritual), gnomic (legal, proverbial, or riddling poetry), mnemonic, communal (work songs, dancing songs, choruses and solo lyrics), societal (praise poetry, dirges) and epic, heroic, or mythical songs. This is undeniably a valid approach, one that is fully justified by the evidence and supported by observation of living traditions today, as we saw in the last chapter. However, it does treat the tradition from the common Germanic point of view, and cites supporting evidence from various times about various Germanic peoples. This is not to say that Heusler does not appreciate local differences or alterations to the tradition in time; he does. But we are concerned here solely with the Anglo-Saxons and are interested in the common Germanic tradition only insofar as it provides a context within which to place the origins of the later Anglo-Saxon tradition. It will suit our purposes, therefore, to adopt a chronological presentation of the material, for then we may attempt to identify significant local changes in the common Germanic tradition and assess the influence of these on the continental ancestors of the English.

A number of classical writers comment on the customs of the Germanic people, but the first to supply any information about their poetry is Tacitus (ca. 55 to 120). The major source within the body of Tacitus's writings is his *Germania*, written in about A.D. 98. It is most unlikely that we can accept statements that Tacitus makes about the Germanic people in general as valid for all the tribes and nations. He has a very hazy knowledge of the tribes beyond the border territories, and although he does consider the individual customs of some tribes, he nowhere mentions the Frisians or the Jutes, and refers to the Angles only in passing. Tacitus's motive in writing the *Germania* was not so much ethnographical as political: he wished to depict for his readers a noble Germanic savage as a pointed contrast to the morally debased Roman of his day. For this purpose he made use of the elder Pliny's *Bella Germaniae* and other books, rather than undertake firsthand field work beyond the Rhine; indeed, we have no evidence that Tacitus ever crossed the Rhine. Wallace-Hadrill assesses the value of the *Germania* for modern historians thus:

> Whether or not Tacitus had ever visited the Rhine frontier, he felt no need to consult those who had. He knew what he had to say, and the material at hand enabled him to say it. It amounts to this: the *Germania* is not only an unsafe guide to future Germanic society, it also affords no solid ground for generalization about Germanic society at large of the historian's own time. It describes the ways of certain Germans, how exactly we cannot tell, at a particular and altogether exceptional moment in their history. [2]

With this caveat in mind, we can proceed to consider the evidence of Tacitus.

The early chapters of the *Germania* (ed. J. G. C. Anderson) deal with the Germanic people in general. In the second chapter Tacitus tells us that "in ancient songs/poems, the only kind of history or chronicle among them ('carminibus antiquis, quod unum apud illos memoriae et annalium genus est'), they celebrate Tuisto, a god born from the earth, and his son Mannus as the source and founders of their people." *Carmen* was used to refer to both poetry and song; with no reference to the performer or the performance, we cannot determine whether these celebrations, *carminibus antiquis*, were chanted or sung, whether they were poems or songs. That they were ancient seems to suggest that they were traditional. It is Tacitus's opinion that their function was historical, but the Germanic performer or his audience might not have agreed; the comment that they are the only form of history among the Germans, however, might be taken to suggest that Tacitus thought that the texts were memorised. It is generally true that in primitive societies those texts that are memorised are of ritual significance—initiation rites, for example, oracular poems or lists of kings (see H. M. and N. K. Chadwick III, 868)—and the mythical content of these performances (the origin of the race and their divine progenitors) lends a measure of support to the inference that these *carmina* were ritual and possibly memorised. It does not appear that they were narrative, however, or that their function was entertainment or instruction: a ritual purpose seems to be suggested, since they are said to "celebrate" the god Tuisto.

When we recall that it is unlikely Tacitus ever heard one of these performances, we may well wonder whether all this discussion is profitable. Nonetheless, if we are to assess the observation as it appears in the *Germania*, we would have to allow that it is susceptible of various interpretations. One reasonable solution seems to me to place these performances within the context of a eulogistic tradition, a tradition like that currently postulated for the primitive Indo-European peoples and current among the contemporary Zulu. The non-narrative eulogy produced by the tribal poet celebrates both living and dead chiefs; the recitation of the eulogies of the chief's dead ancestors ensures their sympathetic interest in the chief. Reference to the founder of the tribe from whom the present chief is descended would not be an unusual element in the eulogies produced by a tribal poet. Constant recitation of the deeds of a chief during his lifetime leads to a verbal stabilization in the performances; these stable passages could be memorised by regular members of the audience, and these passages might well pass into a tradition of memorised (i.e. verbally fixed) transmission. Amongst the Zulu, izibongo of past chiefs are fixed, and their length is directly proportional to the stature of the chief and inversely proportional to the time elapsed since his death: very early chiefs are remembered in very short izibongo. On ceremonial occasions the imbongi recites the izibongo of his chief's forefathers in a genealogical sequence starting with the earliest remembered ancestor. Such practices form a reasonable context within which to place Tacitus's observation about the carmina with which the Germans celebrated Tuisto and Mannus. It is likely, too, that we are to postulate a eulogistic context for the poems (or songs) about the hero Arminius of the Cherusci that Tacitus says are still performed among the Germans ("caniturque adhuc barbaras apud gentis," *Annals* [ed. John Jackson], II, 88), though these may equally well be narrative *Heldenlieder*.

In the third chapter of *Germania*, Tacitus notes that the Germans recollect that Hercules was among them and they sing "He is the first of all strong men" as they enter battle ("Fuisse apud eos et Herculem memorant, primumque omnium virorum fortium ituri in proelia canunt"). The recollections of Hercules' visit need not necessarily be poetic, but the performance as battle approaches is likely to be either a poem or a song, probably the latter. If individuals independently shout out a traditional phrase or two about Hercules, we might label this a poem; it seems more likely, however, that this is a choral performance, a war song sung in unison by the troops advancing into battle. The performance seems to be intended to establish an ideal of heroic conduct for the warriors to emulate, and if it is choral it may in addition foster esprit de corps. If this is granted, the text of the song is likely to be traditional, that is, memorised. The existence of a text or words for the song seems to differentiate this performance from the nonverbal war songs called *baritus* which Tacitus immediately goes on to describe:

> They also have the well-known kind of chant that they call *baritus*. By the rendering of this they not only kindle their courage, but, merely by listening to the sound, they can forecast the issue of an approaching engagement. For they either terrify their foes or themselves become frightened, according to the character of the noise they make upon the battlefield; and they regard it not merely as so many voices chanting together but as a unison of valour. What they particularly aim at is a harsh, intermittent roar; and they hold their shields in front of their mouths, so that the sound is amplified into a deeper crescendo by the reverberation. [trans. Mattingly]

Curiously, most manuscripts read *barditum* and not *baritum*. In his edition, J. G. C. Anderson comments:

> The variant *barditum* has better manuscript authority, but no satisfactory explanation of the word is to be found. It has no connection with the Gallic *bardus*. . . . *Barditus* is probably an incorrect form. A comparison of Tacitus' description with Ammianus 16.12, 43 leaves small room for doubt that the word he used was *baritus* or *barritus*. Ammianus describes the *barritus* as a *clamor* raised just as battle is joined, which begins as a low whisper and gradually swells into a roar like that of waves dashing against rocks (*fractum murmur*, as Tacitus says). Vegetius also calls it a *clamor* which should not be raised until the combat begins (3, 18). The absence of verbal content seems clear from Amm. 31.7,11, where the Germans in the Roman army raise the *barritus*, while the Goths *maiorum laudes clamoribus stridebant inconditis*. The word meant the roar of an elephant, which was called *barrus* from the sound of its voice (Isidor. *Etym.* 12.2,14; Festus, s.v. barrire). The same onomatopoeic word was evidently coined by the Germans for the roar of their *cantus*. The form *barditus* may have been due to a fifteenth-century Humanist who associated the word with *bardus*.

It seems reasonable to accept the emendation of *barditum* to *baritum*, and to take this as a reference to the same kind of performance that Ammianus describes.

The purpose of the baritus is clearly stated in Tacitus; it is equally clear that we are dealing with choral singing, and this is perhaps likely to be the case with the Hercules song as well.

Battle provides the context most frequently cited by Roman historians for the performance of Germanic poetry or song; most Romans knew the Germanic people through military contact, and few historians had the opportunity to live among them and observe their habits and customs on a day-to-day basis. We shall encounter many references to the war songs of warriors in this survey, as well as other references to the baritus, but Tacitus also records the actions of women while their men are fighting: in *Germania*, chapters 7 and 8, we are told that women rally wavering armies with their pleading, exposing their breasts and demonstrating the threat of imminent captivity. These pleas are likely to be ululations and cries such as Xhosa women use to incite their men to further effort while dancing or fighting in a practice known as *ukutshayelela*; when Xhosa women *tshayelela*, they may shout out the traditional izibongo of their menfolk or of their clans, or in the excitement of the moment they may compose spontaneous poetry (see Opland: 1975, 189). The actions described by Tacitus are clearly dramatic, the utterances are likely to be individual rather than choral, and may well be improvised.

Women play a role in another battle described by Tacitus in his *Histories*, IV, 18 (ed. and trans. Clifford H. Moore). The Roman force engages the rebelling Batavians on their island stronghold, and Civilis, the German chief, places his own female relatives as well as other women behind his men. The noise of the German men and women was louder than that of the legions and cohorts. The men sang while the women ululated: "Ut virorum cantu, feminarum ululatu sonuit acies." *Germania*, 8 and *Histories*, IV, 18 afford reinforcing testimonies of the Germanic woman's practice of inciting her menfolk to greater acts of bravery with her ululations during a battle.

Later (*Hist.*, V, 15), in another engagement between the Romans and the Batavians, Tacitus refers—as he does elsewhere—to the singing of the Germans in their camp at night. Superior on marshy ground, the Batavians block the Rhine to produce terrain on which the Romans flounder; they are saved only by nightfall. The Germans spend the night singing and shouting, the Romans raging and threatening vengeance: "Nox apud barbaros cantu aut clamore, nostris per iram et minas acta." These might be entertaining campfire songs to maintain high spirits, but are more likely to be war songs—whether choral or individual performances—designed to foster martial resolve. The "cantu aut clamore" perhaps suggests that the Germans sang together as well as shouted together or individually; perhaps we are dealing here with choral singing punctuated by individual poetic utterances (or "boasts"?).

A similar account of nocturnal singing by Germans on the warpath occurs in the *Annals*, I, 65 (ed. John Jackson). This time the Romans under Caecina are caught in a marsh by the Cherusci under Arminius, and once again the engagement is interrupted by nightfall. Few slept that night, notes Tacitus, though the Germans and the Romans spent their time in contrasting fashion. The Germans, in festive mood ("barbari festis epulis"), filled the low-lying valleys and forests with chants of triumph or fierce sounds ("laeto cantu aut truci sonore"). Again, it is not possible to define the nature of the performance here; there may have been not only war songs to maintain a martial purpose but also victory songs or boasts about the coming encounter. The latter is a practice well attested in later Old English literature such as the *Battle of Maldon*. Once we entertain the thought that the performances may not only be songs in chorus but individual productions, we admit the possibility of poetry. What is referred to here may be a series of individual poetic performances, some memorised autobiographical poems, some improvised boasts, perhaps praise of the performer's forces, and vituperation of the Romans. These would all be acceptable forms of poetry in a eulogistic tradition. It would make sense among the southeastern Bantu; perhaps we have here a series of individual performances similar to those observed among the Sotho, as in the passage cited in the first chapter (see p. 24).

Praise and calumny are recorded before an engagement described by Tacitus in the second book of his *Histories*. The forces of Vitellius, supplemented by German auxiliaries, encounter the forces of Otho at Placentia. At night, "different exhortations were heard: one side exalted the strength of the legions and the army from Germany, while the other praised the high renown of the town soldiers and the praetorian cohorts. The Vitellians assailed their opponents as lazy and indolent, soldiers corrupted by the circus and the theatre; those within the town attacked the Vitellians as foreigners and barbarians" (*Hist.*, II, 21). Tacitus notes that the mutual insult incited the parties more than their praise. The next morning the Germans advanced into battle singing their wild songs ("cantu truci," *Hist.*, II, 22). Now the praise and calumny vented at Placentia could simply be shouts comparable to those raised by youths prior to a ghetto street fight; on the other hand, perhaps the Germans were in the habit of yelling laudatory eulogies in praise of themselves, their forces, or their ancestors before and during a military engagement. Tacitus might be referring to individual performances rather than choral productions coming from German camps at night, or during a battle between the Romans under Sabinus and the Thracians who, true to national custom, gambolled with songs and war-dances ("more gentis cum carminibus et tripudiis persultabant," *Annals*, IV, 47).

It is unlikely that in the heat of battle everyone was at pains to keep in step and in time with his neighbour. It seems more reasonable that the practices referred to in the context of battle are individual eulogistic performances, such as those of the Celts which Diodorus Siculus records in the fourth century: "And when someone accepts their challenge to battle, they loudly recite the deeds of valour of their ancestors and proclaim their own valourous quality, at the same time abusing and making little of their opponent and generally attempting to rob him beforehand of his fighting spirit" (V, 29, trans. J. J. Tierney, 250). Athenaeus quotes Posidonius on the existence among the Celts of special poets who both in peace and war utter eulogies: "The Celts have in their company even in war (as well as in peace) companions whom they call parasites (παρασίτους). These men pronounce their praises before the whole assembly and before each of the chieftains in turn as they listen. Their performers are called bards (Βάρδοι). These are poets who deliver eulogies in song" (ποιηταὶ δὲ οὗτοι τυγχάνουσι μετ᾽ ᾠδῆς ἐπαίνους λέγοντες, VI, 49, trans. Tierney, 248). This is an accurate description of the function of the imbongi among the south-eastern Bantu, but such a figure is not specifically mentioned by Tacitus. Of course, this does not mean that he did not exist: the gambolling Thracians may have been poets exhorting their companions to feats of bravery. Whether or not the throngs around the campfires or in battle contained official poets, the sounds uttered by the Germans probably included eulogistic poetry.

There is no description of poetry or song in Tacitus that has to be interpreted as designed for entertainment (although this is perhaps to be expected, since Tacitus himself probably never encountered the Germans at home in their more tranquil moments); all the passages we have considered could fit into the context of a tradition of eulogistic poetry. In such a tradition there would be official poets whose function was to produce poems about their chiefs on occasions of importance; yet they would not be the only poets in the community. Most men and women would have memorised traditional poems about their ancestors or their clans; some may have memorised poems composed by themselves or by others about themselves or their contemporaries; many might have had the ability to break into spontaneous poetry under the inspiration of the moment and to give vent to their feelings about an occurrence in the immediate past or even in the present. In battle, the official poets might praise the troops, and the women exhort them from the sidelines with a combination of these forms of poetry or with ululations; the warriors themselves might express their feelings in spontaneous poetry or recite poems in praise of their ancestors as a statement of pride or to ensure protection. On occasions of joy many individuals might utter poems—whether improvised or memorised—in turn or simultaneously. Such were the Sotho performances cited in the first chapter. Such is the description of Xhosa warriors returning from a hunt in 1807:

> When the hunting party has returned to the neighbourhood of its village, the one who inflicted the first wound on the lion that was killed, is hidden from view by shields held in front of him. At the same time one of the hunters leaves the troop and praises the courage of the slayer with a screaming voice, accompanied by a variety of leaps, and then returns again, when another one repeats the performance during which the others incessantly shout hi! hi! hi! and beat their shields with knobkirries at the same time. This is continued until one has really reached the village. [Alberti, 77]

And such, in all likelihood, were the Germanic performances witnessed by or reported to Tacitus in the first century. A eulogistic tradition would explain all the references in Tacitus to poetry produced for and in battle by both men and women. The references to carmina about Hercules, Tuisto, or Arminius might be to productions similar to the heroic songs or poems of the later Germanic people like the *Battle of Maldon* or *Ludwigslied*; it is more likely, however, that they too should be placed in a context of eulogy, a likelihood that is strengthened somewhat by a consideration of references to Germanic poetic performances in historians who wrote after the time of Tacitus.

The next historian to provide information about Germanic poetry is Ammianus Marcellinus (ed. and trans. John C. Rolfe) three centuries later. Ammianus, who was born in about 330 in Antioch, was a soldier who wrote accounts of military contact with the Goths from personal experience. He was not a Christian; alive in 391, the date of his death is unknown. His conscious ambition was to succeed Tacitus in eminence as a historian. As we have already seen, Ammianus twice mentions the Germanic baritus. In an encounter between the Alamanni and the Romans in 357, the Alamanni attack, sensing that victory is near. "But as soon as they came to close quarters, the contest continued for a long time on equal terms. For the Cornuti and the Bracchiati, toughened by long experience in fighting, at once intimidated them by their gestures, and raised their mighty battle-cry. This shout in the very heat of combat rises from a low murmur and gradually grows louder, like waves dashing against the cliffs"

(XVI, 12, 43). Later, the Roman troops approach the Goths in Thrace near Salices, where the Goths draw themselves into a wagon laager. When reinforcements arrive, those within the ring of wagons "with frightful outcries ('immaniter fremens,' XXXI, 7, 8) and roused by their furious mood" are eager to engage the enemy, but night intervenes. At daybreak the Roman trumpets sound, and the Goths attempt to reach the high ground after taking oaths together according to their custom ("barbari postquam inter eos ex more iuratum est," XXXI, 7, 10). At this point, the Germans in the Roman army "in unison sounded their war-cry, as usual rising from a low to a louder tone, of which the national name is *barritus*, and thus roused themselves to mighty strength. But the barbarians sounded the glories of their forefathers with wild shouts, and amid the discordant clamour of different languages skirmishes were first tried" ("Barbari veto maiorum laudes clamoribus stridebant inconditis, interque varios sermonis dissoni strepitus, leviora proelia temptabantur," XXXI, 7, 11).

While Ammianus might conceivably have borrowed from Tacitus in his description of the baritus, his description of Germanic custom on entry into battle is unparalleled in Tacitus; it must be judged to be independent testimony and accordingly reliable. Before the battle the Goths swear customary oaths. Whatever the precise nature of the ceremony, it is likely to be related to references in later Old English poetry to boasting or vaunting before battle. It seems to be a ritual ceremony and probably communal, though perhaps there might be an element of individuality in it; it is unlikely that battle was delayed until each soldier recited a personal manifesto concerning his loyalty and resolve, though perhaps there was an oath from the leader and a response from some representatives. More interesting in the light of the preceding discussion is what Ammianus has to say about the Germanic battle cries: these are specifically the praises of their ancestors. Clearly eulogistic, these utterances could conceivably be communal if the ancestors referred to are those of all the nation, though this is unlikely. The wild shouts indicate simultaneous individual productions: each Goth shouted the praises of his own ancestors as he went into battle. This practice is quite distinct from the controlled nonverbal choral baritus. In Ammianus Marcellinus, then, for the first time we have unequivocal confirmation of the existence among a Germanic people of a tradition of eulogistic poetry like that postulated in the preceding chapter.

Both Tacitus and Ammianus testify to the wild, uninhibited behaviour that characterised the oral performances of the Germans just as it impressed early Western observers of the southeastern Bantu productions. Perhaps many Romans shared the attitude of Varus, who thought the Germans "were human only in respect to voice and limbs" (Velleius Paterculus, II, 117). Barbaric, unin-hibited outpourings belonged in the circus or the theatre: it is worth noting that Roman soldiers are abused as "indolent and lazy, soldiers corrupted by the circus and the theatre" in the exchange between the supporters of Otho and Vitellius quoted above. Well-bred Romans rejected the obscenity and unlicenced dis-plays of the circus and the theatre, as well as everything associated with them. By the fourth century the Church Fathers are roundly critical of the luxury and low moral tone, and pronounce condemnations that recur throughout the docu-ments of the church councils in the early middle ages. Even the pagan Am-mianus is critical of the debased tastes of popular culture:

> The few houses that were formerly distinguished for the cultivation of serious pursuits now overflow with the pastimes of inert sloth and resound with singing and piping and harping. In place of the philosopher the singer is called in, in place of the orator the impressario; libraries are shut tight like tombs, but water organs are manufactured, and lyres as big as wagons and flutes and ponderous instruments for gesticulating performers. See how our standards have been debased: not long ago when foreigners were peremptorily expelled from the city because of an expected shortage of food [A.D. 383] and the few practitioners of the liberal arts were thrust out without respite, the companies belonging to actresses of mimes, gen-uine or pretending to be such for the occasion, were retained; 3000 dancing girls with their choruses and an equal number of dancing masters remained, with no question being made concerning them. [XIV, 6, 18 ff.]

Popular Roman entertainments like these were to influence the tastes of some of the Germanic peoples and, as we shall see, will find a place in our history of the Anglo-Saxon oral poet. Up to this point we have no evidence to suggest that the Germans cultivated a similar breed of entertainer; Priscus is the first to pro-vide us with such evidence.

About a century after Ammianus Marcellinus, Priscus of Panium (trans. C. D. Gordon) wrote a history that covered the period 433 to 474, though only fragments now survive. Priscus met many of the characters who people his history in the course of his travels as the secretary of the envoy Maximinus; many passages are eyewitness accounts, and Priscus is generally regarded as a reliable reporter. For the first time we are afforded descriptions of the day-to-day lives of Germanic leaders on their own home ground. For example, in fragment 20, Priscus tells us that he and Maximinus visited Ardaburius the son of Aspar, an Alan who for some time exerted considerable influence at the court of the eastern emperor. After his pacification of Thrace, Ardaburius was made commander of the eastern army by the emperor Marcian. Priscus tells us that after his successful campaign in Thrace, Ardaburius "turned to relaxation and effeminate ease. He took pleasure in mimes and jugglers and all the delights of the stage, and passed the whole day in such shameful pursuits, heedless of the reputation his actions gave him" (Gordon, 14).

Priscus's disapproval of these activities is as patent as that of Ammianus Marcellinus, and is implied in the taunt directed by the Vitellians at the Othonians. The condemnation depends on a context of effeminacy and sexual licence. That a high-ranking German should take pleasure in such entertainments, however, says nothing about common Germanic practice, for Ardaburius was brought up in a Byzantine environment. The musical and dramatic performances associated with the Roman theatre and circus, and consistently condemned in the writings of Christians as well as other Romans, are designed for entertainment only. Priscus presents us with another scene in fragment 8 that describes entertainment, but it is not musical. None of the sources so far cited allows us to conclude that the Germans enjoyed traditional instrumental music during their leisure hours.

In 448 Priscus accompanied Maximinus on a diplomatic mission to the court of Attila. His description of an evening spent with Attila is justly famous: it provides us with our first eyewitness account of a relaxed company of barbarians at home:

> As evening came on pine torches were lit up, and two barbarians, advancing in front of Attila, sang songs which they had composed, chanting his victories and virtues in war [in the Latin of Jordanes, "versus a se factos, quibus eius victorias et bellicas virtutes canebant, recitarunt"]. Those at the feast looked at the men; some took delight in the verses, some, reminded of wars, were excited in their souls, and others, whose bodies were weakened by time and whose spirits were compelled to rest, gave way to tears. After the songs a certain crazed Scythian came forward, who forced everyone to burst out laughing by uttering monstrous and unintelligible words and nothing at all sane. After him Zercon the Moor entered. [Gordon, 95 f.]

The Moor, according to fragment 11, was a hunchbacked cripple with a lisping voice whose very appearance was the object of laughter. His function and that of the "crazed Scythian" was patently to provide amusement for those present at Attila's court. The reaction of the audience to these two is quite unlike their reactions to the performances of the two poets. We are told that the poems were composed by the poets themselves, though we are not told whether they chanted the same words in unison or whether each performed a separate poem of his own composition. It seems most unlikely that the poems would be performed chorally; we probably have to see this as a description of separate, individual performances comparable to Posidonius's description of Celtic bards pronouncing the praises of their chiefs before the whole assembly and before each of the chieftains in turn. (Among the southeastern Bantu, no eulogy, however traditional, is ever performed by more than one person at the same time.) Furthermore, Priscus's comment that the poems were composed by the poets themselves implies that they were not traditional poems (as one would expect if the performers were Germans praising a non-Germanic, Hunnish overlord), but this does not bind us to conclude that the poems were composed in advance for the occasion and committed to memory; they may have been improvised in performance. Their content is plainly eulogistic, dealing with events in which Attila participated (particularly battles) and with his spiritual qualities. Their effect is to incite strong emotions in the audience (see further Hatto: 1973, 27). We have here a description of an evening's formal entertainment of visiting dignitaries. After the torches are lit, there is a recitation of eulogies in praise of the chief by two tribal poets. Thereafter buffoons appear to amuse the guests before dinner.

Another fragment of Priscus provides an account of the funeral of Attila in 453. It is unlikely that Priscus himself was present, but it is possible that he received a report from someone who was, for he furnishes a detailed account of the ceremonies, including a summary of the eulogy uttered on the occasion:

In the midst of a plain in a silk tent his body was laid out and solemnly displayed to inspire awe. The most select horsemen of the whole Hunnish race rode around him where he had been placed, in the fashion of circus races, uttering his funeral song as follows [facta eius cantu funereo tali ordine referebant]: "Chief of the Huns, King Attila, born of Mundiuch his father, lord of the mightiest races, who alone, with power unknown before his time, held the Scythian and German realms and even terrified both empires of the Roman world, captured their cities, and, placated by their prayers, took yearly tribute from them to save the rest from being plundered. When he had done all these things through the kindness of fortune, neither by an enemy's wound nor by a friend's treachery but with his nation secure, amid his pleasures, and in happiness without sense of pain he fell. Who then would consider this a death which no one thinks should be avenged?" After he had been mourned with such lamentations [talibus lamentis] they celebrated a "strava," as they call it, over his tomb with great revelry, coupling opposite extremes of feeling in turn among themselves. They expressed funereal grief mixed with joy and then secretly by night they buried the body in the ground. [Gordon, 110 f.]

The summary of the poem reflects the content of a typical eulogy produced on an occasion of significance. The subject is named, his status is mentioned, and he is placed within a genealogical context. His achievements and his qualities are recorded before attention is given to the specific occasion that has given rise to the poem: the circumstances of Attila's death are set forth allusively (not in explicit narrative), and the poet concludes by appealing directly to his audience in an effort to arouse action or emotion. The implication of the words introducing the summary is that the most select horsemen were also the performers of the poem, though not necessarily the composer. Either a poem was composed for the occasion and taught to the best riders for recitation on their circuits around the body, or the horsemen themselves composed poems as they rode. Physically, it seems unlikely that horsemen galloping as if in a circus race would be reciting a memorised text in unison, although it is conceivable that they might be reciting the same memorised text individually. It is more likely, however, that Priscus's words are not to be taken too literally in the absence of a firsthand eyewitness account, and that the riders uttered individual eulogies in praise of their chief at his funeral, just as Germanic warriors uttered individual eulogies in praise of their ancestors on advancing into battle (see Klaeber: 1927).

Most of the passages quoted so far describe practices among the Germanic peoples of the east. We first hear of Frankish and Burgundian songs in the writings of Sidonius Apollinaris (ed. and trans. W. B. Anderson). Sidonius was born in Lyon in about 430. Both his father and his grandfather—who became the first Christian in his family—had been praetorian prefect in Gaul. In 458 Sidonius delivered a panegyric on Majorian in Lyon that referred to the action of Aetius and Majorian against the Franks. In the course of preliminary maneuvers, Sidonius says, the echoing sound of a barbarian marriage song was heard from a nearby hill, for two yellow-haired Franks were being married amid choral singing

> . . . fors ripae colle propinquo
> barbaricus resonabat hymen Scythicisque choreis
> nubebat flavo similis nova nupta marito.
>
> [*Carm.*, V, 218 ff.]

Clearly this is a reference to traditional songs performed by a number of people in unison, and is distinct from the production of poems by individuals.

Another of Sidonius's poems (*Carm.*, XII), addressed to the senator Catullinus, refers to a period Sidonius spent among the Burgundians; the date and place of composition are unknown, but may be Arles in about 461. Why, Sidonius asks Catullinus, do you ask me to write a poem

> placed as I am among long-haired hordes, having to endure German speech, praising oft with wry face the song of the gluttonous Burgundian who spreads rancid butter on his hair [laudantem . . . quod Burgundio cantat esculentus]? Do you want me to tell you what wrecks all poetry [quid poema frangat]? Driven away by barbarian thrumming [barbaricis abacta plectris] the Muse has spurned the six-footed exercise ever since she beheld these patrons seven feet high. . . . But already my Muse is silent and drawn rein after only a few jesting [iocata] hendecasyllables, lest anyone should call even these lines satire.

The tone of the whole poem is jocular; it is hyperbolic and obviously intended to be amusing. Sidonius places in opposition his refined hendecasyllables and the song of the Burgundian, just as the anonymous author of the *De Conviviis Barbaris* contained in the *Anthologia Latina* does when he slightingly compares the crude utterances of the Goths with the refined poetry of the Romans:

> While the Goths are saluting each other with healths, they make poetry, eat and drink: no one dare recite worthy verses [Inter eils goticum scapia matzia ia drincan: /non audet quisquam dignos edicere versus]. [Wrenn: 1967, 75]

One learns little from this pithy couplet about the function of the Gothic utterances or their manner of presentation, although the condescending attitude of the author is apparent. It is the same attitude that is the focus of Sidonius's twelfth *Carmen*. The Burgundian singer may actually have existed as depicted, or he may be a compound figment of Sidonius's imagination, but one aspect of the performance seems reasonably clear: since Sidonius attributes the absence of his Muse to the barbarian thrumming ("barbaricis plectris"), it is likely that the Burgundians used a stringed musical instrument (although the act of plucking a lyre often serves as a metaphor for the production of poetry, even literate poetry clearly designed to be read—see Bolton: 1979, 28). We cannot deduce from Sidonius's words whether or not the instrument was played to accompany the Burgundian songs that Sidonius had to praise with tongue in cheek, nor are we given any information about the instrument itself. Nonetheless, this is the earliest record we have of the possible existence among the Germans of an instrument that was played with a plectrum. It may be that what Sidonius finds most offensive is the abuse of a Roman instrument in Burgundian hands, for we are not told unequivocally that the instrument and the performance to its accompaniment are traditional. Nevertheless, it seems possible that a stringed instrument was in use among the Burgundians in the middle of the fifth century.

Certainly it was in use among the Goths at the court of Theodoric II, for in a letter to Agricola, Sidonius describes the daily routine of the king, concluding with a description of the evening meal:

> It is true that occasionally (not often) the banter of low comedians [mimici sales] is admitted during supper, though they are not allowed to assail any guest with the gall of a biting tongue [ita ut nullus conviva mordacis linguae felle feriatur]. In any case no hydraulic organs are heard there, nor does any concert-party under its trainer boom forth a set performance in chorus [nec sub phonasco vocalium concentus meditatum acroama simul intonat]; there is no music of lyrist [nullus . . . lyristes . . . canit], flautist or dance-conductor, tambourine-girl or female citharist [psaltria]; for the king finds a charm only in the string music which comforts the soul with virtue just as much as it soothes the ear with melody [rege solum illis fidibus delenito, quibus non minus mulcet virtus animum quam cantus auditum]. [Bk. I, letter 2, sec. 9]

Sidonius's portrait of Theodoric is admiring, and accurate as far as can be determined. Sidonius feels obliged to note that entertainers perform during supper and that the king is fond of stringed music; but he is at pains to dissociate these forms of entertainment from those associated with the circus and theatre. The *mimus* entertains, but he does not raise a laugh by snide insults and slanders of those present; only virtuous music is enjoyed, not extravagant shows and licentious performances. One reasonable inference is that the mimus normally was a biting satirist, and that all the performers mentioned by Sidonius were as unacceptable among well-bred Romans in his time as in the time of Ammianus Marcellinus in the fourth century. This description is as serious as the poem addressed to Catullinus is light-hearted, but as in the latter there is little specific information to be deduced from it. We do not know if the dinner entertainer was a bridled Roman importation or a native Gothic figure, nor can we say very much about Theodoric's favourite music.

Little can be learnt from a brief reference in one of the letters in the *Variae* of Cassiodorus (487–583; trans. Hodgkin). Cassiodorus writes in the person of King Athalaric to Tulum, a Goth who had been elevated to the patrician rank, and comments on fame and reputation among the Goths. The latter passages are obscure and confusing, particularly the reference to Gensimundus, with whose great reputation that of Tulum is now linked. Nonetheless, the phrase that concerns us is clear enough: Gensimundus is said to be a man who is worthy to be sung about throughout the world ("ille toto orbe cantabilis"), a man whose reputation will live forever among the Goths ("vivit semper relationibus"; *Variae*, VIII, 9). While this says nothing about the performance of poetry or song, it does mean that Cassiodorus is aware that among the Goths a man's reputation is often preserved in poems or songs. Whether these are narrative or eulogistic it is not possible to determine. On the other hand, the remarks could derive from a well-defined classical convention.

Another of the *Variae* is a letter from Theodoric to Boethius (II, 40). Clovis, the king of the Franks, had asked Theodoric to send him a harper, and Theodoric writes to Boethius, since "being such a lover of music yourself, you will be able to introduce us to the right man." This opening paragraph is followed by miscellaneous technical notes on music, until Cassiodorus returns to coherence in the final paragraph, urging Boethius to find the harper ("citharoedus"), who may then "go forth like another Orpheus to charm the beast-like hearts of the Barbarians." The request that Clovis directed to Theodoric is significant. Either the Franks had no harper and Clovis turned to the Gothic king to remedy the deficiency, or the Franks had harpers but no one who could perform as the Gothic harpers did. The Gothic harpers must have had a high reputation respected by other Germans, or perhaps the Gothic harpers were using their instruments to accompany a new kind of song: perhaps a tradition of *Heldenlieder* had evolved as a result of Gothic contact with Roman entertainments, and from the Goths it was spreading to the other Germanic peoples. The harper could transfer his activity from one centre to another, entertaining one audience as well as another; a tribal poet could not do this without affecting in some way the intimacy that binds such a eulogiser to his chief. It has often been remarked —especially on the evidence of the extant Old English heroic poems—that the Germanic people enjoyed legends about all the Germanic peoples of the migration period, not just those about their own group: perhaps this taste was the product of itinerant harpers, for on arrival at the Frankish court the Gothic harper would—initially at any rate—command a repertoire of almost exclusively Gothic songs. It is interesting to note in passing from Cassiodorus's letter that Theodoric's attitude to Clovis is that of Roman to barbarian, rather than that of cousin to cousin.

Procopius (ca. 500–ca. 565) was an aide to the Roman general Belisarius, and many of the observations in his *Histories* are based on personal experience. In his account of the Vandal wars, Procopius has King Gelimer respond to a call to surrender in a letter (which is quoted) requesting a lyre (κιθάραν), a loaf of bread, and a sponge. The bread is to satisfy his hunger, the sponge to treat an eye infection; the lyre is to accompany an ode he had composed lamenting his present misfortune (κιθαριστῇ δὲ ἀγαθῷ ὄντι ᾠδέ τις αὐτῷ ἐς ξυμφορὰν τὴν παροῦσαν πεποίηται, ἣν δὴ πρὸς κιθάραν θρηνῆσαί τε καὶ ἀποκλαῦσαι ἐπείγεται; II, 6, 33). The Vandal king in Africa is said to be a skillful lyrist who had composed a song in advance and wished to sing it to the accompaniment of a cithara. This is a classical instrument, although Procopius may be using the classical name for a similar Germanic instrument. The performance would be a song with a fixed text committed to memory, and as such does not strictly find a place in a discussion of the poetic tradition: the content of the song is purely personal and its production evidently does not require an audience. It is an introspective lyric accompanied on a stringed instrument by the singer. Procopius's words are free of approbation. Harps and lyres of various kinds were current in classical Greece and Rome: a performance with a stringed instrument was not in itself to be condemned. However, when the instruments were used in the context of a low theatrical entertainment, that performance merited the censure of well-bred Romans, as we saw in the passages quoted from Ammianus, Priscus, and Sidonius.

Procopius also recounts a battle against the Goths outside Rome in 537, four years after Gelimer's surrender. Belisarius was in charge of the Roman forces, so we may assume that Procopius was present. After an initial skirmish, night fell and the Romans were amazed to hear many laments and great wailings (θρῆνοι πολλοὶ καὶ κωκυτοὶ μεγάλοι) from the Gothic camp, for the engagement had been minor. However, it was later learnt that the Goths had been mourning men of the greatest distinction who were killed in the first charge (VI, 2, 33–36). We are given no details about the nature of the lamentations: they may have been outcries, or they may have been poetic utterances. It is at least possible that the dead Gothic noblemen merited eulogistic laments like those uttered on Attila's death.

We come to Jordanes with high expectations, for his history of the Goths, written in ca. 551, is the first history of a Germanic nation by a member of that nation. Jordanes (trans. Mierow) acknowledges that his work is an abbreviation of the Gothic history of Cassiodorus, although it is based on recollection since Jordanes has no text before him: "The words I recall not, but the sense and the deeds related I think I retain entire. To this I have added fitting matters from some Greek and Latin histories. I have also put in an introduction and a conclusion, and have inserted many things of my own authorship." An examination of the text reveals that this last claim is false: sixteen sources are cited in the course of the history, many of them through Cassiodorus, and little else is original. Jordanes contributed only autobiographical details and links between the passages he quotes from others. Though his work is a collage, one would expect Jordanes only to have included what he knew to be correct; how accurate was his knowledge of the customs of his own people centuries earlier, unfortunately, is a moot point.

Four times Jordanes refers to songs about past heroes that seem to be similar to those Tacitus says the Germans sing in honour of Arminius or Tuisto and Mannus. In narrating the early history of the Gothic people, Jordanes says they moved after a victorious battle at Oium to the farthest part of Scythia, near the Black Sea, "for so the story is generally told in the early songs, in almost historic fashion" ("quemadmodum et in priscis eorum carminibus pene storico ritu in commune recolitur," IV, 28). These ancient carmina are traditional ("in commune") and since they are told in *almost* historic fashion, we are to conclude that they are not pure narratives, which *would* have been in historic fashion. The passage probably describes references to early battles and movements contained in traditional poems with an allusive, elliptical style (characteristic of eulogy); however, the poems may also be memorised lists of itineraries.

A new dimension is introduced into our history of Germanic poetry when Jordanes notes that in earliest times (a reading based on an emendation of *ante quos* to *antiquitus*) the Goths sang to the accompaniment of a cithara songs about the deeds of their ancestors, men whose fame is still great ("Ante quos etiam cantu maiorum facta modulationibus citharisque canebant, Eterpamara, Hanale, Fridigerni, Vidigoiae et aliorum, quorum in hac gente magna opinio est," V, 43). These are evidently narrative songs with stringed musical accompaniment, though it is not clear whether Jordanes is here referring to an ancient custom that is no longer current (if the songs were sung in antiquity and only the fame of their subjects continues). If this is a reference to a Heldenlied (as Heusler positively takes it to be), one might wonder whether it is part of a native tradition or whether it was a foreign introduction in view of the classical cithara used for accompaniment, but Jordanes may have known the name of a native stringed instrument and used the familiar classical term for a similar instrument to refer

to it. Again, if this is a reference to Heldenlieder, it is the earliest statement that
we have about their existence among the Germanic peoples, unless the carmina
that Tacitus referred to were produced to the accompaniment of a musical
instrument, or the virtuous songs Theodoric took delight in were narrative
songs about heroes. Clearly the performances Jordanes refers to are not to be
identified with the strident praises that the Goths yelled out in battle ("barbari
vero maiorum laudes clamoribus stridebant inconditis"; Ammianus, XXXI,
7, 10), for warriors are not armed with harps; yet the content of the performances seems similar.

In the eleventh chapter Jordanes tells of the councilor Dicineus, who gave
the Goths the name Capillati; this name the Goths readily accepted and they
still retain it in their songs ("quod nomen Gothi pro magno suscipientes adhuc
odie suis cantionibus reminiscent," XI, 72). Nothing is said of the performance,
so it is not possible to determine whether songs or poems are referred to here.
A later passage reminds us that it was not only in songs and poems that the deeds
of the ancients could be remembered: Jordanes supplies a genealogical list,
starting with Gapt, who was the first of the heroes, as the Goths themselves
relate in their legends ("ut ipsis suis in fabulis referunt," XIV, 79). These were
clearly prose narratives.

Apart from his quotations from Priscus already discussed above, Jordanes
preserves one other reference to Gothic practices that may be poetic, in the familiar context of death in battle. In 451, a century before Jordanes wrote his
history, Attila's Huns and the Vandals encountered a Roman alliance of Visi-
goths under their king Theodoric, Franks, Saxons, Burgundians, and other
Germanic tribes. After the initial encounter Attila was besieged, and during the
delay in hostilities Theodoric's sons looked for their missing father. When they
found his body, "they honoured him with songs [cantibus honoratum] and bore
him away in the sight of the enemy. You might have seen bands of Goths shouting with dissonant cries and paying honour to the dead while the battle still
raged" ("dissonis vocibus confragosos adhuc inter bella furentia funeri reddidisse
culturam," XLI, 214). This description is probably to be taken—with Procopius's reference to Gothic laments for warriors killed in battle (VI, 2)—in a
eulogistic context. As at Attila's funeral, eulogies were probably uttered as
individual expressions of mourning ("dissonis vocibus").

In the last quarter of the sixth century, Gregory the Great tells the story of
four hundred Christian hostages of the Lombards who refused to worship the
idol of a goat's head. The Lombards sacrificed the head to the devil according to
their custom, and while running in a circle dedicated it to him with a despicable

song ("more suo inmolaverunt caput capiae diabolo, hoc ei currentes per circuitum et carmine nefando dedicantes"; *Dialogues*, III, 28). This clearly describes a ritual sacrifice; the circular running after the death of the victim is perhaps to be likened to the circular riding around Attila's body, and this in turn to the Celtic practice of riding around an enemy in a chariot. The performance may be a song or a poem, produced chorally or individually. References to Frankish wedding songs and Lombardic sacrificial songs remind us that there were uses for poetry or song other than praising persons living or dead.

And finally, before the end of the sixth century, there is the testimony of Venantius Fortunatus (ca. 540 to ca. 600) (*MGH*, IV). In an oft-quoted passage from *Carmen* VII, 8, Venantius says that his praise of Lupus of Aquitaine will incite others to strive to praise him:

> Romanusque lyra, plaudat tibi barbarus harpa,
> Graecus Achilliaca, crotta Britanna canat

> [63–64]

and later he mentions the praise of men that the Germanic peoples confer in their songs or poems ("dent barbara carmina leudos," line 69). Clearly Venantius refers here to songs in praise of people performed to the accompaniment of a stringed instrument. This is confirmed by his statement in the preface thnt "sola saepe bombicans barbaros leudos harpa relidebat." The *harpa* is presented as a characteristically Germanic instrument, the Latin name a simple borrowing from the common Germanic word for the object. This is the earliest reference to the Germanic harp by name, although, as we have seen, stringed instruments are recorded as being in use among the Germans by Cassiodorus, Jordanes, Procopius, and perhaps Sidonius. What is the history and function of the Germanic instrument, and what is its relation to the postulated tradition of eulogistic poetry?

Musicologists differentiate between two types of instruments current in northwestern Europe in the early middle ages, a rounded lyre and a triangular harp. Curt Sachs proposes that of the four instruments mentioned by Venantius, the *lyra*, the *achilliaca* (from $\bar{e}$ *chelys* with false etymology), and the *harpa* are lyres, the *chrotta* is a harp; in a twelfth-century manuscript the harp is labelled *cythara anglica* and the lyre *cythara Teutonica*. The origin of both these instruments is still a matter of some debate. The Germanic *harpa* is generally agreed to be a lyre though descended from the Greek cithara, but the genealogy is obscure. Hortense Panum examined in detail all sources and materials available to her and concluded that " 'chrotta' and 'harp' were the names by which the barbarians (Teutons and Celts) designated the lyre borrowed from the culture of Greece" (140) and "The harp of German antiquity was not a special barbarian instrument, but was actually only the Greek lyre, received at a time when the southern culture on the whole, set its mark upon central and northern Europe" (142). (No attempt is made to indicate exactly when this latter period is likely to have occurred; Rensch does not help.)

In the sources that we have considered above, the first mention of a German's enjoyment of stringed music comes in the middle of the fifth century with Sidonius's description of Theodoric's evening entertainment. The Ostrogothic king is said to favour music which Sidonius is at pains to dissociate from the performances of the circuses and theatres. At much the same time Priscus noted that the Alan Ardaburius surrounded himself with such entertainments; although stringed music is not specifically mentioned, it is likely to have been present, in view of the tone of moral censure common to both Priscus and Ammianus Marcellinus's mention of the licentious delights of the theatres a century earlier. Later, according to Cassiodorus, Clovis of the Franks asks Theodoric to send him a harper. All these passages refer to stringed instruments among the Goths, apparently designed to provide incidental entertainment. In the middle of the sixth century, Jordanes, himself a Goth, explicitly mentions the use of a cithara, a lyre, to accompany accounts of famous heroes; the function of the performances is not alluded to. This is evidently a performance quite different from that mentioned a few years earlier by Procopius in his account of the Vandal Gelimer's surrender. The evidence of Venantius Fortunatus at the end of the sixth century, however, confirms the statement of Jordanes that a lyre was used to accompany songs lauding the exploits of heroes. This constitutes all the evidence we have considered, with the exception of a possible statement about harping among the Burgundians in Sidonius. The songs celebrating heroes mentioned by Jordanes and Venantius are claimed to be traditionally Germanic; the personal lament of Gelimer or the music that Sidonius tells us Theodoric enjoyed could derive from either a Germanic or a classical tradition; the music associated with the theatres is clearly classical entertainment. Most of the sources concern Gothic peoples, who were closely associated with Rome and Byzantium in various ways for some time.

Musicologists claim that the harpa was a development of the Greek cithara: is it possible that all stringed music among the Germanic peoples was the product of contact with the classical culture of the south? The evidence cited above would not contradict this theory, but one should beware of drawing conclusions from the absence of references to harping among the Germans earlier than the fifth or sixth century: Roman authors tended to encounter Germanic peoples in martial rather than domestic situations. Any people that possesses a bow potentially possesses a stringed musical instrument, and the universal currency of the word *harp* among the Germanic languages argues for the early existence of the instrument among the Germanic peoples. However, its use and function in the life of the people may very well have been influenced by contact with classical culture, and the possibility must be allowed that the Germanic Heldenlied, first clearly attested in Jordanes in the middle of the sixth century, was not native to the Germanic peoples. The relation of Heldenlied to eulogy must now be considered.

It seems evident from the sources we have examined that there existed among the Germanic people traditions of eulogistic poetry, of occasional songs, and of prose narratives. Jordanes's reference to what seems to be narrative song accompanied by a lyre poses some problems, however. There is, of course, no problem involved with the existence of such a tradition among the Germans; later it becomes one of the most popular forms, as Heusler noted: "Die folgenreichste Schöpfung der agerm. Poesie war das epische Lied, Heldenlied und Götterlied" (1911, 455). The problem rests in its apparent similarity in content to the eulogistic poems, for Venantius attests that the songs accompanied by a harpa deal with the praiseworthy exploits of people. Why should two such apparently similar traditions coexist? If eulogy is the original form of poetry, why should a tradition of narrative song develop? Heusler accepts the later development of the Heldenlied:

> Die Enstehung des germ. Heldenliedes liegt für uns im Dunkel. Erwägt man, dass es keine primitive, sondern eine verhältnismässig hochstehende Kunstform ist, dass die Zeugnisse mit Jordanes beginnen und dass die historischen Sagennamen bis ins 4. Jh. zurück weisen, so wird man Müllenhoffs Satze betreiten: die Heldendichtung war eine der Neuerungen der Völkerwanderungszeit. [1911, 456]

The tradition has its origin, Heusler proposes, among the Goths, the result, perhaps, of contact with the Roman theatrical entertainers: "Sollte, abgesehen von der allgemeinen Steigerung des Lebensgefühls, die Bekanntschaft mit dem römischen Mimus der befruchtende Anstoss gewesen sein?" (1911, 456 f.; cf. Norman: 1938, 311 f.). Such a solution would accord with the evidence available to us, and would also serve to explain certain aspects of the subsequent development of the tradition. And there is good reason why such a tradition should develop.

Eulogies are not primarily narrative in intent or content; though they can contain sequences of coherent narrative, they are more commonly allusive and elliptical, assuming a knowledge of the narrative content on the part of the audience. Narrative is thus embryonically present in eulogy, but its function is not to tell a story so much as to define a man through a record of his achievements and qualities. Eulogy, as we have seen, plays a part in the ritual life of a people. So too may narrative: in the course of instruction, initiates may learn stories of the origin of their tribe or the deeds of its chiefs, folktales may serve to inculcate in children the traditional values of the society. But the narrative song is more likely to be designed primarily to entertain (perhaps partly to edify or educate), and this is rarely the function of eulogy. For this reason it seems likely that the Heldenlied became popular among the Goths from about the time of the fourth century as a result of their contact with the various entertainments offered in the Roman theatres and circuses. The eulogy provided the raw material and the lyre was already in use; perhaps a type of Roman ballad or the songs of the theatre provided the model and a new form of entertainment evolved, spreading from the Goths to the other Germans.

This is admittedly mere hypothesis, simply one that is in accord with the sparse facts, and it must readily be conceded that other hypotheses are equally possible. One is that a tradition of lyre-accompanied song among the Germans predated their contact with classical civilization; a tradition of lyrical songs seems to lie behind the account of Gelimer's performance, and it is not impossible that there may have been narrative songs too. It is also possible that a Germanic tradition of lyre-song might have been influenced by contact not so much with classical as with Christian culture, in which the figure of David the harper is prominent (see Steger). Although there seems to be no way of resolving the problem decisively, I tend to accept Heusler's suggestion that the Germanic Heldenlied arose as a result of Gothic contact with classical civilization because of the absence of early references to lyre-accompanied narratives (although, as I have pointed out, this may be attributed to the fact that no writer before Priscus had occasion to observe the domestic habits of the Germans) and because of Clovis's request that Theodoric send him a harper.

The testimony afforded by the extant writings in Greek and Latin dating from 100 to 600 serves to confirm the hypothetical reconstruction of the early Germanic tradition advanced in the preceding chapter. Eulogy in praise of ancestors or living nobles appears to be the dominant form of poetry. It is artistocratic in that it is most frequently associated with a king or chief; such ceremonial poetry was probably produced by court poets, although Priscus is the only writer to mention figures who in any way compare with the Celtic bards. This apparent failure of writers to mention a personage who according to our hypotheses was of some importance in tribal life is not too surprising, for few classical writers had the opportunity to witness the domestic habits of the Germanic people and most of them demonstrate a strong bias against native, non-Roman culture. Most frequently one encounters passages describing customs on the battlefield, and these lead to the conclusion that many individuals participated in the tradition of poetry, uttering eulogies to their ancestors during battle. These were probably produced within a magico-ritual context, to strengthen the warrior and intimidate his opponent, and this in turn probably indicates a connection between eulogy and ancestor veneration and a belief in the power of the dead ancestors to influence current events.

Three authors (Priscus, Procopius, Jordanes) mention utterances honouring dead kings or nobles, and these too may be taken as eulogies. Twice Tacitus describes women exhorting the warriors in battle: it is likely that women also participated in the tradition of eulogistic poetry. These poems seem to be both traditional and occasional: there are references to carmina about ancestors or great heroes that are commonly known, and these are probably memorised eulogies passed on from generation to generation, but it is also likely that eulogies were produced for and possibly on specific occasions, and that spontaneous utterances of great emotion on the spur of the moment took poetic form. The performances were individual (never choral), although many people might perform at the same time during a battle or at a funeral; and the performances were unaccompanied by any musical instrument. They were, furthermore, dramatic in that their production was frequently associated with bodily movement.

Alongside this complex tradition of eulogistic poetry there existed a tradition of song, of wedding songs, war songs or sacrificial songs, and (perhaps only later) narrative songs. The songs produced for specific occasions were generally choral, and therefore probably traditional. But there were also individual performances to the accompaniment of a stringed instrument, songs of personal lamentation such as that of King Gelimer or possibly the narrative songs mentioned by Jordanes. These last are distinct from a nonmusical tradition of prose narrative that is also alluded to by Jordanes.

However reasonable these conclusions based on the extant evidence might be, one must be wary of assuming that the preceding paragraphs define a tradition common to all Germanic peoples from the first to the sixth centuries. In particular, one must avoid the error of assuming that these conclusions are necessarily valid for those peoples living in the northwestern corner of the continent, those peoples who in the first century were an aggregation of disparate peoples living in modern-day Holland, Denmark, and Germany and by the sixth century were the slightly more homogeneous Anglo-Saxons living in modern-day England and poised for the advent of the most critical period in their entire literary history, their conversion to Christianity.

The materials available for a reconstruction of the history of the Anglo-Saxons from the first to the sixth century are complex, varied, and inadequate, and few historians have tackled the forbidding task. The most recent attempt is perhaps the most valiant, and certainly the most detailed: for information on the history of this period I rely heavily on John Morris's formidable *The Age of Arthur: A History of the British Isles from 350 to 650.* I do not propose to summarise the history of the period, but merely to single out those developments that might be significant to the even more hazardous reconstruction of the history of the poet in this period. Two facets in particular merit attention: English settlement patterns in relation to the native British population (in order to consider the possibility of influences of the Celtic poetic tradition on the English); and kingship (because of the postulated relationship between tribal poet and king).

The broad outline of events can be swiftly sketched. Early in the fifth century the withdrawal of the Roman troops led to civil war in Britain. Vortigern (ca. 425 to ca. 458) introduced Saxon mercenaries to contain the northern Picts, and proceeded to establish his power in Britain. The British nobility, however, revolted against Vortigern, who then summoned more Saxon mercenaries who in turn successfully rebelled against both factions in ca. 441. A national resistance to the incoming Germanic peoples grew among the British, culminating in the defeat of the English by the British under Arthur at Mount Badon in ca. 495. In the middle of the sixth century the English successfully revolted against the British, establishing strong kingdoms in Northumbria and Kent by the end of the century.

On the Continent, before they crossed the Channel, the ancestors of the English seem to have kept to themselves. In general they did not join the larger federations of Germanic peoples like the Alamanni and the Franci in the second and third century, but in the fourth century they start to emerge with a measure of individuality. At about the same time that Eormanric was establishing his Gothic empire in the east, the Jutes were moving south, leaving Jutland depopulated, and the Franks and Saxons were raiding the coasts of Gaul and Britain.

Between the Jutes and the Saxons, the Angles turned their attention to the northern encroachment of the Jutes. Wiglaet of Angle is said to have killed the Jutish king Amlethus, Wiglaet's son lost Schleswig, but his son Offa was able to secure the Eider as the southern border of the Angles. The peoples of north-western Europe were slowly moving. Morris accepts the identity of the Hengest invited to Britain by Vortigern with the Hengest of the *Fight at Finnsburh*, which would make him a Danish adventurer fighting against Frisians and Jutes before crossing to Britain early in the fifth century.

One of the significant facts that emerges from the history of the ancestors of the English immediately prior to their crossing the Channel is the presence of an established tradition of kingship among all the peoples except the Saxons. In his *Vita Lebuini* Hucbald notes that

> in the old days the Saxons had no king, but appointed rulers over each township. They regularly held a meeting once a year . . . where the leaders met with twelve nobles and as many freedmen and bondmen from each township. There they confirmed the laws, judged important legal cases, and argued upon the plans that would guide them in peace or war during the coming year. [Morris, 318]

Morris comments: "The European Saxons did not establish a permanent monarchy until the ninth century, and the practices of the 'old days' continued to annoy eighth century Franks, who were exasperated at the difficulty of pinning down a multitude of local rulers and assemblies to a binding agreement" (318). And thus in seventh-century England the continuing conflict between the south and the powerful north never came to a conclusion, as "the south altogether rejected Northumbrian supremacy, doggedly renewing their resistance after each defeat. Devotion to a hero king was alien to their past and their present and could not serve as a focus for the union and integration of the English nation" (322).

Hengest's followers were Jutes and Frisians, and were settled widely between the Thames and the Humber. Further north the Bernicians followed Octha, a subordinate of Hengest and said to be his son. Hengest died in about 470, at a time when Ambrosius and Arthur were winning battles. Nennius notes that "the Saxons increased their number and grew in Britain. . . . But when they were defeated in all their campaigns, they sought help from Germany, and continually and considerably increased, and they brought over the kings from Germany to rule over them in Britain." When these kings abandoned the homeland, most of their followers did likewise: Procopius says that early in the sixth century the home of the Angles was vacant, and Bede confirms this in the eighth century. Angles and Saxons joined the Frisians and Jutes in England. The Angles must have been led by their king Icel, a descendant of Offa, and they probably crossed the Channel later in the fifth century as a result of increasing pressure on their homeland from Franks, Danes, and Slavs. The Iclingas were a dynasty, and it is from them that the later kings of Mercia were descended. At about the same time Oesc, the son of Hengest's subordinate in Bernicia, moved south to found the Kentish royal house, the Oescingas.

After the English defeat at Mount Badon, therefore, at the start of the sixth century, there were only two established kingdoms, that of the Iclingas among the Angles and that of the Oescingas in Kent. In 530 Procopius notes that three populous nations occupy Britain, each ruled by a king: the Angiloi, the Frissones, and the Brittones (from whom the island is named). Morris observes that "English tradition confirms Procopius, for it has preserved separate notices of the dates when other kingdoms came into being, all of them late in the sixth century; and it remembered that previously their peoples had been led by notables, not ruled by kings" (281). And of the half-century after Mount Badon, Morris says:

> Throughout Britain the English lived in very small communities each developing a class of notables. Only Kent and the East, and perhaps the Middle Angles, yet combined under a king; some of the small isolated communities may have accepted a local monarchical chief, for the Irish report of the pagan English at Abingdon [the Gewissae] at the end of the fifth century described their chief as a king. . . . Others may have been so ruled, for military insecurity and growing social differentiation encouraged a tendency towards individual authority, that is likely to have developed sooner in some regions than in others. But whatever their internal structure, all the English were surrounded by stronger British neighbours; some of them were doubtless directly ruled by British kings, and all were confined within their borders. [282]

In the early sixth century, therefore, the English settlements had little contact with each other, and neither expanded nor amalgamated, although new immigrants did arrive at this time, such as Franks in Kent and Scandinavians in East Anglia.

If the English were isolated from each other, they also remained isolated from their British conquerors, and nothing demonstrates this fact so dramatically as the effect of the bubonic plague on the population of Britain in the middle of the sixth century: the Irish and the British suffered heavy losses, the English were unaffected. Morris claims that literary and archeological sources serve to explain the English immunity:

> Gildas emphasises that the British were altogether unable to visit the shrines of martyrs 'because of the unhappy partition' of Britain; the British did not journey into English areas. The silence of the Saints' Lives concurs. A couple of Irish stories record Irishmen who preached to pagan Saxons, both of them before the outbreak of the plague; there is little record of British monks among the English except for a single journey, placed in the 590s; and thereafter several continental writers record their astonishment, at the extravagant refusal of the British to have any dealings with the English, refusing even to dine or lodge with them in Rome, or when they met in Britain. Gildas shared their attitude; it never occurred to him that the British should attempt to convert the heathen; instead, he sighed for a Gideon to exterminate them.
>
> The English escaped from infection from the British, because the British refused to have contact with them. They escaped infection from Europe because they did not import from plague-infested areas. What trade they had is indicated by their grave goods; their imports were the ornaments and weapons of northern and northeastern Gaul, and of the Franks of the lower Rhine. These are the regions which Gregory omits from his account of when and where the plague was rampant. [223]

After the plague, isolated English attacks on the British took place, starting with Cynric's raid on Salisbury in 550. Thirty years later, British authority in the south had been destroyed. Several English districts proclaimed their independence and established monarchs, among the East Angles in 571, among the East and South Saxons by kings who died in 587 and 590, among the Mercians in 584. These new kingdoms warred among themselves until Athelbert of Kent established some measure of control late in the century. In the north Athelferth established a similar supremacy a few years later, so that at the start of the seventh century the English could be grouped into "two large and powerful and recent realms." In the middle of the seventh century, when Penda of Mercia killed Oswald of Northumbria, supremacy passed to the Mercians, a domination they were not to relinquish for a century and a half, until after the death of Offa in 796. The Mercian monarchy evolved into a unique system of kings and subkings, a model that was imitated by Charlemagne. Morris describes the system as "a novel concept of kingship, that had learnt to com-

prehend immense diversity within one organic whole. It combined the tradition of Roman imperial authority with a loose hierarchical kingship adapted
from the Irish, and with a secure law of succession inherited from the continental English" (332). After the waning of Mercian power and the rise of Wessex
in the ninth century, West Saxon historians falsified the genealogies "to pretend
that their own royal house was as ancient, as venerable, and as coherent as the
dynasty of the Mercian Angles whom they had replaced" (323), but "the evidence that has already been collected is sufficient to show that no stable and
lasting West Saxon monarchy was erected until the ninth century; then it was
consolidated in the course of war against the Scandinavians, out of the inheritance of the Mercian monarchy" (325).

By about the year 600 the Anglo-Saxons in England had evolved to the
point where fairly stable kingdoms had come into being after domination over
the native British had finally been established. This does not mean, however,
that one can talk of the Anglo-Saxons at this time in any but the most general
terms, for politically and socially there was no uniform structure: each kingdom
had undergone its private period of gestation, each derived from separate backgrounds and was composed of varying populations. As Morris notes, "In the
early seventh century there were as yet no accepted institutions valid for all the
English. Their society and their political government was infinitely varied, its
outline still to be formed" (300 f.). On the individuality of the kingdoms he
comments:

> The ties that bound one man to another varied. The customs of the older
> kingdoms were already hardened, and were little changed by conquest.
> All were conservative, but each had its own conventions. The North Folk,
> the men of Kent, and some of the Middle Angles had settled in a world
> that was still Roman, and their first generations had learnt much from it;
> but many of the Middle and East Angles had come to England in large
> coherent communities, bringing with them ancestral custom, whereas
> Kent was a kingdom formed in Britain from diverse origins, and its situa-
> tion readily exposed it to continuing European influence. [311]

Wessex in particular retained a large proportion of British inhabitants, as is
evident from the number of laws dealing with them in Ine's code.

Many of Morris's conclusions are based on slender evidence, and may well
be disputed by scholars in the future. Nonetheless, he has provided a detailed
and sensitive history of the period, and I have quoted from his book extensively
since it furnishes the most coherent historical foundation on which to base our

discussion of the history of the poet. For we must now consider how much the Anglo-Saxons (whether on the Continent or in England) were influenced by practices that according to the Greek and Roman writers were current among their easterly Germanic relatives, and in what way the poetic tradition was affected by the migration to England.

The most conservative conclusion that can be drawn from the Greek and Latin historians about poetry among the Germanic peoples would seem to be that a tradition of eulogistic poetry existed and was propagated by individuals, and that there also existed a tradition of songs associated with specific occasions that were usually produced chorally. It is likely that these traditions were shared by the ancestors of the English on the Continent, and there is no reason why they should not have been carried with them across the Channel. In other words, one would expect to find among the Anglo-Saxons eulogies produced before and in battle—poems in praise of one's ancestors, or in praise of oneself, or insulting one's opponents—eulogies in honour of the dead at funerals, or spontaneous poems uttered on the inspiration of a particular moment. One would also expect to find among the Anglo-Saxons songs at weddings, war songs, work songs and songs of worship. These might be traditional and choral, or original and individual—composed by a person to express a particular emotion or a reaction to an experience—and they might or might not have had instrumental accompaniment. There are also likely to have been songs or poems used for purposes not recorded in Roman histories but postulated in chapter 2 above: mnemonic poems (like our "Thirty Days Hath September") to preserve wisdom lore or genealogies, and incantations associated with diviners or herbalists. Since the existence of common Germanic traditions of all these forms of folk poetry and song is likely, and since it is to a large extent confirmed in the extant writings from Anglo-Saxon England, we shall pass over consideration of such traditions for the moment and concentrate attention on two figures in particular: the tribal poet and the singer of narrative songs.

The existence of a Germanic tribal poet similar to the Xhosa or Zulu imbongi was hypothesised in the previous chapter on the basis of a comparative study of ancient Indo-European literatures. Such a figure clearly existed among the Celts, as Posidonius and other historians attest; and, as we shall see in a later chapter, he is prominent among the North Germanic peoples as well. In all the Greek and Latin sources we cited earlier in this chapter, only Priscus bears witness to the existence of personages who might be considered to be tribal poets, and that was at the court of the Huns. Nonetheless, the possibility must be entertained that the tribal poet existed among the Germanic peoples as well, a possibility that is strengthened by a consideration of the role of the skald in later Scandinavian society. If the kind of vatic bard that we characterised in the preceding chapter did in fact exist among the Germans, however, it is most likely that he was intimately associated with a sacral king: one should seek him therefore among those peoples with a tradition of strong regnal dynasties.

The presence or absence of a tribal poet does not greatly affect the general tradition of eulogistic poetry. Among the Xhosa- and Zulu-speaking people today, the imbongi is generally associated with a particular chief: he owes loyalty to that chief and travels with him on official visits; there is no figure in southeastern Bantu society comparable to the wandering medieval minstrel. It often happens, however, that people live at some distance from the chief's residence (sometimes in a city hundreds of miles away), and do not involve themselves in his affairs, so that they may grow up never hearing or seeing an imbongi perform. Some chiefdoms (perhaps because they have shrunk in size or influence) do not have an imbongi: their chiefs are perhaps not important enough, or no one with talent has presented himself as an imbongi.

The existence of iimbongi is in some ways a matter of chance, for there is no special craft or guild, and the office is not hereditary. Most practising poets claim to have become iimbongi as a result of inspiration received in a dream, as a result of hearing other iimbongi perform (sometimes their own father), or more recently as a result of reading traditional poems in books. Clearly the presence of an imbongi in a chiefdom enhances the chief's prestige and increases the likelihood that boys may be fired with the ambition of one day becoming an imbongi; but the absence of one—I have met many Xhosas who have never heard a traditional imbongi—does not directly affect the existence of poetic traditions in the community. The men still know the praises of their ancestors or make up izibongo about themselves or their cattle, the women still preserve the traditional izibongo of the clans; at dances or fights the women still yell out snatches of the traditional izibongo, ululate, or improvise poetic encouragement, and men too are still prone to express high emotion in spontaneous poetry.

It is reasonable to assume that a tradition of ritual eulogy existed among the Germanic peoples whether or not there were tribal poets; but it is at least possible that there were tribal poets among the Germanic peoples as among the Celtic or Indic peoples. If they did in fact exist, they are most likely to have been found among the Angles and least likely to have found a place among the Saxons. Strong chiefs with a venerable genealogy attract tribal poets, who confirm their status and their well-being. The Mercian Iclingas are just such a line

of kings; the Saxons lacked kings. The Anglian monarchy moved strongly
across the Channel, bringing with it its customs and traditions. With the exception of the Oescingas, no strong dynastic line established itself in the isolated
pockets of English settlement until the late sixth century, seventy-five years
after Mount Badon. But even the Oescingas took their origin in England from
Hengest's associate, the father of Oesc, who originally settled in the north. Only
when Oesc himself travelled to Kent did he found a dynasty there. Hengest was
probably a Scandinavian leading a smallish party of Danes, Jutes, and Frisians.
The Oescingas were almost as well established a dynasty as the Iclingas—both
dynasties were recognised by Procopius in 530–but their origins differ. Whereas
Icel, the descendant of Offa of Angle, moved across the Channel with his followers, Oesc had to found his own dynasty in England.

It is unlikely that a Jutish or Frisian tribal poet accompanied Hengest when
he accepted Vortigern's invitation, for the Jutish and Frisian kings remained
behind, and Hengest was simply an adventurer (possibly the killer of King Finn
of the Frisians). Of course, there would be nothing to prevent any member of
the band assuming the function of a tribal poet, but on the whole this seems
unlikely, since some time elapsed before Oesc became king. If there was a tradition of tribal poetry among the Danes, Jutes, or Frisians from whom Hengest's
party was drawn, it is likely that it was not continued in England by the original
members of the expedition since there were no kings present, and it is likely that
it had lapsed by the time Oesc established his dynasty. However, individuals are
likely to have uttered eulogies on entering battle, or to have praised Hengest as
they galloped around the body at his funeral. Habits and customs of the general
populace die hard; but a tradition of poetry propagated by tribal poets would
persist only when specialist exponents of the craft continue to practice.

It is highly unlikely that later Frisian or Jutish invaders brought tribal poets
with them, for they and the Saxons proclaimed their fledgling kingdoms only
late in the sixth century. It is unlikely, too, that the presence of Celtic bards at
the British courts led to a resurgence of English tribal poetry: contact between
English and British was never that intimate. However, since the general continental tradition of eulogistic poetry probably perisisted, it is certainly possible
that Anglian poets associated with the Iclingas spawned similar figures in the
neighbouring kingdoms after they had established themselves.

In sum, then, it could be said that if tribal poets existed among the ancestors
of the English, they are most likely to have accompanied Icel to England.
Among the English elsewhere in England any such continental tradition is
likely to have been broken, although it may have revived as a result of contact

between the new English kingships and the Iclingas; the tradition is not likely to have revived or to have been in any way influenced by the Celtic natives, with whom the English had little contact except in battle, whether as allies or opponents.

If the tradition of narrative songs among the Germans was as old as their lyres, there is no reason why the English should not have brought that tradition across the Channel with them. If, however, as Heusler suggested, the Heldenlied arose only as a result of contact with Roman entertainers, then the story is not quite as easy to tell. It seems evident that the ancestors of the English on the Continent had a lyre (Old English *hearpe*), but it is not at all clear that they used it to accompany the recitation of narrative songs. The request of Clovis for a harper may indicate that the new style of harpsong current among the Goths had not yet reached the Franks at about the time that the Battle of Mount Badon was fought in England. If it is true that the Heldenlied was a relative latecomer to the Germanic peoples, initially cultivated among the Goths, then it is almost certain that it was not carried to England by the Anglo-Saxons as a traditional form of entertainment. In the early years of settlement the Anglo-Saxons could have entertained themselves with singing and dancing, or with harping; they almost certainly loved to hear accounts of the adventures of their ancestral heroes. These last were undoubtedly propagated in prose narratives: we need not call them sagas—every nation tells stories. For the germination of the Heldenlied, the Anglo-Saxons would then have to wait for the arrival of wandering minstrels, cousins of those the Goths encountered, or for the advent of texts of cultured narratives, whether Hebrew or Roman in origin. The latter were soon to arrive in the hands of Christian missionaries.

4

The Conversion

The history of the conversion of the Anglo-Saxons to Christianity has been told often enough before (see recently Mayr-Harting), and in any event the process itself is not strictly relevant to my purposes; what is more to the point are the effects of the process. This chapter will therefore bypass the story of the growth of church education or the clash between Celtic and Roman Christian. It will be concerned simply with two matters: the impact on English literature of the introduction of writing for literary purposes, and the effects the new Christian morality had on the oral traditions. The treatment of the former topic will be theoretical, drawing on concepts of oral literature current among folklorists and on my own observations; the latter will employ more conventional documentary sources.

The introduction of writing had a more profound effect on the history of English literature than even the introduction of printing (see Opland: 1980). The change in attitude of audience and artist alike is revolutionary. Written literature brings with it a new kind of artist, a different relation of artist to artifact, an altered function of the artifact in society (see, chosen at random, Clark; Goody; Lord: 1960, chap. 6; Ong; Scheub: 1971). This is not to say that in 597, when Augustine landed in Kent, oral literature went out of business and written literature took over. Oral traditions continue to exist in the Anglo-Saxon world today, some of them probably not far different from those current in England before the Norman Conquest, such as the traditions of jokes, perhaps, superstitions, or proverbial wisdom. The revolution introduced by writing takes place gradually; it also takes place inexorably. Writing as such is not the enemy of oral poetry; it is the altered social conditions or attitudes that writing brings with it that may operate to the detriment of an oral tradition.

What, then, is the character of this literary revolution introduced by the Christian missionaries? What precisely is the difference between an oral poem and a written poem?

In attempting to characterise oral traditions, scholars often make a distinction between improvised and memorised performances. Jan Vansina, for example, proposes such a two-part classification:

> From the formal point of view, it is possible to distinguish between two types of traditions: those which have a fixed form and are learnt by heart and transmitted as they stand, and those which are free in form and not learnt by heart and which everyone transmits in his own way. [22 f.; but see xiii f.]

This bipartite classification proves to be too simplistic to be of great value, for while the fixed form may be easily recognised by verbal stability in transmission, the free form is in practice variable: consecutive performances of a popular joke by the same raconteur, for example, would tend to maintain the punch line in a verbally fixed form, and the measure of verbal fixity would probably rise in proportion to the number and frequency of retellings of the joke; any two consecutive performances of an oft-told joke by the same teller might demonstrate a high proportion of words and phrases in common, thus appearing to be fixed in form, although in the first few versions the form might have been freer.

In their work on the Southslavic tradition of narrative song, Milman Parry and Albert Lord concentrated on the "free" performances and presented a detailed examination of their form. By definition, fixed texts were excluded from consideration in their study, which was concerned only with those songs creatively composed in performance:

> For the oral poet the moment of composition is the performance. In the case of a literary poem there is a gap in time between composition and reading or performance; in the case of the oral poem this gap does not exist, because composition and performance are two aspects of the same moment. Hence, the question "when *would* such and such an oral poem be performed?" has no meaning; the question should be "when *was* the oral poem performed?" An oral poem is not composed *for* but *in* performance. . . .
>
> We must grasp fully who, or more accurately what, our performer is. We must eliminate from the word "performer" any notion that he is one who merely reproduces what someone else or even he himself has com-

posed. Our oral poet is composer. Our singer of tales is a composer of
tales. Singer, performer, composer, and poet are one under different aspects
but at the same time. Singing, performing, composing are facets of the same
act. [Lord: 1960, 12]

Parry and Lord presented a concept of improvisation—composition during
performance—that was set in opposition to memorisation but yet was not equivalent to Vansina's concept of a "free" tradition. While the text of the performance was not fixed, it was not entirely free either, for in order to compose his
song while he was singing it, the singer made use of a stock of ready-made
phrases—formulas—to enable him to say what he wanted to say within the
metrical constraints of his particular tradition. Although the apprentice singer
learnt by heart—that is, memorised—a stock of useful formulas, by the time he
was a professional singer he was free to construct phrases modelled on the formulas—formulaic expressions—and was thus not constrained to repeat the same
words and phrases in successive performances of the same narrative: although
such performances told the same story, they were verbally distinct, as each performance was the unique product of a variable set of circumstances governing
the performance, such as the composition or the reaction of the audience, for
example.

On closer inspection, however, the neat categories break down. The presence of formulas, Lord claims, is one of the distinguishing marks of the text of
an oral performance as he defines it (the other two signs are the presence of
themes—traditional narrative scenes—and the absence of enjambment), and the
determination of a high proportion of such formulas in a text marks it as an oral
performance: "oral epic song . . . consists of the building of metrical lines and
half lines by means of formulas and formulaic expressions and the building of
songs by the use of themes" (Lord: 1960, 4). Yet an especially gifted singer like
Avdo Međedović is apparently not subject to all the terms of Lord's definition of
an oral poet: "We should not be surprised to find a fair number of nonformulaic
expressions in such a talented oral singer as Avdo Međedović. It would be
fantastic to expect that a gifted poet who has thought in poetic form all his life
should not have sufficient mastery of that form to be able not only to fit his
thought into it but also to break it at will" (Lord: 1960, 131).

Once Lord admits one exception, the rigidity of his definitions breaks down:
if a high incidence of formulas indicates an oral text, how can one say objectively
whether a low incidence of formulas indicates a written text or the product of a
highly talented oral poet? What are we to expect of the *Beowulf* poet if Avdo is

free to break his dependence on formulas at will? Again, the distinction between fixed and free (or memorised and improvised) blurs when Lord allows
that "a short song will naturally tend to become more stable the more it is
sung" (Lord: 1960, 100) and that "Some singers, of course, do not change their
wording much from one singing to another, especially if the song is one that
they sing often" (Lord: 1960, 69). Is such a singer an improviser or a memoriser?
Is the song fixed or free?

Alan Jabbour would seem to offer a solution. Jabbour accepts the twofold
division into improvised and memorised performances, but allows a middle
ground:

> If we discover that in a certain oral poetical tradition the variants of a song
> are related only in subject-matter and have no discernible history of word-
> for-word or phrase-by-phrase transmission, we may conclude that the
> tradition is improvisational. It would, however, be more than likely that
> passages would crop up here and there with a considerable number of verbal
> parallels, especially in separate renditions by the same singer, renditions
> from father and son or teacher and pupil, and renditions from the same
> locality. Such cases would require us to qualify our description, using
> the term "primarily improvisational" to show our recognition that memo-
> rial transmission is also taking place. If, on the other hand, we discover
> that in a certain tradition the variants of a song show a history of word-
> for-word or phrase-by-phrase oral transmission from a known or presumed
> archetype, we may describe the tradition as memorial. But considerable
> variation would almost certainly appear in the several texts, such as
> omission, addition, interpolation from other songs, stylizing, form-
> ulizing, or the like. These improvisational traits would compel us to call
> the tradition "primarily memorial." [Jabbour: 1969, 178]

This division of fixed and free (or improvised and memorised) into two pairs
each is a valuable advance on Vansina's or Lord's definitions, for it allows Jabbour to refer to the Southslavic tradition as primarily improvisational—which
settles some of the problems raised above—and the British ballad tradition as
primarily memorial—which would allow us to differentiate between it and, say,
the memorial British nursery-rhyme tradition. Nonetheless, there are limitations in this approach to oral traditions.

Absent from Lord's study of the Yugoslavian guslar is any sense of what a
member of the audience would feel about a performance. This is not necessarily a criticism of the work of Parry and Lord, for that work took its origin

from a desire to understand the form of the Homeric poems; in their field work
Parry and Lord sought the answers to questions that had become significant
from their study of the Homeric texts. But note Lord's reaction to the memoriser:

> The collector even in a country such as Yugoslavia, where published col-
> lections have been given much attention for over a century, some of which
> have become almost sacrosanct, must be wary, for he will find singers who
> have memorized songs from these collections. In spite of authentic manner
> of presentation, in spite of the fact that the songs themselves are often oral
> poems, we cannot consider such singers as oral poets. They are *mere* per-
> formers. Such experiences have deceived us and have robbed the real oral
> poet of credit as a creative composer; indeed to some extent they have
> taken from epic performance an element of vital interest. [Lord: 1960, 14;
> see also 137]

Since the guslari themselves are puzzled by the distinction between improvisation and memorisation (insisting that their variant performances of the same
story are verbally identical, when the collector knows otherwise), one must
conclude that the "element of vital interest" is of interest more to the collector
than to the performer or indeed to his audience. A Yugoslav hearing a memorised performance produced in an "authentic manner of presentation" would
probably not be able to say whether the singer was an improviser or a memoriser—presuming that he cared to distinguish between the two—any more than
the collector, who feels "deceived" when he learns subsequently (either by
comparing two performances of the same singer or by comparing the transcribed text with the songbooks) that he has been listening to a memoriser and
not an improviser. Presumably a memoriser could entertain an audience in a
coffeehouse as well as an improviser could, except that he might not be able to
shorten or lengthen his performance to suit the reaction of his audience as
neatly or easily as an improviser could.

    He may have limitations, but the memoriser does exist; his function in
society may not be radically different from that of the improviser, whatever the
foreign collector's response might be. Indeed, he may play a creative role in the
tradition if his performances encourage others to emulate him. To ignore the
memoriser in one's definition of an oral tradition is to present only a partial
observation of the facts; to deny him a role in the tradition is to invite an un-
balanced definition. I have derived considerable profit from an examination of
the kinds of phrases or sequences an imbongi chooses to memorise: for ex-

ample, when an illiterate Xhosa imbongi who knows no English introduces into his izibongo the lines "Use the school and saving club," or "Sow today and reap tomorrow," the collector can derive a working hypothesis about the tendency of a line of Xhosa poetry towards trochaic tetrameter.

There is, then, little sense in *The Singer of Tales* of the function of the songs in society (but see Lord: 1962), or of the reaction of the society to the songs (see Ben-Amos: 1975 on the necessity for this dimension in the definition of oral traditions). The scholarly categories that Lord imposed on his work caused him to overlook the memoriser, or the singer of lyric songs: we learn little about the interaction between the different traditions of song. Parry's great contribution to Homeric studies was in methodology: he refused to theorise about the nature of the texts but attempted to test his theories in the "living laboratory" of epic singing in Yugoslavia. The thrust of his and Lord's conclusions, however, is directed towards an understanding of the *form* of the poetry in order to understand the process of generation of the Homeric *texts*; medievalists who used their conclusions in general applied them to extant medieval *texts*. Yet, as Bruce Jackson has eloquently put it,

> Art song requires that we perceive the nature of the art involved; folk song requires not only perception of the art but also the generating or supporting musical, social, and historical contexts. Folk song is not simply textual, but *con*textual: it does not exist—save for historians and scholars—on pages in books, or even on shiny black discs. It exists in a specific place at a specific time, it is sung by specific people for whom it has specific meanings and functions. [Jackson: 1972, xvii]

Elsewhere, Jackson characterises the differing responses of the literary critic and the folklorist to the material they study:

> Although the literary critic may focus on the act of creation, he is far more interested in the fact of it—the thing created, the object as forever fixed, the artist's final issue. Most critics consider focus on the creative act ancillary to their main task—analyzing the product—and the reason for that is the product is the only thing that makes the process meaningful in the first place, and it is only the product they can ever possess entirely. The various drafts and their meanings, the psychic states of the artist along the way are never fully open to the critic. Only the finished work is available, and the finished work justifies the attention paid. But for the folklorist, the creative act is part of the product; each redaction of the text, each re-creation of the

event is to some extent controlled or influenced by the situation. And the situation—involving all participants, their physical and psychological relationships to one another and to the material—can be very complex indeed. [Jackson: 1974, x f.]

It is these complex relationships which surround the oral performance and distinguish it from a written production that I wish to explore (see Ben-Amos: 1971; Dundes).

First, there are the physical facts of the performance. The performer is present before his audience: they see him and hear him. He is conscious of his audience and each member of his audience is conscious of him as well as of the rest of the audience, particularly those surrounding him. The oral performance as compared to a text or a transcription of that performance is analogous in some respects to a television show as compared to a radio show. The radio audience hears the voice: it can be distinguished from other voices, it has its own unique accent, timbre, rhythm. The television viewer, on the other hand, hears all this but also sees the performer, perhaps a popular singer swaying to his song, gesturing dramatically, closing his eyes at a tender moment in the lyrics. The television viewer has access to more aspects of the performance than the radio listener has. Yet both lack one significant aspect of the performance, a sense of participation. They miss the thrill of rising to their feet and joining in a standing ovation, of sensing the feeling of excitement running through a crowd, of sweating together in a stuffy room, of laughing together: in other words, in their homes the television viewer or the radio listener may react to aspects of the performance, but they are removed from the essentially social phenomenon that constitutes a live performance. Audience and oral performer participate in a social activity.

The words that the performer utters are thus only one aspect of his performance. A sound film of the performance is already at one remove from the totality of the experience and is unable to capture completely the sense of involvement and participation in the social event. More elements present in the original performance are lost through a tape recording; still more are lost through a transcription of the words. A reader responding to a transcription of an oral performance misses most of the impact of the performance. The bare words may not be able to recapture the communication between performer and audience if the performer mimics different voices while speaking or acts out the events he describes, especially if he allows his gestures momentarily to take the place of words. (This is why different directors may produce totally different effects with the same play, or different actors read the same lines to differing effect: the text of the words alone is only one aspect of the theatrical experience.) The audience responds to the performer: he is there before them on a particular occasion. On another occasion the same performer might not be as impressive: he might have a headache, he might be upset by the weather, the audience might not be as responsive, the atmosphere might be tense. The physical facts of the performance ensure that every performance will be unique. The same fixed text recited to an audience by different performers will sound different; the same text repeated by the same performer on separate occasions will also sound different—here he will stress this word, there he will raise his voice. Still more, a performer operating in a free tradition—a raconteur, perhaps, or an after-dinner speaker—can never exactly repeat any one performance: every performance is unique socially, physically, and temporally.

There inevitably exists a relationship between performer and audience. If he is himself a member of the community, this relationship will be even more intimate and will perhaps manifest itself verbally. If they belong to the same social group, the performer's words will conjure up associations in the minds of his audience that the performer can depend on; he can play on the connotations of words or events, his style can be more elliptical or allusive without sacrificing sense. The audience then reacts not only to the words but to the suggestions residing around and within the words. The performer need not concern himself about being misunderstood: he speaks the same social language as his audience, he has grown up in the same environment as they have, and is a product of the same history that produced them. The audience may involve themselves in the performance, clapping, shouting encouragement, laughing, and this response may egg the performer on to greater efforts: a round of applause may tempt him to repeat the sentiments that earned the applause. The performance is organic; there is a symbiotic relationship between performer and audience. He tailors his performance to the particular audience in front of him; they become involved in his performance. Communication must be immediate and direct; there can be no mystifying introspection. To aid such immediate communication the performance tends to be traditional, it deals in stereotypes. The performance is in the public domain, and it usually concerns the public. Very often the performance has meaning far beyond the words employed: the performer may be dressed up for the occasion, the performance may have a ritual significance, the performer may represent the people or play the part of one of his characters.

In order to illustrate some of the random observations collected above, let us

consider briefly just one example of an oral performer as he operates in his society. Amongst the Banyanga in the Congo Republic there exists a tradition of
narrative dealing with the hero Mwindo. In 1956 Daniel Biebuyck encountered
Shé-kárịsị Rureke, a bard who dictated a complete version of the exploits of
Mwindo: "Rureke sat down with us for twelve days, singing, narrating, dancing, miming, until the present text was completely written down" (Biebuyck,
vi). The text makes fascinating reading, although it is trying, since it requires
heavy annotation to ensure that a European reader will capture some of the
manifold connotations of the words or understand all the allusions: the book
has as its epigraph a couplet from the text, "The tunes [voices] that we sing /
The uninitiated ones [the ignorant ones] cannot understand them." Biebuyck is
careful to distinguish between this particular version that he recorded and the
epic as it is normally performed among the Banyanga. I quote from Biebuyck's
excellent introduction:

> The Nyanga epic is not a text performed only at certain times or on
> highly esoteric ceremonial occasions. There is nothing secret about it; it
> is to be heard and enjoyed by all the people. Normally a chief or headman
> or simply the senior of a local descent group, in order to entertain his people
> and guests, would invite the bard to perform a few episodes of the epic in
> the evening, around the men's hut in the middle of the village. Large
> crowds of people, male and female, young and old, would come to listen
> or rather to be participant auditors. The bard and his collaborators would
> receive food and beer. During the performance, they would receive, not
> only from the host, but also from many auditors, *masabo*—gifts consisting
> mainly of small amounts of *butéá*—money, beads, and armlets. They would
> also receive, like any good musician or dancer or singer, the praises of the
> crowd, praises expressed in words and in gestures (symbolic drying of
> sweat, adjusting of the clothing, pulling of the fingers, and straightening of
> the back of the dancing narrator). There would not be any special fees paid
> to them at the end of the performance, although the bard might receive,
> like any other respected guest, a special farewell gift (*ịkósórwa*). If excite-
> ment ran high and beer and food were plentiful, the narrator would be
> invited to continue parts of the narration on the following evening. The
> interesting point is that the narrator would never recite the entire story in
> immediate sequence, but would intermittently perform various select
> passages of it. Mr. Rureke, whose epic is presented here, repeatedly asserted
> that never before had he performed the whole story within a continuous
> span of days.

. . . Functionally the epic is many things: entertainment, moralization, and explanation of causes, and an interpretation of existing customs; it is a paideia.

Finally, what is presented here as a piece of oral literature is much more than that. It is music, rhythm, song, dance, movement, dramatic entertainment. It is feasting and gift-giving (those who present the gifts dance and gesticulate). It is group solidarity and mass participation. For the bard himself, the act of narrating the story has religious significance. He believes that Kárįsį, deified, wanted him to learn the epic; to perform the drama adequately makes the narrator "strong," protects him against disease and death. The narrator believes he will find in his songs the force that Mwindo himself, the hero of the epic, derives from them. [13 ff.]

This series of extracts exemplifies the social character of an oral performance: the performance is part of an event, it consists of action by the performer and interaction with the audience. The whole context is the performance, not just the words uttered by the performer. Because the Nyanga bard and his audience share the same culture, he can recite discrete extracts from the hero's biography, confident that his audience will place these in the context of their knowledge of the full biography of Mwindo. It is evident, too, that the performer and the performance serve a distinct social function. The extract also demonstrates one of the consequences of the meeting between an oral tradition and writing: the issue may well be a longer and fuller text, a version that could never have any oral existence among the people. What other consequences proceed from the interaction of an oral tradition and the means of recording it?

In some respects the difference between the audience response to a text and to an oral performance can be compared to the difference between the audience response to a recording and to a live performance. A member of the audience at a live performance is subject to stimuli operating on his senses of touch, sight, smell, and hearing; all these contribute to his response. He reacts immediately to the performance, enjoying particularly fine passages as they are produced by the performer. If the performance was distinguished, he has no means available to recreate the unique experience. The recording can capture only one aspect of the performance, the sound, but it can be played over and over again. The audience response to the same recording may alter in time: one's first reaction to any one recording differs from one's reaction on hearing it for the twentieth time—one develops a preference for favourite passages, constantly appreciates more, suddenly hears new things. The reaction on hearing one recording for the twentieth time in turn differs from the reaction on hearing for the first time a recording of the familiar work performed by a different artist: one has a conception of a norm, and one compares and contrasts the unfamiliar interpretation to the familiar as a standard.

In the same way, a reader has a text before him: he responds primarily through his sense of sight, perhaps also of touch. He reacts to letters, to symbols of the spoken word, and to the physical texture of a book, stimuli quite different from those evoking the response of an audience at an oral performance. The reactions of the latter are immediate, ephemeral, and unique; the reader can mull over his text, return to favourite passages, grow in his understanding and appreciation through constant rereading. He may stimulate his own appreciation by reading commentaries on the text; everything returns to the fixed text, stable and permanent. In medieval times, copies of the text might have incorporated errors or interpolations; one hand might be more legible than another, a scroll more difficult to manage than a manuscript. Yet the text itself was established and had a primacy. Not so the oral performance. The reader may read in the privacy of his study; his activity may involve him in personal interaction with no one, it may be entirely asocial. The relation between audience and performance differs radically from the relation between reader and text.

The differing response leads to the development of different forms. In the case of poetry, for example, acrostics can be popular only with a reading audience. Not only can the forms differ, but the attitude of the poet to his poem, and of the poet to his audience alters. An oral performance, like a written poem, may incorporate phrases or passages from other poems; the poet may be influenced in his choice of words by other poets in his tradition. Nonetheless, no one in the audience seeks to ask whose poem it is: the performer is before them, they can see its author. He would not need to claim the poem as his: his performance is just one of many, other poems on the same subject would be different. He does what he does in a manner that has been accepted for generations: he probably does not seriously think about or analyse his craft, nor claim any proprietary right to his artifact. Oral poets are remarkably lacking in objectivity about their tradition: they are themselves the tradition. They can produce a poem on one occasion as well as on another. The thought of possessing—still less of preserving—a poem does not occur to the oral poet before he comes into contact with writing.

The literate poet, on the other hand, approaches his poem with the attitude of a conscious creative artist: he has the time to deliberate, to improve. His ultimate objective is to produce a work that will be as stable as a work of sculpture or a painting. Since it will exist permanently in time, he works at it until he makes it as good as his talent permits. The oral poet produces a performance relevant to a specific occasion and suitable for a specific audience, which he sees in front of him. The literate poet cannot see his audience: he must visualise his readers. He may never see them. The oral poet is kinetically involved in the production of his poem: he cannot be separated from the performance. The literate poet generates a poem that takes on a life apart from him: the poet can be separated from his artifact. The oral poet's audience is physically limited to those who are near enough to hear him perform; his influence on other poets in the tradition is restricted to those with whom he comes in contact. The literate poet's audience is not limited in time or place, not even limited to his own life-span; he has before him as models the poets of all preceding ages. The tribal poet's poems are public: he is a member of the public and his poetry is an expression of the ethos of his society. The literate poet's poems tend to be private, they become introspective and meditative, they become personal; the poet may affect new styles or techniques under the influence of the accessible poetry of foreign cultures.

Some extant Old English poems are clearly intended for readers rather than hearers: the runic riddles, for example, require the reader to say the names of the runes as well as to rearrange the order of the letters the runes represent in order to produce the solution; Cynewulf's signatures are similarly intended for a literate audience. Anglo-Saxons educated in Latin sometimes forego their native tradition and compose Latin poetry, some of it acrostic: the disciples or pupils of Boniface were fond of sending their compositions to Aldhelm or to each other for comment and criticism. Some Old English poems adopt Latin rhyme; some have one verse in English, one in Latin. There is a remarkable amount of experimentation with poetic forms in Anglo-Saxon England (see Bolton: 1977; Derolez). The conversion to Christianity entailed the development of an offshoot of the vernacular tradition of poetry. It also introduced the literate Anglo-Saxon to a new literary culture, to new cultural influences: in Latin the Christian Anglo-Saxon could read epics or philosophical poems. A poet might now have the means to set down a poem the length of *Beowulf*, perhaps drawing on his recollections of discrete oral performances of great moments in Beowulf's life and making of them a coherent biography (like Biebuyck's compilation of the *Mwindo Epic*).

Writing introduced a revolution in literary taste and attitudes, a revolution that ultimately succeeded to the detriment of the vernacular oral poetry. Writing itself, however, is not inherently inimical to the oral tradition. There is no

reason at all why the oral poetic traditions of the Anglo-Saxons should not have
continued unaltered after the conversion to Christianity, unless that process
brought with it a change in social attitudes which affected the oral poetry. The
church never proscribed poetry as such; but fairly soon after the conversion a
new ideal spread among the royal families of England, an ideal that probably
spelt the death of the Anglo-Saxon tribal poet and the radical alteration of his
tradition.

In following the fortunes of the tribal poet whom we presumed to exist
among the Germanic tribes on the Continent, we have looked at the fortunes of
the Germanic sacral kings, for there was probably an intimate connection
between poet and king. If this special relationship survived the migration, it is
most likely to have been preserved among the Anglian Iclingas, who became
the ruling dynasty in Mercia, and least likely to have existed among the Saxons,
who developed a stable monarchy only well after the settlement in England;
tribal poets may have operated amongst the other Germanic settlers in England,
though on balance this is perhaps not so likely, since the earliest settlers were not
led by kings. It is almost certain, however, that if there existed a tradition of
eulogy among the Germanic people—poetry in praise of individuals, their
ancestors, or their tribes—this tradition would be carried over into England by
the invading warriors and settlers. The tribal poet is only one feature of a eulogistic tradition; his presence may be associated with a concept of sacral kingship, but his absence does not deprive the people of their poetry. For the moment, let us concentrate on the hypothetical tribal poet, whose fortune will be
linked to the fortunes of the king. In the seventh and eighth centuries, in the
years immediately following the conversion, the Germanic concept of the role
of the king in society underwent a subtle but profound evolution.

The evolution in the concept of Germanic kingship from continental times
until the ninth century is outlined in J. M. Wallace-Hadrill's *Early Germanic
Kingship in England and on the Continent.* Wallace-Hadrill considers not only
the influence of the philosophies of such writers as Augustine, Gregory, Isidore,
Pseudo-Cyprian and Bede, but also the personal influence of active churchmen
on kings, such as that of Alcuin on Charlemagne and Offa. A king's acceptance
of Christianity did not necessarily entail the immediate abandonment of all
his traditional beliefs—including his belief about himself as king—but in time
the concept of kingship evolved until it was totally Christian, while it yet
retained aspects of the traditional sacral character: "Conversion to Christianity
did nothing to weaken belief, or at least interest, in descent from the gods,
whether descent of peoples or of kings. Indeed, it may have done something to

strengthen it: the sacred character of Christian kingship could be read back into the past" (9). The crucial conversion of Athelbert of Kent did not indicate "his abandonment of all that he understood by paganism. In general, Germanic conversions of this period signified not total abandonment of the pagan gods but acceptance of an additional god" (28). Gregory's instructions to the missionary Augustine are well known (see, most recently, Meyvaert); he wrote to Athelbert, Wallace-Hadrill asserts, "to assure the new convert that a Christian king's gifts were special and came from God, who would render his fame more glorious to posterity. In a word, something is being offered to take the place of the pagan basis, whatever it was, of the king's prestige" (30).

This diplomatic attitude obviously appealed strongly to the Anglo-Saxon rulers. Their conversion brought with it membership in a society far more extensive than the tribal group or kingdom, a society to a large extent controlled by literate clerics at least some of whom were familiar with works of biblical exegesis, philosophy, and theology. Inevitably, "A change in emphasis comes over western kingship in the seventh century; kings move into an ecclesiastical atmosphere; they are required to consider their duties in a fresh light, and may actually have done so" (47). This did not represent a sudden turnabout-face on the part of the church: after the period of missionary activity had passed, the Christian kings were influenced by churchmen who were in turn influenced by an evolving theory of kingship, a theory built on the pagan concept of sacral kingship. The Irish Pseudo-Cyprian, for example, wrote a tract about the conduct of the king. Wallace-Hadrill comments: "The tract's view of kingship is part-Christian, part-pagan; a traditional view is retained in so far as it is compatible with a Christian society, and a little specifically Christian matter is worked into it" (56). There are influences from the Old Testament, but "fundamentally, however, the picture is not Christian at all. The writer sees his king as the embodiment of his people's luck and prosperity, not as the holder of a Christian office" (57).

The Irish saw less of a contradiction between their pagan past and their Christian present than any other western European people. Pseudo-Cyprian's king is sacral: he is the peace of the people, the protection of the country, the defence of the nation, the cure of the ailing, the joy of men, the moderation of the atmosphere, the calm of the sea, the fertility of the soil, a comfort to paupers, the inheritance of sons, the hope of future happiness ("pax populorum, tutamen patriae . . . munimentum gentis, cura languorum, gaudium hominum, temperies aeris, serenitas maris, terrae fecunditas, solacium pauperum, hereditas filiorum et sibimet ipsi spes futurae beatitudinis," 56). At much the same time, in Spain, Isidore conceived of the king as an officer of the church: "Isidore is quite clear, then, that kingship is the exercise of a Christian function, and that what the king holds is neither more or less than a *ministerium*, an office, within the Church" (53 f.). Alcuin was influenced in his thinking by both Pseudo-Cyprian and Isidore, and he in turn influenced Charlemagne's and perhaps Offa's concept of kingship.

In England, the early lives of saints—Cuthbert, Guthlac, Wilfrid—underline the lesson that kings prosper through an association with saints. Wallace-Hadrill examines Bede's concept of kingship and summarises "the lesson of his teaching as exegete and historian" thus:

> Earthly kings are in one respect, the exercise of power, a reflection of the heavenly king; this power they exercise by God's authority and for his purposes, namely the furthering of religion by protecting his priests and monks, encouraging their work, exhorting the faithful by personal example, and by carrying the Gospel, by fire and sword if necessary, into neighbouring territories where it was unknown or misunderstood. It is this that binds together a people into a *Populus Dei* after the manner of the Israelites. It is this that will bring them felicity, prosperity, good harvests, and victory over their enemies. [97]

Of course, the picture is more complicated than would appear from this summary of some of Wallace-Hadrill's arguments. Not every Anglo-Saxon king was an Alfred or an Offa, nor subject to the same intellectual influences. Nonetheless, Wallace-Hadrill's book provides a cultural context—as Morris's book provided a historical context—within which we must try to place the tribal poet and his poetry. The Germanic sacral king was the focus of a cult, and the tribal poet established him in that role. The advent of Christianity did not eradicate all aspects of that pagan cult; Christianity adapted and moderated it so that it became Christian. The king maintained many of his earlier roles: in him resided the luck and well-being of his people, the fertility of the soil, victory in battle. He accepted the additional role of protector of the church: he became more and more like an abbot or a bishop, a Christian ruler concerned about the spiritual welfare of his people. His role in the church remained in essence his role in society, but everything was viewed from within a Christian context. However much he respected his predecessors, however much he enjoyed hearing of their deeds, however much he cared for the traditional poetry of his people, he now drew his strength from God. He was not so much descended from a god as ordained by God.

In the pagan past, the tribal poet may have confirmed the sacral king's power, his poetry may have ensured the sympathetic guidance of the king's ancestors; after the conversion, the pope or the bishop confirmed the king, thereby establishing God's design, and the Mass linked the king to his source of power. The glorious exploits of the pagan king were celebrated by his poet, and perhaps his fame lived on after his death in the eulogistic poetry; Gregory assured Athelbert that it is *God* who would render his fame more glorious to posterity.

Some Christians may have viewed the tribal poet's uninhibited cavortings as distastefully as did Gildas when he censured Maelgwn: "Your excited ears heard no more the praises of God, sung by the gentle voices of Christ's soldiers, nor the melodious chanting of the church, but your own empty praises, shouted by lying thieves . . . shrieking in frenzy," or when he set in opposition the gently modulated tones of Christ's soldiers ("tironum voce sauviter modulante") and the frenzy of the warband's bard bedewing all near him with foaming phlegm ("spumanti flegmate proximos quosque roscidaturo") (Morris, 415). But there was no official opposition of the church to poetry as such, nor to the tribal poet. The place of the tribal poet, his role in relation to the king, was simply usurped by the church. He might remain a public figure, performing his poetry on special occasions, but his poetry would have lost its implicitly sacral character.

Ancestor veneration, of course, did not cease among the Anglo-Saxons on their conversion to Christianity, and it is certain that the ritual songs and poetry of the people continued to play a part in their lives. The eulogistic poetry of the tribal poet may also have continued, but it would no longer have had its former significance. However popular the tribal poet might then have remained, his poetry would not be informed by the same premises or beliefs that formerly sustained the tradition. And although he might continue to perform, the tribal poet would no longer be the tribe's poet, for the people and the king would no longer be united and strengthened by his poetry. It would be relatively easy for him to turn from praising the king to praising God, or, facing hard times, he might turn from praising and criticising the king to flattering the king or entertaining the crowds. But his poetry would then have altered in social function. The modified attitude of the Anglo-Saxon kings to kingship introduced by the Christian missionaries would seem to herald a radical alteration in the tradition of the tribal poet in the seventh or eighth century.

If it be argued that the philosophical development of the concept of kingship as outlined by Wallace-Hadrill and summarised above is too tenuous a basis for such suppositions, that the average king may well have been quite unaffected by this stream of thinking, there is further evidence that can be adduced. Undeniably, Anglo-Saxon kingship had moved into the sphere of the church's influence by the ninth century. After the ninth century there was relative uniformity and stability in Anglo-Saxon kingship, for only the West Saxon dynasty survived the Scandinavian incursions. All the successors of Alfred played an active role in secular life, however much they donated to the church or supported its activities or yearned for the contemplative life. Before Alfred, however, a different attitude often prevailed. Many of the early Anglo-Saxon kings were proclaimed saints or became the focus of a cult; in the first two centuries after the conversion, many Anglo-Saxon kings laid aside their secular duties, abdicated, and entered monasteries or went on pilgrimage. Nor was this monastic ideal confined to reigning kings: princes, princesses, and queens participated.

To present only a few examples (mostly taken from Storms): among the Saxons, Cadwalla of the West Saxons abdicated in 688 and went to Rome, as did his successor Ine in 726; Aldhelm, the great scholar who died in 709, was a member of the royal family. Sebbi of the East Saxons promised on his deathbed to go to Rome, admitting that he would have resigned his throne sooner for that purpose if his queen had been willing to grant him a divorce. In 709 when Coenred of the Mercians abdicated and went to Rome, he was accompanied by Offa, heir to the East Saxon throne. Among the Northumbrians, Hild, the daughter of Hereric, the nephew of King Edwin, became a nun in France with her sister Hereswith before returning to Northumbria to found Streoneshalh (Whitby) and become its abbess. After her death in 680, she was succeeded as abbess by Alfflad, the daughter of King Oswy, who promised on his deathbed to go on pilgrimage to Rome. In 737 King Ceolwulf abdicated and went to Lindisfarne.

There are more examples from among the Mercians and the East Anglians. Athelburg, the daughter of Anna, king of the East Anglians from 635 to 654, became abbess of the monastery of Faremoûtier-en-Brie. Her sister Athelthryth founded the monastery at Ely after her second husband (King Ecgfrith of Northumbria) died. Her sister Seaxburg entered the monastery at Ely after the death of her husband (King Earconberht of Kent) and succeeded Athelthryth as abbess on her death in 680. It was Alfwald, the king of the East Anglians from ca. 713 to 749, who asked Felix to write a life of Guthlac. Guthlac, the son of Pendwald, a member of the Icling royal family, started his career as the hot leader of an Anglo-Saxon warband before renouncing the secular world and retiring to a life of isolation and privation in the fens of Crowland. Here he entertained, and had great influence over, Athelbald, who was king of the Mercians from 716 to 757; Guthlac also had great respect for Abbess Ecgburh, the daughter of King Aldwulf of the East Anglians. Athelbald's predecessor Coenred, who abdicated and went to Rome in 709, had succeeded his brother Athelred as king in 704 when Athelred abdicated to become a monk at Bardney.

This list is not intended to be complete, but simply to suggest that among the Anglo-Saxon royal families of the seventh and eighth centuries existed a Christian fervour that frequently found expression in a retreat to monastic life or in foreign pilgrimage. The motive of each of these people was not equally holy, nor indeed was poetry entirely absent from monastic life; nonetheless, it seems unlikely that royal courts that comprised members subscribing to these religious ideals would cultivate tribal poets with ritual functions. For some time after the conversion, the tribal poets in England must have continued to follow their traditional craft, largely unaffected by the fact that they or the kings they served were now Christian. We are not to assume that because we see their function as essentially pagan they saw themselves in the same light. A Christian tribal poet could continue in the manner of his pagan predecessors, perhaps calling on God to strengthen his king, perhaps praising his Lord as well as his lord, or perhaps simply omitting all Christian references and concentrating on the deeds and actions of his king. Wallace-Hadrill argued that Christian kingship was not so very different from pagan, except in that it operated in a different sphere of influence. Once the new ambience had been absorbed—however gradually—by succeeding generations, it was likely to result in the undermining of the traditional role of the tribal poet.

A consideration of whether the prime factor causing the alteration in this poetic tradition was the espousal of a monastic ideal among the royal families or the gradually altering conception of kingship among the kings themselves may come to the same thing in the end, for Wallace-Hadrill notes, "This is important: those who did most to reinterpret kingship were to be monks, and it is a monastic view of authority, whether of bishop or abbot, that harmonises most comfortably with monarchical power" (73). It seems reasonable to suppose that the pre-Christian tradition of the tribal poet did not survive the monastic influence on the Anglo-Saxon kings that developed after the conversion, and that by the eighth century the tribal poet must have either disappeared or altered radically in function. If the tradition did in fact continue unaltered, it is hardly likely to have survived the ninth century, which saw the destruction of the Anglian royal lines and the emergence of the West Saxon kings as the sole rulers of England (see further Shippey, chap. 8). Similar forces seem to have operated on the Continent. Heusler suggests that in Germany the court poet died out in the eighth or ninth century as a result of the decline of the small princely courts, the unfavourable atmosphere of Christian spirituality, and the competition of the mimes: "Das Erlöschen des alten Hofsängertums setzt für Deutschland ins 8. 9. Jh. und erklärt es aus dem Verfall der kleinen Fürstenhöfe, der Feindschaft der Geistlichkeit und dem Wettbewerb der Mimi" (1911, 462; cf. Frank, 93). The competition of the mimes is something we shall have to consider in attempting to reconstruct the history of oral poetry in England.

If the church never officially proscribed vernacular poetry as such, it was almost universally consistent in its condemnation of the spectacles associated with the Roman theatres (see Axton; Chambers; Marshall; Nicoll; Ogilvy). From the time of Tertullian and Cyprian in the third century, church thinkers and councils alike proscribed actors and admonished Christians for enjoying their performances. The council at Elvira in 300, for example, excluded circus performers or actors from becoming Christians; the council at Arles in 314 prohibited actors from receiving communion. The reason for this opposition lay in the secularity of the mimic performances: the mimes irreverently imitated the figures of society, both high and low, appealing to their audiences for laughter. They mocked emperors, and after the advent of official Christianity they mocked the clerical hierarchy. Obscenity was apparently a consistent element in these theatrical performances, which contained a great deal of robust buffoonery comparable in some respects to the turns of contemporary circus clowns. If this were not sufficient to merit the displeasure of the church, there was also the frequent operation of off-duty actresses as courtesans and off-duty theatres as brothels. The performers commanded various skills, but after the theatres ceased to be used and the players took to the roads and courtyards, the skills multiplied: there were jugglers, dancers, mimes, harpers, puppeteers, and acrobats—whatever tricks were likely to appeal to the audiences. Such troupes could travel freely, for their performances were largely spectacles, designed to appeal to the eye with action and to the ear with music; only to a lesser extent did they rely on words.

This form of entertainment associated with the Roman theatre or circus was classical in origin; a firm tradition can be traced back to ancient Greece, and many scholars argue for continuity of the tradition right through the Middle Ages. Through their contact with Roman civilization, some of the Germanic peoples seem to have developed a taste for such entertainments. There probably were figures among the Germanic people who amused audiences, similar to those in Priscus's description of an evening spent with Attila, but these are likely to have been individuals; the Roman troupes were organised under a leader, often controlled by an impresario, and in the first few centuries of the Christian era concentrated their activities in theatres or circuses. In the middle of the fifth century, Salvianus of Marseilles testifies to the popularity of the mime at Marseilles and Rome, and considers the barbarians superior to the Romans in that they had no such scenic displays (Nicoll, 141). But if they originally lacked organised public entertainment, the Germanic people soon developed a taste for it, however reluctantly their rulers might have admitted it. Councils and decrees are consistent in their condemnation of theatrical performers right up to the seventh century and on. It is in the seventh century that Isidore of Seville enters in his *Etymologiae* some theatrical definitions that greatly influence subsequent medieval glosses and glossaries.

Evidence for the nature of the performances in the Middle Ages is sketchy, although the presence of the performers is regularly attested to. During the Middle Ages much that is written referring to performers and performances is derived from traditional sources rather than firsthand experience, and many errors and misconceptions can be demonstrated in the medieval writings. It is unlikely, for example, that Isidore had ever witnessed a performance in a theatre, though he may have seen travelling performers, perhaps on a raised public platform. Evidence for this contention, advanced by Allardyce Nicoll, is contained in Isidore's theatrical definitions, in which he refers to theatres in the past tense but to actors and mimes in the present. Nicoll concludes:

> It seems highly probable from these definitions that, while Isidore knew of theatres only as disused buildings, he was personally acquainted with the activities of the *histriones* and the *mimi*. It is noticeable, also, that in another section of his work Isidore distinctly refers to mimic obscenity as a thing with which the Christian of his time should have naught to do. All this goes to prove that acting of a kind was being continued in his time, with performers who had carried over from classic days the old tradition of mimic impersonation with its "imitation" of life and its secular tendencies. [146]

The history of the mime in Spain is less important for the moment than Isidore's definitions themselves, for, as Mary Marshall puts it, "Isidore's information on the Roman theatre, his definitions of theatrical terms, formed the general basis of medieval knowledge on these subjects" (8).

Isidore (ed. Lindsay: 1911) defined a theatre as a semicircular structure used for the presentation of spectacles, and also as a brothel: "Theatrum est quo scena includitur, semicirculi figuram habens, in quo stantes omnes inspiciunt.

. . . Idem vero theatrum, idem est prostibulum, eo quod post ludos exactos meretrices ibi prostrarentur" (XVIII, 42). The "scena" was a house-shaped construction inside the theatre which had a platform (the "orchestra") where comic and tragic performers sang or recited, and where actors and mimes danced or cavorted: "Scena autem erat locus infra theatrum in modum domus instructa cum pulpito, qui pulpitus orchestra vocabatur; ubi cantabant comici, tragici, atque saltabant histriones et mimi" (XVIII, 43). The orchestra also served as a place where dancers could perform or where two people could exchange words. To this platform poets, tragic and comic performers ascended to the contest, and while they sang or recited, others mimed with gestures: "Orchestra autem pulpitus erat scenae, ubi saltator agere posset, aut duo inter se disputare. Ibi enim poetae comoedi et tragoedi ad certamen conscendebant, hisque canentibus alii gestus edebant" (XVIII, 44). Mimes imitated human affairs, expressing the plays ("fabulas") of poets with physical gestures: the author recited the text before they acted it, and the texts were designed to be suitable for mimic interpretation (XVIII, 49). Thus (XVIII, 45) "tragedians are those who sang (or recited) the ancient deeds and crimes of wicked kings with dolorous voice while the people looked on. [XVIII, 46] Comedians are those who presented the deeds of private men by words or (and?) action (*dictis aut gestu*) and related the seduction of virgins and the loves of harlots. Mimes are so called from a Greek name because they are imitators of human actions (*rerum*); for they had their *auctor* who, before they gave their mimic performance, told the tale. For the stories were so composed by the *poetae* that they were most suitable for acting out by gestures" (Ogilvy, 604). It is not clear whether Isidore considered the "auctor" and the "poeta" to be one and the same person, or whether the auctor recited what the poeta composed, as in the later (erroneous) tradition associated with Terence and his friend Calliopius; nor is it clear how many of the people named in his definitions—if any—Isidore had seen in action. Nonetheless, it is the definitions themselves and the conception of Roman theatrical performances they present that is reflected in later vernacular glosses, including the Old English glosses we shall discuss in a later chapter.

The theatres were dead, but the performers associated with them were not. Whether the Anglo-Saxons had met up with travelling entertainers on the Continent before the fifth century or whether they encountered them for the first time only after the migration is a debatable point not susceptible of resolution. This much is clear: these entertainers were certainly in England from the eighth century onwards and quite possibly even from the seventh (see the following two chapters). One of the consequences of the conversion of the Anglo-

Saxons to Christianity was the readmission of Britain to the Roman world. One of the features of this Roman world was the existence of the professional entertainer, associated with fixed places of public entertainment in the early period, and wandering about Europe after the closing of the theatres. It is unlikely that the presence of such travelling troupes in England in itself caused an alteration in the tradition of the tribal poet (if it still survived); other social factors saw to that. But the existence of public entertainers may have offered the poets a new direction when they came to be thrown off their traditional course. The serious tribal poet, a vatic figure supporting a sacral ruler, was doomed by the monastic influence exerted in royal circles in seventh- and eighth-century England. The poet himself could apply his talent to a modified form of his poetry designed for entertainment; perhaps he acquired a harp and started singing narrative songs, perhaps he continued praising—now flattering—lords and ladies in his audience. Or, if the tribal poet still existed, perhaps the travelling troupes found place for a performer who took the traditional poet on at his own game. The precise course of history is not ever likely to be clear; nonetheless, the arrival in England of *mimi, scurrae, histriones,* and *citharistae,* the *ioculatores* and the *saltatores,* descendants of the Roman theatrical performers, may have set the stage for the blurring of the distinction between tribal poet and entertaining singer to which the later Old English glosses beat testimony (see chap. 9).

One objection to this scenario must be entertained before we pass on. If it is possible that the tradition of narrative song or poetry started to take shape in England only in the seventh and eighth centuries, how are we to account for the seemingly traditional diction of the extant Old English reflexes of this tradition? One of the firmest contentions of Parry and Lord is that oral formulas evolve over a long period of time, they gradually become accepted as part of the general tradition because they have proved their usefulness. Since no one would deny that the extant Old English poetry is formulaic, are we not therefore dealing with an archaic tradition whose diction evolved over the course of many centuries, of necessity indicating an origin during the continental period? Do the formulas common to all the Germanic traditions not demonstrate a common Germanic origin for the narrative tradition (see Kellogg; Whallon)?

There are a number of responses to these objections. First, Lord's study is essentially synchronic rather than diachronic. Concerned primarily with the form of the songs, Lord devoted relatively little attention to the alteration of the tradition in time (see Lord: 1960, 115). Although there are some brief comparisons between texts collected in the 1930s and texts collected in the 1950s (sometimes from the same singer), no detailed analysis has been published which would allow us to assess the effect of the extended passage of time and altered social environments on the diction of the poetry. Occasionally in *The Singer of Tales* Lord suggests that the guslar's songs might have served a social function more serious than entertainment: "The poet was sorcerer and seer before he became 'artist.' His structures were not abstract art, or art for its own sake. The roots of oral traditional narrative are not artistic but religious in the broadest sense" (1960, 67); "There is some evidence to indicate that singers do not ornament unimportant points in their stories. Halting places on journeys, scenes of hospitality, both here and in Homer, may deserve the emphasis given them neither because they are realistic pictures of heroic life nor because they are artistically useful in showing passage of time, but because the archetypal journey in epic was of a ceremonial nature and its stages were marked by significant events and meaningful encounters" (1960, 109); "Indeed this poetry has more often been aristocratic and courtly than of the folk. It would seem even from its origins to have belonged to serious ceremonial occasions, to ritual, to celebration" (1960, 6). But we are never presented with a calculus of change in oral tradition, the Southslavic tradition is presented to us as essentially static.

Second, Lord studied only one restricted aspect of the tradition, the songs of the improvising guslar: there is no discussion of the diction of memorised songs or of lyrical or any other songs current in the community. Poets grow up in a society, they are subject to the influence of various verbal traditions. Could the diction associated with one genre be utilised for another? In the Anglo-Saxon frame of reference, could the diction of a newish tradition of narrative song derive from a tradition of eulogistic poetry? Lord supplies no data on which to found any assumption about the interaction of contemporary traditions within the same community.

To turn from Lord to Anglo-Saxon studies: it must be admitted that to argue that Old English poetic formulas presuppose an archaic tradition is to argue from weak premises and on weak grounds. For example, there exists the strong possibility that the Xhosa eulogistic tradition has altered in the last few decades from a primarily memorial to a primarily improvisational tradition (see Opland: 1974): the verbal or artistic expressions of a people can be shown on this evidence to be capable of rapid alteration if social conditions are in a state of flux. Some literate Xhosa poets I have met perform as oral poets but also write poetry; I have no way of telling whether phrases that recur in both their oral and written poetry are oral "formulas" or phrases they have written into their poetry in imitation of their oral style or phrases they have absorbed into their oral performances only after composing them for publication. In other words, the Xhosa tradition may well have altered radically in the last half-century, and there is no clear-cut distinction in form between some oral and literate productions. Anglo-Saxon scholars are by no means agreed on what constitutes a formula in Old English poetry—is the basis syntactic, metrical, melodic, verbal, or semantic (see Miletich)? It is by no means clear what we mean when we say that extant Old English poetry is formulaic, and even if we grant that the poetry is formulaic, there is no firm evidence that this means that it must derive from an antique tradition. While considerable profit has been derived from the examination of the diction of Old English poetry in the wake of Magoun's articles, it is noteworthy that relatively few Old English narrative themes have been identified. As crucial to Lord's definition of oral poetry as the formula was the absence of enjambment and the thematic construction of the narratives; yet in Old English poetry we have "the sea voyage," "the battle," perhaps "feasting in the hall," and very little else. On this evidence it might well be argued that the extant Old English poetry clearly did *not* derive from an antique native narrative tradition.

In any event, even if a tradition of narrative poetry developed in England only after the seventh and eighth centuries, we still have four centuries of Anglo-Saxon England left, time enough for the evolution of a traditional diction. There is no reason at all why the diction of the eulogistic poetry should not have formed the basis of a new narrative tradition: I have already suggested that narrative is embryonically present in eulogy. Nor need we suppose that there was no narrative poetry at all before the seventh century. The harp certainly existed, and it may have been used to accompany ballads or short lays. All that is suggested here is that after the eighth century there is good reason to believe that there might have appeared a professional singer of narrative songs; amateurs may have existed before this time, but the professional entertainer is something different. His livelihood depends on his ability to please his audience, and his talent ensures that he will purvey the best possible product. A new kind of performer appears in England; perhaps his presence inspires the development of native English singers, perhaps he himself is influenced by the existence of native English poets and assumes aspects of their tradition. It is a notable fact that Old English narrative poetry draws largely on continental heroes for its subject matter; this may indicate that the narrative tradition in England was originally the business of continental travelling performers, though it may indicate nothing at all if the scribes recorded only the continental tales in the belief that Englishmen would always remember their own heroes.

In general, one may conclude that the conversion of the Anglo-Saxons to

Christianity ushered in a new attitude to literature on the part of artist and audience alike, a revolution in the history of English literature unrivalled in scope and impact by that caused by any other subsequent single event or set of events. After the introduction of writing, Anglo-Saxons were influenced by classical literature and ideas, and their own poetry could be recorded for the first time. Writing itself was not inimical to the oral traditions, which in many respects must have continued unaltered, though the altered moral ideals of the rulers and patrons of literature led to a significant modification of the oral poetic tradition, particularly as it affected the tribal poet. Finally, in the wake of the conversion to Roman Christianity came the wandering entertainers, the purveyors of new kinds of amusement and diversion.

All this is hypothetical, supposition based on comparative studies of other literary traditions or other disciplines: so far no documentary evidence has been produced from Anglo-Saxon England. It is only after the seventh century that such evidence comes into existence. It is time now to turn from hypothesis to the extant facts. From this point on we shall be concerned with an examination of evidence in Old English and Latin that survives from Anglo-Saxon England.

5

The Seventh Century

The two centuries from 600 to 800 constitute a period of transition in the history of English literature. Before 600 the Anglo-Saxons were pagan and effectively preliterate (for runes seem to have had a limited currency and in any case do not appear to have been used originally for recording works of literature); after 800 the Anglo-Saxon kingships, with the exception of the Wessex line, were destroyed by the Vikings. If there was a flourishing tradition of pagan royal poetry before 600, it could accordingly have survived intact in the ninth century only in the courts of the West Saxon kings; but as we have seen, the Saxons are not likely to have supported a tradition of tribal poets, and even if they did, the poets' sacral function would probably have been undermined by the monastic theology of kingship. It is likely, therefore, that the early centuries of the Christian era witnessed the radical alteration of the tradition perpetuated by tribal poets among the Anglo-Saxons.

The introduction of Christianity entailed the admission of the Anglo-Saxons to the society of western Europe, and perhaps led to the appearance in England of those wandering troupes of entertainers that commonly aroused the censure of European ecclesiastics. One of the results of the conversion was the production of a body of written literature which, as we have seen, is significantly different in many respects from an oral literature. Literate Anglo-Saxons took to writing poetry in Latin, some wrote in English, and some combined the two languages; some worked within the classical tradition, but some extended the native English tradition. It is unlikely, however, that this written poetry, whether in Latin or English, was ever very popular. We have no strong evidence to indicate that it was ever intended for dissemination among the illiterate population at large; it seems to have been the pursuit of a literate elite, designed primarily to entertain or edify that elite clerical class or perhaps a lay aristocracy. All the extant writings in Anglo-Latin and most of the extant works in Old English can readily be seen to emanate from this literate and Christian body of authors; we are fortunate indeed if we find any descriptions of purely secular, nonclerical performances or transcriptions of such performances. Yet traditions of secular poetry and song almost certainly existed before the conversion, and many manifestations of these traditions are likely to have continued among the general populace.

The tenor of the conversion was laid down by Gregory the Great, who counselled a policy of assimilation: in a letter to Mellitus, he asks him to tell Augustine that "the temples of the idols in that country should on no account be destroyed. He is to destroy the idols, but the temples themselves are to be aspersed with holy water, altars set up, and relics enclosed in them. For if these temples are well built, they are to be purified from devil-worship, and dedicated to the service of the true God. In this way, we hope that the people, seeing that its temples are not destroyed, may abandon idolatry and resort to these places as before, and may come to know and adore the true God" (Bede, *Eccl. Hist.*, trans. Sherley-Price, I, 30). In spite of the good intentions of the missionaries, the conversion undoubtedly introduced severe tensions among the Anglo-Saxons. Bede narrates the early growth of the mission to the East Saxons, the conversion of King Sigeberht, the establishment of Cedd as bishop, and then the sudden murder of the king:

> To the great joy of the king and all his people, the Gospel of eternal life made daily headway throughout the province for a considerable time until, at the instigation of the Enemy of all good men, the king was murdered by his own kinsman. This horrid crime was committed by two brothers, who on being asked their motive, had no answer to make except that they hated the king because he was too lenient towards his enemies, and too readily forgave injuries when offenders asked pardon. This then was the fault for which the king was killed, that he sincerely observed the teachings of the Gospel. [III, 22]

No doubt the murderers felt compelled to resort to so drastic a step because they were witness to the erosion of traditional custom under Sigeberht. The rift between pagan and Christian must have yawned painfully wide in seventh-century England. In his life of Cuthbert, Bede tells the story of a party of Jarrow monks trapped helplessly on rafts in a storm-tossed river Tyne:

> While the monks opposite were watching in sorrow, the peasants began to

jeer at their way of life, as though they deserved such misfortune for spurn-
ing the life of the ordinary man and introducing new, unheard-of rules of
conduct. Cuthbert stopped their insults.

"Do you realise what you are doing? Would it not be more human of
you to pray for their safety rather than to gloat over their misfortune?"

But they, boors both in thought and speech, fulminated against him.

"Nobody is going to pray for them. Let not God raise a finger to help
them! They have done away with all the old ways of worship and now
nobody knows what to do." [chap. 3, trans. J. F. Webb]

Cuthbert kneels to pray, the storm immediately abates, and the peasants recant;
Bede claims to have this story from a Jarrow monk who heard one of the peasants who was involved recount it on a number of occasions. We would not read
of the peasants' hostility to the monks if it were not a vital element in the story
of one of Cuthbert's miracles; the reasons for the murder of Sigeberht are
provided to make of him a martyr for the faith. Obviously, one rarely reads of
the peasant or the pagan Anglo-Saxon's attitude toward Christianity in the
extant documents.

The first permanent Christian mission station among the Xhosa was established in 1823. The effects of the conversion and the rift that it introduced into
Xhosa society are still apparent today (see Hutchinson; Pauw: 1965 and 1975).
Those who converted were *amakholwa*, the believers; those who remained
pagan were *amaqaba*, those who smeared themselves with traditional ochre. The
amakholwa adopted European dress, assumed a new name in baptism, abjured
dances and traditional gatherings, entered school, and spurned the amaqaba as
their inferiors. Christian women at a funeral I attended recently cooked for
themselves and the guests and totally ignored and kept themselves rigidly segre-
gated from the pagan women.

The effect of the conversion on written literature is pronounced. The Xhosa
were introduced to writing by Christian missionaries, whose early tasks included transcribing the Xhosa language in the Roman alphabet and translating
the Bible into Xhosa. The early printing presses were in the hands of the missionaries, and this meant that early printed literature written by Xhosas tended
to be didactic, suitable for prescription in schools, or emasculated by imitation
of European models. The imbongi has the licence to use ribald language, to
criticise with impunity excesses of behaviour in his chief or his fellows. Today
open criticism of the missionaries is voiced by the imbongi in his oral izibongo
(see, for example, Opland: 1975, 202); rarely in the published literature do we

find similar sentiments openly expressed. Even today, when nonsectarian publishers are printing vernacular books, the books that are published are designed
for prescription in schools, since there is as yet a limited Xhosa reading public.
Some Xhosa antiquarians did collect traditional poetry in the early years of this
century, but they edited it for publication. The result is that the poetry that
appears in print tends to be an emasculated or westernised reflex of the oral
tradition.

In an analogous way, one would expect the Old English literature written
on vellum in the early centuries of Christian England to reflect the attitudes
and sympathies of that section of society from which the authors and the intended audience were drawn. A Christian Anglo-Saxon of course did not cease
to be an Anglo-Saxon. It is abundantly clear, for example, that monks preserved an enthusiasm for secular feasting and song, an enthusiasm that was
constantly decried in ecclesiastical correspondence and conciliar pronouncements; certain literary attitudes in the early saints' lives might be reflexes of a
secular tradition. But in general the extant sources for our study of the oral
poet immediately after the conversion are written from a Christian point of
view and testify to a clash between secular and Christian tastes or a movement
towards accommodation. Secular poetry is apparently held to be undesirable,
and one reads accounts of secular poetry—as one reads accounts of pagan opposition to Christianity—only when the Christian faction may be seen to have
triumphed. There are no references to purely secular performances except in a
Christian context or in the course of a narrative leading to a conclusion in
harmony with Christian sentiment. In the few accounts extant from the seventh
century, one is aware of conflict between the Christian and secular poetic traditions, of accommodation of secular to Christian tastes, of transition and assimilation.

Perhaps the earliest authentic reference to what might be poetic activity in
England occurs in Eddius Stephanus's *Life of Wilfrid*, written between 710 and
720 (ed. Colgrave, trans. Albertson). Eddius is generally believed to have known
Wilfrid intimately and to have accompanied him on at least two of his journeys
to the Continent. If he was not with Wilfrid during the events he narrates in
chapter 13, it is likely that he received an account of the incident from Wilfrid
himself or from an eyewitness. The passage refers to Wilfrid's return to England in about A.D. 666:

> Then as they were sailing across the British sea from Gaul with Bishop
> Wilfrid, and the clerics were singing and chanting psalms in chorus to

praise God and to keep time for the oarsmen [canentibus clericis et psal-
lentibus laudem Dei pro celeumate in choro], suddenly in mid-ocean a
violent tempest blew up and the wind shifted against them, just as it had
against the disciples of Jesus on the sea of Galilee. [chap. 13]

The boat is blown toward the shore of the South Saxons, and is met by a swarm
of hostile pagans bent on booty. Wilfrid tries unsuccessfully to ransom his
party.

They refused, like Pharaoh, to let the people of God go, and arrogantly
maintained that everything cast upon land by the sea belonged to them as
their own personal property. Meanwhile the high priest of their idolatry
[princeps sacerdotum idolatriae] stood like Balaam, on a high grave-
mound in full view of the pagans and strove with all his strength to curse
the people of God and bind their hands with the spell of his magic [male-
dicere populum Dei, et suis magicis artibus manus eorum alligare nitebatur].
[chap. 13]

One of Wilfrid's men takes up a stone blessed by his companions and, like
David, hurls it at the head of the sorcerer as he stands cursing ("ad cerebrum
magi exprobrantis illisit") and topples him lifeless, like Goliath, from the grave-
mound.

I shall return to this passage and that immediately following it in the next
chapter when I have occasion to discuss briefly the saints' lives written in the
eighth century. For the moment, two aspects of the passage concern us: the
rowing song and the cursing priest. The first is particularly interesting, as it
clearly alludes to Christians singing a psalm in chorus. There is nothing unusual
in this, of course, but what is striking is the function of the psalm, "pro celeumate." The *celeuma* is strictly an exhortatory or joyful song (see Prinz and
Schneider), but more specifically it is used as an aid to navigation; a song "to
keep time for the oarsmen" is a reasonable translation (cf. the Old English
glosses *sæleoðes: celeumatis*, and *lewisplega: cereuma vel celeuma, idem et toma, i.
leta cantatio*: see Padelford). In other words, it is a form of work song. Although
the rowers or sailors are likely to have been Gauls, the passengers are Anglo-
Saxons, and they sing in chorus a song to expedite the business of sailing. It is
possible that this was a traditional Anglo-Saxon practice, that Anglo-Saxons
often sang in chorus as they rowed. Singing such songs in chorus implies a
memorised traditional text; but Wilfrid's companions apparently did not care
to use the traditional words, and they substituted a text introduced by the new

Christian religion. It may be that they used the psalm and its melody, or they may have fitted the text to the traditional melody; whatever the truth of the matter, they chose not to sing the traditional English text but employed instead a liturgical text or song for a nonliturgical purpose. This calls to mind Alfric's urging his audience not to chant spells over plants but to bless them with God's words ("Ne sceal nan man mid galdre wyrte besingan, ac mid Godes wordum hi gebletsian," Thorpe, I, 476; cf. Frank, 66).

It seems reasonable to infer that there were traditional rowing songs among the Anglo-Saxons, that some early Christians considered secular songs unsuitable for performance (or at any rate less desirable than Christian songs), and that we have here an example of an attempt to accommodate the old and the new traditions. This postulated antipathy on the part of Christians towards non-Christian literature receives confirmation of sorts from the writings of Bede (see Blair; Raby, 170). However well-read he himself might have been in both Christian and non-Christian Latin poets, Bede apparently felt that Christians should not read the pagan poets: in *De arte metrica* he refers to the works of such authors as Porphyrius, which it is disagreeable for us to touch because they are pagans ("Reperiuntur quaedam et in insigni illo volumine Porphyrii poetae, quo ad Constantinum Augustum misso meruit de exilio liberari, quae, quia pagana erant, nos tangere non libuit"). Wilfrid's companions apparently felt much the same way about secular songs. (In 1825, Thomas Philipps visited an early mission station and recorded in his diary that "They sang several hymns, some of which were words adapted to [Xhosa] tunes": Keppel-Jones, 283.)

The second point of interest in Eddius's narrative concerns the "princeps sacerdotum idolatriae" of the South Saxons, who takes up a position apart from the combatants high on a barrow and attempts to rob the Christians of their strength. Although not much is known of the pagan worship of the Anglo-Saxons, they may have had priests, like the high priest Coifi who plays a role in Bede's description of the acceptance of Christianity in Northumbria (II, 13). This magus may be one of those, and if so there is nothing more to be said. However, perhaps one ought to consider whether his curses might not have been poetic, and whether he might not have been a tribal poet. Certainly his station on a barrow—a spot closely associated with the pagan cult of ancestor veneration (see Davidson: 1950)—and his performance in the context of battle harmonise with our hypothetical reconstruction of the function of the tribal poet, whose sacral poetry would conjure the sympathetic attention of the ancestors to the situation confronting their descendants; the poet's battle poetry would exhort his companions and rob their opponents of power. It may

well be that in the eyes of Wilfrid's companions such a person could be identified with Balaam; or it may even be that priest and tribal poet were one. We
may have here a description of an Anglo-Saxon tribal poet in action. Yet
it is unlikely that Eddius would call him a pagan priest if he were not one,
for surely Wilfrid's companions would recognise a pagan priest when they
saw one. On balance, it seems probable that the man described here is a priest
and that he was performing the function of a priest, though it is certainly possible that the priest may have chanted poetry; he may have been performing
the function of, or may indeed have been, a tribal poet. If this last is accepted, it
should be noted that this passage then provides evidence that would contradict
the hypothesis that there were not likely to be any tribal poets among the Saxons
in the seventh century.

Wilfrid features in another seventh-century allusion to the practice of poetry
or song in England. In October 679 Pope Agatho held a council in Rome with
seventeen bishops and thirty-five priests to discuss English church affairs and in
particular to prepare for the visit of John the Precentor to England; John subsequently reported on this meeting at the Council of Hatfield in 680. Wilfrid
was probably in Rome at the time of the council, although his problems were
not explicitly mentioned in the pronouncements. The members of the Roman
council seem to have had knowledge of local conditions in England. They issued
statements on the number and arrangement of the English bishops, on John the
Precentor's impending visit, and on the behaviour of the English clergy; on the
latter topic they resolved as follows:

> Statuimus etiam atque decernimus, ut Episcopi vel quicunque ecclesiastici
> ordinis religiosam vitam professi sunt, armis non utantur, nec citharoedas
> habeant, vel quaecunque symphoniaca, nec quoscunque jocos vel ludos
> ante se permittant, quia omnia haec disciplina sanctae ecclesiae sacerdotes
> fideles suos habere non sinit. . . . [Haddan and Stubbs, III, 133]

Faithful priests are to spurn arms, harpers, shows, jokes, and games; they are not
to use the former and not to entertain the other four. Throughout the Anglo-
Saxon period English ecclesiastics write to colleagues, whether secular or
regular, warning them to beware the evils of drunkenness, feasting, and flashy
dressing. So consistent are these specific admonitions that one is led to conclude
that these were firmly entrenched features of Anglo-Saxon life. It is reasonable
to assume that the cultivation of harpers, musicians, actors, and entertainers
alluded to in the council's statement was, like the bearing of arms, a fault that
the council had been informed the English ecclesiastics were guilty of and for

which they needed to be admonished. These musicians and entertainers might
have been foreign minstrels or they might have been traditional English performers. The former seems to be suggested by the use of the words *symphoniaca*
and *ludos*, though the Romans might have used such words describing practices
familiar to them to refer to English practices they thought were similar. The
argument for classical performers is not strong, however, for there is no explicit
mention of mimi, joculatores, or scurrae, figures associated with the Roman
theatres. This conciliar statement may be taken as testimony to the fondness of
the seventh-century Anglo-Saxons for harpers, though we are not told whether
the harpers produced songs or narrated stories to the accompaniment of the
harp: the citharoedas supplied music, but we are unfortunately not told whether
at the same time they sang songs, Heldenlieder or otherwise.

There remain to be considered accounts of two seventh-century English
poets, both of singular significance because they exemplify the transition from
the native to the Christian tradition. Each in his own way, Cædmon and Aldhelm drew on native resources to compose poems or songs on Christian themes.
We will start with Cædmon, since he stands closer to the native poetic tradition
than does Aldhelm.

The story of Cædmon can be found in Bede's *Historia Ecclesiastica Gentis
Anglorum* (ed. Colgrave and Mynors), completed in 731. Bede places Cædmon
in Whitby in the monastery of the abbess Hild, "in huius monasterio abbatis-
sae." Hild established the community at Whitby in 657, and she died in 680, so
657 must be the terminus a quo for Cædmon's association with Whitby; we
have no way of knowing when he died, however, but since he is said to have
lived a secular life to advanced old age ("siquidem in habitu saeculari usque ad
tempora prouectioris aetatis constitutus") before becoming a monk, we may
assume that he died not long after taking monastic vows at Hild's suggestion.
His vision and his literary career may thus reasonably be placed roughly between the years 660 and 680. Bede probably entered Benedict Biscop's new
foundation at Wearmouth as a seven-year-old boy in about 680, and probably
joined Ceolfrith two years later at Jarrow, where he remained for the rest of
his life. A. H. Smith argues for the reliability of Bede's account of Cædmon:

> In view of his accuracy and skill as an historian there can be little doubt
> that Bede believed the hymn to be Cædmon's: if he followed his usual
> practice, he had it from some trustworthy source, either an eyewitness or
> some written description made by such an eyewitness at Whitby. It is not
> known whether Bede had ever been at [Whitby], but we know that he

visited York in 733 and he may have been in Yorkshire before the *Historia Ecclesiastica* was written. And a connexion with [Whitby] is clearly suggested by Bede's use of a Life of Gregory the Great, without doubt composed by a Whitby monk. [12]

Smith also examines and rejects the theory that the Old English version of the hymn is a translation of Bede's Latin paraphrase and concludes: "We cannot therefore doubt that Bede was actually paraphrasing a poem already in existence" (13). I accept the view that Bede translated an Old English poem, and that this poem was originally produced by Cædmon in circumstances such as Bede describes. I am less inclined to accept the reliability of the Old English version of Bede's History, which was produced almost two centuries after Cædmon flourished: I shall have occasion here to refer to the Old English text, but that text cannot tell us any more than what a late ninth-century scholar (probably Mercian) thought was current practice in late seventh-century Northumbria (see Whitelock: 1962).

The following passages in Bede's account (ed. Colgrave and Mynors; Miller; trans. Whitelock: 1955) are relevant to our study:

> In the monastery of this abbess there was a certain brother who was specially marked out by the grace of God, so that he used to compose godly and religious songs [carmina religioni et pietati apta facere solebat; Old English he gewunade gerisenlice leoð wyrcan, þa ðe to æfestnisse 7 to arfæstnisse belumpen]; thus, whatever he learned from the holy Scriptures by means of interpreters, he quickly turned into extremely delightful and moving poetry, in English, which was his own tongue [quicquid ex diuinis litteris per interpretes disceret, hoc ipse post pusillum uerbis poeticis maxima suauitate et conpunctione conpositis in sua, id est Anglorum, lingua proferret; swa hwæt swa he of godcundum stafum þurh boceras geleornode, þæt he æfter medmiclum fæce in scopgereorde mid þa mæstan swetnisse 7 inbryrdnisse geglængde 7 in Engliscgereorde wel geworht forþbrohte]. By his songs [cuius carminibus; for his leoþsongum] the minds of many were often inspired to despise the world and to long for the heavenly life. It is true that after him other Englishmen attempted to compose religious poems [religiosa poemata facere temtabant; ongunnon æfæste leoð wyrcan], but none could compare with him. For he did not learn the art of poetry [canendi artem didcit; he þone leoðcræft leornade] from men nor through a man but he received the gift of song [canendi donum; þone songcræft] freely by the grace of God. Hence he could never compose any foolish or

trivial poem [friuoli et superuacui poematis; leasunge ne idles leoþes] but only those which were concerned with devotion and so were fitting for his devout tongue to utter. He had lived in the secular habit until he was well advanced in years and had never learned any songs [nil carminum aliquando didicerat: he næfre nænig leoð geleornade]. Hence sometimes at a feast, when for the sake of providing entertainment, it had been decided that they should all sing in turn, when he saw the harp approaching him, he would rise up in the middle of the feasting, go out, and return home [Vnde nonnumquam in conuiuio, cum esset laetitiae causa decretum ut omnes per ordinem cantare deberent, ille, ubi adpropinquare sibi citharam cernebat, surgebat a media caena; Ond he forþon oft in gebeorscipe, þonne þær wæs blisse intinga gedemed, þæt heo ealle scalde þurh endebyrdnesse be hearpan singan, þonne he geseah þa hearpan him nealecan, þonne aras he for for-scome from þæm symble].

On one such occasion, he left the place of feasting (domu conuiuii; þæt hus þæs gebeorscipes) and went to the stable to look after the cattle whose care had been entrusted to him for the night, and fell asleep there. He then dreamt that someone stood before him, greeted him and addressed him by name:

'Cædmon,' he said, 'sing me something' [canta mihi aliquid; sing me hwæthwugu]. Cædmon answered, 'I cannot sing; that is why I left the feast and came here because I could not sing' [Nescio cantare; nam et ideo de conuiuio egressus huc secessi, quia cantare non poteram; Ne con ic noht singan; 7 ic forþon of þeossum gebeorscipe úteode, 7 hider gewat, forþon ic naht singan ne cuðe]. Once again the speaker said, 'Nevertheless you must sing to me.' 'What must I sing?' said Cædmon. 'Sing,' he said 'about the beginning of created things' ['At tamen' ait 'mihi cantare habes.' 'Quid' inquit 'debeo cantare?' Et ille 'Canta' inquit 'principium creaturarum'; Hwæðre þu meaht singan. Þa cwæð he: Hwæt sceal ic singan? Cwæð he: Sing me frumsceaft]. Thereupon Cædmon began to sing verses which he had never heard before in praise of God the Creator [Quo accepto responso, statim ipse coepit cantare in laudem Dei Conditoris uersus quos numquam audierat; Þa he ða þas andsware onfeng, þa ongon he sona singan, in here-nesse Godes Scyppendes þa fers 7 þa word þe he næfre gehyrde], of which this is the general sense: 'Now we must praise the Maker of the heavenly kingdom, the power of the Creator and his counsel, the deeds of the Father of Glory and how He, since He is the eternal God, was the Author of all marvels and first created the heavens as a roof for the children of men and then, the almighty Guardian of the human race, created the earth.'

A number of manuscripts of the Latin text add in the margin or at the foot of the page at this point the Old English version of the hymn: four contain a Northumbrian and seven a later (West Saxon) version. The five extant manuscripts of the Old English version of Bede substitute at this point the later version of the hymn. The Northumbrian version reads as follows:

> Nu scylun hergan   hefaenricaes uard,
> metudæs maecti   end his modgidanc,
> uerc uuldurfadur,   sue he uundra gihuaes,
> eci dryctin,   or astelidæ.
> He aerist scop   aelda barnum
> heben til hrofe,   haleg scepen;
> tha middungeard   moncynnæs uard,
> eci dryctin,   æfter tiadæ
> firum foldu,   frea allmectig.

Bede immediately follows his summary of the hymn with an apology for the translation:

> This is the sense but not the order of the words which he sang as he slept [non autem ordo ipse uerborum, quae dormiens ille canebat; the Old English texts, of course, omit the apology]. For it is not possible to translate verse [carmina], however well composed, literally from one language to another without some loss of beauty and dignity.

Bede then continues his narrative of Cædmon.

> When he awoke, he remembered all that he had sung while asleep and soon added more verses in the same manner, praising God in fitting style [Exsurgens autem a somno, cuncta quae dormiens cantauerat memoriter retenuit, et eis mox plura in eundem modum uerba Deo digni carminis adiunxit; Þa aras he from þæm slæpe, 7 eal, þa þe he slæpende song, fæste in gemynde hæfde. 7 þæm wordum sona monig word in þæt ilce gemet Gode wyrðes songes togeþeodde].
>
> In the morning he went to the reeve who was his master, telling him of the gift he had received, and the reeve took him to the abbess. He was then bidden to describe his dream in the presence of a number of the more learned men and also to recite his song [dicere carmen; þæt leoð singan] so

that they might all examine him and decide upon the nature and origin of the gift of which he spoke; and it seemed clear to all of them that the Lord had granted him heavenly grace. They then read to him a passage of sacred history or doctrine, bidding him make a song out of it, if he could, in metrical form [si posset, hunc in modulationem carminis transferre; gif he meahte, þæt he in swinsunge leoþsonges þæt gehwyrfde]. He undertook the task and went away; on returning next morning he repeated the passage he had been given, which he had put into excellent verse [optimo carmine quod iubebatur conpositum reddidit; þy betstan leoðe geglenged him asóng 7 ageaf, þæt him beboden wæs].

Hild then urges him to forsake his secular life and enter the monastery, which he does. There he is taught sacred history ("seriem sacrae historia").

He learned all he could by listening to them and then, memorizing it and ruminating over it, like some clean animal chewing the cud, he turned it into the most melodious verse: and it sounded so sweet as he recited it that his teachers became in turn his audience [at ipse cuncta, quae audiendo discere poterat, rememorando secum et quasi mundum animal ruminando, in carmen dulcissimum conuertebat, suauiusque resonando doctores suos uicissim auditores sui faciebat; Ond he eal, þa he in gehyrnesse geleornian meahte, mid hine gemyndgade; 7 swa swa clæne neten eodorcende in þæt sweteste leoð gehwyrfde 7 his song 7 his leoð wæron swa wynsumu to gehyranne, þætte seolfan þa his lareowas æt his muðe wreoton 7 leornodon]. He sang [canebat; song] about the creation of the world, the origin of the human race, and the whole history of Genesis, of the departure of Israel from Egypt and the entry into the promised land and of many other of the stories taken from the sacred Scriptures: of the incarnation, passion, and resurrection of the Lord, of His ascension into heaven, of the coming of the Holy Spirit and the teaching of the apostles. He also made many songs [multa carmina faciebat; he monig leoð geworhte] about the terrors of future judgement, the horrors of the pains of hell, and the joys of the heavenly kingdom. In addition he composed many other songs [et alia perplura; and swelce eac oðer monig] about the divine mercies and judgements, in all of which he sought to turn his hearers away from delight in sin and arouse in them the love and practice of good works.

Bede then proceeds to relate the blessed death of this religious and pious man, and concludes

and his tongue which had uttered so many good words in praise of the
Creator also uttered its last words in His praise (illaque lingua, quae tot
salutaria uerba in laudem conditoris conposuerat, ultima quoque uerba in
laudem ipsius; Ond seo tunge, þe swa monig halwende word in þæs scyppendes lof gesette,—he ða swelce eac þa ytmæstan word in his herenisse),
as he signed himself with the sign of the cross and commended his spirit
into God's hands.

Bede's story of Cædmon is the most detailed contemporary account of the
career of an Anglo-Saxon oral poet, and accordingly merits lengthy quotation
and particular attention. It should be noted before we start our discussion that,
strictly speaking, we may not be able to arrive at definitive conclusions about
the nature of the poetic tradition from Bede's narrative; all that we can really
hope to determine is what Bede thought the nature of the tradition to be. The
fact that Bede is himself an Anglo-Saxon does not necessarily mean that he is an
accurate commentator on the Anglo-Saxon poetic tradition: as Lord notes, and
as I have observed, even the oral poets themselves frequently lack objectivity
about their art or the nature of their tradition. Bede spent most of his life in the
monastery of Jarrow, but it is not necessary to assume therefore that he never
heard Old English traditional songs or poems. He seems to demonstrate a familiarity with native poetry when he writes in his *De re metrica*, perhaps of the
difference between classical and English poetry, that similar to metre is rhythm,
which is a harmonious arrangement of words not counted according to regular
metre but by the number of syllables judged orally, like the works of vernacular
poets ("Videtur autem rhythmus metris esse consimilis qui est verborum modulata compositio non metrica ratione sed numero syllabarum ad judicium aurium
examinata, ut sunt carmina vulgarium poetarum," VII, 242), and his disciple
Cuthbert, as we shall see, testifies to his personal knowledge of and skill in
composing English poetry. On these grounds we should have to conclude that
Bede's evidence is certainly admissible, though on certain points—such as the
distinction between improvisation and memorisation, for example—he may not
discriminate as nicely as modern scholars have learnt to do. I shall divide my
discussion of Bede's account of Cædmon into three sections: first, we shall look
at the convivium that supplies the traditional context for Cædmon's career;
next, we shall look at Cædmon himself; and finally we shall consider the short
poem that Bede tells us Cædmon composed in a dream.

We are not told where the convivium takes place or who is present. Cædmon leaves the house ("domu conuiuii") and goes to the stables; the Old English version translates *conuiuio* as *gebeorscipe*, a beer-party, and *domu conuiuii* as *þæt hus þæs gebeorscipes*. The house may or may not be a part of the monastery complex; Cædmon's companions may or may not be associated with the monastery, they may or may not be exclusively males. It is implied, however, that the gathering is purely secular since the hymn seems to be set up as a pious reaction to the entertainments of the party, but this is only an inference. There is nothing in the description of the party itself that marks it as secular: harps, as we shall see, were not entirely silent in monasteries, and the monks frequently feasted and entertained themselves or were entertained by others. In his Life of Cuthbert (trans. Webb), for example, Bede has the saint censure his companions for their feastmaking on Christmas day: "As things went on and we were enjoying dinner," Cuthbert recollects, "feeling convivial and telling stories, I broke in again to warn them to be earnest in prayer and vigils and to be ready against all temptation" (chap. 27).

One is led to believe that the performances at the party Cædmon attended were "foolish and trivial," since Bede tells us that Cædmon could never compose such songs ("friuoli et superuacui poematis"), but again this is an inference; one can conclude at least that foolish and trivial poems—that is, purely secular, not specifically Christian poems—did exist. We cannot read much into the Old English version's ascribing Cædmon's departure from the party to shame ("for forscome")—whether the shame was occasioned by the triviality of the entertainment or by his inability to perform—since Bede's Latin supplies no such explicit motive. It is clear, however, from Bede's reference to the convivium that such gatherings took place regularly, that the function of the performances was entertainment, and that each performance was an individual production accompanied by the performer on the lyre ("cum esset laetitiae causa decretum ut omnes per ordinem cantare deberent"). As such, we must label these performances songs and not poems. There is no need to assume that Cædmon's friends were chanting spontaneous poems on the spur of the moment (see Magoun: 1955); it is far more likely that they were performing in turn memorised, traditional songs. It may be that Cædmon did not participate in this activity because he spurned the secularity of the lyrics or because he could not play the lyre; the reason Bede gives is that he had never learnt any songs ("nil carminum aliquando didicerat"), clearly implying that the songs had to be learnt—that is, that they were traditional, memorised performances. In his dream Cædmon tells his interlocutor that he left the party because he could not sing ("quia cantare non poteram"), apparently confirming what Bede tells us, that he had never learnt any songs, or that he had never learnt how to sing. Bede's description of the convivium thus indicates that there was a tradition of memorised songs performed by ordinary people (not specially trained artists) to the accompaniment of a lyre (cithara); we are left to infer that the songs were purely secular, though we cannot determine whether they were narratives— whether "lays" or "ballads"—or lyrical songs. King Gelimer of the Vandals sang to his own harp accompaniment; apparently seventh-century North-umbrians could do the same.

We turn now to Cædmon himself. First, Bede seems to indicate that Cædmon remained illiterate all his life. He never reads for himself, but always gathers his knowledge of biblical narrative by listening to others read to him ("quicquid ex diuinis litteris per interpretes disceret; exponebantque illi quendam sacrae historiae siue doctrinae sermonem, praecipientes eum, si posset, hunc in modulationem carminis transferre; At ipse cuncta, quae audiendo discere poterat . . . in carmen dulcissimum conuertebat"); he always sings or makes songs or dictates his songs (this last being an addition of the Old English version: "suauiusque resonando doctores suos uicissim auditores sui faciebat; 7 his song 7 his leoð wæron swa wynsumu to gehyranne, þætte seolfan þa his lareowas æt his muðe wreoton 7 leornodon").

In other words, Cædmon is a purely oral poet or singer. His performances, whatever their subject matter, are as much a part of Anglo-Saxon oral tradition as are the performances of his erstwhile drinking companions. Unlike these companions, however, Cædmon is never said to play a harp to accompany his compositions: if one wishes, one may infer that he did in fact perform after his dream in a style identical to that of his companions at the party before the dream, but this inference relies on no textual support. At all times, however, Bede implies that Cædmon's performances, like those of his companions, participate in a memorial tradition; with the exception of the hymn itself— which we shall examine in detail shortly—there is no evidence anywhere in the account of any spontaneous, improvised performance (see Fry: 1975). On the contrary, Bede tells us that Cædmon had never *learnt* any songs ("nil carminum aliquando didicerat"), that he remembered the words of the hymn ("memoriter retenuit"). Bede does say in his introduction that Cædmon turned what he heard into charming poetic form quickly ("post pusillum"), implying little delay, but this is a relative term; on the two occasions when Bede gives an account of such delays, they are in fact quite long in duration: the monks test his ability by reading a passage to him, he goes home, and only the following morning returns with a finished product; and later Cædmon is likened to a clean animal memorising and ruminating over the story ("rememorando secum et quasi mundum animal ruminando") before being able to turn it into poetic form.

All indications are that Cædmon generally required a period of meditation for his compositions, like Celtic bards with blankets over their heads, or like Egil (trans. Jones) labouring through the night to produce a *drápa* in praise of Erik: "Egil composed the whole *drápa* and had so got it by heart that he could recite it in the morning" (chap. 59). One might well question Bede's ability to discriminate between improvisation and memorisation, but there can be no doubt that the text supports the view that Bede believed that Cædmon was a memoriser: hence it is worthy of remark that Cædmon's hymn did not derive from a memorial tradition, that Cædmon produced verses that he had never heard before ("coepit cantare . . . uersus quos numquam audierat"). Bede apparently accepts as normal practice the transmission of words that have been heard elsewhere, he apparently conceives of this Anglo-Saxon tradition as being oral and memorial (see Fritz: 1974). Two centuries later, the Anglo-Saxon translator accepts the memorial character of the tradition in adding that Cædmon's teachers wrote down his words from dictation and learnt them ("æt his muðe wreoton and leornodon").

Technically, since they accompanied themselves on a musical instrument, I have referred to the productions of Cædmon's friends as songs. Do Cædmon's compositions fall within the same tradition? First, as we have seen, the performances at the convivium are accompanied by a lyre, whereas all Cædmon's performances seem to have been unaccompanied. The distinction between song and poetry is one that we have set up as a distinction in function and performance: the text of a song recited without musical accompaniment (whether vocal or instrumental) would be a poem, the text of a poem set to music and so performed would be a song; it is quite possible that the same "metre" might be employed for both songs and poems. This distinction may or may not be useful to us, but it is perhaps unfair to expect Bede to observe a similar distinction. *Carmen*, as we have noted, is used for both "a song" and "a poem," but although *carmen* is the word most frequently used by Bede in his narrative, it is not the only word used: Cædmon composes only "carmina religioni et pietati apta;" he puts the scriptural stories into delightful "uerbis poeticis;" men's minds are inspired by his "carminibus;" others after him compose "religiosa poemata;" he never composes "friuoli et superuacui poematis;" he had never learnt any "carminum;" in his dream he produced "uersus" which he had never heard; Bede acknowledges the impossibility of translating "carmina;" when he awakes, Cædmon adds to his hymn more "uerba carminis;" he is asked to recite his "carmen;" he is asked to transfer a given text "in modulationem carminis," and he does this the next morning "optimo carmine;" he later turns stories into "carmen dulcissimum" and he makes "multa carmina" about various scriptural subjects.

While *carmen* might refer to what we would call a poem or a song, *uerbis poeticis*, *poemata*, and *poematis* seem to indicate poetry; the use of these words might in turn suggest that *carmen* as applied to one of Cædmon's compositions should be translated "poem." Similarly, when one inspects Bede's choice of verbs, *canere* and *cantare* are found to be the most popular (*canendi artem, canendi donum, cantare, canta, cantauerat, canebat*), though once Bede uses *dicere* when the learned men ask Cædmon to repeat his hymn. Now *canere* and *cantare* could be used to refer to the performance of both poems and songs, but *dicere* seems to indicate a nonmusical context. Thus Bede's nouns and verbs are generally used to refer to both song and poetry, but some few, by their restriction to contexts generally free of musical accompaniment, would seem to indicate that Bede believed that Cædmon was not singing songs so much as uttering or reciting poems. This evidence cannot be taken as conclusive, of course, if Bede appreciated no difference between the two activities, but it draws a measure of support from a consideration of the social function of the performances referred to.

In that Cædmon's companions at the party accompany their performances on a lyre whereas he apparently never makes use of a musical instrument, Cædmon's hymn and his subsequent compositions might be held to participate in a tradition significantly different from that of his companions' performances; the difference might well be that they produce songs whereas he produces poems, whatever similarities there might be in the form of the productions. Apart from an apparent difference in the technique of performance, though, there is a marked difference in the social function assigned to the performances. Clearly, the main—if not the only—function of the songs at the party is to provide entertainment (they are produced "laetitiae causa"); this is never the function of Cædmon's poems. Bede makes it quite clear that Cædmon's poems were designed to provoke action or a state of mind in his audience. Apart from the religious character of the poems, Bede says that "by his poems the minds of many were often inspired to despise the world and to long for the heavenly life," and that in all his poems "he sought to turn his hearers away from delight in sin and arouse in them the love and practice of good works."

Now one might remark of this simply that Cædmon's poems were didactic, and leave it at that; or one might care to argue that in attempting to arouse action in his audience, in exhorting his hearers to conform to an ideal of social behaviour (in this case Christian), Cædmon is performing one of the functions of the hypothetical tribal poet we have discussed in the preceding chapters. And if this is conceded, one might go further and note that Cædmon's inspirational poetry is produced in praise of God, exhorting his hearers to loyalty for and obedience to Him just as the tribal poet serves to arouse in his audience loyalty for the chief or king he serves: Bede states explicitly that Cædmon's hymn was composed "in praise of God the Creator," that Cædmon added to it more words "praising God," and that at the end of his life "his tongue which had uttered so many good words in praise of the Creator also uttered its last words in His praise." There would seem to be ample justification on this evidence for considering Cædmon not as the praise-poet of a lord, but as a praise-poet of the Lord.

If we read Bede's text literally, we would have to conclude that Bede supplies the summary of a poem that is not identical to the poem Cædmon produced in his sleep, for he tells us that between the dream and the first repetition of the poem to the learned men Cædmon added more words to the poem ("eis mox plura in eundem modum uerba Deo digni carminis adiunxit"). Clearly Bede conceives of the poem as fixed in Cædmon's mind, so that mental alterations or improvements can be made to the established text, or further phrases added to it. This is apparent from Bede's statement that Cædmon retained in his mind the poem that he had produced while asleep ("cuncta quae dormiens cantauerat memoriter retenuit"), but Bede's opinion is also confirmed by a study of the extant texts of Cædmon's hymn: Alan Jabbour has argued persuasively that the manuscript variants are consonant with a memorial transmission of the text. Either Cædmon altered his text slightly in the course of time, or the variants arose independently of the author in the process of oral transmission; it is demonstrable, however, that the short hymn was memorised and passed on by word of mouth, just as the Old English version of Bede tells us Cædmon's later compositions were memorised ("æt his muðe wreoton and leornodon").

As to the initial performance, it is clear that this is to be considered unique, unlike any subsequent performance that Cædmon was to give. Cædmon produces his poem immediately, with no delay, and the performance would accordingly have to be considered spontaneous; but, as we have seen, when those who command his performances are ordinary men not heavenly visitors in a dream, Cædmon requires time to prepare his poetry. The circumstances of the dream can in no way be considered normal as far as Cædmon's career is concerned, and his composition of the hymn cannot be considered typical of his subsequent habits of composition. The dream inspiration to produce poetry, however, as has been frequently noted, is hardly unusual, but is common to poetic traditions throughout the world. To the "analogues" of the Cædmon story that have already been surveyed—stories of Mahomed, the *Heliand* poet, Hesiod, and many others—I could add five more from among the Xhosa- and Zulu-speaking peoples in South Africa (see Andersson: 1974; Lester).

As to the hymn itself, it is clear that although Cædmon is asked to compose a poem about the beginning of created things ("Canta . . . principium creaturarum"), the result is not a narrative of the creation. In fact, the poem is not a narrative at all, although it does tell us that God created the heavens and then the earth. Cædmon's hymn is far more at home in a tradition of eulogy than in a tradition of narrative poetry: it is not so much an account of the creation as it is a poem in praise of God the Creator ("in laudem Dei Conditoris"). Like most eulogies, its subject is a person whose various alternative names (or praise names) are employed to provide a statement of the subject's moral and physical characteristics and to allude to his achievements and the events he participated in. God is referred to as the Maker of the heavenly kingdom, the Creator, the Father of glory, eternal God, and almighty Guardian of the human race: he has strength and powers of mind; and he created for men heaven and earth. Further, the function of the poem is obviously to praise God and to exhort the audience to loyalty towards God: the main clause is *nunc laudare debemus*.

In other words, it may very well be that in Cædmon we have the first Anglo-Saxon to extend a native tradition of eulogistic poetry in praise of chiefs and kings to poetry in praise of God. If this is in fact so, it would seem to argue for the existence of a tradition of tribal poetry in praise of rulers among the seventh-century Northumbrians: Cædmon may have been drawing on a tradition adopted by some of the early Northumbrian kings who spent periods of exile or study among Celtic peoples as a result of their contact with and observation of the Celtic tradition of tribal poetry; or he may have been drawing on a native Anglian tradition common to the Northumbrians and the Mercians; or, of course, as is reasonable, he may have been drawing on a Christian tradition (see Blake; Fritz: 1969).

Whatever the character of the tradition within which Cædmon initially operated, he succeeded in establishing the legitimacy of his English poetry among his monastic colleagues. If purely secular poetry was looked down upon in some Christian circles—as seems to be indicated by Eddius's account of the use of a psalm as a rowing song, and by attitudes expressed by Bede in his *De re metrica* and in his introduction to the story of Cædmon—Cædmon initiated the acceptance of vernacular poetry as long as it was composed by a Christian or expressed Christian themes—as long, that is, as the poems were "carmina religioni et pietati apta" and not "friuoli et superuacui poematis." If the conversion was followed initially by a period of rejection of vernacular poetry as secular and pagan, Cædmon's poetry would have allowed the pious Anglo-Saxon monk to indulge freely any sublimated affection he might bear for his native poetic tradition.

Curiously enough, Cædmon has his counterpart among the Xhosa. Ntsikana was a figure of considerable political importance and influence in the affairs of the Eastern Cape frontier, a man who probably heard the preaching of the white missionary Van der Kemp, and who later underwent conversion of his own accord as a result of a vision (see Bokwe; Holt). Ntsikana won over a small group of converts and taught them a hymn he had composed; some time after his death (ca. 1821), the first white missionaries to the Xhosa heard Ntsikana's converts singing this hymn and for the first time transcribed the text. In style and intent the hymn is indistinguishable from the traditional izibongo:

> You are the great God, who is in heaven.
> You are the very One, shield of truth,
> You are the very One, stronghold of truth,
> You are the very One, forest-refuge of truth,
> You are the very One, who dwell in the heavens,
> Who created life, created it above.
> This creator who created, created the heaven,
> This maker of the stars and the Pleiades.
> A star would flash, telling us.
> This maker of the blind, does he not make them on purpose?
> The trumpet sounded, calling us.
> He who in his hunting pursues souls.
> He who gathers together squabbling flocks.
> He the leader who has led us.
> He whose great blanket we wear.
> He whose hands are pierced.
> He whose feet are pierced.
> Your blood, why is it flowing?
> Your blood, it is shed for us.
> This great price, have we requested it?
> This home of yours, have we requested it?

Not only does Ntsikana's hymn, like Cædmon's, demonstrate the use of a traditional form to express the new Christian themes, it also provides an example of a traditional poem set to music that is now almost exclusively encountered as a song: it is today performed by a choir or a congregation, not by an imbongi. A. C. Jordan has written (1973b, 51) of Ntsikana's hymn that it is "the first literary composition ever to be assigned to individual formulation—thus constituting a bridge between the traditional and the post-traditional period"; Cædmon's hymn shares the same position in the history of English literature.

Cædmon may be a crucial transitional figure in that his poetry embodies the happy marriage of an essentially sacral tradition of vernacular eulogy to the new Christian theology; he may also be one in that in his subsequent career he exploited the established eulogistic tradition in order to produce explicitly narrative poetry. It may be that at the time of his dream Cædmon knew no form of poetry other than eulogy: when he is asked in his dream to compose a poem about the beginning of created things he produces a eulogy praising God as Creator. When he appears before Hild's monks, however, they read a passage of Scripture to him and ask him to turn it into poetic form ("exponebantque ille quendam sacrae historiae siue doctrinae sermonem, praecipientes eum, si posset, hunc in modulationem carminis transferre"). The terms of reference of this assignment are much more rigid than those offered him by his heavenly visitor. Hild later instructs him to be taught the whole course of sacred history ("iussitque illum seriem sacrae historiae doceri"), and it is this that he turns into "carmen dulcissimum" after ruminating like a clean animal. The list of subjects of Cædmon's poems that Bede supplies supports the view that in the course of his monastic career Cædmon produced in English poems that followed his scriptural exemplars—poems, in other words, that are likely to have been narrative, even though, like his hymn, their function might still have been to exhort his hearers to a love of God.

We have seen that Shé-kárįsį Rureke, the Nyanga bard who dictated the Mwindo epic to Daniel Biebuyck, had never before produced the biography of his hero in the coherent and connected form in which Biebuyck collected it, but he did so at Biebuyck's request; I have collected from a Xhosa imbongi a magnificent unpremeditated narrative poem on a subject he would not normally sing about and had in fact never sung about, but he produced the poem with little hesitation because I asked him to do it (see Opland: 1975, 200). It may be that Cædmon produced in English narrative poems on scriptural subjects because he was asked to do so by the monks of Whitby. A tradition of eulogistic poetry could provide the material for the production of narrative poetry. As I have argued in a previous chapter, narrative is embryonically present in eulogy; all that is required for the development of a narrative tradition out of a eulogistic tradition is an impetus: perhaps, in this case, the Whitby monks supplied that impetus. Whether or not Cædmon was able to draw on a native tradition of explicitly narrative poetry or song, it is evident that he produced such poetry on scriptural subjects, and in so doing inspired many others to imitate his example ("Et quidem et alii post illum in gente Anglorum religiosa poemata facere temtabant, sed nullus eum aequiperare potuit"). Almost all of the extant Old English poetry is Christian or biblical; it may be that the very existence of this poetry is directly attributable to the singular success achieved by Cædmon in exploiting the secular native poetic tradition for pious ends.

Bede's account of Cædmon is a source of unparalleled importance in any attempt to reconstruct the history of oral poetry in Anglo-Saxon times. Bede was far closer in time to his subject than William of Malmesbury was when he wrote about Aldhelm; yet William's early twelfth-century account of Aldhelm is our main source of evidence for Aldhelm as an oral poet. Of course we have much of Aldhelm's poetry and many of his letters, but these are all in Latin: for our knowledge of Aldhelm as an English poet we are almost entirely dependent on William. Aldhelm's dates are approximately 639 to 709, and William of Malmesbury completed the first version of his *Gesta Pontificum Anglorum* (ed. Hamilton) in 1125, yet, in spite of the intervening passage of some four centuries, there is reason to credit the reliability of William's evidence. William was, like Bede, a careful historian, conscious of the need to assemble reliable testimony on which to base his histories. He professed a particular personal devotion to Saint Aldhelm, and at Malmesbury enjoyed the advantage of access to records and documents associated with Aldhelm's abbacy. He may also have been the recipient of oral traditions concerning Aldhelm, but for his account of Aldhelm's English performances, he seems to have relied on written testimony:

> Although fully instructed in literature, he did not neglect poems [songs?] in his native language [nativae quoque linguae non negligebat carmina]; so much so that there was never at any period anyone to equal him, as the book of Alfred (which I spoke about above) attests. He was able to create poetry in English, and to compose a song [poem?] and to sing or recite that in the appropriate manner [Poesim Anglicam posse facere, cantum componere, eadem apposite vel canere vel dicere]. Finally, Alfred records that Aldhelm composed a trivial poem/song, which is still recited/sung

among the people [Denique commemorat Elfredus, carmen triviale, quod adhuc vulgo cantitatur, Aldelmum fecisse], adding the evidence which he gives to argue that so great a man undertook with reason things that might seem frivolous. [V, 190]

William then proceeds to narrate an anecdote, which, since it is presented in indirect speech, may be taken to be the very evidence that Alfred cited in mitigation of Aldhelm's involvement in apparently frivolous pursuits ("his quae videantur frivola"):

> The people at that time, being semi-barbarous and too little interested in divine sermons, used to run off home immediately after the mass had been sung. And so the holy man positioned himself in the way of those who were leaving on a bridge which connected the town and the country as if he were someone professing the art of singing/reciting [quasi artem cantitandi professum]. Having done this more than once he earned the sympathy and the attention of the people. Once he had gained that, by gradually inserting scriptural phrases between the light-hearted [sensim inter ludicra verbis Scripturarum insertis], he led the people back to sanity; if he had considered acting strictly and with excommunication, he would assuredly have accomplished nothing.

Before we examine the text itself for the evidence it yields, we have to consider its relation to an alternative version of Aldhelm's performances. In his twelfth-century life of the saint, Faricius writes:

> At that time, the people of that district, perverse in their behaviour although subject to our faith, did not attend church nor give sufficient heed to the authority of the priests: the flattering man [vir blandus], exhorting them with persuasive words and often (when the opportunity arose) weaving in divine phrases [divina ... eloquia retexens], fertilised the laity with wholesome precepts after they had been discreetly gathered together in the church. In this way he imitated the Teacher of nations, who first offered milk to the ignorant and later fed the strong on solid food. [Migne, PL, 89, p. 67]

For ("namque"), Faricius continues, Aldhelm, imitator of the apostles ("apostolorum imitator"), went to meet a large crowd of merchants outside Malmesbury ("extra urbem veniebat obviam") on one sabbath day. Positioned on a bridge, he supplied divine nourishments ("super pontem stando tandiu divina

subministrabat pabula"), with the result that some of the merchants temporarily
forsook their business and voluntarily followed Aldhelm to church, where they
listened reverently to the divine service ("sancta reverenter auscultabant offi-
cia"). After this they returned to their business and later travelled home with
their souls nourished by the divine services they had attended.

   This passage bears some resemblances to William of Malmesbury's account
of Aldhelm's poetic activities. In both, Aldhelm positions himself on a bridge in
the path of people whom he lures into the church; in both he is said to have
introduced religious matter gradually into a predominantly secular context. But
there is nothing in Faricius's account that refers specifically to poetry or song,
and the basic situations presented by Faricius and William differ: in Faricius the
merchants gathering for business on a Sunday are induced first to attend church,
whereas in William habitual churchgoers are induced to return for the sermon.
There is perhaps some similarity between Faricius's "Eo tempore illius provin-
ciae populas perversus opere" and William's "Populum eo tempore semibar-
barum," but whereas in Faricius the laity "ecclesiam non frequentabat, nec
sacerdotum satis curabat imperium," in William the people "parum divinis
sermonibus intentum, statim, cantatis missis, domos cursitare solitum." In view
of the existence of the similarities, one must investigate the relation between
Faricius's account and William's before proceeding to examine William's text,
in order to consider the relative reliability of the two versions of the story.

   Faricius was a Lombard physician from Tuscany who became abbot of
Abingdon. His life of Aldhelm was written before William commenced work
on his biography of the saint, and was known to William. In fact, William is at
pains to establish the superiority of his work: as a monk of Malmesbury, he
claims, he is better informed than Faricius was, and in addition Faricius laboured
under the disadvantage of being a foreigner (V, Prologue). For this particular
passage William supplies his source of information, whereas Faricius gives no
authority; we shall shortly consider William's source of information, but for the
moment let us see how William's version stands in relation to that of Faricius.

   William's account is at once more detailed than and significantly different
from Faricius's; since William knew the earlier biography, one may assume
that he chose to provide an independent version because he felt he had more
reliable sources of information. Either William depended only on Faricius, or
both William and Faricius depended on varying oral traditions, or one relied on
an oral tradition whereas the other consulted an extant "Handbook," or both
used the Handbook. William makes explicit his dependence on the Handbook:

it is possible that Faricius had read it and based his account on a later recollection of his reading, whereas William—whose account seems to be a paraphrase of some written source—worked either directly with the Handbook or shortly after he had read it. However, this would not explain the difference between Aldhelm's audience in the two accounts, merchants in one and parishioners in the other. One might resolve the difference as follows: Faricius seems to imply, and William explicitly says, that on various occasions Aldhelm addressed a lay audience and won their attendance at church by gradually introducing religious into secular matter. If Faricius and William had a common source for this anecdote, whether oral or written, it may have cited the merchants as well as the departing congregation as examples of the audiences that Aldhelm used to win over by his eloquence: Faricius may then have chosen to refer to the merchants, and William to the congregation. As such, the two accounts might not be contradictory.

In any event, Faricius's account does not necessarily cast any aspersions on the reliability of William's: it is unlikely that William depended exclusively on Faricius and imaginatively embroidered the details he found there. It is possible that William presented Alfred's Handbook as his source merely as a conventional fiction, but this is unlikely since he clearly had a deep devotion to Aldhelm and was at some pains to assemble documentary evidence in support of his facts; he insists too, in his introduction, that he will not produce any unattested statements in his biography of Aldhelm. Since William knew Faricius's version and believed his own to be superior, it seems reasonable to conclude either that William had access to independent information or that both used the same basic source but gave it different emphases. Since Faricius does not refer to poetry or song, we may now take William's account as our sole source of information on Aldhelm as an oral poet.

As his source of information William cites the book of Alfred "de quo superius dixi": in §188 William had discussed the relation of Aldhelm to the royal house of Wessex, and referred to Alfred's Manual as evidence: "Qui enim legit Manualem librum regis Elfredi, reperriet Kenten, beati Aldhelmi patrem non fuisse regis Inae germanum, sed arctissima necessitudine consanguineum." William's reference to this book here and in his *De Gestis Regum Anglorum* (II, 123; ed. Stubbs) allows us to suppose that it may have been identical to the "enchiridion, id est manualem librum" mentioned by Asser (89, 20). In Asser, it is not clear whether this "Handbook" is the same as a book of psalms and sermons that Alfred carried with him and to which he asked Asser to contribute extracts that appealed to Alfred. Certainly, as R. M. Wilson has put it, "William's description of the book leads to some difficulties; he makes use of it to correct a statement that Aldhelm's father was the brother of King Ine, and he gives it as his source for Alfred's opinion that Aldhelm was the greatest of the Old English religious poets. Material such as this is hardly what we should have expected to find in the *Handbook* from the description of it given by Asser" (66). It seems reasonable to assume that William used a book which he believed to have been assembled by King Alfred and which he identified with the *enchiridion* mentioned by Asser. It is possible that this book was actually at Malmesbury, since Faricius, who was a cellarer at Malmesbury before becoming abbot of Abingdon, seems to refer to it in his genealogical statement on Aldhelm: he says that Kenten, Aldhelm's father, was the brother of King Ine, who was "virum probum, sanctitate lautum, honestate magnificum, antiquissimis Anglicanae linguae schedulis saepius ex interprete legendo audivimus." Whether or not this book was one of those referred to by Asser, William seems to have based this entire passage on its evidence (see Whitelock: 1969).

Believing the book to be Alfred's, he says that in Alfred's opinion Aldhelm was without peer as a vernacular poet. The next sentence of the passage as quoted above refers to Aldhelm's ability to compose and perform, and then comes a sentence starting "Denique commemorat Elfredus": the import of the *denique* is that William is summarising the contents of the book at this point, and that the reference to Aldhelm's ability as a performer is also dependent on Alfred's book. Alfred seems to excuse Aldhelm's participation in an apparently trivial activity on the grounds that he turned that activity to evangelical ends: the account of Aldhelm's performances on the bridge are dependent on the clause "Denique commemorat Elfredus" and introduced by "aditiens causam qua probet rationabiliter tantum virum his quae videantur frivola institisse."

It seems reasonable, therefore, to accept the fact that William's account of Aldhelm's performances is basically a summary of the contents of a book he believed to be Alfred's. If this is in fact so, and the book was Alfred's, the statements concerning Aldhelm would have been written down some two centuries after the events occurred. Alfred himself enjoyed English poetry, and it is likely that he had read or heard poems of Aldhelm's composition: one may accept therefore the fact that Aldhelm did not neglect *carmina nativae linguae*. One has to wonder, though, about the statement that there never was at any period any poet the equal of Aldhelm ("nulla umquam aetate par ei fuerit quisquam"): Bede's statement that Englishmen attempted to compose religious poems but that none could compare with Cædmon ("sed nullus eum aequiperare potuit") would seem to contradict this, unless Aldhelm was held to have had no peer as a composer of secular poetry; of course, the statements are in contradiction only if Alfred (if it was indeed he) had read or heard Bede's account of Cædmon by the time he expressed his opinion of Aldhelm, but even then he may have trusted his own personal judgement above Bede's secondhand testimony.

As to Aldhelm's ability to compose and perform, that could derive from the anecdote of the performances on the bridge. The anecdote itself is likely to have been orally transmitted to Alfred, and as such must have been subject to mutations in the course of two centuries of transmission. The account may accordingly be generally accurate in its details, or—if Alfred heard vaguely that Aldhelm used to perform in public—it may be a description of the way Alfred assumed Aldhelm would have performed. In other words, if the latter is correct, it may be a description of a scene more common in the ninth century than in the seventh. In any event, the text we quoted above represents at best a twelfth-century summary of a ninth-century account of a series of seventh-century performances.

As with other sources, we are confronted with the problem of *carmina*: are they songs or poems? There may be the hint of a solution to this problem in the sentence "Poesim Anglicam posse facere, cantum componere, eadem apposite vel canere vel dicere." If *poesim* and *cantum* refer to separate phenomena and are not synonyms for the same activity—in other words, if William (or Alfred) appreciated a distinction between the two—then we may be justified in translating *poesim* as poetry and *cantum* as song. Certainly there seems to be opposition rather than identity implied in the phrase *vel canere vel dicere*, that is either sing (a song) or recite (a poem), and perhaps this view is strengthened by the use of the plural *eadem* (indicating two separate objects): *idem* might have suggested that a poem was a song and it could be either sung or recited, whereas *eadem* might be taken to imply that Aldhelm could compose an English poem as well as an English song, and that he also knew how to perform both appropriately, singing one or reciting the other.

If this interpretation is not strained (and I am merely suggesting it as a possibility rather than arguing for it), and one can attribute the inversion of the word order to the stylistic choice of chiasmus ("poesim . . . cantum . . . vel canere vel dicere," assuming that *dicere* refers to *poesim* and *canere* to *cantum*), then we are justified in concluding that William was sensitive to a distinction between poetry and song and that *carmen, cantitatur,* and *cantitandi* refer to songs and singing. In this case we can bring no external criteria to bear on the problem, since there is no mention of any musical instrument to accompany the performances. This same sentence provides reason to believe that composers of poetry and song were not always the performers of their compositions; as we saw, Cædmon's hymn was probably propagated orally, and the monks (in the Old English version of Bede) wrote down Cædmon's other compositions and learnt them.

We are told that Aldhelm once composed a trivial song, and that this is still commonly sung in William's day ("adhuc"): if this statement is accurate, it affords clear evidence of the existence of a memorial tradition of song, though it is not at all clear how William knew that the song referred to by Alfred was the same as the song sung in his day unless Alfred actually quoted it. It is clear, however, that Alfred apparently considered the singing of such a song to be, on the face of it, beneath a churchman's dignity, for he adds an apology for Aldhelm's behaviour. The singing of secular songs is referred to with words like *triviale, frivola,* and *ludicra,* indicating its low status and possibly its function of entertaining. Aldhelm succeeds in attracting the attention of the crowds by seeming to promise them a purely secular entertainment: one need not read "quasi artem cantitandi professum" as indicating the existence of a guild of liveried professional musicians, he simply sang in public, "like someone professing the art of singing." We have seen that among the Germanic peoples there were choral war songs and wedding songs, and that among the Anglo-Saxons there probably were rowing songs. There is no reason at all why there should not also have been solo singers: indeed, Cædmon's friends seem to be just such. Their performances may not have been radically affected by the presence or absence of accompaniment on a musical instrument. Aldhelm seems here to earn the people's confidence as a public entertainer, perhaps, or a public singer, and as he grows sure of his audience, so he introduces his Christian message, and ultimately succeeds in winning not only their attention to his songs but also their attendance at the priest's sermons.

Aldhelm and Cædmon were contemporaries, the former a West Saxon, the latter a Northumbrian. If the accounts of both in William of Malmesbury and Bede may be taken as accurate in detail, then it appears that both extended traditional secular techniques to encompass Christian subject matter, but Cædmon seems to have worked within the tradition of eulogistic poetry and Aldhelm within the tradition of popular song. This interpretation may well depend on an overliteral reading of the texts, however, and it may be that both operated within similar traditions. Certainly Aldhelm seems to have incited his audience to action, one of the functions we have assigned to the eulogistic poet; however, he seems to have attained this end only by means of a gradual process ("eo plusquam semel facto"), first winning their confidence and attention ("plebis favorem et concursum emeritum") and then week after week gradually inserting the Christian content that ultimately succeeded in urging the congregation to attend the sermon. A tribal poet works on the emotions of his audience and, if successful, elicits an immediate response. On balance, therefore, it seems probable that Aldhelm sang songs on the bridge, whether traditional or of his own composition, whereas Cædmon's hymn was a eulogistic poem.

Aldhelm's writings themselves yield nothing of interest for our purposes. The first and last letters of the thirty-six lines of the preface to his riddles spell out the message "Aldhelmvs cecinit millenis versibvs odas" supplying evidence —if it were needed—that the verb *canere* could be used to refer to literate poems. In this preface Aldhelm stresses the fact that his inspiration comes from God, for he has not slept on Parnassus and dreamed strange dreams:

> Cynthi sic numquam perlustro cacumina, sed nec
> In Parnasso procubui nec somnia vidi.
> Nam mihi versificum poterit Deus addere carmen
> Inspirans stolidae pia gratis munera menti;
> Tangit si mentem, mox laudem corda rependunt.
>
> [12–16]

There is no need to associate this praise of God with any secular eulogistic tradition, or to see Aldhelm's separation of himself from dreamers on Parnassus as an oblique reference to current accounts of secular Anglo-Saxon poets' dream inspirations to perform: Aldhelm is writing in a purely classical tradition of influence. Nor does Adilwald's letter to Aldhelm (*MGH*, 3) appending three poems suitable for singing ("trina cantati modolaminis carmina") tell us anything about the performance of Anglo-Saxon oral poetry. A first glance at the manuscript of the Leiden Riddle, a translation of Aldhelm's *De Lorica*, does raise some hopes, because it has some musical neumes written over the first line, but closer inspection reveals that the neumes were probably scribbled in a different hand below the text which ended halfway down the folio, and that the Leiden Riddle was written below that in yet a third hand: the neumes accordingly have nothing to do with the riddle (see Parkes). If not for William of Malmesbury's account of Aldhelm singing on the bridge, we would have no reason to believe from Aldhelm's writings that he ever composed or performed in English.

One last item is worth a brief note before we leave the seventh century. Theodore's Penitential (ed. McNeill and Gamer) condemns incantations, divinations, and auguries. These incantations may simply be magical spells, and their proscription is common in ecclesiastical documents throughout the Anglo-Saxon period. If, however, the incantations are metrical, charms such as survive in later manuscripts, then we should take this as a reminder in passing that poetry existed in various forms and performed various functions in Anglo-Saxon England: if we concentrate on tribal poets and wandering entertainers, we should not at the same time forget the persistent popular traditions of (perhaps metrical) proverbs, charms, and wisdom lore.

Extant evidence of oral poetic practices in the seventh century attests to the complexity of the Anglo-Saxon tradition. One reads of songs both choral and solo, accompanied by a lyre and unaccompanied; the function of the solo performances seems to be entertainment, whereas choral songs seem to serve other functions, such as keeping time for rowers. One can perhaps infer from the story of Cædmon the existence of a native tradition of eulogistic poetry in Northumbria. The most prominent theme running through all these references is one of opposition, assimilation, and accommodation. Clearly there were many Christians who spurned the native traditions of secular poetry and song, feeling obliged to use a psalm as the lyrics of a rowing song; the church also officially proscribed musical entertainments in monasteries and Theodore condemned incantations associated with witchcraft and augury. There seems to have existed a general Christian climate of opinion which felt that Christian poetry and song ought to supplant the products of the secular traditions, and which apparently frowned upon the context of entertainment and licence that usually accompanied such performances. However, secular poetry or song as such was not condemned, and this led to variations in the attitude of churchmen to the secular traditions: Bede argues against quotation from pagan poets, whereas Aldhelm felt bound by no such strictures.

The first generations of converts seem therefore not to have presented a unified attitude towards their native traditions, and it is perhaps in this context of uncertainty that we are to judge as significant the attempts at accommodation: Wilfrid's monks continue to sing in the traditional manner to keep time for the rowers, but they use the words of a psalm. The two most significant figures, however, are Aldhelm and Cædmon, who, each in his own way, one in the south the other in the north, exploit the secular traditions for Christian ends. Aldhelm uses traditional singing techniques to convey a Christian message; Cædmon uses the secular tradition of eulogy to praise God. Their subsequent influence, however, differs: although he might have performed in English, Aldhelm's reputation rests largely on his Latin poetry, and many contemporaries send copies of their Latin compositions to him for correction or for comment. Cædmon's influence is felt within the field of English literature, and from that point of view his achievement may be held to be more significant than Aldhelm's. The enthusiasm that Cædmon's poetry evoked may have been a product of the belief that he was divinely inspired, but it may also be because it provided a convenient solution to a seventh-century problem: if there were those converts who reluctantly felt that as Christians they had to lay aside their secular poetic traditions, Cædmon showed them how they might reconcile their Christianity and their affection for native poetry. It is Cædmon who extended the English tradition of praising one's lord to praising the Lord: there is no essential difference, and the secular poetic tradition might henceforth happily accommodate Christian subject matter (see Huppé).

Unfortunately, there are relatively few texts extant from the seventh century, so these assumptions may well be incapable of firm proof. There are a greater number and variety of texts revelant to our study extant from the eighth century, to which we can now turn our attention.

6

The Eighth and Ninth Centuries

Almost all the extant evidence relevant to the study of the Anglo-Saxon oral poet in the eighth century refers to monastic or ecclesiastical contexts; two references to practices associated with eighth-century kings are found in twelfth-century works and are of debatable reliability. The overwhelming body of evidence is to be found in ecclesiastical correspondence or synodal pronouncements, and these bear such striking similarities to each other that they might almost be considered conventional: that they reflect a real state of affairs, however, is not seriously in doubt, and they are accordingly of value as testimony to the monastic taste for secular performances. One letter, that of Cuthbert to Cuthwin, is of singular interest, since it provides us with the only reliable description of a specific eighth-century performance. The earliest extant glosses, Epinal, Erfurt, and Corpus, probably date from this century, but since they do not yield information on specific performances, their evidence—valuable as it is—will be considered in a later chapter on the words for poets and poetry.

If the seventh century witnessed an initial period of ecclesiastical opposition (however reluctant) to secular poetry and song, an opposition that was to a large extent undermined by the example of the likes of Aldhelm in the south and Cædmon in the north, the eighth-century sources bear testimony to the predilection of ecclesiastics for secular entertainment. The consistent admonitions against the contexts within which such performances were produced seem to bear witness to their popularity. If immediately after the conversion the Christian Anglo-Saxon was unsure of what his attitude to secular poetry and song ought to be, the eighth-century ecclesiastic generally seems to have been less doubtful; if the seventh century saw the first steps towards assimilation and accommodation between the secular and Christian traditions, the eighth-century clerics exploited to the full the licence that such pioneering efforts afforded them to pursue their secular tastes as Christians. It is perhaps to such a mood of the times that we may attribute the quantity and general tenor of the saints' lives that were written in this century (see Colgrave: 1958).

The earliest English saint's life is the anonymous life of Cuthbert (perhaps written between 698 and 705) used by Bede for his prose and verse versions; just as early may be a life of Gregory the Great by an anonymous monk of Whitby. These were followed by Eddius's life of Wilfrid (710–20), lives of Ceolfrith (716–25) and Guthlac (730–40), Bede's Lives of the Abbots (ca. 730), Willibald's life of Boniface (ca. 768), and Alcuin's life of Willibrord (ca. 789); and these names by no means exhaust the list of eighth-century hagiographical works produced in England. It is generally believed that such works are the product of an aristocratic influx into the monasteries. Thus Clinton Albertson, who translates seven of the eighth-century lives in his *Anglo-Saxon Saints and Heroes*, writes in his introduction, "All the biographies that follow in this book are a testimony to the astounding number of young Anglo-Saxon nobles, warriors even in the royal *comitatus*, who fairly flooded into the monasteries as the Heroic Age turned into the Golden Age" (19). He cites as examples Benedict Biscop, a warrior serving Oswy who became a monk at age twenty-five; Cuthbert, probably also a noble warrior of Oswy who became a monk at seventeen; Eastorwine, a relative of Benedict Biscop who served in Ecgfrith's comitatus and became a monk at twenty-four; Ceolfrith, who was the son of a thane of Oswy and became a monk at seventeen; Wilfrid, a nobleman who entered a monastery when he was fourteen; and Guthlac, who spent his youth as the leader of a warrior band and became a monk at age twenty-four.

The generally heroic tenor of the saints' lives is attributed to a traditional secular ethic turned to Christian themes, another example of literary accommodation. Albertson writes: "Perhaps the most interesting thing about this amazing Heroic Age of English monasticism is that, once realized for the widespread and special phenomenon it was it makes the heroic cast of Anglo-Saxon literature so much more understandable. The latter is not due solely to the general influence of early Christian Latin literature and spirituality. These noble young monks brought with them into the cloister the heroic songs and sagas that the aristocratic families had been bred on" (20). Again, in a footnote to this passage, Albertson comments on the didactic purpose of "the old heroic songs and sagas they had learned from their childhood. These were the oral textbooks that taught the heroism they were to live. One of the reasons why heroic poems are found in monastic manuscripts may simply be that they were used in the education especially of noble lay-students living in the monasteries" (20). And later, writing of the monks, he says, "These warriors of the spirit . . . were nurtured on a diet of great deeds done by the saints, just as the king's warriors and nobles were trained to greatness by the songs and sagas of the heroes" (78), though Albertson is careful to point out that the hero-saint is "not a peculiarly Anglo-Saxon phenomenon" (22).

Certainly one encounters instances in the saints' lives that seem to be indicative of accommodation between secular and Christian ideals, as when Bede writes of Benedict Biscop in his *Lives of the Abbots*:

> He was descended from a noble family among the Angles, but by no less a nobility of mind he was found worthy to be forever raised into the society of angels. In fact though he served as a soldier in the personal *comitatus* of King Oswy and was rewarded with a landed estate befitting his rank, yet at about the age of twenty-five [i.e. about 653] he abandoned property bounded by time in order to acquire an eternal estate. He turned his back on earthly military service with its reward of gifts tainted with time in order that he might serve as a soldier of the true King and thus win an everlasting kingdom in the heavenly city [chap. 1, trans. Albertson, 225 f.]

or when we read in the life of Ceolfrith:

> In fact on one occasion when he had prepared to receive the king with a most sumptuous banquet, and some unexpected wartime emergency had arisen and prevented his coming, Ceolfrith's father gave thanks to divine providence and straightway decided that all the poor, the pilgrims, and the enfeebled be called in from all round to the feast. What was to have been offered to the earthly king and his young followers, he offered now to the supreme King in the person of his lowly ones for the sake of his eternal reward. [chap. 34, trans. Albertson, 268]

This conscious establishment of parallels between secular and Christian ideals is reminiscent of the technique of *The Seafarer*:

> Forþon nis þæs modwlonc   mon ofer eorþan,
> ne his gifene þæs god,   ne in geoguþe to þæs hwæt,
> ne in his dædum to þæs deor,   ne him his drythen to þæs hold,
> þæt he a his sæfore   sorge næbbe,
> to hwon hine dryhten   gedon wille.
>
> [*ASPR*, III, 39–43]

[Yet no man in the world's so proud of heart,
So generous of gifts, so bold in youth,
In deeds so brave, or with so loyal lord,
That he can ever venture on the sea
Without great fears of what the Lord may bring.]

[trans. Hamer]

Forþon ðæt bið eorla gehwam   æftercweþendra
lof lifgendra   lastworda betst,
þæt he gewyrce,   ær he on weg scyle,
fremum on foldan   wið feonda niþ,
deorum dædum   deofle togeanes,
ðæt hine ælda bearn   æfter hergen,
ond his lof siþþan   lifge mid englum
awa to ealdre,   ecan lifes blæd,
dream mid dugeþum.

[*ASPR*, III, 72–80]

[Therefore for every warrior the best
Memorial is the praise of living men
After his death, that ere he must depart
He shall have done good deeds on earth against
The malice of his foes, and noble works
Against the devil, that the sons of men
May after praise him, and his glory live
For ever with the angels in the splendour
of lasting life, in bliss among those hosts.]

[trans. Hamer]

Commenting on this last passage, Bertram Colgrave, the foremost expert on the early English saints' lives, writes: "The poet is here apparently expressing an idea which is common enough in Old English heroic poetry; he is referring to the glory which will survive the hero's death, the prize sought after by all heroic warriors. But the poet proceeds to show that he is not really referring to this, the pagan ideal, at all, but rather to the ambition of the Christian Saint, the *miles Dei* who is taking the place of the heroic warrior. . . . This passage seems to me to indicate clearly the transition from one ideal to the other" (Colgrave: 1958, 36). Such passages succeed through establishing parallels between the Christian ethic and the native.

Two examples may be cited to illustrate the accommodation of the heroic ideal in the saints' lives. In the preceding chapter I quoted extracts from Eddius's life of Wilfrid dealing with the stranding of Wilfrid's party on the hostile South Saxon shore. After narrating how the pagan magus toppled lifeless like Goliath from the mound, Eddius (trans. Albertson) continues:

> Thereupon the pagans rushed into position for battle, but they launched their host against the people of God in vain. For the Lord fought on the side of the few. Just as Gideon, at the command of the Lord, with 300 men slew 120,000 Midianite warriors in one attack, so these men of our holy bishop's retinue, although few in number (they were 120 men, the same number as the years in Moses' age), were well armed and courageous. Holding a council of war among themselves they made a pact that no one would turn his back on anybody and drop out of the fight, but that all would act so as to win either death with honor or life with victory. Then St. Wilfrid the bishop and his clergy knelt down and raised their hands to heaven, and again brought down the help of the Lord. [chap. 13]

Thus, like Joshua fighting the Amalekites, Wilfrid's small party repulses three onslaughts and escapes a fourth after Wilfrid succeeds in importuning God to bring in the tide before its due time so that they may embark and flee. As a second example, we may offer Willibald's description of the martyrdom of Boniface on 5 June 754. At daybreak the Christian camp falls under attack:

> Brandishing spears and shields, a vast throng of the pagans burst into the camp. At once Boniface's escort rushed to arms on all sides and ran out against them. They stood poised to defend the saints—later martyrs—against this mindless mob of raging people, when the hero of God suddenly stepped out of his tent. At the first sound of the crowd's furious onslaught he had called the band of clergy to his side and taken up the saints' relics which he always had with him. Now he immediately scolded his followers and forbade any fighting. "Do not fight them, lads. Lay down your weapons. What we are taught by the Gospel is true, and we must not give back evil for evil, but good for evil. This now is that very day we have long dreamed of. That moment of freedom we have yearned for is right here. So be heroic in the Lord and suffer this royal Grace of his will gladly. Keep your trust in him and he will set your souls free."
> Then he turned to the priests and deacons and other clerics standing beside him, God's sworn men all of them, and spoke to them like a father:

"My hero brothers be bold of heart. Have no terror of these slayers of the
body, for they have no power to kill the soul, which lives forever. Take
cheer in the Lord and fix the anchor of your hope in God, because in another instant he will give you your eternal reward and lead you to your
rightful seat in the great hall of heaven among the fellowship of the angels
noble beyond earthly measure. Do not surrender yourselves to the doomed
love of this life. Snare not your heart with the base and hollow blandish-
ments the heathen do. But submit courageously to this brief instant of
death so that you may reign with Christ forever."

While he was lovingly urging his disciples on to the martyr's crown
with these heartening words, suddenly the raging storm of pagans over-
whelmed them with swords and every sort of weapon, and stained the
bodies of the saints with the blood of a happy death. [chap. 8]

Similarities in style and tone between these two extracts and the extant
Anglo-Saxon heroic poetry will be immediately apparent to anyone familiar
with, say, *Beowulf* and *The Battle of Maldon* (see also Bolton: 1979, 168–70). In
Eddius there is the constant establishment of parallels with a body of venerable
biblical traditions (David and Goliath, Moses, Gideon, and Joshua are invoked),
just as the *Beowulf* poet constantly refers to analogous situations from Germanic
tradition; the council of war, and particularly the pact "that no one would turn
his back on anybody and drop out of the fight, but that all would act so as to
win either death with honour or life with victory," would find a most congenial
home in *Beowulf* or *Maldon*. Similarly, in Willibald the leader haranguing his
troops before battle is strongly reminiscent of Byrhtnoth's address before the
battle at Maldon, and the use of heroic phrases ("the hero of God," "God's
sworn men," "My hero brothers") and even anticipation ("They stood poised
to defend the saints—later martyrs") can be easily paralleled in the extant Old
English heroic poetry; instead of sitting like warriors feasting in their lord's
hall, the priests will take their places in the great hall of heaven among the fellowship of the angels (cf. *The Dream of the Rood*, 139–44).

There is, however, one significant difference in approach between the passages quoted from Eddius and Willibald. Both, apparently, depict scenes that
are intended to recall similar situations in secular productions—both, that is,
seem consciously to establish parallels with secular situations and to exploit
secular traditions; but whereas Eddius creates a heroic scene in order to stress the
heroism of his subjects (in addition to their dependence on God and their reli-
ance on the efficacy of Wilfrid's prayers), Willibald creates a heroic scene but in

it reverses our expectations of heroic conduct. In Eddius the party acts and fights heroically; in Willibald the same heroic context is established, but Boniface's harangue is not an incitement to martial fervour but precisely the opposite, an encouragement to submit passively. Christian writers who used the secular traditions could exploit to extend, as in those passages quoted above from *The Seafarer*, or exploit to deny, as in the Willibald passage and the following extract from *The Seafarer*:

> Þeah he græf wille   golde stregan
> broþor his geborenum,   byrgan be deadum,
> maþmum mislicum   þæt hine mid wille,
> ne mæg ðære sawle   þe biþ synna ful
> gold to geoce   for godes egsan,
> þonne he hit ær hydeð   þenden he her leofað.
>
> [96–102]

> And though a brother
> May strew with gold his brother's grave, and bury
> His corpse among the dead with heaps of treasure,
> Wishing them to go with him, yet can gold
> Bring no help to the soul that's full of sins,
> Against God's wrath, although he hide it here
> Ready before his death while yet he lives.
>
> [trans. Hamer]

Whether they evoke a secular context to reinforce parallels with Christian situations or in order to demonstrate how Christian teaching diverges from secular ethic, these Christian writers work in a period when they *can* exploit secular traditions, and it is possible that seventh-century figures like Cædmon and Aldhelm had served as initiators in this literary breakthrough. The eighth-century English hagiographers clearly felt no qualms about depicting their saints as heroes, and this testifies to the presence of heroic ideals in the monasteries. But one major problem remains: where did these writers get their heroic conceptions from? Does the heroic cast of the saints' lives derive from a tradition of poetry like *Beowulf*, as is commonly assumed, or does *Beowulf* derive from a flourishing tradition of eighth-century saints' lives?

The generation of *Beowulf* in the form we now have it has concerned many critics of the poem, and it is not my intention to enter that debate. I should like to point out, however, that the case for a venerable tradition of Germanic narrative poetry or song is by no means proven. Passages in Tacitus, Jordanes, and other early writers may refer to such a tradition but, as we have seen, they may equally well refer to a tradition of eulogistic poems. Without denying the possibility of the existence of a tradition of narrative poetry or song, it is also possible that there were tales and legends, that there were songs of various kinds (work songs, wedding songs, personal songs), but only eulogistic poems (whether performed by individuals, male or female, or by tribal poets; whether spontaneous or memorised): such poems might have been the only kind of formal history among the early Germanic people. The first extant references we have to Anglo-Saxon performers are to Aldhelm and Cædmon. We are given no indication of the character of Aldhelm's performances—whether songs or poems—though if he intended to attract crowds wandering home from church it might be argued that he was adopting the role of a popular entertainer, and therefore was singing songs. Cædmon's first poem is a eulogy, but subsequent productions seem to have been, at the request of his mentors, more explicitly narrative. This is the earliest unambiguous reference to narrative productions among the Anglo-Saxons. It is possible that Old English narrative poems are the product of an interaction between a tradition of (Latin) written literature and the secular tradition of eulogy: it is possible, as Alistair Campbell (1962) has suggested, that the Old English epics are of monastic origin.

Where, then, would the heroic cast of the eighth-century saints' lives have come from? Colgrave has demonstrated the dependence of the early Anglo-Saxon hagiographers on earlier Latin saints' lives, such as Athanasius's *Life of Antony* translated into Latin by Evagrius, Jerome's *Life of Paul the Hermit*, Sulpicius Severus's *Life of St. Martin*, and Gregory's *Dialogues*; certainly protagonists in early Christian literature were often cast in a heroic mould. There is no need to deny the possibility of secular influence on the hagiographical conception of the Anglo-Saxon saint, but we must be careful not to assume without question that the eighth-century Anglo-Saxon saints' lives were influenced by a venerable tradition of secular narrative poetry or song.

Whether or not such a secular narrative tradition existed, Anglo-Saxons had a conception of ethical conduct. As is often pointed out (e.g. Whitelock: 1951, 14), Alcuin wrote to Charlemagne recommending to him one Torhtmund, who had "faithfully avenged" the murder of his lord, and Aldhelm writes to Wilfrid's monks urging them to follow him into exile like a faithful comitatus:

> Behold, if laymen, ignorant of the divine knowledge, abandon the faithful lord whom they have loved during his prosperity, when his good fortune

has come to an end and adversity befallen him, and prefer the safe ease of their sweet native land to the affliction of their exiled lord, are they not regarded by all as deserving of ridicule and hateful jeering, and of the clamour of execration? What then will be said of you if you should let the pontiff who has fostered you and raised you go into exile alone? [Whitelock: 1955, 730 f.]

It is not necessary to argue that Aldhelm was here writing under the influence of a secular tradition of heroic epic: all Anglo-Saxons had access to traditional conceptions of ethical norms, and Aldhelm had access to Christian depictions of heroic behaviour. Nor is it necessary to assume that the eight-century saints' lives took their heroic cast from a tradition of secular poems such as *Beowulf*: such a tradition may itself derive only from the eighth century.

We may start our review of the eighth-century sources with Bede. In 734 he wrote a letter to Archbishop Egbert of York (ed. Colgrave and Mynors, trans. Whitelock: 1955), in the course of which he inveighed against certain lax practices in the monasteries, urging Egbert to take action against them:

I do not speak thus as if I knew you to do otherwise, but because it is rumoured abroad about certain bishops that they serve Christ in such a fashion that they have with them no men of any religion or continence, but rather those who are given to laughter, jests, tales, feasting and drunkenness, and the other attractions of the lax life [illos, qui risui, iocis, fabulis, commessationibus et ebrietatibus, ceterisque uitae remissioris illecebris subigantur], and who daily feed the stomach with feasts more than the soul on the heavenly sacrifice. I should like you to correct such, if you find them anywhere, by your holy authority. [Whitelock, 737]

In conclusion, Bede notes that he has concentrated mainly on one abuse:

These things I have said briefly against the venom of avarice. For the rest, if we should wish to deal in like manner with drunkenness, feasting, loose living, and the other pollutions of this kind [de ebrietate, commessatione, luxuria, et ceteris huiusmodi contagionibus], the length of this letter would be immoderately extended. [Whitelock, 745]

It is true that Bede does not explicitly refer to poetry (*pace* Godfrey: 1974, 135), but these extracts from his letter to Egbert are quoted here as examples of a persistent prejudice on the part of some prominent eighth-century ecclesiastics against the kind of situation that did on occasion give rise to secular perform-ances. As we have seen, Bede's sentiments are also expressed in the seventh century by the Council at Rome on English affairs, which forbade ecclesiastics from using arms, "nec citharoedas habeant, vel quaecunque symphoniaca, nec quoscunque jocos vel ludos ante se permittant," and in his life of Cuthbert, Bede quotes the saint's objection to the frivolous atmosphere at a Christmas dinner where his companions were "feeling convivial and telling stories."

Censure of clerical and monastic affection for feasting, drunkenness, and flashy clothes in particular recurs so frequently that one begins to suspect that they are merely traditional complaints; there can be no real doubt, however, that a basis for such complaints existed. Most of them are to be taken as offences against discipline: it is not the games and entertainments as such that elicit censure so much as the context of licentiousness in which such amusements were produced. It was suggested in chapter 5 that the Council at Rome was referring to performers and performances associated with the wandering entertainers, the mimi, scurrae, jocistae, and their company; those eighth-century sources that refer to such performances would seem to confirm the possibility that we are to connect the performers more with Cædmon's friends at the convivium than with Cædmon himself, that we are to consider them as entertaining singers rather than more serious poets.

Before we leave Bede to look at the other ecclesiastical statements about poetry and song, we must consider the account of his master's death by Bede's pupil Cuthbert (not to be confused with the saint). In his letter to his fellow pupil Cuthwin, Cuthbert gives an eyewitness account of Bede's last days (ed. Colgrave and Mynors; see Smith: 1933; and, most recently, Chickering). Bede spent the day instructing Cuthbert and others and singing the psalms ("in psalmorum cantu") whenever his strength permitted. He used to quote Paul, "It is a fearful thing to fall into the hands of the living God" and other scriptural sayings ("canebat autem sentenciam sancti Pauli apostoli dicentis 'horrendum est incidere in manus Dei inuentis,' et multa alia de sancta scriptura") designed to make his hearers reflect on their last hours. "And in our own language—for he was familiar with our songs, speaking about the terrible departure of the soul from the body ("et in nostra quoque lingua, ut erat doctus in nostris car-minibus, dicens de terribli exitu animarum e corpore")：

> Fore thaem neidfaerae   naenig uuiurthit
> thoncsnotturra,   than him tharf sie
> to ymbhycggannae   aer his hiniongae

huaet his gastae   godaes aeththa yflaes
aefter deothdaege   doemid uueorthae

[*ASPR*, VI]

which translated means 'Before setting forth on that inevitable journey, none is wiser than the man who considers—before his soul departs from here—what good or evil he has done, and what judgement his soul will receive after departing.' " He also sang antiphons ("cantabat antiphonas") to comfort himself and those present, and from time to time he quoted Paul and Ambrose. After he had finished translating the last sentence of John's gospel, he sat on the floor of his cell, sang ("cecinit") the Gloria through, and died.

We are concerned here with the five-line Death Song. Not all of the many extant manuscripts of Cuthbert's letter include the Old English text; of the twenty-nine manuscripts that do, eleven have the Northumbrian version quoted here, seventeen have a later West Saxon version, and one is intermediate between the two. The large number of extant manuscripts of the letter attests to the general veneration in which Bede was held; the comparatively large number of texts of the Death Song accordingly argues for a widespread belief that these were the words uttered by Bede a few days before his death.

Cuthbert says that Bede was familiar with English poems/songs ("doctus in nostris carminibus"). What exactly *doctus* means is not clear: given the early age of his entry into monastic life, it is unlikely that Bede had been instructed in the art of secular performances, and in any event, considering the prejudice he expresses against non-Christian poetry, even if he had learnt a number of texts, it is unlikely that any public performances he might have given could ever be judged typical of secular performances. We may assume that Bede knew some Old English texts—or was familiar with them if he had not himself committed them to memory—but that these texts were almost certainly pious and Christian. No finite verb is assigned to the uttering of the Death Song; the participle *dicens* introduces the sentence. Did Bede sing or recite the text: were the carmina with which he was familiar poems or songs? Cuthbert refers to much singing: of psalms ("in psalmorum cantu"), of quotations from Paul ("canebat sentenciam"), of antiphons ("cantabat antiphonas") and the Gloria (" 'Gloria patri' cecinit"). It is possible that all these might have been sung, but it seems more likely that the quotations from Paul (mentioned twice), other scriptural writings, and Ambrose were spoken not sung: their purpose was to make those present reflect on their death ("in quibus nos a somno animae exsurgere precogitando ultimam horam amonebat") and—what may be the same thing—to comfort them and himself ("ob nostram consolationem et suam"). It is in the context of these utterances that the Death Song must be placed.

There are three possibilities concerning its generation: either Bede composed the poem on the spur of the moment, or he had composed it at an earlier time and committed it to memory, or he had not composed it at all but had learnt it from someone else. The last would harmonise with the context of citing passages from Paul and elsewhere on the subject of death, but there is no reason why Bede should not have composed the words himself either well in advance of his reciting them or in the last days of his life. Although there is no evidence one way or another, I prefer to believe that here Bede was quoting from memory a text of his or someone else's composition, rather than that he spontaneously produced the Death Song with no premeditation. It does not seem possible to determine from the Latin whether Bede sang a song or recited a poem. Since it was widely held that Bede uttered the Old English text, however, it is clear that Bede had no reservations about secular poetry or song as such, but only about non-Christian performances or the licentious occasions on which they might be produced. Such occasions were clearly of concern to the synodal council that met at Clofeshoh in 747, twelve years after Bede's death.

The decrees of that council (ed. Haddan and Stubbs) bear witness to the intrusion of secular ideals into monastic life, a situation apparently similar if not identical to that supposed by Albertson to provide the context for the production of the heroic saints' lives. Canon 7 warns monks against being concerned with empty dreams of glory ("inanis gloriæ cupiditatibus occupantur"); Canon 16 condemns the widespread practice of celebrating major feasts with vanities, games, horse-racing, and feasting ("non admixtis vanitatibus, uti mos est plurimis, vel negligentibus, vel imperitis, id est, in ludis et equorum cursibus, et epulis majoribus"); Canon 19 condemns vanity in dress; and Canon 21 inveighs against intemperate drinking and scurrilous entertainments while eating ("sed pura ac sobria sint eorum convivia, non luxuriosa neque deliciis vel scurrilitatibus mixta"). These statements serve to reinforce the suggestions of lax discipline and high living in the monasteries culled from the decrees of the Council on English affairs at Rome, from Bede's quotation of Cuthbert's rebuke of his companions, and from Bede's letter to Egbert. They all provide a context within which to place the performance of secular poetry and song. For our purposes, Canons 12 and 20 are far more directly to the point.

Canon 12, *Item ut Presbyteri simplici voce et modesta Sancta canant in Ecclesiis*, concerns the singing of the church service and provides us with one of our only descriptions—albeit biased—of the secular style of performance. Priests ought not to babble in church in the style of secular poets in case with tragic noise they mar and confuse the composition and division of the sacred words ("ut presbyteri sæcularium poetarum modo in ecclesia non garriant, ne tragico sono sacrorum verborum compositionem ac distinctionem corrumpant vel confundant"), but they should strive after a simple and holy melody according to the custom of the church. Apparently the normal style of delivery of secular poetry was held to be a rushed babbling with words run together; the performance may also have been histrionic, if we may take the "tragicus sonus" as suggestive of a "theatrical" performance. Again, there is no condemnation of secular poetry as such, but only a differentiation between the possibly uninhibited, excited style of the secular poet and the plain, simple, and dignified style expected of the chanter of the liturgy.

The use of *tragicus* implies a familiarity with Roman theatre. It is unlikely that classical Latin plays were performed formally in England at this time, but it is almost certain that by this time those offshoots of the Roman theatres, the wandering mimes, jugglers, musicians, and purveyors of general entertainment had become welcome visitors. It is likely that the Council on English affairs in Rome in the seventh century referred to such performers; Canon 20 of the Council of Clofeshoh in 747 explicitly condemns them. Bishops are urged to ensure that monasteries in their dioceses house quiet men labouring for God and do not serve as shelters for the skills of entertainment—that is, for playwrights, harpers, musicians, and clowns ("et non sint ludicrarum artium receptacula, hoc est, poetarum, citharistarum, musicorum, scurrorum"). It is clear that these performers are not drawn from the ranks of the monks themselves, but are visitors from the secular world, for the canon goes on to condemn the access that secular persons have to the interiora of monasteries where they do not belong ("ut non habeant sæculares quique vagandi licentiam per inconvenientia sibi loca, vel discursus per interiora monasterii domuncula") in case they steal, or see or hear things that might give rise to rumours: familiarity with lay people is harmful ("Nam satis nociva atque vitiosa consuetudo est illa laicorum familiaritas"), particularly in monasteries of nuns not living strictly according to the rule.

The poetae, citharistae, musici and scurri, then, are itinerant entertainers, and are most probably to be seen as individual performers travelling together in professional troupes. I would suggest that the "poeta" here referred to is not the secular Anglo-Saxon poet, but the poet of Isidore's definition of *orchestra* (quoted in chapter 3 above) who recited while others acted ("Ibi enim poetae comoedi et tragoedi ad certamen conscendebant, hisque canentibus alii gestus edebant"), the "poet" who wrote the script for mimic performances: "the stories were so composed by the *poetae* that they were most suitable for acting out by gestures." This canon of the Council of Clofeshoh, then, does not refer to Old English secular poets, but to the troupes of wandering entertainers who took to roaming about western Europe after the closing of the Roman theatres or to similar English troupes; the performances themselves are not condemned, so much as the presence of the performers (as lay people) in the monasteries and the disruption of discipline they encouraged. It is evident that eighth-century Anglo-Saxon monasteries welcomed such entertainers and encouraged their performances, and that this tendency is viewed as another example of the rampant secularisation in the monasteries that the council was at pains to extirpate.

The citharoedi mentioned by the Council of Clofeshoh may have been wandering musicians, but this does not mean that the monks did not enjoy music produced among themselves. Witness a letter written to Lul in 764 by the abbot of Wearmouth and Jarrow, that same Cuthbert who was present at Bede's death (trans. Whitelock: 1955). Cuthbert is sending to Lul copies of Bede's prose and verse life of Saint Cuthbert; at the same time he asks Lul to send him a glass-maker, "because we are ignorant and destitute of that art." He continues: "It would delight me also to have a harpist who could play on the harp which we call 'rottae'; for I have a harp and am without a player. If it be not a trouble, send one also to my disposal. I beg that you will not scorn my request nor think it laughable." It is likely that Cuthbert intended the harp to be used nonliturgically, for secular music, since if it were to be used for religious purposes he would surely have said so and would not then have considered the possibility of Lul's scorning his request. It is curious that Cuthbert should send to the Continent for a harper: from Bede's account of the convivium that Cædmon left, we would conclude that harpers could be found in Northumbria. Perhaps the secular tradition had died out among amateurs, or perhaps Cuthbert is after all requesting a liturgical harper or psalmist trained on the Continent. We need not dwell on this puzzling request: we may assume that it provides testimony of the fondness of at least one abbot for music. We have no way of knowing how Cuthbert intended his harper to operate, whether he intended him (Saxon or Anglo-Saxon) just to play the instrument or to play and sing to its accompaniment.

Lul was Boniface's successor at Mainz. Associated with Boniface is the short text of a proverbial saying in poetic form that provides additional testimony to the memorisation of poetry in Anglo-Saxon times (*ASPR*, VI). A tenth-century manuscript in Vienna contains copies of Boniface's letters, of letters that passed between other eighth-century ecclesiastics, and of some anonymous correspondence. In one of the latter letters, a monk writes to an important (unnamed) church dignitary attempting to dissuade him from a course of action. He tells him to remember the Saxon proverb ("Memento saxonicum uerbum")

> Oft daedlata   dome foreldit,
> sigisitha gahuem,   suuyltit thi ana.

(In his notes, Dobbie states that "no satisfactory translation exists," but he suggests: "Often a sluggard delays in his [pursuit of] glory, in each of his victorious undertakings; therefore he dies alone"—p. 176.) Dobbie comments in his introduction to this *Proverb from Winfrid's Time*, which he calls "the oldest extant verse proverb in English":

> The letter is assigned by Dümmler to the period 757–786. Of the origin of the proverb nothing is known; it may have been taken from a longer Anglo-Saxon poem which is no longer extant, as suggested by Wülker, or it may have been an independent composition. In the latter case, it may be compared with the highly sententious tone of BEDE'S DEATH SONG, composed only a few years earlier. [lxviii]

It is clear in any event that poetry was memorised, and that proverbial wisdom found expression in poetic form, as in the *Maxims*. This in turn serves as a reminder that poetry performed diverse functions in Anglo-Saxon society, and that eulogy—however dominant it might have been—was not the only form of Old English poetry.

In the ecclesiastical sources extant from the eighth century, we have only to consider Alcuin's letters before passing on to discuss two twelfth-century references to eighth-century practices. The letter that Alcuin wrote to Hygbald in 797 is one of the most commonly quoted sources of information on poetry in Anglo-Saxon England, but in one respect it poses a problem. Alcuin wrote many letters to people in England, to colleagues, ecclesiastics, bishops, kings, and laymen. He frequently finds occasion to express his criticism of lax morals and most frequently singles out for condemnation immoderate drinking, fasting, and a fondness for unclerical clothing. Apart from his letter to Hygbald in 797, however, there are surprisingly few references to secular performances in English monasteries; in fact, the only other example I have been able to find is so vaguely worded that it is not at all clear whether he is in fact referring to such entertainments: in his letter to Eanbald of York in 796, he urges the archbishop to see to it that his monks prefer sobriety to drunkenness, divine texts to inanities and jesting ("Non sint ebrietatis sectatores, sed sobrietatis amatores, ut ex illorum bonis exemplis edificentur plurimi. Non inaniloquium uel scurilitas, sed sancta ex ore eorum audiatur psalmodia").

Alcuin frequently opposes virtues and vices in this style, as he does in the famous passage from his letter to Hygbald. The terms of his admonitions recur so often that they tend to read like clichés: with regard to the second sentence just quoted, for example, compare the sentence in one of his letters to king Athelred: "Ueritas audiatur ex ore tuo, non falsitas." Now the fact that such admonitions recur in his letters, even the fact that they are couched in similar expressions, need not be taken to suggest that the vices he condemns are imaginary: there would surely be no point in writing to someone urging him to stamp out drunkenness in the monasteries if those monasteries were models of sobriety, and in any event, as we have seen, Alcuin's concern with these particular vices draws support from the decrees of the Council of Clofeshoh in 747 and other statements in ecclesiastical documents. What is perhaps surprising, though, is that of all the letters he wrote to people in England, Alcuin chose only once to refer specifically to secular entertainments in the monasteries. He had occasion to do so often enough. Nor could we offer in explanation Alcuin's unfamiliarity with such practices: they are often condemned in his correspondence with continental ecclesiastics. E. K. Chambers cites the following examples:

> Alcuin, *Ep.* cclxxxi (793–804), to a disciple in Italy, 'melius est Deo placere quam histrionibus, pauperum habere curam quam mimorum'; *Ep.* ccl (801), to the monks of Fulda, 'non sint [adulescentuli] luxuriosi, non ebrietati servientes non contemptuosi, non inanes sequentes ludos', . . . *Ep.* clxxv (799), to Adalhart, Bp. of Old Corbey, 'Vereor, ne Homerus [Angilbert] irascatur contra cartam prohibentem spectacula et diabolica figmenta. quae omnes sanctae scripturae prohibent, in tantum ut legebam sanctum dicere Augustinum, "nescit homo, qui histriones et mimos et saltatores introducit in domum suam, quam magna eos immundorum sequitur turba spirituum." sed absit ut in domo christiana diabolus habeat potestatem' (the quotation from Augustine cannot be identified): *Ep.* ccxxxvii (801), also to Adalhart, 'quod de emendatis moribus Homeri mei scripsisti, satis placuit oculis meis . . . unum fuit de histrionibus, quorum vanitatibus sciebam non parvum animae sui periculum imminere, quod mihi non

placuit, . . . mirumque mihi visum est, quomodo tam sapiens animus non intellexisset reprehensibilia dignitati suae facere et non laudabilia.' [35 f.]

Alcuin's dislike of such entertainments is patent (see Bolton: 1979, 111–17), yet he seems to have mentioned them in only one letter to England. Even when he wrote to the same Hygbald and his monks immediately after the sack of Lindisfarne in 793, he failed to refer to secular performances in the monastery, though he admonishes his readers to spurn vain clothing and drunkenness:

> Do not glory in the vanity of raiment; this is not a glory to priests and servants of God, but a disgrace. Do not in drunkenness blot out the words of your prayers. Do not go out after luxuries of the flesh and worldly avarice. . . . Let your company be of decent behaviour, an example to others unto life, not unto perdition. Let your banquets be in soberness, not in drunkenness [sint tibi epule non in ebrietate, sed in sobrietate]. Let your garments be suitable to your order. Do not adapt yourself to the men of the world in any vain thing. [trans. Whitelock: 1955, 778 f.]

The letter he wrote in 797 is also critical of drunkenness.

In 797 Alcuin wrote a letter to Hygbald bishop of Lindisfarne (*MGH*, Ep. 4), in which he urged among other things a proper care for the poor: it is better to feed paupers from your table than actors and prodigals ("Melius est pauperes edere de mensa tua, quam istriones vel luxoriosos quoslibet"); the sentiment and choice of words recalls Ep. 281 (quoted above), "melius est Deo placere quam histrionibus, pauperum habere curam quam mimorum." This leads to a denunciation of drunkenness and immoderate dress ("Insania est vestimentorum pompa et assidua aebrietatis luxoria"); Hygbald should serve as an example of sobriety and continence ("In te enim exemplum sit totius sobrietatis et continentiae"). The oft-quoted passage follows immediately. The words of God should be read when priests are eating. The reader should be heard, not the harper; the sermons of the Fathers, not the songs (or poems?) of the laity. What has Ingeld got to do with Christ? The house is small; it cannot hold both of them. The king of heaven wants nothing to do with damned pagans holding the title of king; for the one eternal King reigns in heaven while the other pagan king is damned and cries in hell. The voices of readers should be heard in your houses, not the uproar of merry-makers in the streets:

> Verba Dei legantur in sacerdotali convivio. Ibi decet lectorem audiri, non citharistam; sermones patrum, non carmina gentilium. Quid Hinieldus cum Christo? Angusta est domus: utrosque tenere non poterit. Non vult

rex cęlestis cum paganis et perditis nominetenus regibus communionem habere; quia rex ille aeternus regnat in caelis, ille paganus perditus plangit in inferno. Voces legentium audire in domibus tuis, non ridentium turbam in plateis. [p. 183]

Much scholarly energy has been expended on Ingeld and Christ: the passage is usually taken as evidence for the performance of ballads or Heldenlieder concerning legendary or heroic figures like Ingeld in the eighth-century Anglo-Saxon monasteries; from this inference it is an easy step to produce this passage as evidence for the performance of Anglo-Saxon poetry in monasteries. A number of points are worth noting, however. First, the crucial opposition of sermons to secular performances, of Ingeld to Christ, does not appear in the text as printed by Migne from the edition of Frobenius: the text in *PL* 100 reads "Ibi decet lectorem audire, non citharistam. Angusta est domus. . . ." Second, it is not at all clear that Ingeld stands as an exemplum of the popular hero. Alcuin has, in the passage immediately preceding this, inveighed (characteristically) against drunkenness and vanity in dress; the presence of the harp may be taken as symbolic of the community's lack of "sobrietas et continentia"; Ingeld may be taken as a type of drunkenness, or paganism. Third, even if we allow that heroic songs of Ingeld accompanied by a harp are referred to here, there is no connection between this kind of performance and that of the Anglo-Saxon poet we have been discussing. It seems clear to me that this passage refers to wandering popular entertainers, those mimi and histriones that I have tried to separate from the eulogising poet. That such entertainers were welcome visitors in Anglo-Saxon monasteries is suggested by the Council on English affairs in Rome and confirmed by the Council at Clofeshoh in 747, and one need not argue this point further. It remains to be said, however, that, as has been noted, similar admonitions are not unusual in Alcuin's letters, though this is the only reference to such practices in a letter to England; further, it is difficult to establish to what degree such admonitions depended on St. Augustine's injunction against mimes and dancers (see Bolton: 1979, 114), to what degree they had become traditional or conventional in ecclesiastical circles, to what degree they refer to actual practices, or to what degree this particular letter ascribes without evidence to the monks of Lindisfarne a vice Alcuin saw fit to criticise in his continental colleagues.

Two twelfth-century sources of information on the eighth century provide us with information on oral poetry and song. Both deal with the relations between Offa of Mercia and Athelbert of East Anglia which led to the murder and martyrdom of the latter while on a visit to the former. The *Vitae Duorum Offarum* (trans. C. E. Wright) tells of Athelbert's arrival and Offa's temptation by his Lady Macbeth-like wife to murder his guest. Offa spurns his wife's evil suggestion and sits down to dinner:

> Meanwhile, his violent disquiet of mind having subsided a little, Offa suavely concealed these things, and the kings took their places at the table for the feast, where they spent the whole day in great delight refreshed with royal meat and drink, with timbrels and harp and song [in timpanis, citharis, et choris, diem totum in ingenti gaudio expleuerunt].

One cannot rely too heavily on twelfth-century descriptions of eighth-century social practices: the author may have assumed that contemporary practices were current in earlier times. But the passage presents no grave problems: it reinforces the impression gained from numerous other sources that a meal or a feast provided the usual context for the production of music to the harp as a form of entertainment. Sidonius's description of a day spent with Theoderic confirms this, as does Bede's description of Cædmon's friends and perhaps Alcuin's letter to Hygbald in 797.

An early twelfth-century life of Athelbert provides a more interesting text for discussion (see James). As Athelbert is about to set out on his fateful journey to Offa's court, he turns to his companions and blesses the name of God. Then he continues:

> "For travellers it is often no small pleasure when divine poems are recited there rhythmically [Itinerantibus non modica crebo leticia, dum illic diua poemata modulando recitantur]. And so the man who produces for us royal songs will be presented with a bracelet [Ergo nobis qui ediderit carmina regia armilla donabitur]." Without delay, two who were endowed with the skill of singing began to sing in the joy of their hearts [duo canendi prediti scientia in cordis leticia psallere ceperunt]. They were songs [carmina] about the same king's royal ancestry [de regis eiusdem regia prosapia]. Delighted by these, the king immediately took a bracelet from his arm and gave it to those who were singing the songs [modulantes carmina], and promised much more on his return to his own country.

It seems that here Athelbert attests to the practice of singing religious songs/poems on a journey, but expresses a preference for secular productions. The implied opposition between *diua poemata* and *carmina regia* depends on construing *regia* with *carmina* and not with *armilla* (a royal bracelet for songs); but this seems the more likely reading in view of the fact that the two men do produce songs/poems about the king's family ("regia prosapia") which the delighted Athelbert immediately rewards with the promised gift. M. R. James, who edited this text, notes that later writers, like Osbert of Clare and Giraldus Cambrensis, who used this text omitted reference to the carmina "perhaps as tending to encourage frivolity." Osbert and Giraldus may well have been slightly embarrassed by the preference of the saint and martyr for a secular over a religious performance. If this is so, the incident is likely to be an authentic tradition by virtue of its being a kind of "difficilior lectio." The sources of the life, the earliest extant account of Saint Athelbert of East Anglia, are unknown.

On the assumption that we have here a generally reliable—albeit twelfth-century—account of an eighth-century incident, we may proceed to examine the text more closely. If *illic* in the first sentence is taken to refer conceptually to *itinerantibus*, that is to mean "while travelling," we may have an example here of a practice similar to that mentioned by Eddius, the use of religious texts to accompany a nonreligious activity like rowing or, in this case, riding. Athelbert, at any rate, seems to accept that religious poems are usually recited while on a journey, perhaps to pass the time. And seems to express a wish to hear not these religious poems but royal ones. In other words, if Wilfrid's monks substituted a religious text for a secular rowing song, Athelbert here seems to call for just the opposite. He is perhaps saying, "Let's leave aside for the moment these religious performances and have a good old-fashioned poem about my family." It may well be that such poems were not old-fashioned, that they were still current in spite of the threat of usurpation by religious lyrics. Nonetheless, it is possible that the poems are genealogical in content, though they may equally well be narrative poems—ballads—about the deeds of the king's ancestors.

These are sung (*psallere* does not necessarily imply musical accompaniment) rhythmically—chanted—with joy by two members of the king's party. We cannot say whether they produced separate performances or whether they sang together. They do not seem to be official poets or singers, for the king would then have directed his request to them specifically instead of issuing a general invitation: the statement that he would reward with a bracelet the man who sang a royal poem seems to imply that he was not sure there would be anyone who could in fact produce such a poem. At all events, he is delighted with the response to his invitation and immediately plays the customary role of royal ring-giver.

If the source is reliable, and if the productions are eulogistic poems—though they could equally well be narrative songs—then we have crucial testimony to the state of one aspect of the secular poetic tradition at the end of the eighth century (Athelbert was murdered in 792). All our sources of evidence extant from the eighth century refer to practices in an ecclesiastical context, with the exception of the *Vitae Duorum Offarum*, which is too vaguely phrased to be of much help except as corroborating evidence, and this text from the anonymous life of Saint Athelbert. We have postulated the existence of a general tradition of eulogistic poetry in which most Anglo-Saxons knew poems about themselves, their relatives, or their ancestors, and a tradition of eulogistic poetry produced by a tribal poet in praise of a sacral ruler. We have argued for the likelihood that this latter tradition came to be threatened as a result of the conversion to Christianity. Clearly, the life of Saint Athelbert provides testimony that this East Anglian king no longer sponsored a court figure like the tribal poet—or, less likely, that he did in fact do so but that this personage did not accompany him on this particular journey—but that he harboured recollections of (eulogistic) poetry produced in honour of the king and his ancestors. He feels that his royal mission to Offa provides a suitable occasion for the production of such poems, but he is not sure whether any members of his party can still produce them. He issues a general invitation, then, and is delighted when two men respond successfully. The two do not have to be tribal poets themselves—clearly they were not—nor do they have to be improvising poetry on the spur of the moment: there could well have existed in the past traditional— that is, memorised—poems in praise of a ruler's dead ancestors which many people could recite but which the tribal poet performed as part of his duty and function. In other words, one may here have testimony to the last stage in the extinction of the East Anglian tradition of eulogistic poetry produced in praise of sacral kings by tribal poets. At the end of the eighth century, King Athelbert realises that Christian performances are supplanting secular poetry associated with the king; as he sets out with his royal entourage for the court of Offa, he recollects that this is an occasion for the production of poetry under the old dispensation and, bowing to his impluse, he offers a reward to anyone who can produce a royal—not a Christian—poem. The poems that he was pleasantly surprised to hear in response may have been among the last ones uttered in praise of an Anglo-Saxon ruler until after the Vikings had settled in the Danelaw.

Eighth-century sources would seem to indicate that secular songs were popular among clerics and lay people alike, whether such songs were produced by professional entertainers or by talented amateurs (lay or clerical); the tribal poet would seem to have disappeared from the royal courts, his function perhaps usurped by the church; a tradition of poetry in praise of individuals might well have persisted among the general populace, just as poetry continued also to be used for the preservation of traditional lore or proverbial wisdom and perhaps for charms and incantations. Our sources from the ninth century are less numerous but they serve to deny none of these hypothetical trends.

Extant texts from the ninth century are in short supply; we shall consider here information on only two figures, King Alfred and Cynewulf. Although in the past some doubts have been expressed as to the authenticity of Asser's biography of Alfred, W. H. Stevenson and Dorothy Whitelock have argued persuasively in favour of the genuineness of the work, the composition of which Stevenson puts in 893. Asser drew heavily on extant sources of information in his compilation, but for the chapters that concern us he seems to have had no written authority, so we may assume that they derive from his own personal observations of conditions at Alfred's court and anecdotes presumably narrated to him by Alfred himself. The biography seems to have been abandoned in an incomplete state during Alfred's lifetime, since it refers to nothing later than 887; its opening dedication to Alfred makes it extremely unlikely that the biographical information it purveys would constitute a gross falsification. In chapter 21, therefore, when Asser lays aside the *Chronicle* and turns to "the little that has come to my knowledge concerning the character of my revered lord, Alfred, king of the Anglo-Saxons, during his childhood and boyhood," he is likely to be drawing on reliable sources of information, probably the king himself. Asser tells us in the next chapter that

> by the unworthy carelessness of his parents and tutors, he remained ignorant of letters [illiteratus] until his twelfth year, or even longer. But he listened attentively to Saxon poems day and night, and hearing them often recited by others committed them to his retentive memory [Sed Saxonica poemata die noctuque solers auditor, relatu aliorem saepissime audiens, docibilis memoriter retinebat].

We are not, unfortunately, given any information about the nature of these poems or their performance: clearly they are orally produced and by no means in short supply. If Asser is correct in asserting that Alfred committed the poems to memory, then he must have heard the same texts repeated on a number of occasions, in other words, he must have heard poems that were themselves memorised and repeated verbatim at each performance; Alfred would then be participating in this memorial tradition. We are not told anything about the performers: they may have been tribal poets attached to the court or they may have been amateur laymen. The former is unlikely, in view of the fact that Asser on a number of occasions—as we shall see—refers to poetry in Alfred's court, but never to court poets; one may assume that such personages were not in attendance.

There is no need to assume that because Alfred was the son of a king the poems he heard were associated with the kingship, though of course they may well have been. As a West Saxon boy living in 860, Alfred could have heard poems uttered by others in praise of themselves or their friends and relatives, poems in praise of descent groups or even animals; or, by this time, he may have heard poems performed by wandering entertainers. Alfred could have attended feasts and beer-parties and heard songs sung to the accompaniment of a harp. One cannot argue that a serious scholar like Alfred would hardly concern himself with frivolous poems, for at this stage he is not yet twelve, he is illiterate, and seemingly unlikely ever to succeed to the kingdom. This passage attests to Alfred's fondness from an early age for vernacular performances, and to a flourishing tradition of West Saxon poetry (of indeterminate character) in the middle of the ninth century.

Apparently the virtue Asser wishes to draw attention to in this pasage is Alfred's retentive memory, for he continues in the next chapter to provide an explicit example of just this.

> *Chap. 23.* When, therefore, his mother was one day showing him and his brothers a certain book of Saxon poetry [quendam Saxonicum poematicae artis librum] which she held in her hand, she said: "I will give this book to whichever of you can learn it most quickly." And moved by these words, or rather by divine inspiration, and attracted by the beauty of the initial letter of the book, Alfred said in reply to his mother, forestalling his brothers, his elders in years though not in grace: "Will you really give this book to one of us, to the one who can soonest understand and repeat it to you [intelligere et recitare]?" And, smiling and rejoicing, she confirmed it, saying: "To him will I give it." Then taking the book from her hand he immediately went to his master, who read it [(magistrum adiit et legit), but Stevenson suggests that *et* is an error for a compendium for *qui*]. And when it was read, he went back to his mother and repeated it [Quo lecto, matri retulit et recitavit].
>
> *Chap. 24.* After this he learnt the daily Course, that is the services of the hours, and then certain psalms and many prayers. He collected these into

one book and carried it about with him everywhere in his bosom (as I have myself seen) day and night, for the sake of prayer, through all the changes of this present life, and was never parted from it. . . .

In his notes to this passage, Stevenson argues plausibly that the mother must have been Osburh and not Judith, and that the incident is best placed in Alfred's early boyhood: "There is nothing improbable in the statement that a clever boy, whose keen intellect cannot but have been sharpened by his visit to Rome in 853, learned by heart a book of poems in his fifth or sixth year." The anecdote, if genuine—and there is no reason why Alfred himself could not have told the story to Asser—provides information on a number of points. Perhaps the most significant is that by the middle of the ninth century vernacular poetry existed in manuscript, moreover in a manuscript of sufficient quality to contain an initial letter that would capture the fancy of a young boy. This much we may infer from the significant addition to the Old English translation—produced later in the century—of Bede's *Ecclesiastical History*: we have already noted that the ninth-century translator has "ðæt þa sylfan his lareowas æt his muðe wreoton and leornodon" for Bede's "doctores suos uicissim auditores sui faciebat." The reference to transcription from Cædmon's mouth, not found in Bede's Latin, is intelligible only if the translator knew of the existence of manuscripts of poetry presumed to be Cædmon's. The passage in Asser provides the earliest extant reference to the preservation of vernacular poetry in manuscript.

What was the nature of these poems? If it was not possible to say anything definite about the nature of the oral poems mentioned in chapter 22 that Alfred heard as a boy, there is at least some slight indication that the poetry Alfred learnt from his mother's book was religious. Asser says that Alfred felt challenged by his mother's offer, "immo divina inspiratione." Asser might have meant this to be read as a kind of hagiographical phrase in his account of the precocious powers of memory his king was blessed with, but it seems somewhat unlikely that he would have used the phrase if Alfred were learning secular poetry. The manuscript itself was apparently a handsome production, and this was likely to have contained religious poems; in addition, Asser immediately passes on to record Alfred's feat of memorising "celebrationes horarum," "psalmos quosdam," and "orationes multas." The evidence is hardly conclusive, but the context suggests that the prize Alfred won contained vernacular poetry but religious rather than secular compositions.

These passages from Asser afford evidence that vernacular poetry was committed to memory; whether an illiterate Anglo-Saxon heard traditional poetry produced by other illiterates or whether he heard the poetry read from a book made little difference, apparently: he could learn the text however it was produced and having done so could continue to participate in a memorial poetic tradition. From his early youth, then, Alfred has a marked predilection for vernacular poetry. This is confirmed by subsequent passages in Asser referring to the education of Alfred's children.

With the exception of chapter 29, chapters 26 to 72 are based on the *Chronicle*; chapters 73 and 74 deal with Alfred's physical infirmity, and chapter 75 then takes up the account of Alfred's family. Five surviving children are mentioned.

> Athelweard, the youngest, was given over by the divine counsel and the admirable prudence of the king to the pleasures of literary studies [ludis literariae disciplinae], along with almost all the children of noble birth of the whole country, and also many of humble birth, under the diligent care of masters. In that school, books of both languages, Latin, that is, and English, were assiduously read, and they had leisure for writing; so that before they had the strength for manly pursuits, namely hunting and other pursuits which are fitting for noblemen, they were zealous and skilled in the liberal arts.

Two other children, Edward and Alfthryth were carefully brought up in the royal court, where they remained.

> Nor, indeed, are they allowed to live idly and carelessly without a liberal education among the other occupations of this present life which are fitting for nobles; for they have learnt carefully psalms and Saxon books, and especially Saxon poems, and they frequently make use of books [nam et psalmos et Saxonicos libros et maxime Saxonica carmina studiose didicere, et frequentissime libris utuntur].
>
> *Chap. 76.* Meanwhile the king, in the midst of wars and frequent hindrances of this present life, and also of the raids of the pagans and his daily infirmities of body, did not cease, single-handed, assiduously and eagerly with all his might, to govern the kingdom, to practise every branch of hunting, . . . to recite Saxon books, and especially to learn by heart Saxon poems, and command others to do so [et Saxonicos libros recitare, et maxime carmina Saxonica memoriter discere, aliis imperare]. He was also in the habit of hearing daily the divine office, the Mass, and certain prayers and psalms, and of observing both the day and the night

hours, and of visiting churches at night-time, as we have said, in order to pray without his followers knowing.

These passages confirm the information derived from the earlier passages quoted that books of vernacular poems existed; these poems were learnt by Alfred's children, by Alfred himself, and, at his command, by others. It was suggested above that the book of poems mentioned in chapter 23 contained religious rather than secular compositions. It is also likely that the Latin and English books used by the young princes would have contained matter acceptable to the undoubtedly clerical schoolmasters, and the coupling of "psalmos et Saxonicos libros" seems to bear this out. Yet we have to note that chapter 23 ends with a description of Alfred's memorising a book of vernacular poetry and chapter 24 immediately adds that he also learnt religious material; in much the same way, chapter 76 mentions Alfred's memorisation of vernacular poems and then Asser immediately passes on to note Alfred's regular observance of church services. One might argue that Asser believed the vernacular poems to be religious and that this reminded him of Alfred's involvement with religion, mention of the one evoking mention of the other by association; or one might equally well argue that Asser knew the vernacular poems to be secular and felt he had to compensate for this somewhat embarrassing exercise by immediately mentioning Alfred's involvement with the official religious literature and liturgy.

The distinction here between secular and religious is not artificial: it would be interesting to know whether Alfred learnt the presumably religious poems of Aldhelm—who William of Malmesbury tells us was Alfred's favourite poet— or poems of the likes of Cædmon, or whether he was concerned to preserve the traditional oral poetry and song of the West Saxons, whether eulogies in praise of eminent people or popular songs. Certainly this seems to have been a concern of Charlemagne, as we hear from Einhard (trans. Turner): in addition to transcribing traditional laws, "he also had the old rude songs that celebrate the deeds and wars of the ancient kings written out for transmission to posterity" (chap. 29). Although Asser—and perhaps even Alfred—knew Einhard's biography, there is no reason to believe that Asser was, in his biography, ascribing to Alfred deeds that Einhard had attributed to Charlemagne: Alfred's method is essentially different, though his motives may have been the same. Up to this point in time, Alfred remains illiterate in Asser's biography; his literary upbringing is accordingly a participation in an oral tradition. Whether he hears poems performed traditionally or read from books, he still *hears* them and does not read them for himself. His reaction is to learn the texts and to command others to learn them: preservation for Alfred lies in committing these texts to memory in the traditional manner, not in placing them in books.

It may therefore be that the "carmina Saxonica" were traditional and secular, poems such as Athelbert of East Anglia wished to hear on his journey to Offa's court; it may be that Alfred took upon himself the task of preserving these since there was in his court no official whose duty it was to undertake this task— Asser frequently mentions poetry in his biography, but nowhere does he mention a poet. If this argument from silence may be accepted, then it would seem to support the hypothesis that there were no tribal poets among the Saxons, or that, even if there were, their tradition had died out by the ninth century.

Alfred's fondness for vernacular poetry passed into tradition, for we read in later sources a story of his entering the Danish camp in the guise of a minstrel to spy out their plans during the period he spent on Athelney island. The chronicle that purports to be written by Ingulf, William the Conqueror's one-time secretary, tells us that Alfred, pretending to be a minstrel, took his harp and entered the tents of the Danes ("rex ipse fingens se esse iocultorem, assumpta cithara, tentoria Danorum adijt," C. E. Wright, 145), where he gained access to the enemy's secrets, and having satisfied himself, returned undiscovered to Athelney. A similar story is told by William of Malmesbury in his *Gesta Regum,* II, 121 (ed. Stubbs): Alfred enters the Danish tents in the guise of a minstrel ("sub specie mimi subiens tentoria") where he entertains the king at their meals like a professional ("ut joculatoriæ professor artis, etiam in secretiora triclinii admissus"), all the while gaining access to all he cares to learn through his eyes and ears; after a few days, satisfied with his knowledge, he returns to Athelney.

It is generally accepted that this is a popular legend comparable with the story of Alfred's burning the cakes, and of little historical value. As we shall see, it is not the only tale William tells of a war leader disguising himself as a minstrel and entering the camp of his opponents. It may be held to have a factual basis in accounting for Alfred's remarkable triumph over the Danes at Edington after his expulsion from Wessex and his virtual exile in the Somerset marshes; the *Chronicle* does testify to his activity in his period of exile, constantly striking the Danes with punitive hit-and-run raids, but his ultimate triumph must have been based on an effective system of espionage, a fact perhaps accorded legendary status in the story of his entering the Danish camp. His disguise as a minstrel might reflect a knowledge of Alfred's love of secular performances, but it also might simply be that the figure of Alfred attracted to himself a popular story of a similarly disguised spy.

The story of Alfred's exploit seems to have been a popular oral tradition, since William and pseudo-Ingulf seem to present verbally independent accounts: the independence cannot be insisted on, however, for although pseudo-Ingulf gives Alfred a harp and William does not, and William places him at the Danish king's table for a few days, whereas pseudo-Ingulf omits this detail, both have him entering the Danish tents ("Regis enim Danorum . . . subiens tentoria" in William, "tentoria Danorum adijt" in pseudo-Ingulf) and remaining in the encampment until he had satisfied himself ("cum ex omnibus quæ nosse desiderarat animo satisfecisset suo" in William, and "cum suo desiderio satisfecisset" in pseudo-Ingulf). A detailed examination of the source of the legend and the relation between these two texts is not called for here, however; whether or not they reflect post-Conquest conceptions of Anglo-Saxon practices, one may accept that by the ninth century there were wandering entertainers (individuals or troupes) who were popular figures welcomed both among laity and clergy and whose performances often accompanied dining or feasting. There is little reason to insist, on this evidence, that Alfred ever played a harp to accompany his recital of "Saxonica carmina," though of course there is no reason why he should not have done so.

Alfred initiated or himself undertook the translation of a number of Latin texts into English, and some of these, particularly the Boethius, frequently refer to poetry and its performance; since they are translations of Latin works, however, they do not refer to Anglo-Saxon poetic practices, so their evidence will not be considered here but in a later chapter on Old English words for poets and poetry.

Finally, in our discussion of sources from the eighth and ninth century, we must briefly consider Cynewulf, not because his extant work tells us anything about oral poetry, but because, as a literate poet, he functions in a tradition distinctly different from the oral poetic tradition. Cynewulf's is the first set of undated poetry we are considering, but scholars are in general agreement that he wrote in the ninth century. He is known to us through runic signatures that he contrived to introduce—with varying degrees of success—into the conclusion of four poems: *The Fates of the Apostles* and *Elene* in the Vercelli Book and *Christ II* and *Juliana* in the Exeter Book. All four poems treat Christian themes and all are based on Latin originals; a comparison of the Old English with the Latin texts demonstrates similarities not only of content but also of structure and sometimes syntax, and suggests that Cynewulf was himself competent in Latin and read the originals himself (see, for example, Chase). It would not be necessary to argue the case for Cynewulf's literacy, were it not that Magoun, faced with the formulaic quality of Cynewulf's diction, felt constrained to con-

clude awkwardly that Cynewulf was accordingly an oral poet and hence illiterate. If Cynewulf's treatment of his sources is not sufficient evidence of his
literacy, also to be considered are his frequent references to books and writings
and his runic signatures.

His references to books are particularly interesting. Apart from phrases like
Elene 825 f. ("Sint in bocum his wundor þa he worhte on gewritum cyðed,"
"the wonders he wrought are revealed in writings in books") and 1254 ("swa ic
on bocum fand," "as I found in books"), and *Christ II* 785 ("Us secgað bec,"
"books tell us") and 792 f. ("þæt me hælend min on bocum bibead," "what my
Saviour commanded me in books"), which do not recur in the same form, there
are phrases like "on Godes bocum," "in God's books," which occurs twice
(*Elene* 204 and 290), and "þurh halige bec," "through holy books," which
occurs four times (*Fates of the Apostles* 63, and *Elene* 369, 670, and 852). These
last would seem to merit classification as formulas. Similarly, with reference to
Christian concepts, "wuldorcyninge(s)" occurs three times in Cynewulf's
poetry (*Elene* 1304, 1321, and *Juliana* 248) and often in the extant corpus (*Andreas* 418, 1430, *Guthlac* 596, 793, 849, *Resignation* 17, *Genesis* 1384, *Riddle 39* 21,
Vainglory 50, and *Beowulf* 2795); "engla Ordfruma" occurs in *Fates of the
Apostles* 28 as well as in *Andreas* 146, *Creed* 6, and *Christ and Satan* 21, 237, 657;
and "Petrus and Paulus" occurs in *Fates of the Apostles* 14, *Juliana* 304 and also
Menologium 122. This brief list is by no means exhaustive, but its implications
are significant. A. H. Smith wrote of Cædmon's hymn:

> In its relationship with the rest of Old English poetry Cædmon's Hymn
> appears to display no great originality, for, though it is technically ac-
> curate, nine or more of its eighteen half-lines can be paralleled in other
> poems. But in Cædmon's time when Northumbria had been converted to
> Christianity for only half a century these phrases belonging to Christian
> poetry could scarcely have become conventional, as they certainly were in
> later Old English; on the contrary, the poem represents the beginnings of
> such a diction and its freshness and originality must have been felt a genera-
> tion or more after its composition. [14 f.]

One might accept this argument for Cædmon's, but one cannot apply the
same reasoning to Cynewulf's poetry some two centuries later. Many of the
formulas in Cædmon's hymn might have been based on existing secular formulas, but the formulas referring to books or to Apostles could not possibly
derive from a pre-Christian oral tradition. Cynewulf's formulas may be taken
to demonstrate the relative rapidity with which a purely Christian formulaic

diction arose after the conversion, and this has relevance to our earlier discussion about the antiquity of the Old English tradition of narrative poetry. The presence of formulas in poems like *Beowulf* does not necessarily mean that *Beowulf* derives from an ancient tradition of narrative poetry. Formulas current in a tradition of narrative might have been adopted and adapted from an existing tradition of eulogy; the adaptation and assimilation of formulas from one tradition into another, or the generation of formulas for new concepts is, on the evidence of Cynewulf's poetry, not necessarily a process requiring an extended period of time: a poem like *Beowulf*, for all its formulaic diction, or Cædmon's biblical narratives, could have been produced in seventh- or eighth-century England even if there never had been an ancient tradition of Germanic Heldenlieder known to the Anglo-Saxons.

Cynewulf, from his own testimony, was a poet quite different from the pre-Christian oral poet. For his source material he relied exclusively on books, and the books that inspired him to write were biblical or exegetical: the concerns of Anglo-Saxon poetry were no longer Germanic alone. The literate poet produces an artifact that takes on a life independent of himself, whereas the oral poet, as we have seen, cannot be divorced from his poetry: hence the literate poet can observe his artifact objectively and assume a proprietary right to it. The oral poet need not announce to his audience that it is he who is reciting the poem: they can see him before them. Cynewulf signs his name to his poems: he assumes that he will be unknown to his audience, but through the signature, he says, you can now know the name of the person who was once unknown to you:

> Nu ðu cunnon miht
> hwa on þam wordum wæs   werum oncyðig.
>
> [*Fates of the Apostles*, 105–06]

Clearly the poems of Cynewulf are designed to be read: it is difficult to understand how else the runic signatures might appeal to an audience. As compared to an oral poem, therefore, Cynewulf's poems appeal to his audience primarily through a different sense, they take on a life independent of the author and achieve a permanency that outlives their creator; hence Cynewulf may use them to solicit the prayers of his readers: he asks those who enjoy his composition to solicit the aid and solace of the Apostles for him in his sadness, and to desire his comfort:

> Nu ic þonne bidde   beorn se ðe lufige
> þysses giddes begang   þæt he geomrum me

> þone halgan heap   helpe bidde,
> friðes ond fultomes . . .
> Sie þæs gemyndig,   mann se ðe lufige
> þisses galdres begang,   þæt he geoce me
> ond frofre fricle.
>
> [*Fates*, 88–91, 107–09]

Cynewulf is, of course, not the first poet of his kind, but the picture he gives us of himself working on his poetry (presumably alone in his cell) at night, aged and ready for death, weaving his compositions with the skill of words, pondering and carefully searching his mind,

> Þus ic frod ond fus   þurh þæt fæcne hus
> wordcræftum wæf   ond wundrum læs,
> þragum þreodude   ond geþanc reodode
> nihtes nearwe
>
> [*Elene*, 1236–39]

differs radically from the picture the *Beowulf* poet gives us of the king's thane riding back from the lake and chanting Beowulf's praises: the one is isolated and writes personal poetry, the other is part of a crowd and produces poetry referring to a man known to all his audience. Cynewulf is quite a different poet from the thane, though he stands much closer to Cædmon (see Opland: 1980).

Broadly speaking, the extant texts relating to the performance of poetry during the eighth and ninth centuries allow us to believe that the sacral poetry of a vatic tribal poet—if it existed—tended to disappear; that wandering minstrels performing (among other things) songs to the accompaniment of a harp were welcomed both inside and outside the monasteries; that biblical epics came to be written in the monasteries, perhaps as a pious extension of the oral tradition of eulogy (in which narrative was embryonically present). Clearly poetry continued to be propagated orally, and it seems most likely that such poetry was in the main memorised and transmitted in a fixed form (as is indicated by *The Proverb from Winfrid's Time*, for example, or Asser's account of Alfred's interest in vernacular poetry); with the sole exception of the twelfth-century life of Saint Athelbert referring to the late eighth century, there are no references to eulogistic poetry in honour of living sovereigns or dignitaries. This general picture alters radically after the Viking settlement in England.

7

The Last 150 Years

In the history of early English oral poetry, the period from about 900 to the
end of Anglo-Saxon England is set apart from the eighth and ninth centuries
by virtue of the Scandinavian influence on the Anglo-Saxon traditions of oral
poetry. This influence is unlike any that may have been exerted by the Celtic
or Latin traditions. Celtic influence may have been felt in West Germanic
poetry during the continental period, but since I have advanced in my second
chapter the hypothesis that the early Germanic tradition of court poetry, like
the Celtic, was essentially eulogistic, there seems little point in considering the
possibility of interanimation between the two traditions while they coexisted
on the Continent. After their arrival in England, the Anglo-Saxons assumed
an identity of their own, distinct from the common Germanic stock, and at
two stages in the early period there is the possibility of Celtic influence, during
the sixth century and during the seventh. In the fourth chapter I considered
improbable any Celtic influence being felt in the sixth century before the
Germanic settlers achieved dominance, on the grounds that there was relatively
little social intercourse between Celt and Anglo-Saxon then. The many scholars
or kings in exile who spent periods of time in Ireland or at centres of Irish
culture like Iona during the seventh century may well have adopted Celtic
tastes in literature, they may even have learnt to perform Celtic songs or poems,
but it seems unlikely that they would initiate a radical alteration in a whole oral
tradition on returning to their own people.

The influence of Latin literature on English was of course profound, but
that influence was largely demonstrated by those literate Anglo-Saxons who
wrote their poetry. There is a strong possibility that new genres of oral poetry
developed, as we saw when we considered the case of Cædmon, and written

poetry exhibiting the influence of Latin or Christian themes and techniques may have been learnt and passed back into the oral tradition, as seems to be clear from Asser's accounts of Alfred's fondness for vernacular poetry. Some few oral poets may have been bilingual, like Aldhelm, and their oral poetry may well have been strongly influenced by classical models. Certainly, it is likely that the introduction of Christianity led to the radical alteration in the seventh and eighth centuries of the tradition of sacral eulogy honouring reigning monarchs, but on the whole the influence of Latin literature permeates through writing (see Bolton: 1977; J. J. Campbell: 1966 and 1967; Derolez).

The Scandinavian influence differs from the Celtic and Latin: with the settlement of the Scandinavians in England, intimate social intercourse took place between the Anglo-Saxons and members of another Germanic group. In circumstances such as then existed, cultural symbiosis took place, as is evidenced by the number of Scandinavian words that entered the English language; very few Celtic words were adopted (see Baugh and Cable, §55). If these Germanic settlers supported a strong tradition of oral poetry, and if the language of their poetry was moreover intelligible to their English cousins, the stage was set for Scandinavian influence to be felt on the traditions of Anglo-Saxon oral poetry.

As we saw in the second chapter, scholars readily accept that the geographically extreme Celtic and Indic cultures are the most conservative of the Indo-European group. In the same way, the North Germanic people are the most conservative of the Germanic linguistic family; geographically isolated in the northwest of Europe, they developed their traditions free from the influence of Christian and Latin culture until the tenth century. Their traditions of oral poetry bear strong resemblances to the hypothetical structure posited in the second chapter and accordingly strengthen the possibility of its accuracy. The sagas bear abundant testimony to the activity not only of the skalds but also of the everyday Scandinavian.

If the sagas are to be believed, it was not uncommon for people to break into poetry on the spur of the moment; such improvised stanzas, independent in their own right and the product of a unique occasion, are called *lausavísur*. A problem immediately presents itself: how can a thirteenth-century author commit to writing a snatch of poetry uttered spontaneously and presumably only once by someone living in the tenth century? It is reasonable to assume, as we shall see, that there existed a strong oral tradition of memorised poetry, poetry that sometimes included reference to the author and the circumstances of composition; any participant in this tradition could construct a prose context for the verse and incorporate it into a saga. But the saga writers would not have attributed widely to people the ability to compose poetry spontaneously if such an ability were not feasible. In his recent dissertation on lausavísur, Russell Poole discusses the apparent ability of Egil to compose spontaneous verse in a passage we will consider later in this chapter, and of Hild the wife of Ragnvald the Jarl, who pleads in vain with Harald Fairhair to remit his sentence of out-lawry on her son Rolf (in the saga of Harald Fairhair, chap. 24) and utters a poem at the conclusion of her plea. Poole writes:

> The *lausavísa* is a democratic form. Poets and princes may use it, but so may Swedish berserks, dead men, three-year-old children, and other seem-ingly inarticulate persons. The Egill and Hildr scenes illustrate this point in a mild way. Egill was a professional poet—we have fragments of his *encomia* to prove it—whereas Hildr was not. Her name will not be found anywhere in the medieval catalogues of court skalds; we have no other verses by her. The speaking of a verse, whatever the alacrity or surprise value of the delivery, was no remarkable feat in itself. Anyone in the com-munity, it seems, could do as much. Nor is there any hint in the medieval texts that something miraculous might be involved—that (say) a shaman or spirit is speaking *through* the person who improvises. Although Snorri speaks of Sigvatr's 'facility in numbers' as an exceptional gift [Saga of St. Olaf, chap. 160], his own *Heimskringla* and the prose works of medieval Iceland and Norway in general compel us, if we take them literally, to attribute the same facility to a much wider circle of people. [12 f.]

Of course, we need not take the sagas literally when they claim to preserve a poem uttered once, and once only, three centuries earlier, but we may well accept that they testify to the ability of the everyday Norwegian or Icelander to produce poetry spontaneously, a practice still current in contemporary Iceland (see Rich).

Alongside this tradition of spontaneous poetry in which potentially every-one participated, there clearly existed a tradition of memorised poetry handed on in a fixed form. Poems recorded in different sagas occasionally have sections in common: poets may have incorporated into their original compositions relevant extracts from traditional poems maintained in the common stock. The poems of the famous skalds must have been subject to fixed memorial transmis-sion. Snorri testifies to this in arguing for the admissibility of these poems as historical evidence. In the preface to *Heimskringla* (trans. Laing) he writes:

> Iceland was settled in the time that Harald Fairhair was the king of Norway. There were scalds in Harald's court whose poems the people know by

heart even at the present day, together with all the songs about the kings who have ruled in Norway since his time; and we rest the foundations of our story principally upon the songs which were sung in the presence of the chiefs themselves or of their sons, and take all to be true that is found in such poems about their feats and battles: for although it be the fashion with scalds to praise most those in whose presence they are standing, yet no one would dare to relate to a chief what he, and all those who heard it, knew to be false and imaginary, not a true account of his deeds; because that would be mockery, not praise.

Snorri is clearly aware of the memorial character of this tradition as he is of the vicissitudes to which it is subject. He discriminates between poems that are likely to have been faithfully transmitted as composed, and those that have been altered in transmission: he remarks at the end of the preface, "But the poems seem to me least corrupt, if the metrical rules are observed in them and if they are sensibly interpreted."

Thus, in Norway and Iceland at least, it seems evident that there were traditions of spontaneous poetry and of memorised poetry in which many people participated. Drawing on both traditions, over and above them, there were poets known as skalds. These were men (never women) whose poetry celebrated the characters and deeds of rulers and other distinguished men. Of their compositions Lee Hollander writes:

> Skaldic poetry is not elegiac-epic, i.e. it does not tell a story or dwell on mournful reflections, as does so much of West Germanic poetry; nor is it dramatic-dialogic like the Old High German *Hiltibrantsliet* and so many Eddic lays—in fact, this difference is the very touchstone of Skaldic poetry. And it is not didactic, in any sense. But it is largely odic, encomiastic, frequently satiric, sometimes lyric, in a fashion that has no counterpart in other Old Germanic poetry. [19]

In fact, the skalds purvey what I have referred to in earlier discussions as eulogistic poetry. Their function is complex, but they seem to have had a commitment to the truth, as Snorri testifies in the passage quoted above from his preface: the skalds did not simply praise and flatter, for they could not distort or exaggerate facts or introduce fanciful incidents in reference to the careers of the subjects of their poems: "that would be mockery, not praise." In commenting on the skald's relation to his prince, Hollander quotes Finnur Jónsson:

> once he was accepted at court, in the *hirð*, "there frequently sprang up a

relation of devotion and friendship—the prince on his part honoring and respecting the skald, often making him his confidential adviser and pleni-potentiary; the poet in his turn aiding him with friendly and sincere coun-sel. He was hardly ever found among those who flattered and humored the king. In fact, it is characteristic of the skalds that they knew how to preserve their independence of opinion and maintain an attitude of frank-ness and self-possession which inspired respect." Both their works and their lives substantiate this proud and fine relation. There are scores of instances recorded by them when the ruler was criticized, warned, ex-horted, excoriated by his skald, who thus sometimes incurred the wrath, and sometimes earned the gratitude, of his sovereign. [6]

If the skald does not always in fact enjoy the licence to criticise with impunity, he is frequently treated as if it is generally accepted that criticism is as much a part of his trade as praise: he is a truth-teller, in whose poetry the achievements and characters of the subjects of his compositions will be immortalised.

For all his skill and status, the skald undergoes no formal training, nor does he serve a term of conscious apprenticeship. Yet his poetry is highly stylised and intricate. Hollander notes that "skalds were proudly conscious of their art. Though not formally taught, it certainly was seriously cultivated and debated, both as to technique and contents and as to the mode of reciting—music did not enter in it at all, in strong contrast with the Continental lyric" (6). All the forms of Scandinavian poetry we have been discussing were solo productions unaccompanied by music, although singing and harping were not unknown to the North Germanic peoples (see Jónsson).

We have, then, in early medieval Norway and Iceland a complex tradition of poetry that is distinct from song. Many people memorise traditional poems, some apparently produce poems on the spur of the moment; in this tradition, the dominant figure is the skald, a man of considerable importance associated with the court, whose poetry celebrates kings, rulers, and other worthies (see Turville-Petre). This latter tradition of eulogistic skaldic poetry, strong in the tenth and eleventh centuries, weakens in the twelfth. In the introduction to her edition of Old Norse court poetry, the most sensitive scholarly introduction to the art of the skald, Roberta Frank writes:

> In the course of the twelfth century, one hears the complaint that skaldic craftsmanship is no longer rewarded or appreciated; the court prefers fiddles and pipes to *dróttkvætt*. This is the burden of Einarr Skúlason's stan-za [no. 16 in the collection] on the gifts he didn't receive from Sveinn

svíðandi, king of Denmark. It is a complaint echoed around 1184 by the poet Máni at the Norwegian royal court: jugglers and minstrels are usurping the position of a suddenly unfashionable skald. [93]

Readers will perhaps by now have noted the remarkable similarity between the traditions of medieval Scandinavian oral poetry as outlined above and of contemporary Xhosa oral poetry as outlined in the first chapter of this book: with the exception of the last point on the weakening of the skaldic tradition, every feature of the Scandinavian tradition I have drawn attention to is also a feature of the Xhosa tradition (although it is true that the metre and techniques of the poetry differ). This, of course, proves nothing about either Xhosa or Scandinavian poetry, but I believe it makes more plausible the use of the contemporary Nguni traditions in Africa as analogues of the Anglo-Saxon tradition.

Obviously, the Scandinavian traditions themselves provide more credible material for comparison with the Anglo-Saxon tradition; yet scholars have rarely pushed the comparison to its logical conclusion. It is almost universally assumed that the Scandinavian tradition is unique among the Germanic peoples, that the skald's poetry "has no counterpart in other Old Germanic poetry," in Hollander's words (19). It is generally accepted that the skald was a solo eulogiser, while the Anglo-Saxon scop was a harping entertainer. Thus Lars Lönnroth, for example, has to draw a distinction between the Anglo-Saxon and the Scandinavian poetic traditions: in his discussion of *Norna-Gésts þáttr*, he writes:

As a performer, Norna-Gest is related to the scop of West-Germanic tradition. *The scop's singing of epic tales to the happ* [my italics], however, seems to have been divided here in three separate acts: harp-playing, story-telling in prose, and poetic recitation. There are many indications that harp-playing was known in medieval Scandinavia, and at least in one other case it is clearly associated with poetry, but it is never known to accompany the recitation as in the hall of Heorot. On the whole, it seems unlikely that music played any important role in Norse poetic tradition, except in magic and ritual singing. Only a few Eddic lays that are in some way associated with magic are clearly characterised as "songs" in medieval texts. (5)

There is no reason to believe that the Anglo-Saxon tradition was radically different from the Scandinavian, no reason at all to insist, as we shall see, that the Anglo-Saxon scop sang epic tales to the harp. At an early stage it is likely that there was a similarity between the Scandinavian traditions and the traditions of those Germanic people on the Continent whose descendants would become the Anglo-Saxons; the main point of divergence between the Scandinavian and the Anglo-Saxon traditions of oral poetry will readily be seen to be that the English counterpart of the skald in the seventh and eighth centuries found his popularity usurped by wandering entertainers and his function usurped by the church, whereas the skald experienced a similar threat only in the twelfth century.

After the period of Scandinavian settlement in England, there was constant traffic between England and the Scandinavian countries. Many skalds visited England, and in poems they composed reference is often made to English kings or to events that took place in England (see Alistair Campbell: 1971a). For example, in *Heimskringla* in the Saga of St. Olaf alone, we read poems on the battle of London during Athelred's reign by Ottar the Black and Sigvat (chap. 13), another on the battle of Ringmere Heath (chap. 14), and yet another on Canterbury (chap. 15), we read of Sigvat's and Bersi Scaldtorfuson's visit to Cnut in England (chap. 131) and Sigvat's poems referring to a subsequent visit (chap. 146), of Sigvat's poems about his relation to Cnut, uttered after Olaf had questioned his loyalty (chap. 160), of Thorarin Praisetongue's brush with Cnut (chap. 172), and of Thormod the Skald's recitation of Bjarkamal before the battle of Stiklestad (chap. 208); in the saga of Harald Hardrada, mention is made of a poem about Earl Waltheof composed after the battle of Hastings (chap. 96). The list is by no means complete: the references are many. We are not strictly concerned, however, with Old Norse poetry that refers to England; it is sufficient to note that practising skalds visited England. That they performed in England is evident from two sagas which we must look at briefly before passing on to consider the effects of this activity on the English tradition.

In his account of the murder of Ragnar Lothbrok in 878, Roger of Wendover says that the legendary Viking was shipwrecked off the coast of East Anglia and made his way to Edmund and "was received with honour and for some time remained at his court, and, since the Danish language is similar to English speech, Lothbroc began to relate to the king by what chance he was cast ashore in England" (trans. C. E. Wright, 139). Whether or not we accept the historicity of Ragnar's shipwreck, we may comfortably accept Roger's aside about the mutual intelligibility of Old English and the Old Norse languages. Travelling skalds could perform in England in the expectation that their English audiences would be able to understand at least as much of their poetry as audiences at home did. In the sagas devoted to them, we learn that Egil Skallagrim's son and Gunnlaug Serpent-Tongue served English kings not only as retainers but also as skalds. I do not intend to examine these two sagas in great detail, because, strictly speaking, they are relevant not so much to a study of Anglo-Saxon oral poetry as to a study of oral poetry in Anglo-Saxon England. Nonetheless, they do merit attention since they provide accounts of the kind of practices that might well have evoked imitation by English poets.

Egilssaga (trans. Pálsson and Edwards) refers to events that occurred between ca. 860 and 1000. It is possible that the saga was written by Snorri Sturlason, who was born in 1179 and was murdered in 1241 (see Jones: 1960, 16–23); if the saga was Snorri's work it is likely to have been written between 1220 and 1225. The author exhibits considerable confusion about English affairs, particularly in his chronology, but there is no reason to doubt that Egil did visit the court of King Athelstan (see Jones: 1952). The historical accuracy of the author's account of Egil's exploits in England is not insisted on here; the saga is referred to merely to provide an example of the kind of performance that skalds might have given at English courts. Chapter 50 of the saga tells of the arrival of Egil and his brother Thorolf at Athelstan's court, where they are prime-signed at the king's request. They are placed in charge of the Norwegians in the English army, and successfully engage the forces of the Scottish king. Then at the battle of Vinheiðr, which might well be Brunanburh, Egil commands Athelstan's division and Thorolf the second division of the English army, despite Egil's objections. Thorolf is killed in the successful engagement and as Egil buries him he chants two poems. Then he joins Athelstan's victory feast and sits sulking morosely. Athelstan tries to mollify him with a present of a gold ring; Egil accepts the ring on the blade of his sword and produces a poem:

> The King in his coat
> Of steel sets this gold coil,
> This ring, on my right arm
> Where falcons have rested:
> The gift hangs glowing,
> My arm its gallows:
> Honour was earned
> By the feaster of eagles.
>
> [chap. 55]

Egil cheers up, even more so when Athelstan rewards him for his participation in the battle and offers handsome compensation for Thorolf. Egil thanks the king in another poem. Egil spends the winter with Athelstan where he is highly honoured by the king, and where he composes a drápa about the king

for which he is given by the king two gold rings and the king's own cloak.
The drápa contains the following lines:

> The royal warrior rises
> Above his realm,
> The pride of three princes
> Ælla's stem overpowers;
> Countries are conquered
> By Athelstan the King,
> All kneel to the noble
> And generous knight

and has as its refrain

> Now the Highlands, deer-haunted,
> Lie humbled by Athelstan.

[chap. 55]

These stanzas are highly suspect (apart from anything else, Athelstan was
not descended from Alla of Northumbria, as Egil would surely have known
had he spent much time with the king), but it is probable that Egil stayed in
Athelstan's court, that he there performed poetry in praise of the king as he was
accustomed to do in Iceland or Norway, and that he was rewarded for his
poetry. The saga emphasises the high regard in which Athelstan holds Egil; the
king time and again urges Egil to remain with him permanently, but Egil
declines. Later he returns to England, where he falls into the hands of his
enemy Erik Bloodaxe in York and ransoms his head by producing a poem
vaguely in praise of Erik. He makes his way to Athelstan, where he reports on
his dealings with Erik in a poem, and again leaves for home against the urgings
of the king.

Like Egil, Gunnlaug visited England in the course of his wanderings:

At that time King Ethelred, the son of Edgar, ruled England and was a
good prince; he was spending that winter in London. The language in
England was then one and the same as that in Norway and Denmark, but
when William the Bastard conquered England, there was a change of language; from then onwards, French was current in England, since he was of
French extraction.

Gunnlaug at once went into the king's presence and gave him a bold
and courteous greeting. The king asked what country he was from, and

Gunnlaug told him. 'And I have sought this meeting with you, my lord, because I have made a poem about you, and I should like you to listen to it.'

The king said he was willing, and Gunnlaug recited the poem in a good confident manner. In the refrain he says this:

> All the host stands in awe of the generous
> prince of England as of God;
> the race of the war-swift king and all the race of
> men bow to Ethelred.

The king thanked him for the poem, and as a reward for it he gave him a cloak of precious cloth lined with excellent furs and with an embroidered border down to the hem. He also made him one of his retainers, and Gunnlaug stayed with the king for the winter and was well thought of. [chap. 7, trans. Quirk, in Foote and Quirk]

Both sagas depict the kind of scene that could have occurred in aristocratic circles in England after the Viking settlement.

Egil's *Hofuðlausn*, the poem he performed before Erik Bloodaxe as a ransom for his own head, is end-rhymed, "the first poem so to be composed by any Norse skald" (to quote Gwyn Jones): "to Egil must be given the glory of introducing a new kind of poetry to the North" (Jones: 1960, 14 and 15; cf. Jones: 1952, 143). Scholars are generally agreed that Egil first encountered the form in England, whether through Latin hymns or Old English poems is not certain. It is at any rate clear that in England Anglo-Saxon and Norse poets could meet and hear each other perform; if Egil could carry home with him the influence of poetry he had encountered during his stay in England, Anglo-Saxon poets could also be inspired to emulate the performances of the skalds who visited them or lived with them. Such interanimation of traditions requires a seedbed of intimate social intercourse in order to germinate. Conditions were not favourable during the reign of Alfred, when the Scandinavians were recent enemies settled in their own part of the country; nor were conditions favourable during the reign of Edward the Elder, engaged as that king was on the reconquest of the Danelaw. But by the time of Athelstan the situation had altered.

Athelstan was king of all England, he had married his daughter to Sihtric of York and fostered Hakon the son of Harald Fairhair. Not all Scandinavians in England were well-disposed toward Athelstan, of course, but a climate did exist in which free social intercourse between Englishman and Scandinavian flourished. Athelstan controlled Northumbria after Sihtric's death in 927, but in the reign of Edmund the Northumbrians revolted and tried to take Mercia. It was not until the expulsion of Olaf Cuaran and the death of Erik Bloodaxe that Northumbria passed out of Viking hands, and during the reign of Edgar, Anglo-Danes were accepted as officers of church and state. Relations between Englishman and Scandinavian certainly fluctuated, but from the time of Athelstan conditions were generally favourable for literary cross-fertilization to take place. What were the consequences for the Anglo-Saxon traditions of oral poetry?

According to the reconstruction attempted in the preceding chapters, we could expect to find in England at the start of the tenth century a tradition of memorised poetry: biographical or autobiographical eulogies, proverbs, charms or incantations, religious poems and hymns, or traditional genealogical poems. People may yet have retained the ability to burst into spontaneous poetry under the inspiration of a particular moment. Such traditions are of the people, and are not likely to have been radically altered by the Scandinavian settlement. The charms may have incorporated references to some Norse figures, pieces of Norse wisdom lore may have been adopted and naturalised (see Grattan and Singer, 52–62). Nor would the tradition of minstrelsy have altered much: wandering harpers might have included Scandinavian heroes in their repertoire of songs, the jugglers and mimes would perform for a penny as well before Scandinavians as before an English audience. There may have been harpers among the Scandinavian settlers, and they may have exchanged tunes or songs with their English counterparts, but on the whole there does not seem to have been as strong a tradition of harp-song among the North Germanic peoples as there was among the Anglo-Saxons: it is likely, therefore, that if one tradition influenced another in this sphere, the English tradition was dominant.

It is also likely that at this time in the Anglo-Saxon oral tradition there existed no counterpart for the skald: I have suggested above that the tradition of the Anglo-Saxon tribal poet was threatened after the conversion by Christianity itself and by the new attitudes of the nobility, so that the poet who eulogised a sacral king was bound to disappear as a figure of prominence in Anglo-Saxon society. In any event, he is not likely to have found a home among the West Saxons, whose dynasty was not well-established and certainly could not claim continuity with a continental line; since one result of the Viking raids and settlement was the effective eradication of all English royal lines save that of Wessex, it is unlikely that, even if in fact the tribal poet continued to operate into the ninth century in the non-West Saxon courts, he would have survived into the tenth century. Accordingly, it is in this sphere that Scandinavian practices can be expected to have had the greatest influence on the English tradition.

One cannot base too strong an argument on the extant evidence, since it is certainly true that another effect of the Viking raids was to destroy or halt the productions of monastic scriptoria, so that very few ninth-century manuscripts survive; the bulk of extant Old English poetry is now found in manuscripts of the tenth century probably attributable to the monastic revival that flourished in particular in the reign of Edgar. Nonetheless, it is true that one type of poetry does start to appear in the reign of Athelstan and continues to surface sporadically up to the death of Edward the Confessor, a type that can plausibly be held to have emerged as a result of skaldic influence. Strictly speaking, we are not so much concerned with the history of written literature as with the history of oral poetry, but the appearance of poetry in the *Anglo-Saxon Chronicle* may well be a reflection of trends in the oral tradition. Dobbie (*ASPR*, VI) prints six of these poems: the *Battle of Brunanburh* (937), the *Capture of the Five Boroughs* (942), the *Coronation of Edgar* (973), the *Death of Edgar* (975), the *Death of Alfred* (1036), and the *Death of Edward* (1065). With the exception of the *Death of Alfred*, these are all in regular metre; Sedgefield (1904, xx f.) lists seven other *Chronicle* entries containing "Poems of irregular metre": King Edgar's Reign (959), King Edgar's Death and Persecution of Monks (975), Death of Edward the Martyr (979), Laying Waste of Canterbury (1011), Edward Atheling (1057), Margaret Wooed by Malcolm (1067), William the Conqueror (1086). The greatest of these poems is undoubtedly the *Battle of Brunanburh*. Comparing it to the *Battle of Maldon*, Dobbie wrote: "The *Battle of Maldon* is a sober, highly detailed narrative. . . . The *Battle of Brunanburh* on the other hand, is an unrestrained song of triumph, in which the poet seems to know little, and care less, of the actual course of events, but gives full play to his feelings of exultation at the victory over a foreign foe. In style and diction the *Battle of Brunanburh* follows the older poetry rather closely, and yet it is not quite in the old heroic tradition" (*ASPR*, VI, xl). That divergence Dobbie failed to account for, though Campbell had not only characterised it but hinted at its source: the poem is

> one of a group of poems preserved in the *Chronicle* (937, 941, 973, 975 lines 1–12, and 1065), which are to be described as panegyrics upon royal persons, arising out of the commemoration of events in which they were concerned. Each poem takes its rise from a single event, in the first two a

victory, in the third a coronation, in the last two a death. Such poems must have been a popular form of composition with certain poets of the age. Parallels must be sought among the poems of the Norse skalds rather than in the earlier Old English poetry. Such poems . . . are extremely careful in metre and style, full of evidence that the poets had meticulously studied earlier Old English verse, and are equally distant from the doggerel of the popular poems of the *Chronicle*, and the vigorous, but often careless, verse of the *Battle of Maldon*. In the two latter styles of writing we have natural, unfettered developments of the old style, but in the poems now under consideration we have an artificial preservation, or rather, perhaps, resurrection of the old style. [Alistair Campbell: 1938, 37 f.]

Dobbie notes that the *Battle of Maldon* is "a sober, highly detailed narrative," but implies criticism of the *Brunanburh* poet who "seems to know little, and care less, of the actual course of events"; Campbell is sensitive to the underlying difference:

> The poet's subjects are the praise of heroes and the glory of victory. When this is realised, the oft-repeated criticism, that he does not greatly add to our knowledge of the battle, falls to the ground. It was not his object to do so. He was not writing an epic or a 'ballad.' He was writing a panegyric, and a sufficient number of similar poems of the period are preserved to show that this was then a regular form of composition. . . . [41 f.]

This group of poems, as far as we know without precedent in the written literature of the Anglo-Saxons, celebrates an event: they do not describe or tell the story of the event, but are produced on the occasion. They treat people (usually rulers) who are in the public domain, people known to poet and audience alike; they apportion praise and sometimes blame (the leaders of the antimonastic reaction, 975; and the murderers of Edward, 979), they celebrate the deeds and achievements of their subjects, as well as their characters, in an elliptical, allusive, non-narrative style. They are, in short, eulogies, like those purveyed by Norse skalds and Xhosa iimbongi.

There seems little reason to doubt that such eulogies, dating as they do from the reign of Athelstan, came to be written down as a result of the presence in England of Norse skalds; it is rather more difficult to say whether or not the presence of these Norse eulogisers influenced Anglo-Saxon oral poets. It may well be that the tradition of Anglo-Saxon ritual eulogy in praise of a sacral king was dead by the time the Vikings settled in England, but some form of eulogistic

court poetry may well have continued, perhaps propagated by popular minstrels in imitation of the traditional tribal poets; even if such a continuation or
mutation of the tradition did not take place, a tradition of eulogistic poetry may
well have persisted—a tradition of poetry in praise of oneself, one's relatives or
ancestors, whether or not there were public figures who uttered eulogies in
praise of the rulers on ceremonial occasions. In addition, there is likely to have
been a tradition of memorised poetry, poems like Cædmon's hymn or Christian
poems or poems such as Alfred insisted his children be taught. Norse skalds in
England would perform in their own language with its distinctive metres; there
is no reason why Anglo-Saxons, drawing on their living oral traditions, should
not be able to produce similar poetry in *their* traditional form. Individual Anglo-
Saxons, operating on the precedent of the skalds, might have been induced to
imitate the skalds whether or not they were conscious of the fact that in so doing
they were reviving a native tradition dormant for some centuries.

Such poetry would not have had its original ritual significance, but its prop-
agators could have assumed from the Norse model the licence to criticise with
impunity and the function of eulogising rulers and dignitaries on official occasions. Such a reanimated tradition, perhaps taking its impetus from the example
of those Norse skalds who lived and performed in England, would be continuing, perhaps after a hiatus, a tradition of poetry related not so much to the
narrative *Beowulf* as to the eulogistic poem that the king's thane produces in
praise of Beowulf's defeat of Grendel. Such a reanimated tradition of eulogistic
poetry in praise of rulers might then have ensured the legitimacy of written
poems such as those that were entered in the *Chronicle*. The hypothesis seems
reasonable: such poetry could have been—ought to have been—produced about
Alfred; its absence in the *Chronicle* entries treating Alfred's reign may be due to
its lack of currency as a form in the oral tradition, this in turn confirmed *a
silentio* by Asser.

The hypothesis that an oral tradition of Anglo-Saxon eulogistic poetry in
imitation of the skaldic tradition was revived during the reign of Athelstan is
reasonable; one piece of evidence rescues the theory from the realms of hypothesis. William of Malmesbury had already started writing about the reign
of Athelstan in his *Gesta Regum* when he came across a contemporary Latin
poem about the king. This he proceeded to incorporate into his work:

> Concerning this king, a firm opinion is current among the English, that no
> one more just or learned administered the State. A few days ago I dis-
> covered that he was versed in letters, from a certain very old book, in which

the author struggled with the difficulty of his matter, unable to express his meaning as he wished. I would append here his words for the sake of brevity, if he did not range beyond belief in praise of the prince, in that kind of expression which Tullius, the king of Roman eloquence, in his book on rhetoric calls bombastic. The custom of that time excuses the diction; the affection for Athelstan, who was still alive, lends colour to the excess of praise. I shall add, therefore, in a familiar style a few matters which may seem to augment the record of his greatness. [§132, trans. Whitelock: 1955, 278 f.]

William goes on to draw information from the poem, twice quoting extracts from it. Curiously enough, it is evident that Athelstan was not alive at the time of composition of the poem, for the last line William quotes refers to Olaf Cuaran's succession to rule in York after the death of Athelstan. It may be that William's addition of a few matters "in a familiar style" explained his editorial treatment of the bombastic original, and that he himself touched up the poem and added the last lines, or it may simply be that he was momentarily mistaken: the quotation of the conclusion of the poem comes only at the end of §135, some pages after he had stated that Athelstan was alive at the time of composition. Whatever the truth of this matter, there is no reason to doubt that William is here quoting a poem written by a clerical contemporary of Athelstan who may have been an eyewitness of the events he describes; certainly a bombastic style is characteristic of Athelstan's charters ("the foggiest court-Latin any country or any age produced" in the words of Christopher Brooke, 139).

We have seen before—and we shall continue to remark on it—that poetry and song often form part of descriptions of joyful feasting. The first extract of the poem William quotes deals with just such an occasion, the coronation of Athelstan at Kingston. William introduces the extract with the worlds: "Hence, at the glory of such happy events and the joy of that day [pro tantorum successuum gloria, et illius diei lætitia], the poet exclaims, not without cause: A royal son prolonged a noble line, when a splendid gem illumined our darkness, the great Athelstan, glory of the country, way of rectitude, noble integrity, unable to be turned from the truth. Given at his father's command to the learning of the schools, he feared stern masters with their clattering rod, and, avidly drinking the honey of learning, he passed not childishly the years of childhood." This eulogistic poetry may have been composed in Latin by the clerical poet in imitation of the kind of poetry produced at Athelstan's court by Egil and other skalds, although it certainly has its precedents in the classical tradition (see

Garrison). What concerns us more for the moment is the poet's description of Athelstan's coronation feast in 925:

> The nobles assemble and place the crown, pontiffs pronounce a curse on faithless men; fire glows among the people with more than wonted festivity, and by various signs they disclose their deepest feelings. Each burns to show his affection to the king; one fears, one hopes, high hope dispels fear; the palace seeths and overflows with royal splendour. Wine foams everywhere, the great hall resounds with tumult, pages scurry to and fro, servers speed on their tasks; stomachs are filled with delicacies, minds with song [Deliciis ventres cumulantur, carmine mentes]. One makes the harp resound, another contends with praises [Ille strepit cithara, decertat plausibus iste]; there sounds in unison: 'To thee the praise, to thee the glory, O Christ' [In commune sonat, 'Tibi laus, tibi gloria, Christe']. The king drinks in this honour with eager gaze, graciously bestowing due courtesy on all.

At the feast there is poetry and song; there seems to be choral singing of anthems to Christ, perhaps to balance the praises of the king. It is not clear whether or not the harper sings to the accompaniment of his music, but what is clear is that the harper and the man who utters praises (presumably eulogies in praise of the king) are quite different people: they try to outdo each other in performance. On this evidence it seems likely that an oral poet uttered eulogies at Athelstan's coronation feast; it is at least possible that such English poetry once again became a feature of court life from the reign of Athelstan.

William of Malmesbury (*Gesta Regum*, 131, trans. Whitelock: 1955) records a legend about another tenth-century harper. In a passage strongly reminiscent of his account of Alfred's entry into the Danish camp in disguise, William tells of a sortie undertaken by Olaf Cuaran while the opposing armies were manoeuvring before the Battle of Brunanburh:

> When Olaf perceived such danger to threaten, he cunningly undertook the role of a scout; laying aside the trappings of kingship and taking in his hands a harp, he reached the tent of our king, where, singing before the entrance and now and then touching the resounding strings with a sweet loud sound [pro foribus cantitans, interdum quoque quateret dulci resonantia fila tumultu], he was easily admitted, professing himself a minstrel who earned his daily livelihood by this art [professus mimum qui huiusmodi arte stipem cotidianam mercaretur]. He captivated the king and the companions at his board for some time with the musical harmony, while

in the midst of his playing he scrutinized everything with his eyes. When satiety of eating had put an end to these delights and the nobles' conversation turned again to the stern business of waging war, he was ordered to depart and received a reward for his song [precium cantus accepit].

Although it is by no means certain that Olaf Cuaran took part in the Battle of Brunanburh, there is no need to reject this anecdote out of hand, despite its similarities to the story William tells of Alfred. The very least that can be said is that William believed that there were travelling professional minstrels in England two hundred years before he wrote his histories, and, as we have seen, this belief receives corroboration from other sources of evidence. If we could rely fully on the veracity of this tale, we would have an invaluable description of the minstrel's technique, for William notes that Olaf sang and intermittently (interdum) struck a loud sequence of notes on the harp: evidently the harp did not provide continuous musical accompaniment to the words of the song, but was used for musical interludes. This must have been a technique that seemed reasonable to William, either from his own observation of twelfth-century minstrels or from oral evidence on earlier practices; unfortunately, we have no way of knowing which. It is not beyond belief that twelfth-century performers in William's day preserved unaltered an earlier tradition of harp-song, so that William's description of Olaf's technique might be taken as accurate for tenth-century harpers. Olaf should not be confused here with the tenth-century oral eulogiser: his performance is clearly designed to provide an entertaining background to a meal, and is one of its delights (deliciis).

Before we leave William, we should comment on two further points. In his account of Edgar's reign, William records a meeting between Edgar and Kenneth of Scotland which took place after a jocular remark of Kenneth's had been exaggerated and broadcast by a mimus ("a quodam mimo sinistra aure acceptum," II, 156). Clearly the travelling entertainer was still mimicking personalities of his day, and enjoyed considerable currency. Second, we should note that in his account of Athelstan's reign, William produced evidence derived from cantilenae, a source of information that we shall return to comment on at the end of this chapter. William considers the evidence of these songs less reliable than that of written records but includes their testimony for the sake of completeness:

Thus far relating to the king [Athelstan] I have written from authentic testimony [Et hæc quidem fide integra de rege conscripsi]: that which follows I have learned more from old ballads, popular through succeeding

times [cantilenis per successiones temporum detritis], than from books
written expressly for the information of posterity. I have subjoined them,
not to defend their veracity, but to put my reader in possession of all I
know. First, then, to the relation of his birth. . . . [II, 138]

Such narrative songs—ballads—may well have been composed during or
shortly after the reign of Athelstan; they may well have formed part of the
repertoire of wandering minstrels whose audiences learnt them and passed
them on to others, ensuring their popularity two centuries later.

One celebrated harper of the tenth century was no wandering minstrel.
The earliest extant life of Saint Dunstan (ed. Stubbs: 1874) was written ca. 1000
by a continental Saxon priest, known only as Author B, who enjoyed Dunstan's
friendship towards the end of the saint's life. Dunstan, who was related to the
royal line of Wessex, received his early education at Glastonbury, and joined
his uncle Athelm at Canterbury in 923 when Athelm succeeded Plegmund as
archbishop of Canterbury. The young and talented Dunstan spent much time
at the court of Athelstan where his accomplishments aroused the envy of his
relatives, who spread the foul rumour that Dunstan had learnt from medical
books and trained men, not works of benefit for the salvation of souls, but
songs (or poems) of ancient heathendom, and that he performed the frivolous
incantations of charms from histories ("dicentes illum ex libris salutaribus et
viris peritis, non saluti animarum profutura sed avitæ gentilitatis vanissima
didicisse carmina, et historiarum frivolas colere incantationum nænias,"
Auctore B, 6). In response, Dunstan invokes David; Dunstan probably had a
reputation as a harper, and the precedent of David could certainly be invoked
in support of the legitimacy of harping. Dunstan's opponents, however, were
able to insinuate that his knowledge of vernacular poems or songs embraced
non-Christian material, and that these ancient and traditional texts, whether
learnt from books or through oral transmission, were associated with paganism. Clearly, at the time of Athelstan there was poetry and there was poetry:
popular secular traditions could yet cast aspersions on all poetry or song. The
rumours were trenchant enough to secure Dunstan's banishment from Athelstan's court in 935.

The life of Dunstan written ca. 1085 by Osbern, precentor of Christ Church,
Canterbury, depicts Dunstan as actually harping for the king when he saw him
exhausted by worldly duties, by which activity he cheers the king and the
princes; Osbern has Dunstan singing psalms to the accompaniment of tym-
panum, harp, and other musical instruments ("psallebat in tympano sive in

cithara, sive alio quolibet musici generis instrumento," 9). Although Osbern is generally unreliable, Dunstan's facility with the lyre is attested by the more trustworthy Author B (trans. Whitelock: 1955), who relates a miracle that occurred on Dunstan's return to Glastonbury:

> Among his sacred studies of literature he also diligently cultivated the art of writing, that he might be sufficient in all things; and the art of harp-playing [artem . . . citharizandi], and skill in painting likewise; and, so to speak, he excelled as a keen investigator of all useful things.

Because of this reputation, a neighbouring noblewoman invited Dunstan to design a religious stole for her.

> When he came to her for this work, he usually brought with him his *cythera*, which in the native language we call 'harp,' that he might at times delight himself and the hearts of his listeners in it [sumpsit secum ex more cytharam suam quam lingua paterna hearpam vocamus, quo se temporibus alternis mentesque ad se tendentium jocundaretur in illa, *Auctor B*, 12].

The harp is hung against the wall, and one day, of its own accord, it plays a Christian melody of jubilation ("jubilationis modulum"), the melody of an antiphon ("antiphonæ melodiam"). The twelfth-century biography by Eadmer mentions that this miracle was the occasion of rumours put before the king by Dunstan's enemies, proving his association with the devil (*Eadmer*, 6). It is Eadmer, too, who notes explicitly what we may assume from the wording of the accusation in *Auctor B*, 6, that Dunstan sang in English as well as Latin (presumably):

> Dunstan was accustomed to play on musical instruments, in the knowledge of which he was distinguished in no ordinary way, and to lull not only his own, but the minds of many from the turbulent affairs of the world and toward the meditation of celestial harmony as much through the sweetness of his words (which he alternated, sometimes in his mother tongue, sometimes in another, [modo materna modo alia lingua]) as through the harmonious melody he expressed on those instruments. [*Eadmer*, 4, Stubbs: 1874, 170]

William of Malmesbury has a similar passage in his biography of Dunstan. Interesting too is a passage in Author B, repeated in the later biographies, concerning a vision Dunstan had of his mother's divine marriage, in which, like

Cædmon, he is addressed by a heavenly visitor, who teaches Dunstan the text of a hymn that is subsequently transcribed.

It is not necessary to cite additional examples. It is clear that Dunstan was a gifted and versatile young man, and that harping was only one of his many accomplishments. He may have learnt this skill from the Irish scholars that Author B tells us were at Glastonbury (chap. 5), but he plays an English instrument, a hearpe. Whether or not he played before the king (Author B does not explicitly say so), he had at the court the reputation of being a skilled harper. His repertoire probably contained both English and Latin texts. Dunstan, however, does not produce eulogistic poetry: his songs are designed to relax (and probably edify) his audience, they are incidental, and they are never said to refer to contemporary figures or events. His subjects, where they are mentioned, are religious. Nonetheless, it is evident that vernacular harp-song, however Christian, could easily be associated with a secular, non-Christian tradition, an indication that such a secular tradition did exist. Dunstan's accusers do not charge him with performing incantations or charms to the accompaniment of a harp, but imply that someone who sings English songs is not far removed from someone who dabbles in heathen folklore; we should not take their insinuations too seriously.

That there yet existed a tradition of purely secular, even heathen, song seems to be suggested by a tenth-century proscription by Alfric, who warns priests not to go to funerals unless invited, but instructs them, if they do go, to forbid the heathen songs of the laity and their loud laughter: "forbeode ge þa hæðenan sangas þæra læwedra manna and heora hludan cheahhetunga" (*Canons of Alfric*, 35, cited in Fowler, 41). Alfric's opposition to secular custom extends to the practice of boasting, for in his *Sermo de Memoria Sanctorum*, he lists as the seventh "laughter" *iactantia*, or idle boasting: "se seofoða leahter is iactantia gecweden, þæt is ydel gylp on ængliscre spræce, þæt is ðonne se man bið lofgeorn and mid licetunge fænð, and deð for gylpe gif he hwæt dælan wille."

Reference to boasting raises the question of whether this formalised practice among the Anglo-Saxons could have included the utterance of poetry. Although Alfric's condemnation of "iactantia" or "ydel gylp" cannot be taken as an expression of his opposition to secular poetry, the translator of Boethius seems at one point to indicate that boasting might take poetic form: in the first poem of Book I, Boethius in prison contemplating his present condition cries out, "Why, my friends, did you boast of my happiness so often? [Quid me felicem totiens iactastis amici?]" The Old English version (I, 2) reads:

> Forhwam wolde ge,   weoruldfrynd mine,
> secgan oððe singan   þæt ic gesællic mon
> wære on weorulde?
>
> [*ASPR*, V, 16–18]

The translation of *iactastis* as "secgan oððe singan" might simply be an expansion for purposes of alliteration, but the phrase is used in Old English poetry in passages that deal with poetry or song, as in *Widsith* 54 ("Forþon ic mæg singan ond secgan spell") and *Christ* 667 ("Se mæg eal fela singan ond secgan þam bið snyttru cræft bifolen on ferðe"). Perhaps the fullest accounts of the practice of boasting in Anglo-Saxon England are to be found in *The Battle of Maldon*, a poem that refers to an encounter between Viking raiders and an East Saxon force that took place in 991.

In the opening passage of the poem as we now have it (the beginning is lost), the poet tells us that Edric put aside the pleasures of hawking and turned to the battle filled with martial resolve now that he gripped his sword and shield; now that he had to fight in the presence of his lord, he fulfilled his vow

> beot he gelæste
> þa he ætforan his frean   feohtan sceolde.
>
> [*ASPR*, VI, 15–16]

This vow or promise (*beot*) would seem to have been uttered some time before the battle in a gathering consisting of the lord and his warriors, if we can assume that it was uttered in a situation like that alluded to later in the poem. After the leader Byrhtnoth has fallen, some of his warriors flee the battlefield, heedless, the poet tells us, of the many kindnesses Byrhtnoth had shown them. But Offa had warned Byrhtnoth in the meeting place when they held a council that many men spoke boldly who would not stand firm in the time of need:

> Swa him Offa on dæg   ær asæde
> on þam meþelstede,   þa he gemot hæfde,
> þæt þær modiglice   manega spræcon
> þe eft æt þearfe   þolian noldon.
>
> [198–201]

Whether or not the bold promises were uttered at the same *gemot* that Offa addressed, it seems clear that prior to the battle warriors had in some way vowed not to desert their lord in battle, that they would fight with him or die. In contrast to the cowards who fled after Byrhtnoth's death, those who remained to fight on were resolved to avenge Byrhtnoth's death or die in the attempt ("lif forlætan oððe leofne gewrecan," 208). As they fight, a succession of warriors exhort their companions with resolute speeches. The first, young Alfwin, refers more explicitly to the context in which the vows were uttered before the battle:

"Gemunan þa mæla   þe we oft æt meodo spræcon,
þonne we on bence   beot ahofon,
hæleð on healle,   ymbe heard gewinn;
nu mæg cunnian   hwa cene sy.
Ic wille mine æþelo   eallum gecyþan,
þæt ic wæs on Myrcon   miccles cynnes;
wæs min ealda fæder   Ealhelm haten,
wis ealdorman,   woruldgesælig.
Ne sceolon me on þære þeode   þegenas ætwitan
þæt ic of ðisse fyrde   feran wille,
eard gesecan,   nu min ealdor ligeð
forheawen æt hilde.   Me is þæt hearma mæst;
he wæs ægðer min mæg   and min hlaford."
Þa he forð eode,   fæhðe gemunde. . . .

[*ASPR*, VI, 212–25]

"Remember all the speeches that we uttered
Often when drinking mead, when we made vows
Upon the benches, heroes in the hall,
About hard strife. Now may whoever has
True courage show it. Here will I reveal
My genealogy to all. I come
From a great family in Mercia;
Alderman Ealhelm was my grandfather,
Wise, prosperous, and honoured in this world.
The thanes among that race shall not reproach me
That I intend to leave this troop and go
Home to my land now that my lord lies dead,
Cut down in battle. My grief is the greatest,
For he was both my kinsman and my lord."
Then he advanced, and set his mind on war. . . .

[trans. Hamer]

The vows were apparently uttered in the lord's hall while the warriors were drinking; it is not clear whether the drink accompanied the oathmaking. Towards the end of the poem, Edward the Tall says in boasting words (*gylp-wordum*) that he has no intention whatever of fleeing now that his lord lies dead:

> Þa gyt on orde stod   Eadweard se langa,
> gearo and geornful,   gylpwordum spræc
> þæt he nolde fleogan   fotmæl landes,
> ofer bæc bugan,   þa his betera leg.

[273–76]

Later still Offa is killed. Nevertheless, he had fulfilled the vow he made to his generous lord that they would either return home unharmed or die on the battlefield; like a proper retainer he lay dead alongside his lord:

> Raðe wearð æt hilde   Offa forheawen;
> he hæfde ðeah geforþod   þæt he his frean gehet,
> swa he beotode ær   wið his beahgifan
> þæt hi sceoldon begen   on burh ridan,
> hale to hame,   oððe on here crincgan,
> on wælstowe   wundum sweltan;
> he læg ðegenlice   ðeodne gehende.

[288–94]

Clearly, we are dealing here with the utterance of oaths before battle, perhaps solemnified by drinking, perhaps taking the form of an alternative ("We shall die in battle or return home safely"; cf. "I shall avenge my lord or die in the attempt"). We are reminded of the account in Ammianus Marcellinus of an encounter between Romans and Goths in Thrace: at daybreak, after an initial skirmish, the Romans sound their trumpets and the Goths attempt to reach high ground after taking oaths together according to their custom ("barbari postquam inter eos ex more iuratum est," XXXI, 7, 10). The Anglo-Saxon *beot* and its relation to Scandinavian custom has been treated in detail by Stefán Einarsson, who surveys the occurrences of *beot* and *gylp* in Old English. The two words, he concludes, "seem to mean the same thing; but it is probable that *gielp-* stresses the glory of the adventure, something to boast of, whereas *beot-* stresses the fact that it is a promise, a vow" (Einarsson: 1934, 976). This distinction would seem to be borne out by the preference for *gylp* in religious writers such as Ælfric when referring to the sin of pride or vainglory;

certainly, as Einarsson notes, *beot, gylp*, and related words are used to refer to circumstances other than the custom of uttering vows.

A survey of the Anglo-Saxon and Scandinavian evidence would seem to suggest that the custom was associated with ceremonial drinking; in Saxo, for example, we read of a pledge that whatever was promised through drunken mouths over drink would be fulfilled bravely, as would the vows sworn by Jupiter and the gods ("Omnia quae poti temulento prompsimus ore, fortibus edamus animis, et vota sequamur per summum jurata Jovem, superosque po-tentes," Einarsson: 1934, 980). This would seem to link the vows not only with drink but also with religious belief. Einarsson (p. 983) quotes a passage from *Heimskringla* that describes a feast called by Svein after the death of his father Harald. At the start of the feast Svein drinks the cup of memory to his fa-ther ("minni hans") before taking up his high seat, and swears at the same time to attack Athelred in England before the passage of three years. All the Joms-vikings drink a brimming cup after this, then another to Christ and a third to Michael. Then Earl Sigvald drinks to the memory of his father and swears an oath; and he is followed by others. If this incidence of drinking characterised such ceremonies, one can appreciate the admonition in *The Wanderer* that a warrior should not be too quick to boast before he has learnt the limits of his abilities; before he makes a vow, he should pause until he can assess how he would react in a crisis:

> Wita sceal geþyldig . . .
> ne næfre gielpes to georn   ær he geare cunne.
> Beorn sceal gebidan   þonne he beot spriceð
> oþ þæt collenferð   cunne gearwe
> hwider hreþra gehygd   hweorfan wille.
>
> [*ASPR*, III, 65–72]

The passage in *Heimskringla* is interesting, since it links the vows with a remembrance of an ancestor; if these ancestors in turn link the warrior with the gods, then the passage in Saxo and the evidence of Snorri would seem to rein-force the view that the vows were connected with ancestor veneration and probably ritual. *Fagrskinna* confirms the ceremony of succession as described in *Heimskringla*: many draughts are drunk "to Thor or to other Gods of theirs while they were yet heathen" (Einarsson: 1934, 984) and these are followed finally by the Bragi-cup. Brage was the god of poetry (*Heimskringla, Yng.*, 40), and this brings us back to a consideration of whether the practices alluded to in *The Battle of Maldon* might be poetic.

There is no reason why an oath should be poetic, but an oath involving the conjuration of the ancestors might well include a recitation of the eulogy of the ancestors if that eulogy participated in a system of ancestor veneration as out-lined in my second chapter. Contemporary Zulus and Xhosas still recite the eulogies of their ancestors in order to conjure their presence and invoke their aid or intercession with the great spirit; the drinking of beer is an essential in-gredient of such ceremonies (on Xhosa ritual beer-drinks, see McAllister). It is certainly possible that formal oaths were accompanied by a recitation of the eulogy of the warriors' ancestors. Distinct from these customary vows before battle, however, are the utterances of the warriors during battle. The mutual encouragement of the participants in the battle at Maldon need not be poetic, although if Anglo-Saxons were accustomed to utter spontaneous poetry as an expression of high emotion, it is possible that they were. More interesting, per-haps, is the speech of Alfwin, which refers to his grandfather's rank and quali-ties. Realistically, one would presume that Byrhtnoth's retainers would know his genealogy, especially if he was a Mercian related to Byrhtnoth and serving him. What Alfwin says of his grandfather is typical of the content of eulogies; it bears comparison in content with what Beowulf's retainers say about him at his funeral. One is reminded, too, of Ammianus Marcellinus's statement that the Goths entered battle shouting the glories of their ancestors ("Barbari veto maiorum laudes clamoribus stridebant inconditis," XXXI, 7, 11). It seems high-ly likely that these shouts would be ritual and poetic; warriors could well have uttered the eulogies of their ancestors to ensure their protection, just as they could also have uttered eulogies in praise of themselves as an expression of pride or self-confidence—boasting, if you like. This latter possibility seems to be evidenced in *The Battle of Finnsburh*: one of the warriors at the door of the hall identifies himself and his clan, refers to his qualities and his deeds, and baits his audience to attack him. My name is Sigeferth, he says, a Secgan noble, a re-nowned adventurer; I have endured many a tough, grievous battle; fate has decreed for you one of two results from our meeting:

> "Sigeferþ is min nama," cweþ he   "ic eom Secgena leod,
> wreccea wide cuð;   fæla ic weana gebad,
> heardra hilda.   Ðe is gyt her witod
> Swæþer ðu sylf to me   secean wylle."
>
> [*ASPR*, VI, 24–27]

I am not suggesting that *The Battle of Maldon* and *The Battle of Finnsburh* pre-serve the actual words uttered by Alfwin and Sigeferth; the poets had to cast their material in their own fashion. I am suggesting, however, that Alfwin and Sigeferth both utter in battle something referring to themselves or their ancestors and that these utterances are consonant with a tradition of eulogy. In the light of the hypothesis advanced in chapter 2 on the basis of the comparative study of other poetic traditions, and the evidence of Ammianus Marcellinus in particular, I take them as confirmation that Anglo-Saxon warriors uttered poetic eulogies in the context of battle. These eulogies may also have formed a part of the ritual ceremony of oathmaking; the beot or gylp, at least in part, may have taken poetic form. *The Battle of Maldon* suggests that a popular tradition of eulogy continued right to the end of the Anglo-Saxon period.

To continue with the evidence extant from the last century-and-a-half of Anglo-Saxon England: Kenneth Sisam once remarked (1953b) that "The scribbles on the blank leaves of old manuscripts are always worth notice, because the broken scraps that were running in the minds of scribes or readers floated to the surface when a new pen had to be tried" (195). One such scribble (dated to the tenth, possibly the eleventh, century by Neil Ker, p. 304) in a manuscript of Alcuin's letters bears testimony to the memorisation of vernacular poetry in this period. Written across the upper margin of both leaves of folio 87ᵛ and folio 88 of B M Harley 208 is the caroline alphabet from *a* to *z* followed by "&7 þæð" and then "Pater noster . . ." down to "adueniat reg." In the lower margin the same hand has written "hwæt ic eall feala ealde sæge." (This interesting scribble was remarked on by Robinson: 1971.) It is likely that the scribbles in both upper and lower margins are pen trials written at the same time. The scribe wrote out the alphabet, the Paternoster as far as space would allow, and continued in the lower margin with the opening words of a song or poem he knew. The fact that he chose to write the alphabet and the Paternoster suggests that the lower margin entry was also memorised: the "Hwæt ic . . ." formula suggests that this is the opening of a text (cf. *Andreas, Beowulf, Exodus, Juliana, Vainglory*). The author of this lost song or poem clearly used the same formula as the *Beowulf* poet used in l.869 ("se ðe ealfela ealdgesegena"); one can only regret that the scribe apparently found the point of the quill not to his liking and broke off after penning only one tantalising line. The line seems to suggest that the text was secular ("Lo! I [have heard] very many ancient stories . . .") rather than religious; the scribe must have been Christian. One does not wish to fashion a critical theory on the basis of a one-line fragment, but it seems clear that this text was memorised, and that one Anglo-Saxon monk at the end of the tenth century had committed to memory a secular poem or song.

In the early eleventh century, perhaps between 1005 and 1007, Wulfstan produced a document apparently intended to serve his cause of educational reform, the so-called *Canons of Edgar*. In the words of Roger Fowler, its most recent editor, this collection of admonitions "is designed to control the morality of the secular clergy and to provide guidance on their duties. These duties are seen as responsibilities towards the laity: the priest must minister to his flock and exhort them to virtue. . . . The *Canons of Edgar* is thus aimed at the reform of the laity through the reform of the previously neglected and neglectful secular clergy" (liii). Canon 58 exhorts priests to spurn drunkenness and to discourage it in others ("And riht is þæt preostas beorgen wið oferdruncen and hit georne belean oðrum mannum"), then Canon 59 reads:

> And riht is þæt ænig preost ne beo ealusceop [thus Junius 121; Corpus 201
> had *ealascop*], ne on ænige wisan gliwige mid him sylfum oðrum mannum,
> ac beo swa his hade gebyrað, wis and weorðfull.

A priest should not be an ale-poet, nor amuse himself or others in any way, but he should be wise and honourable as befits his station. Later, according to Fowler (lxi), Wulfstan rewrote the *Canons* specifically for the secular clergy in the northern diocese and produced what is called the *Laws of the Northumbrian Priests* (ed. Liebermann): Canon 41 conflates the *Canons of Edgar*, 58 and 59, and prescribes a penalty for the priest who lives in a drunken manner or becomes an entertainer or an ale-poet: "Gif preost oferdruncen lufige oððe gliman oððe ealascop wurðe, gebete þæt."

Now it is not at all clear what an ealascop is. I shall discuss the Old English words for poets in a later chapter, and one of these is *scop*. Presumably an ealascop was a poet who performed while others drank ale, though we do not know if he performed in alehouses or during private banquets. It is clear, however, that Wulfstan considered the kind of performer so designated to be an entertainer, for he links him in the *Canons* to the person who entertains, and in the *Laws* to drunkards and gleemen. The verb *gliwigan* of the *Canons* and the noun *gliman* of the *Laws* share the same root, *gliw*, whose meaning we shall have occasion to discuss later; for the moment it is sufficient to note its use in the context of joy and entertainment, especially musical. Wulfstan himself offers a good example of this usage in one of his homilies, where he associates harps, pipes, and various entertainments with the beer-hall: "Hearpe and pipe and mistlice gliggamen dremað eow on beorsele; and ge Godes cræfta nan ðing ne gymað" (Bethurum, 217). Clearly, Wulfstan exhorts priests not to become entertainers while others drink beer. This conclusion is confirmed by those passages which Fowler takes to have been possible sources of this canon:

Theodulf's *Capitula* XIII and *Canones Hibernenses* X suggest a context of licentious secular feasting and entertainment; Alfric's third Pastoral Letter says simply "Ne ge gligmenn ne beon" (Fowler, 38f.). It is apparent that such entertainers existed; that Wulfstan saw fit to prohibit priests from participation in such performances may indicate that the eleventh-century clergy were as fond of such amusements as were their seventh- and eighth-century predecessors.

Our last set of evidence from Anglo-Saxon England centres upon Cnut. As we have seen, there is no doubt at all that Cnut enjoyed the services of many skalds, and numerous Norse poems praising or at least referring to him are extant. It is quite likely that this king of England's reputation was perpetuated in English eulogies, though none has survived. There is, however, in the twelfth-century *Historia Eliensis* (cf. C. E. Wright, appendix 5) the story of Cnut approaching Ely in a boat and hearing the monks singing the divine office.

> He exhorted the others in their boats to gather round him and to sing in jubilation with him [secum jubilando canere]; he himself, expressing with his own lips the pleasure in his heart, composed a ballad in English in these words [cantilenam his verbis Anglice composuit], the beginning of which is
>
> > Merie sungen ðe Muneches binnen Ely.
> > ða Cnut ching reu ðer by.
> > Rowe cnites noer the land.
> > And here we þes Muneches sæng.
>
> which in Latin means "Sweetly sang the monks in Ely as Cnut the king rowed nearby; now men row nearer the shore and let us all hear the singing of the monks," and the other words which follow, which to this day are sung publicly in chorus and remembered in old sayings [quae usque hodie in choris publice cantantur et in proverbiis memorantur]. [*Hist. El.* II, 85]

The source is late, but there is no reason to disbelieve that the Danish Cnut could improvise a song on the inspiration of the moment. The four lines that are recorded are not in the recognizable form of Old English poetry, so perhaps it is best to consider this a sung ballad improvised by Cnut (with no instrumental accompaniment), a song that entered tradition and was still sung by groups of twelfth-century Englishmen or quoted in anecdotes about Cnut.

That such cantilenae existed in the twelfth century is attested especially in the writings of William of Malmesbury. We have seen that he appended to his account of Athelstan's reign the less reliable information derived from cantilenis. He also mentions that Edgar's reputation is impugned in ballads ("in-famias . . . magis resperserunt cantilenæ," II, 148), and of Cnut's daughter's marriage to the German emperor Henry he says that the splendour of the cere-monies is still sung about in the streets in ballads ("nostro adhuc seculo etiam in triviis cantitata," II, 188). C. E. Wright believed that these ballads were not composed at the time of the events described in them, but that oral legends circulated which formed the basis of later ballads. That may well be; but there is no reason why such ballads should not have been composed from the time of Athelstan on, for they could easily have formed part of the repertoire of wander-ing minstrels. It is clear that harpers existed in Anglo-Saxon England, but we know nothing of the form of their songs: the ballads may have been identical to the poetry in form, or they may have been looser metrically, like Cnut's song about the monks in Ely.

This concludes our chronological survey of references to the oral poetry of Anglo-Saxon England, but it does not conclude our study of the Anglo-Saxon traditions of oral poetry. We have yet to weigh the evidence of the undated poetry, and then finally to consider the Old English words for poets and poetry.

8

The Evidence of the Poetry

This chapter will deal with the testimony of the extant undated poetry concerning oral poetry in Anglo-Saxon England; references in the poetry to poets or poetic activity will be considered here, as distinct from the usage of words relating to poets or poetry, which is the subject of the following chapter. We have seen from the evidence cited in the preceding chapters that a tradition of popular eulogistic poetry could have existed throughout the Anglo-Saxon period, and that poetry is likely to have been employed for wisdom literature and lore of various kinds. Two dominating figures emerge from the throng, however: the tribal poet, a vatic soothsayer originally ritually related to a sacral king, whose tradition weakens and probably atrophies during the eighth and ninth centuries, but might have enjoyed a late revival as a result of the activity of the Scandinavian skalds; and the (wandering) harper, whose function is entertainment, who is a popular figure in monasteries and market places, and who, when associated with the scurrilous itinerant jugglers and actors, merits the consistent censure of the clerical hierarchy. It has been suggested that these two latter figures were originally distinct, though some merging of the traditions might have taken place during the eighth and ninth centuries, when the tribal poet's status declined.

The distinction between tribal poet and harper was manifested in function and performance: the poet eulogised contemporary personages whereas the harper entertained audiences professionally; the poet performed solo without accompaniment whereas the harper sang to the accompaniment (whether occasional or continuous) of his instrument. The harper may have purveyed songs dealing with contemporary personages, but his songs would probably have been explicitly narrative and could be appreciated by all his diverse audiences;

the poet would tend to produce elliptical, allusive eulogies susceptible of immediate interpretation by an audience that was familiar with the events and personalities referred to. Thus the poet and his audience shared a community of experience, which was not necessarily true of the relation between the professional itinerant entertainer and his audience. All the evidence so far presented would tend to support such a dichotomy; the evidence in the following chapter will serve to confirm it still further. In the present chapter I shall assume as a working hypothesis what will become evident from the following chapter, namely, that the eulogising poet was called a *scop* and the (wandering) entertainer was a *gleoman* (*gliwman*, *gligman*), the scop being the creator and the gleoman the glee-man. First we shall consider *Beowulf*, *Widsith*, and *Deor*, perhaps the most frequently cited sources of evidence on Anglo-Saxon oral poetry, and then we shall pass on to consider the evidence presented by the other extant poetry. At all times we must bear in mind the constraints on the admissibility of the extant poetry as evidence concerning poetry as set out in the first chapter of this study.

Beowulf, of course, is about Scandinavians: can one accept the evidence it presents as an accurate representation of Anglo-Saxon practices? It is clearly historical in that the Christian author is describing pagan personalities: to what extent did the poet artificially reconstruct a setting he thought to be in harmony with the age in which his heroes lived? Did the poet actually witness a ship burial or a funeral like Beowulf's? If not, did he derive his information from hearsay or from a venerable oral poetic tradition or from written sources? Problems like these necessarily underlie any attempt to solicit information from *Beowulf* about Anglo-Saxon behaviour (see Girvan: 1971). The questions cannot be answered with assurance. One cannot ignore them; on the other hand, one has no alternative but to ignore them and to approach the text as if they did not exist, to examine the poem on the assumption that its evidence is somehow relevant to Anglo-Saxon society. I shall in fact discuss those passages that refer to poets and poetry on the (assumed) understanding that they refer to practices current among the Anglo-Saxons or their continental ancestors at some time or another. The poet was an Anglo-Saxon, and presumably his audience (whether auditors or readers) would not tolerate the irresponsible ascription to Germanic peoples of outlandish customs even though the heroes were not themselves Anglo-Saxon. If we work on the assumption that the customs described are Anglo-Saxon, we should nonetheless remember that this is only a convenient assumption.

We are on safer ground when we accept that *Beowulf* is a literary creation, a poem exhibiting the creative sensibility of an artist. One may assume that the author wrote what he wrote by the conscious exercise of his creative powers rather than by the passive acquiescence to a binding tradition that presented to him all the materials in his composition; that he was, in other words, more poet than transmitter or collater. That he worked within a tradition is not open to doubt; it is likely, however, that he was master rather than slave of that tradition (see, for example, Bonjour; Brodeur). We shall have to allow for the poet's creative judgement when we consider his references to what might be poetic activity: on four occasions he describes such activity in the Danish king's hall, and these passages bear striking similarities to each other, similarities that set them clearly apart from the references to what might be poetic activity in the community outside the hall (see Opland: 1976). Let us first examine the depictions of poetry or song in Heorot.

The first reference to a poet occurs in a generalised description of the joy in the hall that aroused Grendel's enmity. The powerful spirit suffered in the darkness because each day he heard the loud sounds of joy in the hall: there was the music of the harp, the clear performance of the scop. The man who knew how to narrate the origin of men long ago spoke, he said that the Almighty created the earth:

> Ða se ellengæst   earfoðlice
> þrage geþolode,   se þe in þystrum bad,
> þæt he dogora gehwam   dream gehyrde
> hludne in healle;   þær wæs hearpan sweg,
> swutol sang scopes.   Sægde se þe cuþe
> frumsceaft fira   feorran reccan,
> cwæð þæt se ælmihtiga   eorðan worh[te] . . .
>
> [*ASPR*, IV, 86–92]

After the account of the creation, the *Beowulf* poet returns to the company. In this way, he says, the retainers lived happily in joy until a hellish fiend began to perpetrate sin:

> Swa ða drihtguman   dreamum lifdon
> eadiglice, oððæt an ongan
> fyrene fre[m]man   feond on helle.
>
> [99–101]

Clearly the poet is attempting to sketch briefly the pristine state of happiness that existed in Heorot before Grendel's first onslaught (parallel to that pristine

state of creation before the onslaught of sin). It is usually assumed that lines
89–91 introduce a summary of a poem on the creation produced by the scop to
the accompaniment of his harp. The Old English poetic technique of variation
being what it is, this is certainly a justifiable reading. However, it is also possible that not one but three activities are referred to here: the playing of the
harp, the performance of the scop, and the narrative of the creation by someone
who knew how to tell this story. Considered from this point of view, the passage reminds one of Lars Lönnroth's summary of Norna-Gest's performance on
Christmas in the hall of Olaf Tryggvason:

> Norna-Gest entertained them by first playing his harp and then telling
> various stories about Sigurd the Volsung and other heroes he had met. He
> also showed some heroic relics that he carried with him; the golden ring of
> the Volsungs and a strand from the tail of Sigurd's horse, Grani. Episodes
> from the Volsung legend are included in the *þáttr* as told by Norna-Gest
> himself. At various points in the prose narrative, Norna-Gest lets his char-
> acters speak in verses, which are in fact verbatim quotations from two well
> known dialogue poems in the Edda, *Reginsmál* ("The Sayings of Regin")
> and *Helreið Brynhildar* ("Brynhild's Ride to Hel"). [Lönnroth, 4]

As we have seen, Lönnroth proceeds to compare this Scandinavian performance
with Anglo-Saxon practices, taking the *Beowulf* poet's descriptions of entertainment in Heorot as the norm:

> As a performer, Norna-Gest is related to the scop of West-Germanic tradi-
> tion. The scop's singing of epic tales to the harp, however, seems to have
> been divided here into three separate arts: harp-playing, story-telling in
> prose, and poetic recitation. There are many indications that harp-playing
> was known in mediaeval Scandinavia, . . . but it is never known to ac-
> company the recitation as in the hall of Heorot. [5]

One might well argue from the passage in *Beowulf* that in fact Norna-Gest's
threefold performance *is* paralleled in Heorot: there is a harper, a scop (who
does not sing epic tales to the harp) and someone who tells (in prose) the story
of the creation. The line from the poem William of Malmesbury cites on
Athelstan's coronation, "Ille strepit cithara, decertat plausibus iste," clearly
refers to two separate performers; "þær wæs hearpan sweg, swutol sang scopes"
might also refer to two separate performances.

The second reference to a scop in *Beowulf* occurs after the Geats arrive and
settle down to their places at the feast in Heorot. A thane went about his duty

carrying a decorated ale-cup and pouring the bright drink. From time to time a scop performed clearly in Heorot; there was the joy of warriors, no small band of Geats and Danes:

>   Scop hwilum sang
> hador on Heorote.   Þær wæs hæleða dream,
> duguð unlytel   Dena and Wedera.

[496–98]

This passage reveals little about the scop or his performance; it may or may not be relevant that this time there is no mention of a harp. It may be that as a resident Danish scop he was kept busy singing the praises of the newly arrived heroic strangers, that the Geats provided him with the opportunity of performing eulogies in their honour, but this is mere inference. There are, however, some interesting similarities with the preceding passage: both describe the performance of the scop as clearly audible (*swutol*, 90; *hador*, 497). This may indicate that all activity ceased while the scop performed, that his utterances were not merely background entertainment. Both passages clearly are intended to suggest joy in the hall: both contain the key word *dream* (88 and 497), both use the same formula *þær wæs* ¹ × ¹ ("þær wæs hearpan sweg," 89; "Þær wæs hæleða dream," 497). This last element springs to mind again when we read, after the tense taunting of Beowulf by Unferth, that there was (once again) the laughter of warriors, the noise resounded, the words were joyous; Wealhtheow comes forward with the ale-cup and serves Hrothgar and Beowulf:

> Ðær wæs hæleþa hleahtor,   hlyn swynsode,
> word wæron wynsume . . .

[611–12]

If we put together these three passages, clearly intended to suggest the joy in Heorot, we note apart from the *þær wæs* formula common to all three, the presence of noise, joy, or laughter and the sound of voices (whether of warriors, harper, scop, or story-teller); in the last two passages the pouring of drink is also mentioned. To a remarkable degree, these elements are also present in the anonymous Latin poet's description of Athelstan's coronation festivities quoted by William of Malmesbury; they are present, too, in the third depiction of poetry or song in Heorot.

After Beowulf has defeated Grendel, a celebration is held in Heorot, during which Hrothgar presents gifts to Beowulf and his companions. There were performance and music both together before Hrothgar, the joy-wood was touched, a gid was often uttered, when Hrothgar's scop along the meadbench had to speak hall-joy about the followers of Finn when the sudden attack fell on them. The poet then summarises what is known as the Finn episode, an elliptical account of the Fight at Finnsburh, and then returns to the scene in Heorot: the leoð, the gleoman's gyd, was finished, joy sprang up again, the bench-noise resounded, cup-bearers poured wine from wondrous vessels:

> Þær wæs sang ond sweg   samod ætgædere
> fore Healfdenes   hildewisan,
> gomenwudu greted,   gid oft wrecen,
> ðonne healgamen   Hroþgares scop
> æfter medobence   mænan scolde
> be Finnes eaferum,   ða hie se fær begeat . . .
>   Leoð wæs asungen,
> gleomannes gyd.   Gamen eft astah,
> beorhtode bencsweg;   byrelas sealdon
> win of wunderfatum.
>
>   [1063–68, 1159–62]

My summary of lines 1063–68 is stilted and awkward, in part because various meanings can be elicited from the passage, depending on the meanings assigned to words like *sang, sweg,* and *gid.* Before we discuss the interpretation, it should be noted that the poet's introduction of the Finn episode has always been held to be awkward: Klaeber, for example, says, "Scholars are not at all agreed on the punctuation and construction of these lines [1066–70]." Line 1063 says that there was *sang* and *sweg* together. Since line 89 associated *sweg* with the harp and line 90 associated *sang* with the scop, line 1063 might be taken to mean that harper and scop were one and that the sang and sweg were simultaneous, or that harper and scop were separate individuals but that here they performed a duet, or that harper and scop were separate and they performed separately but at the same point in the proceedings. The latter would not entail a forced reading of "samod ætgædere": harper and poet vie one against the other at Athelstan's coronation feast, and one could say that there were both harping and poetry together before Athelstan. *Gomenwudu* (1065) as a kenning for a harp occurs only in *Beowulf,* here and in line 2108. *Gid* (1065) is a loose term: Donald K. Fry, in his recent edition of the Finn fragment and episode, glosses *gid* in Old English (not just in the passages he edits) as "song, poem, tale, formal speech, saying, riddle. . . . Generally applied to oral, traditional knowledge" (65). In other words, it could be applied to the performance of a harper, a poet, or a story-teller. The word occurs ten times in *Beowulf*. On five occasions (151, 868, 1065, 1160, 2105) it could conceivably mean either song, poem, or tale; twice it could mean either song or poem (1118, 2108); once it is a variation of the noun *sang* (2446); and twice it clearly can mean only tale (when Hrothgar tells Beowulf about Heremod, 1723, and when Beowulf reports to Hygelac, 2154).

Most editors have a comma at the end of 1065, making the introduction of the Finn episode dependent on the preceding three lines, in other words, making the Finn episode an example of the harp-singing in the presence of Hrothgar. It is possible, however, as I suggested in chapter 1, that line 1065 could end with a full stop, making 1066–70, the introduction of the Finn episode, independent of the preceding lines and in fact solving some syntactic as well as musicological problems. Taken as a unit on its own, lines 1063–65 could serve as a signal to the audience that the poet is describing joy in the hall: as in the previous passages we have quoted, there is the *þær wæs* formula (1063), there is joy (*gomen* here, rather than *dream*) and there is *sang*; as in line 89, there is a harp and *sweg*. While all this joy was current, *then* (1066) the scop had to utter hall-joy about the followers of Finn ("healgamen . . . mænan scolde be Finnes eaferum"). I take this to mean that, as part of the entertainment, the scop was requested to narrate the story of how Finn and his men were caught in a surprise attack when it was his fate to fall in Frisia; 1066–70 is then the request, and at 1071 the poet begins his summary of the scop's performance, which is produced solo, free of harp accompaniment. It is not normally his function to narrate stories, but he has the ability to do so, since the eulogistic form can be turned to explicit narrative; Hrothgar's scop, a eulogiser, can produce a narrative on demand, just as Cædmon complied with the request to produce narratives. Reference to Finn and his exploits might be made in the course of his day-to-day performance of eulogies, but perhaps in honour of the Geats, Hrothgar asks his scop to turn his talents to the story of Finn (Beowulf's recent defence of Heorot against Grendel suggesting Finn's defence of the Frisian hall). The episode as summarised is elliptical and allusive: the audience would know the story, and in any event, this is just how a eulogiser would handle the story within his tradition.

This is admittedly leaning rather heavily on the evidence: it must be readily conceded that the text would certainly support the generally accepted reading that the scop played a harp to accompany his narrative song about Finn. This last would seem to be indicated by the poet's statement at the conclusion of the Finn episode, that the leoð had been performed, the gleoman's gyd. Clearly, "gleomannes gyd" (1160) is a variation of "leoð" (1159), that is the Finn episode, and is therefore likely to be the "gid" of 1065, which in turn seems to make "gid oft wrecen" and "gomenwudu greted" concurrent activities. If this is admitted, then it is likely that the gleoman of 1160 is "Hroþgares scop" (1066). Of course, this must be conceded as a possibility, even a strong possibility, but one should note that the weight of external evidence tells against it. Our hypothetical reconstruction of the oral tradition in the preceding chapters would have the vatic scop distinct from the entertaining gleoman; that working hypothesis, however, draws concrete support from the evidence presented in the following chapter. With only two exceptions (both glosses, to be discussed in the next chapter), it is only here in this passage in *Beowulf* that the scop and the gleoman seem to be identified; there is no other reference to singing or poetry in Anglo-Saxon England that compels us to equate the two.

Such a consideration leads us to seek an explanation of the usage in *Beowulf* that would free the scop from identification with the gleoman. As we saw in the fifth chapter, it is likely that the tradition of the scop underwent a radical alteration as a result of the development of a Christian theology of kingship and of a monastic ideal among the royal families in the seventh century. By the eighth century, therefore, the scop who wished to continue as a public performer may have tended to fall together with the wandering entertainer, producing narrative poems or songs for entertainment. We have no agreement among scholars about the date of *Beowulf* (see John, 389–93); perhaps it was composed in the eighth century or later by a poet who was not sensitive to the distinction I am making between scop and gleoman because both were entertainers at the time he wrote, though he may have known that the scop was originally a tribal poet associated with a chief or king (he is referred to as "Hroþgar's scop"). Another argument might well be that the *Beowulf* poet does not exactly equate scop and gleoman, although he does equate the scop's performance of the Finn episode and a gleomannes gyd: if for the sake of entertainment in the hall ("healgamen") Hroþgar requested his scop to narrate the story of Finn, something he would not normally do, the scop may well have acceded to his king's request and in so doing produced a performance typical of an entertainer, a gleoman.

As a third explanation of the apparent identification of scop and gleoman in this passage—and this seems to me the most convincing—we should recall that the author was a poet, that he was creating poetry not social history. We have already seen that his descriptions of joy in the hall share verbal echoes: it may be that as a poet he wished to establish in the minds of his audience an association between the *þær wæs* formula, and words like *dream, gamen, gid, sang,* and *sweg* indicative of noise, laughter, and the sound of voices, so that any future collocation of these elements would evoke these earlier scenes describing joy in the hall. In lines 2105 to 2119, for example, a passage shortly to be discussed, one finds once again the formula *Þær wæs gid and gleo* (2105) and a collocation of the words *gid* and *gleo* (2105), *hearpan* and *wynne* (2107), *gomenwudu* and *gyd* (2108).

After Beowulf has returned to Geatland, the harp is mentioned three times in the poem; in each passage there is a formula indicating the absence of joy, music, or a harp metrically equivalent to the *þær wæs* formula indicating their presence in the earlier passages, and there is a collocation of at least three of the verbal elements connotative of joy in the hall. In the lament of the last survivor, he bemoans the absence of the sources of aristocratic joy, a fast horse, a good hawk, and the happiness of the harp, the entertainment of the joy-wood: "Næs *hearpan wyn, gomen gleo*beames" (2262f.). When Beowulf reflects before his fight with the dragon, he talks of the desolate mood of the old man surveying his executed son's deserted home. There is no sound of the harp, joy in the dwellings, as there once was: "Nis *þær hearpan sweg, gomen* in geardum, swylce ðær iu wæron" (2458f.). Finally, in a highly evocative passage that draws in exile formulas (see Greenfield: 1955) and references to funeral pyres and to the beasts of battle (all heavily connotative of sadness, loss, or disaster), the Geatish woman is threatened by slavery now that Beowulf has laid aside laughter, happiness, and joy-mirth; accordingly, many a spear will be brandished, clasped with fingers, cold in the morning, the sound of the harp will not waken the warriors, but the dark raven will tell the eagle how he and the wolf fed themselves on the slain corpses:

> Þa sceall brond fretan
> æled þeccean,   nalles eorl wegan
> maððum to gemyndum,   ne mæg scyne
> habban on healse   hringweorðunge,
> ac sceal geomormod,   golde bereafod,
> oft nalles æne   elland tredan,
> nu se herewisa   hleahtor alegde,
> *gamen* ond *gleodream*.   Forðon sceall gar wesan
> monig, morgenceald,   mundum bewunden,
> hæfen on handa,   nalles *hearpan sweg*
> wigend weccean,   ac se wonna hrefn
> fus ofer fægum   fela reordian,
> earne secgan   hu him æt æte speow,
> þenden he wið wulf   wæl reafode.
>
> [3014–27; italics mine]

This passage is one of the highlights of the whole poem, a superb evocation of imminent disaster and destruction and the loss occasioned by Beowulf's death (see Bonjour: 1957). The effect is contributed to by the poet's reference to the absence of those elements that he has established as connotative of joy, *gamen*, *gleo*, *dream*, *hearpe*, and *sweg*. Line 3021a tautologically packs into one half-line three synonyms for joy which the hero has laid aside; since *gleodream* is a hapax legomenon, one is led to conclude that the poet coined the compound because each of its elements connoted the scene of joy in the hall that he had established earlier in the poem: *gamen* occurs in lines 1066, 1160, 2108 and is said to be absent in 2263 and 2459; *gleo* occurs in 1160 and 2105 and is said to be absent in 2263; and *dream* occurs in 88, 99, and 497.

If it is true, as I suggest, that the poet is evoking a connotation of joy through the concatenation of verbal elements he has established earlier in the poem as associated with joy in the hall, and that *gamen*, *gleo*, and *dream*, each meaning joy and each occurring not less than three times in the passages we have discussed, are key words in this artistic play, then we may have an explanation of the apparent identification of scop and gleoman in the frame of the Finn episode. The word *gleoman* appears once only in the poem, in line 1160, where it carries alliteration: it may be that the use of *gleoman* in 1160 was dictated more by a desire to introduce the suggestive element *gleo* into a scene describing joy in the hall (as in 2105, 2263, and 3021) than by a respect for sociological veracity.

In sum, then, although it is reasonable to accept that for the *Beowulf* poet a scop was also a gleoman, this identification of the two figures is not unequivocally supported by other references to the scop in the poem, and the identification can be assailed with literary arguments drawn from a consideration of the use of *gleo* in the poem as a whole.

In three passages, then, the poet describes the joy in Heorot (see Hume). When Beowulf returns to Geatland he reports back to Hygelac, and his account of his adventures includes a reference to the scene in Heorot after his conquest of Grendel, in other words, the same scene that the poet himself had earlier described. In Beowulf's version, there is no reference to the Finn episode nor to a scop. The meaning of the passage is more obscure than many commentators are prepared to allow. Dobbie prints it as follows:

> Þær wæs gidd ond gleo.   Gomela Scilding,
> felafricgende,   feorran rehte;
> hwilum hildedeor   hearpan wynne,
> gomenwudu grette,   hwilum gyd awræc
> soð ond sarlic,   hwilum syllic spell

rehte æfter rihte   rumheort cyning.
Hwilum eft ongan,   eldo gebunden,
gomel guðwiga   gioguðe cwiðan,
hildestrengo;   hreðer [in]ne weoll,
þonne he wintrum frod   worn gemunde.
Swa we þær inne   ondlangne dæg
niode naman,   oððæt niht becwom
oðer to yldum.

[*ASPR*, IV, 2105–17]

Dobbie's note on this passage is fuller than that of most editors. His punctuation implies that "gomela Scilding" (2105) is the same as "rumheort cyning" (2110), Hrothgar, who plays a harp, since 2105 to 2110 is one sentence (in fact, his note allows that "gomela Scilding" may even be the scop of 1066, and that both he and Hrothgar may perform to the accompaniment of a harp). The "gomel guðwiga" of 2112 belongs to a sentence running from 2111 to 2114, and one may infer that he is not the same person as the "gomela Scilding" (the note allows that the "gomel guðwiga" is not Hrothgar, though he may be the same person as the "gomela Scilding"). Klaeber has 2105 to 2114 as one sentence, suggesting that all the actions describe the same activity. Thus Klaeber's punctuation would suggest that Hrothgar plays the harp to accompany his meditations on old age (Klaeber cites the precedent of King Gelimer of the Vandals) and that all this is "gidd ond gleo," whereas Dobbie's punctuation has Hrothgar at times playing the harp and singing while at other times an old warrior speaks about his youth ("gioguðe cwiðan"). A comparison of two recent translations demonstrates how obscure the passage really is. Talbot Donaldson, working from Klaeber's edition, translates as follows:

> There was song and mirth. The old Scylding, who has learned many things, spoke of times far-off. At times a brave one in battle touched the glad wood, the harp's joy; at times he told tales, true and sad; at times he related strange stories according to right custom; at times, again, the great-hearted king, bound with age, the old warrior, would begin to speak of his youth, his battle-strength. His heart welled within when, old and wise, he thought of his many winters. Thus we took pleasure there the livelong day until another night came to men.

Burton Raffel, working basically with Klaeber's edition but consulting also Dobbie and Wrenn, produces a freer translation in poetry:

There were songs, and the telling of tales. One ancient
Dane told of long-dead times,
And sometimes Hrothgar himself, with the harp
In his lap, stroked its silvery strings
And told wonderful stories, a brave king
Reciting unhappy truths about good
And evil—and sometimes he wove his stories
On the mournful thread of old age, remembering
Buried strength and the battles it had won.
He would weep, the old king, wise with many
Winters, remembering what he'd done, once,
What he'd seen, what he knew. And so we sat
The day away, feasting. Then darkness
Fell again . . .

According to Donaldson's reading, Hrothgar is the "gomela Scilding" of 2105, but he is not the "hildedeor" of 2107, a man who plays the harp. Hrothgar is the "rumheort cyning" and the "gomel guðwiga," but he neither harps nor sings, he merely speaks of his youth and reflects on it. Raffel differentiates Hrothgar from the "gomela Scilding," though it is Hrothgar who plays the harp while he improvises autobiographical narratives. On the evidence of this passage, could or would a king play a harp, is the performance improvised or memorised, is it poetry (unaccompanied by a harp) or song (accompanied)? The passage does not furnish unambiguous replies to any of these questions. Since it is open to varying interpretations, one cannot cull from this passage primary evidence of poetic activity in Anglo-Saxon England. Clearly a harp is played in Heorot, but we cannot say from this passage whether it was played by the same person who meditated on old age, or whether it accompanied those reflections, or even whether the "syllic spell" was "soð ond sarlic," or whether it was about the "gomel guðwiga's" youth, or even whether it was produced in prose or verse. The poetic medium here does not lend itself to the deduction of incontrovertible sociological evidence.

The passages in *Beowulf* discussed above contain the only references in the poem to a harp, a scop, or a gleoman, but they are not the only references in the poem to what might be considered poetic activity: the descriptions of the warriors' return from the lake after the defeat of Grendel, and of Beowulf's funeral are still to be examined. But the descriptions of poetic activity in these latter passages differ significantly from the descriptions in those passages we have already discussed. Inside Heorot the account of the creation, the Finn episode, and the ruminations on a past youth are didactic or entertaining or elegiac productions. They refer to the individual experience of one member of the community or to events that neither performer nor audience witnessed. The performers produce set pieces that are incidental to the occasion: they could presumably have produced other pieces for the edification or entertainment of the audience, or they could produce these same pieces on some other suitable occasion. The performances are tangential and do not refer to the situation that confronts the performer at the time. The poems (if such they are) in the hall seem to be designed primarily for entertainment, and as such form part of the set depictions of joy in the hall. The performances outside the hall are quite different from these in character and in function.

On the morning after Beowulf's fight with Grendel, the retainers ride out to the lake to view the signs of Grendel's defeat. Old and young retainers ride joyfully back from the lake on their horses (853–56). Lines 916–18 mention that at times they raced their horses across the sandy ways, by which time much of the morning had passed. It is reasonable to assume, therefore, that the section of the poem between these two passages (856–915) refers to incidents that took place while the warriors were returning from the lake on horseback. "Ðær wæs Beowulfes mærðo mæned" (856f.), there, while the retainers were returning on horseback, Beowulf's deed was discussed; many often said ("monig oft gecwæð") that there was no finer warrior alive, no one more worthy to be a king (857–61), though in so doing they were not disparaging their own king Hrothgar (862f.). (This is a realistic depiction of the conversation Danish warriors might hold in the circumstances.) At times, on level stretches, the warriors raced their horses (864–67); at other times (that is, when they were not racing) a thane of the king found new words to depict Beowulf's exploit; he mentioned every famous deed of Sigemund that he had heard of, and referred to Heremod as well:

> Hwilum cyninges þegn,
> guma gilphlæden,   gidda gemyndig,
> se ðe ealfela   ealdgesegena
> worn gemunde,   word oþer fand
> soðe gebunden;   secg eft ongan
> sið Beowulfes   snyttrum sytrian
> ond on sped wrecan   spel gerade,
> wordum wrixlan.   Welhwylc gecwæð

þæt he fram Sigemundes   secgan hyrde
ellendædum,   uncuþes fela,
Wælsinges gewin,   wide siðas, . . .

[867–77]

Now this is a famous crux, and has been commented on by many scholars interested in early English poetry, but let us note immediately that the poet does
not tell us that the performer is a scop (though he could have had *scop* for *þegn*
in 867, since the line alliterates on *c*), and there is no mention of a harp. If, however, the *cyninges þegn* of 867 is *Hroþgares scop* of 1066, then it is clear that on
occasion he performed without musical accompaniment. All the passage tells
us explicitly, however, is that he is a retainer of the king, a man distinguished
for his knowledge of *ealdgesegena*, a man mindful of many a *gyd*, a man
gilphlæden.

Ealdgesegena would seem to be ancient legends like those of Sigemund and
Heremod; *gyd* in *Beowulf* could mean "song," "poem," or "prose tale."
Gilphlæden is more problematical: Klaeber glosses the word as "covered with
glory, proud," although he expounds the compound as "vaunt-laden" and
quotes Gummere's note, "a man . . . who could sing his *bēot*, or vaunt, in
good verse." It is clear that the three phrases *guma gilphlæden, gidda gemyndig*,
and *se ðe ealfela ealdgesegena worn gemunde* are variations of *cyninges þegn*, but it is
not clear exactly what *gilp-, gidda*, and *ealdgesegena* refer to. It is likely that
these are historical facts or narratives, but are they prose or poetry? Is the thane
merely a man knowledgeable of the history of his people, or is he a man who
has by heart a number of poems or songs treating that history? If Gummere's
suggestion is entertained, *gilphlæden* may mean that the thane knew many
traditional eulogies about various people, since the bēot or gilp could be simply
an autobiographical poem or the praises of ancestors that Germanic warriors
uttered on entry into battle.

Whatever the character of his information about past events, the poet says
that the thane found new words truly bound ("word oþer fand soðe gebunden").
This passage is as notorious a crux as that dealing with Hrothgar, a harp,
and reflections on an old man's youth, but in the case of the latter passage no
consensus has emerged from scholarly debate and none seems likely to in
view of the ambiguities of the poetic medium; in the interpretation of this
passage, however, there is a scholarly consensus. Though there are dissentients
(see, for example, Eliason: 1952), Dobbie expresses the generally accepted
interpretation thus: "The *cyninges þegn* 'found other words properly bound

together.' . . . . It is widely held that the word *oþer* here means 'new' and that this passage provides evidence for the improvisation of lays in Anglo-Saxon times" (159). It is clear that the "cyninges þegn" is a man knowledgeable of past events; whether or not he memorises these in poetic form, he stirs up again Beowulf's exploit and quickly creates an apt (or "ready" or "skilful," *gerade*) account, shuffling with words, making use of his knowledge of the careers of Sigemund and Heremod. Let us examine the content of this performance more carefully.

Many scholars wonder whether we are here dealing with one poem (about Beowulf, Sigemund,. and Heremod) or with three (one about each of the individuals); one scholar (Creed: 1966b) has even seen in the phrase *welhwylc gecwæþ* a statement of a new poetic principle which implies that the thane performed on horseback "a 'cyclic poem' or poems." There is no need at all to have any more than one poem here, certainly not a cycle of narratives about Sigemund (let alone Beowulf and Heremod). The problems arise from a desire to place the performance in a narrative tradition; the problems are resolved when we view this performance in the context of a eulogistic tradition, as indeed it seems reasonable to do from the discussion in the preceding chapters of this book. The thane is not entertaining his companions as they trot back from the lake, he is giving vent to his emotion in spontaneous poetry, and his emotion is occasioned by the particular social situation in which he finds himself. The poet has established the stimulus for the performance quite carefully. The party has travelled to the lake and viewed the scene. On their return the retainers discuss Beowulf's glory ("mærðo"), they assert that there is no better warrior alive anywhere on earth ("suð ne norð be sæm tweonum ofer eormengrund oþer nænig under swegles begong selre nære rondhæbbendra," 858 ff.), no one more worthy of being king ("rices wyrðra"). It is within this specific social context that the thane, drawing on his knowledge of ancient stories, performs. He utters a eulogy in praise of Beowulf. He skilfully rehearses his conquest of the monster; he refers to every famous deed of Sigemund that he has heard of, and he reviews the career of Heremod.

The poet tells us that the performance is generated by Beowulf's exploit: what are Sigemund or Heremod doing in it? I believe the thane does not explicitly narrate the adventures of Sigemund, he alludes to all the highlights of his career in a manner typical of eulogy, but, according to the poet's summary of the performance, he emphasises Sigemund's defeat of a dragon; he does not tell, the story of Heremod's career, he refers to it elliptically, stressing the promising start and the inglorious conclusion of his reign. The party of retainers have been discussing Beowulf's defeat of Grendel; they have asserted in particular that there is no finer warrior alive, nor anyone better fitted to be king. The thane produces a spontaneous poem about Beowulf that arises from this discussion: Beowulf's exploit is treated, his prowess is placed alongside that of another legendary monster-killer, and his potential as a king evokes the admonitory example of a promising young king who ultimately oppressed his own people. The performer here functions as chronicler and social commentator; there is nothing in his performance that is not typical of eulogistic poetry. Sigemund and Heremod serve as metaphors for Beowulf: his prowess is as great as Sigemund's, but he should beware of inviting a fate similar to Heremod's (see Kaske). In both cases the real referent is Beowulf: the "cyninges þegn" produces a spontaneous eulogy in praise of the young Geatish hero.

At the end of the poem the Geats place the dead Beowulf on a pyre, lamenting the hero, their dear lord ("hæleð hiofende, hlaford leofne," 3142). They kindle a fire to burn his body; sad in spirit they speak of their heart-pain, the death of this lord ("Higum unrote modceare mændon, mondryhtnes cw[e]alm," 3148 f.). These laments are reminiscent of the references to Germanic funeral ululations and laments in the classical histories discussed in the third chapter, but we have no way of knowing whether these expressions of grief were poetic or not. They may have been songs such as Ælfric enjoins priests to discourage. One such lament may well be referred to in the lines that follow, though the manuscript is defective at this point and the passage requires editorial reconstruction:

> swylce giomorgyd   [Ge]at[isc] meowle
> [. . . . . . .]   bundenheorde
> [so]ng sorgcearig   s[w]iðe geneahhe
> þæt hio hyre [heofun]g[da]gas   hearde ond[r]ede,
> wælfylla worn,   werudes egesan,
> hynðo ond h[æ]f[t]nyd.
>
> [3150–55]

One cannot derive much information from a text that rests so heavily on conjecture, but it seems clear that a woman is here uttering a lament that incorporates images of terror and destruction (see Mustanoja: 1967). We are not told whether or not the poem or song refers to Beowulf, though it is occasioned by his death and is produced at his funeral just as Hildeburh laments her brother and son at their funeral ("Ides gnornode, geomrode giddum," 1117 f.).

After the body has been burnt, the Geats spend ten days building a mound

high on a cliff in honour of Beowulf. The ashes are placed inside the wall they
have raised, together with the dragon's hoard, and all is covered with earth.
Then twelve sons of nobles tried in battle rode around the mound expressing
their sorrow and mentioning their king; they praised his nobility and passed
judgement on his glorious accomplishments; it is fitting for a man to honour his
lord with words in this way, to hold him in affection after his death. And so the
Geatish hearth-companions mourned the fall of their lord; they said that he
was the mildest and gentlest of kings, kindest to his subjects and most eager to
earn a good reputation:

> Þa ymb hlæw riodan   hildediore,
> æþelinga bearn,   ealra twelfe,
> woldon [ceare] cwiðan   ond kyning mænan,
> wordgyd wrecan   ond ymb w[er] sprecan;
> eahtodan eorlscipe   ond his ellenweorc
> duguðum demdon,   swa hit ged[efe] bið
> þæt mon his winedryhten   wordum herge,
> ferhðum freoge,   þonne he forð scile
> of lichaman   [læded] weorðan.
> Swa begnornodon   Geata leode
> hlafordes [hr]yre,   heorðgeneatas,
> cwædon þæt he wære   wyruldcyninga
> manna mildust   ond mon[ðw]ærust,
> leodum liðost   ond lofgeornost.

[3169–82]

As with the previous passage, it is not at all clear whether the activity referred
to here is to be considered as poetry or song or either; both the nobles and the
woman utter words unaccompanied by musical instruments. The verbs used,
song (3152), *cwiðan* and *mænan* (3171), *wrecan* and *sprecan* (3172), and *cwædon*
(3180), do occur in passages that are commonly accepted as referring to poetry
or song—as in the passage describing the king's thane (*wrecan*, 873, and *gecwæð*,
874), or the scop (*sang*, 496; *wrecan*, 1065; *mænan*, 1066)—so it is at least possible
that the activity is poetic. But the passage affords unusual evidence in that there
are twelve people involved: are they singing in chorus? The same problem
confronted us in our discussion of the funeral obsequies of Attila (see Klaeber:
1927; Schrader). The solution posed there applies here too: it seems most likely
that the twelve retainers are uttering individual eulogies in honour of Beowulf.
This is not seen as in any way unusual: on the contrary, the poet states that it is

fitting that a dead lord be praised in this way. The retainers refer to Beowulf's moral attributes and to his deeds; they assess (*demdon*, 3174) his career. Little violation is done to the text in interpreting their performances as eulogies, expressions of the same tradition within which the king's thane worked. Like him, the twelve retainers could be uttering spontaneous poems, and if this is conceded, it should be noted that they are none of them scops. Clearly poetry was not the exclusive preserve of a specialised class: all levels of society participated in the tradition, and, as among the Scandinavians, it seems as though it was not unusual for an Englishman (or woman) to produce spontaneous poetry on the inspiration of the moment.

In *Beowulf* the harp is not heard outside Heorot; yet, as we have seen, at least two activities (that of the thane and those of the retainers) may well be considered poetic. The descriptions of the performances inside the hall are conventional and stylised; the descriptions of the performances outside the hall are more convincing depictions of social practices. Outside the hall the laments are occasioned by the death of Beowulf (or Hnæf), the thane's poem is a celebration of Beowulf's victory: each of the performances outside Heorot is in response or refers to an event that has taken place within the community, an event that both performer and audience witnessed or participated in. These performances, in other words, are socially integrated and relevant to the situation confronting the performer at the moment of performance. If they can be accepted as descriptions of Anglo-Saxon practices, they can be taken as further confirmation of the existence of a tradition of eulogistic poetry among the Anglo-Saxons, a tradition in which all Anglo-Saxons potentially participated. Such a tradition, bearing strong similarities to what we know of the medieval Scandinavian traditions, has formed one of the working hypotheses of the preceding chapters.

When we turn to *Widsith*, we are confronted with even graver restraints on the acceptance of the evidence than *Beowulf* was subject to. Not only are we dealing with the problems of poetic technique and diction but also with a most unusual kind of poetry; perhaps we are dealing with a song. Did the author of *Widsith* as we have it set three mnemonic lists in an autobiographical framework? What are we to make of the patent absurdity of the autobiographical claims? There is nothing else quite like *Widsith* in the Old English corpus, but there are a number of analogues in Old Norse and Celtic literature, and the most convincing explanation of *Widsith*'s form is one that seeks to understand it by comparison with its analogues; as Margaret Schlauch puts it, "The Celtic and Oriental parallels to *Wīdsīð* form an enlightening general background to the study of the poem; the Scandinavian parallels, which are closer and perhaps directly connected with it, are indispensable for an understanding of it" (Schlauch: 1931, 986 f.).

These analogues, one of the most important of which is *Norna-gests þáttr*, serve to establish "the figure of a Far-Wanderer who recounts the events of an impossibly long life for the entertainment of his auditors" (977). In the Norse analogues, the longevity of the speaker is attributable to the action of magic or divine power; in some the speaker is Oðinn himself. The analogues present striking parallels to the three lists that form much of the substance of *Widsith*; it must have been relatively easy for an author who was familiar with the Far-Wanderer productions to attribute the speaker's knowledge of so many people to his wanderings in the role of professional entertainer. There can be no doubt that the autobiographical sections of *Widsith* are a fiction and intended to be patently so. We are not concerned with the *þular* so much as with the pseudo-autobiographical framework, and we can consider the evidence that the framework provides on the reasonable assumption that the speaker is a member of a profession familiar to the author and his audience.

We have so far considered two major figures in the Anglo-Saxon oral poetic tradition, a tribal poet associated with a sacral ruler (scop) and a wandering professional minstrel purveying entertainment (gleoman). It should be acknowledged at the start of our discussion of *Widsith* that the word *scop* does not occur anywhere in the poem; in fact, Widsith seems to be identified as one of the "gleomen gumena," the entertainers of men, who go wandering through many lands ("scriþende . . . geond grunda fela," 135 f.). We are justified in believing that we are dealing here with a wandering minstrel travelling from place to place in search of a livelihood and not with a vatic poet who serves one lord and one community; yet many of the functions Widsith assigns to his performances seem more characteristic of the eulogiser than of the entertainer. Let us consider those passages that refer to Widsith's profession.

He is introduced as the person who has visited most nations on earth; he often received handsome treasure in a hall ("oft he on flette geþah mynelicne maþþum," 3 f.). Presumably, the treasure he received was payment for his performances, and such performances were produced in a hall. Widsith travels from court to court earning money: his audiences are aristocratic. We are not told of any performances in the marketplace, but it is perhaps reasonable to assume that Widsith could expect the royal personages he visited to be in a position to offer him the most substantial rewards. Widsith speaks, and supplies a list of rulers and their subjects, commenting in particular on Offa of Angle. And so, he says, he travelled through many countries, separated from his relatives, performing a service far and wide ("folgade wide," 53). For this reason (as a result of his experiences) he is in a position to perform and provide an account before a company in a mead-hall of how the highborn people were generous in their gifts to him:

> Forþon ic mæg singan   ond secgan spell,
> mænan fore mengo   in meoduhealle
> hu me cynegode   cystum dohten.
>
> [*ASPR*, III, 54–56]

This passage confirms his custom of performing to aristocratic audiences in their halls. The verb *singan* was used in *Beowulf* of the scop's performances, but it is of such general application that one cannot insist on a translation "sing" here; the combination *singan and secgan* may suggest that Widsith's performance consisted of both melody and words, or it may describe an activity somewhere between singing and speaking, chanting perhaps, or it may not be significant of anything specific at all, since *singan and secgan* is a fairly common formula (see L. F. Anderson, 39). Widsith then lists the nations he has visited, and mentions that he received an armlet from the Burgundians, and from Guthhere a pleasing treasure as payment for his performance: he was no selfish king ("me þær Guðhere forgeaf glædlicne maþþum songes to leane. Næs þæt sæne cyning!"66 f.). (Norna-Gest went one better, and actually produced for examination the armlet he received from Sigurð.) He was with Eormanric all the time (*ealle þrage*, 88). The Gothic king treated him well, giving him a solid gold armlet, which Widsith gave on his return home to his own lord Eadgils as payment (*leane*, 95) because Eadgils gave Widsith's father's plot of land to Widsith ("þæs þe he me lond forgeaf, mines fæder eþel," 95 f.). We are not told that Eadgils gives Widsith the land for his services as a minstrel; it lies within the lord's prerogative to grant land to a subject, and in any case, Widsith pays Eadgils for the land. Widsith also received an armlet from Ealhhild (the wife of Eormanric).

There follows a passage in which the word *þonne* starts every third line three times; as with the passage in *Beowulf* introducing the Finn episode, subtle distinctions emerge from considering the possibility that *þonne* might be either an adverb or a conjunction. Krapp and Dobbie punctuate the passage as follows:

> Ond me þa Ealhhild   oþerne forgeaf,
> dryhtcwen duguþe,   dohtor Eadwines.

Hyre lof lengde   geond londa fela,
þonne ic be songe   secgan sceolde
hwær ic under swegle   selast wisse
goldhrodene cwen   giefe bryttian.
Đonne wit Scilling   sciran reorde
for uncrum sigedryhtne   song ahofan,
hlude bi hearpan   hleoþor swinsade,
þonne monige men,   modum wlonce,
wordum sprecan,   þa þe wel cuþan,
þæt hi næfre song   sellan ne hyrdon.

[97–108]

In lines 88–92 Widsith claims to have been with Eormanric all the time
(throughout his reign, according to Malone: 1962); Eormanric gave him a
golden armlet of great value measured in shillings (scillingrime, 92). In lines
93–96 Widsith asserts that he gave this ring to Eadgils, "my protecting lord"
(minum hleodryhtne, 94), on his return home. Lines 97–98 announce that
Ealhhild gave him another one (presumably another armlet, such as her husband
Eormanric gave him). Line 99 says that her fame spread through many lands. If
þonne of line 100 is a subordinating conjunction, as the punctuation implies, it is
dependent on lengde of line 99, and one is to infer that Ealhhild's fame spread
when Widsith had to say in performance where on earth he knew the best gold-
adorned queen distributing gifts—in other words, that Widsith's performances
spread the fame of Ealhhild. This is a likely reading in view of Widsith's earlier
statement that he could express before the company in the hall how the aristocrats were generous in their gifts to him (54–56). One is to assume that wherever
he went Widsith felt compelled to acknowledge ("secgan sceolde") in his performances that Ealhhild was the most generous queen he had met, and thereby
he extended her reputation; this presumably did not offend the foreign queen
who might have been in his audience, or perhaps it was designed to sting her
into emulation of Ealhhild's generosity.

As punctuated, however, the passage from 88 to 111 is rather awkward,
marked, as Malone put it "by a systematic shift of scene (or, if you will, a
backward and forward movement)" (36). Malone divides the passage into six
sections: (1) Eormanric gives Widsith the armlet; (2) Widsith gives this to his
lord Eadgils on his return home; (3) Ealhhild gave Widsith a similar gift; (4)
Widsith sang Ealhhild's praises in many lands; (5) Widsith and Scilling (a harp
or a harper: see below) performed before their lord to the acclaim of discrimi-

nating men; and (6) from Eormanric's court Widsith travelled through the Gothic empire. As such, sections 1, 3, and 5 occur at Eormanric's court, sections 2, 4, and 6 "elsewhere" (not quite "a backward and forward movement"). This is awkward, and implies that Widsith's *sigedryhten* (104) is Eormanric, whereas in line 94 his *hleodryhten* is Eadgils; moreover, the performance with Scilling that supposedly elicits the acclaim of Eormanric's men reads very like a one-time performance of a visiting minstrel rather than the performance of someone who remained with Eormanric throughout his long reign.

These difficulties can be resolved by taking 99 to 108 as a unit, referring to a performance Widsith gave before Eadgils on his return home. Widsith gives Eadgils Eormanric's ring, Eadgils asks who was the most generous queen he had met on his travels, Widsith then, at the request of his lord, puts his reply in the form of a performance to the harp: "Eormanric gave me a handsome ring which I gave to my lord [hleodryhten], his wife gave me another, so that when I was asked to say in a song [be songe secgan sceolde] who was the most generous queen I had met I named her; and so her fame spread when I had to name her, when Scilling and I sang before our lord [sigedryhten]; this command performance was acclaimed by those who heard it." As such, both *þonne* in line 100 and *Ðonne* in line 103 become temporal subordinating conjunctions dependent on *lengde* (99), and *þonne* (106) becomes an adverb meaning "then, that is, after the performance referred to in lines 99 to 105."

Now I am not arguing for this interpretation, nor am I suggesting that the passage as generally punctuated represents the most reasonable reading; I am trying to demonstrate once again that the passage is by no means clear and that one should be wary of arguing absolutely from the evidence supplied by the extant poetry. One may assume with some confidence that Widsith performed on at least one occasion together with a harp or harper. Scilling (103) would be a reasonable name for a minstrel's harp, especially in view of the *Riming Poem*'s "scyl wæs hearpe" (27); Scilling could also be the name of a harper who complemented Widsith's performance. Scholars may prefer one or the other explanations, but their views will be subjective; there seems no way of conclusively resolving the crux.

Similarly, the concluding passage in which, presumably, the poet as distinct from his fictional creation Widsith speaks of minstrels is not explicit on one crucial point. And so, the poet says in conclusion, the minstrels of men move through many countries wandering at the dictates of their destinies, they express their need, they utter words of thanks, south or north they always encounter a person who appreciates songs (*gyd* again), who is generous with gifts, who wants to increase his reputation among the retainers, who wants to assert his claim as a warrior, until everything crumbles, light and life together; he achieves praise, he holds a towering reputation on earth:

> Swa scriþende   gesceapum hweorfað
> gleomen gumena   geond grunda fela,
> þearfe secgað,   þoncword sprecaþ,
> simle suð oþþe norð   sumne gemetað
> gydda gleawne,   geofum unhneawne,
> se þe fore duguþe wile   dom aræran,
> eorlscipe æfnan,   oþþæt eal scæceð,
> leoht ond lif somod;   lof se gewyrceð,
> hafað under heofonum   heahfæstne dom.

[135–43]

Lines 135–39 are straightforward enough: minstrels travel in search of someone who appreciates their art, they claim poverty, perform, and thank the generous donor for the payment. It is clear that the person (*sumne*, 138) they encounter is also *gydda gleawne* and *geofum unhneawne* (139), and also the *se* of 140 and 142. Lines 140 to 143, however, assign to the potential donor qualities different from those in the preceding lines: he is generous and discriminating, but he is also desirous of ensuring his reputation. This last is a quality attributed to Beowulf, for example. Is 140–43 another way of saying "a good ruler," or is the quality as essential to the minstrel's success as open-handedness and a love of minstrelsy? In other words—and this is the crux—does the minstrel ensure the patron's *dom*? Certainly the minstrel needs a liberal audience: Widsith frequently comments on the payments he received for his performances. But does the ministrel serve the patron's desire for glory as a warrior, does he sing the praises of his patrons? This is a reasonable assumption, since Widsith comments on Offa's valorous deeds, for example; but it is an assumption, the poet does not make the connection explicit in his conclusion; it is still up to the patron to earn glory on earth (*lof se gewyrceð*, 142) but the poem does not explicitly state that it is for the minstrel to perpetuate it.

There are, then, problems involved in the interpretation of the evidence afforded by *Widsith*. But let us take the line of least resistance and assume that the poet created a character, Widsith, who was a representative of a profession familiar to his English audience (in other words, that one may accept the accuracy of the professional depiction); that Widsith was a wandering minstrel (gleoman) who performed professionally in halls (i.e. for aristocratic audiences) to the accompaniment of a lyre; and that his songs referred to people, their deeds and qualities in a way that enhanced their reputation. If this be accepted, what does the poem tell us about oral poetry in Anglo-Saxon England? That minstrels offered their entertainment in England we know from the Council of Clofeshoh in 747 and perhaps from the Council on English affairs in Rome in 679. The creator of *Widsith* may have been Christian (all we have to go on is a reference to God in line 133), but certainly the man who transcribed the song or poem was Christian: it is interesting therefore to note that at least one Christian believed that there was no necessary opposition between minstrelsy and official Christianity. Councils or ecclesiastics may condemn the context of inebriation within which minstrels performed or the licentious character of certain performances, but there is nowhere any proscription of harpers as such: the abbot of Lindisfarne may encourage a harper to visit the monastery, or Dunstan may learn to play the harp as part of his liberal education, though harping still carries an aura of permissiveness about it that requires Cuthbert to excuse his request to Lul or allows Dunstan's opponents to spread malicious rumours. Whoever commissioned the compilation of the Exeter Book or originally transcribed *Widsith* evidently felt no deep-seated qualms about recording what purports to be the autobiography of a minstrel.

As a minstrel Widsith travels widely, visiting courts of sympathetic aristocrats in order to earn his livelihood; he is a professional entertainer. The emphasis in *Widsith*, however, is more on his professional need to earn payment than on his providing entertainment. The latter feature is not overly emphasised. If the lists of names are intended to be an announcement of a bill of fare, a repertoire of subjects he can sing about, we are nowhere explicitly told so: this is an assumption that has no textual justification. If Widsith gives a short account of Offa's career in passing, this does not necessarily mean that he can offer a song about Offa. Let us assume that, for all his hyperbolic travels, Widsith is a typical English minstrel. If so, we must account for the apparent content of his performances. Twice Widsith explicitly tells us that his performances concern the generosity of nobles he has visited (54–56), in particular the generosity of the queens (100–02); this is the only information he gives us about the content of his songs. It may be that the last four lines of the poem referring to *lof* and *dom* are to be taken as implying that minstrels like Widsith can contribute to a warrior's reputation, but this is not explicitly stated. However, for the sake of argument, let us assume that *Widsith* tells us that the gleoman performs the function of a scop in praising the exploits and establishing the fame of rulers; this would seem to imply that we are to accept the symonymity of *scop* and *gleoman* in *Beowulf*. It is not at all clear, as we have seen, that the scop in *Beowulf* ever struck a harp, and we are told of only one occasion on which Widsith performed to musical accompaniment, and even then we cannot say whether he played the instrument or not. But let us override even that objection, and assume that one implication of the evidence of *Widsith* is that scop and gleoman were identical figures, and that they played a harp to accompany their narrative songs for entertainment: how would this conclusion affect our reconstruction of the history of oral poetry in Anglo-Saxon England?

The reference to Offa of Angle has often been taken as an argument to place the composition of *Widsith* in the eighth-century Mercia of Offa, descendant and namesake of the continental king. As we saw in the third chapter, Mercia is of all the kingdoms the most likely to have enjoyed a strong tradition of sacral eulogy in praise of the king ceremonially performed by a tribal poet; we also suggested in the fifth chapter that such a tradition was likely to be affected by the conversion of the Mercian kings to Christianity, by the pervasive monastic ideal among the royal family in the seventh century, and by the supplanting of the ritual function of the tribal poet by the church and its sacraments. If that hypothesis is correct, the seventh-century scop (assuming he is the tribal poet) would need to turn elsewhere if he wished to continue exercising his talent. He might alter his style and assume a different role in society, turning his skill in eulogy to the service of explicit narrative for the entertainment of his audiences, but professional entertainers (gleomen) were by then already current. One result might have been a tendency of the traditions of the scop and the gleoman to fall together, so that the wandering harper offered for the diversion of his host flattering songs honouring him.

Traditions of eulogy have been exploited for mercenary ends by wandering performers. Among the Hausa of northern Nigeria, for example, there are traditions of eulogy (*roko*) in honour of the king, the ancestors, and commoners; the king supports praise-singers (*maroka*) who form part of his official entourage (see M. G. Smith; Gidley). The individual *maroki*, however, seeks a livelihood by wandering from village to village. On arrival in a village, he seeks information about the wealthy villagers from the local maroki, then takes up a position that will ensure him the largest audience and the presence of prominent people.

> He begins by calling the name of the person he intends to praise several times, working into a rhythm and thence into the individual's praise-song.

This continues for some time with increasingly frequent and direct demands for gifts. Normally the person addressed, if already out of sight, continues to remain so as long as possible and sends out his gift by a boy. The *maroki* now chants his thanks, *godiya, na gode, na gode*, then announces the amount of the gift. If it is clearly adequate by community standards, he concludes his address to the first individual with a brief repetition of his praise-song and a recommendation of the donor to Allah, and turns his attention to a second individual near by. If either of the persons addressed sends a gift which the *maroki* regards as inadequate, then this is announced, and the voice-pattern changes from singing to a rhythmic declamation in an unnatural pitch. Innuendo marks the alteration initially, but later, to indicate impatience at tardiness in the arrival of an appropriate gift, this innuendo becomes sharper, harsher, and its delivery takes a staccato form. This is virtually an ultimatum and rarely fails to produce surrender from the individual addressed, who has probably had more than he can stand already.

The content of a solo declamation consists in statements of the individual's ancestry, their notability, his prosperity and influence, the number of his dependants, his fame, and its range. If he has any well-known and important political connexions, such as clientage with a senior official capable of protecting him, these are alluded to indirectly. If the declamation becomes hostile, the same themes recur, though with unfavourable emphases and connotations. Insinuations about the ancestry of the person addressed are made at this time and, for many commoners at whom this type of declamation is directed, this may imply slavery. Unfavourable references to the individual's meanness, fortune (*arziki*), treatment of his dependants, occupation, reputation, and possible disloyalty to his community or political patrons are also liable to be made. The ultimate insult—imputation of ambiguous paternity—is never openly mentioned, but overshadows the process of increasing pressure. [M. G. Smith, 39]

This account is quoted here not only because it demonstrates how a tradition of eulogy may be used for praise as well as calumny, but also because it illustrates how such a tradition can be exploited to serve mercenary ends. Left to his own resources, the scop may have wandered from court to court in search of his livelihood, and in so doing may well have become identified with the professional gleoman; in turn, the gleoman may have absorbed into his performances

aspects of the scop's tradition. *Widsith*, in its references to the generosity of patrons, can be placed alongside the opening gambit of the Hausa maroki. If this
is taken as reasonable, then an eighth-century date for the composition of *Widsith* would be in accordance with our hypothetical reconstruction of the history
of the Anglo-Saxon oral poet.

If *Widsith* does not mention a scop, *Deor* does. The speaker announces at
the conclusion that he was once the scop of the Heodenings, a man dear to his
lord. This may be taken as tending to confirm the assumption that the scop
was a poet attached to a lord and serving a community, a tribal poet. For many
years, he says, he held a secure office and enjoyed the loyalty of his lord, but
now Heorrenda, a man skilled in leoþ, has succeeded to the land-right which
his lord had formerly given to Deor:

> Þæt ic bi me sylfum   secgan wille,
> þæt ic hwile wæs   Heodeninga scop,
> dryhtne dyre.   Me wæs Deor noma.
> Ahte ic fela wintra   folgað tilne,
> holdne hlaford,   oþþæt Heorrenda nu,
> leoðcræftig monn   londryht geþah,
> þæt me eorla hleo   ær gesealde.
>   Þæs ofereode,   þisses swa mæg!
>
> [*ASPR*, III, 35–42]

We are not so much concerned with the interpretation of *Deor* as with what it
tells us about the scop. We may accept the general view that line 42, which
recurs at the end of five preceding references to calamity, is a refrain that Deor
finally applies to his own misfortune: the unhappiness of those events has passed,
so now may mine. Unfortunately, the short autobiographical statement of a
scop tells us little about his art or calling. Clearly he was associated with a lord
apparently on some official basis, since he has been supplanted by Heorrenda.
The supplanting may be merely in the lord's affection, but it is more likely to
be in the office of scop, since Heorrenda is called a man skilled in *leoþ*, poems or
songs. The reference in lines 40–41 to *londryht* may then imply that the lord
gave his scop land; when his scop was replaced by a successful rival, the land
passed to the successor along with the office. This reading in turn may be taken
to imply that Widsith's land was granted in exchange for his services. However,
we noted that the latter reading was not implicit in the text; similarly, we are
not explicitly told that Heorrenda succeeded to Deor's land, thereby supplanting
him and causing him to move. We *are* told that Heorrenda received the same

rights to land Deor had received; we are not told that Deor had to move off it at all.

As scop, Deor may have been offered land with certain rights and privileges; as his successor, Heorrenda may have been offered a different plot of land but with the same rights and privileges: Bosworth and Toller gloss *land-riht* as "the law of the land, the rights and privileges belonging to the inhabitant of a country," and expound the use of the word in *Deor*: "Heorrenda was now admitted, as Deor had been before, to the rights of a native, and had succeeded in attracting to himself the favour before shown to Deor." In *Beowulf* Wiglaf predicts that all the cowards who fled from Beowulf, stripped of their right to land (*londrihtes*, 2886), will have to go wandering; in other words, they are exiled, refused permission to go on living in Beowulf's chiefdom. In the same way, Heorrenda is now attracted to the chief of the Heodenings and granted the right to settle, the same right that Deor was once granted: Deor does not say that Heorrenda was granted his *land*, thereby enforcing Deor's eviction, merely that he was granted the *privileges* of a landholder. So all we are left with is the information that Deor (if indeed that is the name of the speaker) claims to have been a tribal poet ("ic hwile wæs Heodeninga scop," 36) enjoying a relation of affection with his lord, that he served his lord for some time, and that now a rival has appeared on the scene.

In sum, however popular *Widsith* and *Deor* have been as sources of information on the practice of poetry in Anglo-Saxon England, attractive as they may be as the basis of scholarly theories, they offer us little reliable information about the early English scop and gleoman.

When one turns to the remaining corpus of extant Old English poetry for information on poets and poetry, one finds little primary material. There are a number of passages associating music and joy, there are a few passages depicting performances at a feast, and there are three passages referring to the gifts God bestows on men that include poets and harpers in the lists. Finally, the extant poetry itself provides evidence of its memorisation, and its genre may sometimes be taken to be indicative of practices within the oral tradition. Curiously enough, all the passages we shall look at are found in the Exeter Book (*ASPR*, III).

In *Guthlac*, in the passage describing the hermit's death, there is a strong association between music and joy. Throngs of angels sang a victory song; melody, the joy of the holy ones filled the air. The saint's old dwelling was suffused with rejoicings, with sweet aromas and heavenly wonders, with the voices of angels. Far more attractive and joyful than any earthly tongue can describe, the aroma and the melody, wave upon wave of heavenly voices and holy song were made manifest, the peerless glory of God:

> Engla þreatas
> sigeleoð sungon,   sweg wæs on lyfte
> gehyred under heofonum,   haligra dream.
> Swa se burgstede wæs   blissum gefylled,
> swetum stencum   ond sweglwundrum,
> eadges yrfestol,   engla hleoðres,
> eal innanweard.   Þær wæs ænlicra
> ond wynsumra   þonne hit in worulde mæge
> stefn areccan,   hu se stenc ond se sweg,
> heofonlic hleoþor   ond se halga song,
> gehyred wæs,   heahþrym godes,
> breahtem æfter breahtme.

[1314–25]

The poet is here describing the chorus of heavenly voices that rejoiced at Guthlac's death. Though there is no harp, there are elements in this passage that make it strongly reminiscent of those passages in Heorot describing joy in the hall, the hall in this case being Guthlac's *burgstede*. As in *Beowulf*, there are key words for joy (*dream* and *wyn*) and for song or melody (*sweg* and *song*). These elements are present, too, in a long passage in *The Phoenix*.

The Old English poem on *The Phoenix* is interesting because it is a rather faithful translation of a Latin poem by Lactantius. In one of the finest articles that emerged as a reaction to Magoun's application of the theories of Parry and Lord to Old English poetry, Larry Benson examined the diction of *The Phoenix*, clearly the work of a literate author, and showed it to be highly formulaic; Benson argues convincingly that the clerical poet employed traditional diction by choice, since he did not find the Old English formulaic phrases in Lactantius's Latin, that he did so "not because the demands of the meter or the pressures of oral composition prevent the poet from pausing to select some more suitable phrase but because this phrase *is* suitable, is part of a poetic diction that is clearly oral in origin but that is now just as clearly a literary convention" (339). One might produce as evidence in the same argument the poet's translation of a passage describing the bird's song at daybreak. In Lactantius's Latin (ed. Garrod) there are brief references to music and song:

tollitur ac summo considit in arboris altae
uertice, quae totum despicit una nemus,
et conuersa nouos Phoebi nascentis ad ortus
exspectat radios et iubar exoriens.
atque ubi Sol pepulit fulgentis limina portae
et primi emicuit luminis aura leuis,
incipit illa sacri modulamina fundere cantus
et mira lucem uoce ciere nouam;
quam nec aedoniae uoces nec tibia possit
musica Cirrhaeis adsimulare modis,
et neque olor moriens imitari posse putetur
nec Cylleneae fila canora lyrae.
postquam Phoebus equos in aperta effudit Olympi
atque orbem totum protulit usque means, . . .

[39–52]

The Old English poet expands on this passage, giving it his own emphasis, and his original treatment of the Latin is significant. As soon as the sun rises high over the sea, the poet says, the bright phoenix leaves its tree in the forest. It quickly flies up and sings ("swinsað ond singeð," 124) in the sky. Then the bird's manner is beautiful, its spirit is full, it exults in joys (*blissum*); it traffics in eloquence with a clear voice more wonderfully than any man on earth ever heard. The melody of that music ("hleoðres sweg," 131) is sweeter and more joyful than any human song: nothing on earth equals it, neither trumpets nor horns, the sound of the harp, the voices of men, organs, the rhythm of harmony ("sweghleoþres geswin," 137), a swan's feathers, or any of those joys that God created to delight men. And so it sings rejoicing with happiness, until the sun has sunk in the south:

Sona swa seo sunne   sealte streamas
hea oferhlifað,   swa se haswa fugel
beorht of þæs bearwes   beame gewiteð,
fareð feþrum snell   flyhte on lyfte,
swinsað ond singeð   swegle togeanes.
Ðonne bið swa fæger   fugles gebæru,
onbryrded breostsefa,   blissum hremig;
wrixleð woðcræfte   wundorlicor
beorhtan reorde,   þonne æfre byre monnes
hyrde under heofonum,   siþþan heahcyning,
wuldres wyrhta,   woruld staþelode,

heofon ond eorþan.   Biþ þæs hleoðres sweg
eallum songcræftum   swetra ond wlitigra
ond wynsumra   wrenca gehwylcum.
Ne magon þam breahtme   byman ne hornas,
ne hearpan hlyn,   ne hæleþa stefn
ænges on eorþan,   ne organan
sweghleoþres geswin,   ne swanes feðre,
ne ænig þara dreama   þe dryhten gescop
gumum to gliwe   in þas geomran woruld.
Singeð swa ond swinsað   sælum geblissad,
oþþæt seo sunne   on suðrodor
sæged weorþeð.

[120–42]

There are many verbal elements in this passage that have occurred in passages
we have already discussed, verbs like *swinsian*, *singan*, and *wrixlan*, nouns referring to music like *sweg*, *hleoþor*, *song*, *hearpe*, *hlyn*, and nouns referring to joy
like *blis*, *wyn*, *dream*, and *gliw*; there is the presence, too, remarked on in previous discussions, of the voices of men and the clear voice of the performer. Perhaps the verbal elements in this passage remind one most strongly of the three
lines from Widsith:

Ðonne wit Scilling   sciran reorde
for uncrum sigedryhtne   song ahofan,
hlude bi hearpan   hleoþor swinsade . . .

to which compare the half-line *beorhtan reorde* (*Phoenix*, 128), the use of *swinsian*
twice (lines 124 and 140) and *hleoþor* twice (131 and 137) and the appearance of
song (132) and *hearpe* (135). It is not necessary to argue that the poet of *The Phoenix* knew *Beowulf* or *Widsith*, but it is likely that a traditional association (not
necessarily of native origin) existed between music and joy, and that this association tended to be expressed poetically in certain words which (necessarily)
recur in those passages treating joy or music or both. It should be noted once
again that God gives music to man for his delight: music and musical instruments are by no means evil in themselves, although in certain contexts musical
performances might evoke ecclesiastical censure.

   The *Gifts of Men* once again associates the harp with entertainment, referring
to the instrument which the gifted man handles dexterously as a *gleobeam*, a
glee-wood:

> Sum mid hondum mæg   hearpan gretan,
> ah he gleobeames   gearobrygda list.

[49–50]

A passage in *The Seafarer* bears close comparison to the extracts quoted from *The Phoenix*, *Guthlac*, and the references to the harp in *Beowulf*: if the harp is associated with joy, its absence connotes the absence of joy, a connotation that can only be depended on if there is a traditional association of harping with entertainment and happiness. The seafarer establishes his life of hardship as one of separation from the joys of the hall: for joy I had the song of the wild swan, for the laughter of men I had the sound of the gannet and the rhythm of the curlew, for mead I had the singing seagull:

> Hwilum ylfete song
> dyde ic me to gomene,   ganetes hleoþor
> ond huilpan sweg   fore hleahtor wera,
> mæw singende   fore medodrince.

[19–22]

Once again there is drinking and the voices and laughter of men, *song, sweg, hleoþor* and *gamen*. The seafarer is deprived of these joys, deprived of lord (25), he is not in the dwellings proud and flushed with wine (27–30); but he thinks of the relentless tossing of the waves, not of the harp, ring-giving, the joy of a woman, or the pleasures of the world:

> Ne biþ him to hearpan hyge   ne to hringþege,
> ne to wife wyn   ne to worulde hyht,
> ne ymbe owiht elles,   nefne ymb yða gewealc.

[44–46]

Clearly the harp, music, laughter, and ring-giving are all associated with the joy and comfort a retainer experiences in his lord's hall.

These associations are present again in *Maxims I* and the *Riming Poem*. The former presents many problems of interpretation; in the passage that mentions a harp, the poet seems to say that wise words befit every man, the gyd befits a minstrel, and widsom (?) befits a man. Whether this implies that the gleoman's gyd is wise, or whether these lines are in any way connected with what follows, is not at all clear. There are as many mentalities as there are men on earth; each man has his own mind. Then the man who knows many a leoþ, or who can play the harp, experiences less longing; he has the gift of entertainment, which God gave him:

> Wæra gehwylcum wislicu   word gerisað,
> gleomen gied   ond guman snyttro.
> Swa monige beoþ men ofer eorþan,   swa beoþ modgeþoncas;
> ælc him hafað   sundorsefan.
> Longað þonne þy læs   þe him con leoþa worn,
> oþþe mid hondum con   hearpan gretan;
> hafað him his gliwes giefe,   þe him god sealde.
>
> [165–71]

It is not clear whether a leoþ is performed to the accompaniment of a hearpe, but the recurrent association of hearpe and gliw seems to gain support from this passage. The performance of songs and the music of the lyre (perhaps both together) are viewed as consolations to man.

The *Riming Poem* furnishes yet another example of the association of music and joy. In his happy, mindless days the poet enjoyed the pleasure of material things and the company of men. The warriors were sharp, the harp resounded loudly, the music swelled, the melody rang out and by no means diminished:

> Scealcas wæron scearpe,   scyl wæs hearpe,
> hlude hlynede,   hleoþor dynede,
> sweglrad swinsade,   swiþe ne minsade.
>
> [27–29]

We have the harp, *hleoþor*, and *swinsian* again, though no joy. *Gomen* does occur in line 24 (gomen sibbe ne ofoll), but the manuscript has *gomel*. Although joy is not explicit, the scene is set "in healle" (15), and is likely to have drawn on the traditional depiction of joy in the hall.

In the sources we examined in previous chapters, we frequently noted the presence of poetry or song as an accompaniment of feasting in a building, whether the lord's hall or the monks' refectory. The poem quoted from the *Anthologia Latina,* for example, made this connection among the Goths, who drank each other's health and uttered poetry while feasting ("Inter eils goticum scapia matzia ia drincan"). This scene obviously bears a relation to the passages describing joy in the hall we have discussed above; it appears without any harp or connotation of joy in *Vainglory*, though this latter connotation is perhaps deliberately avoided by the didactic poet. With its opening reminiscent of *Beowulf* ("Hwæt, me frod wita on fyrndagum sægde, snottor ar, sundorwundra fela!"), the poem seems to evoke heroic images and situations, but it does so to condemn them. Such a situation is the drunken feast, when many proud battle-smiths are eager to talk publicly in the wine-hall, they sit at the feast, they utter a *soðgied*, they exchange words, they want to test what sort of resistance they will find among the men in the building, when wine excites the warrior's heart. Waves of noise arise, a din in the assembly, speeches resound variously:

> . . . þonne monige beoð   mæþelhegendra,
> wlonce wigsmiþas   winburgum in,
> sittaþ æt symble,   soðgied wrecað,
> wordum wrixlað,   witan fundiaþ
> hwylc æscstede   inne in ræcede
> mid werum wunige,   þonne win hweteð
> beornes breostsefan.   Breahtem stigeð,
> cirm on corþre,   cwide scralletaþ
> missenlice.
>
> [13–21]

The drunken warriors trail their coats in the beer-hall; in so doing they vie with each other in shouting *dissonis vocis*. It may be assumed that the *breahtem*, *cirm*, and *cwide* that resound in the alcoholic haze are the verbal efforts of the drunken *wigsmiþas* to pick a fight (16–19), and are in turn the product of the activities described in the clauses *soðgied wrecað, wordum wrixlað*. Are they shouting, or are they uttering poetry? They are hardly drinking each others' healths in this scene, but can it be said that they *scapia matzia ia drincan*? To approach a reply, we must consider the poetic contexts of *wrixlan*.

In the extant poetry, *wrixlan* occurs with reference to colour (*Phoenix* 294 and *Elene* 759), but more frequently with reference to speech of some sort. *Maxims I* says that "Gleawe men sceolon gieddum wrixlan" (4), which tells us nothing, since wise men could convey their wisdom in poetry or orations. On three occasions the context seems to suggest ordinary discourse: Wulfgar announces that Beowulf wishes to exchange words ("wordum wrixlan," 366) with Hrothgar; in the physical destruction of the body after the departure of the soul, the torn tongue cannot exchange intelligent words with the unhappy soul ("forþan hie ne magon huxlicum wordum wrixlian wið þone werian gast," *Soul and Body I*, 114f., "Forþon heo ne mæg horsclice wordum wrixlan wið þone wergan gæst," *Soul and Body II*, 109 f.); and warriors talk of their horses ("wrixlaþ spræce," 57) in *The Rune Poem*. Occasionally the context suggests music or poetry, as in the passages quoted above from *The Phoenix* ("wrixleð woðcræfte," 127) and *Beowulf* ("wordum wrixlan," 874). *Riddle 60* seems to invoke the context of feasting in the hall as in *Vainglory*, as the reed (now a pipe) entertains the diners: the reed scarcely thought, while growing near the beach, that though lacking a mouth it would ever speak and exchange words across the mead-benches:

> Lyt ic wende
> þæt ic ær oþþe sið æfre sceolde
> ofer meodubence muðleas sprecan,
> wordum wrixlan.

[7–10]

Of course, lines 9 and 10 may have no connotation of song or poetry if, though itself a musical instrument, the reed is simply likening its performance to dinner conversation. *Riddle 8*, however, clearly plays on the connotation of musical entertainment and raucous joy in the hall, and uses *wrixlan* with *woþ* (as does the *Phoenix* poet). The nightingale or jay says he speaks through his mouth with many voices, he sings with skill (cf. *Phoenix*, 133), often he varies the eloquence of his head ("wrixle geneahhe heafodwoþe"), he cries loudly, holds his note, does not conceal his voice (*hleoþor*). He refers to himself as an evening-poet of old who brings joy to men in towns when he storms with his pliant voice; the men sit huddled over in silence in their houses. He invites his readers or listeners to identify him, and calls himself one who, like a female entertainer, loudly imitates a minstrel's song and announces many welcome things to warriors with his eloquence:

> Ic þurh muþ sprece mongum reordum,
> wrencum singe, wrixle geneahhe
> heafodwoþe, hlude cirme,
> healde mine wisan, hleoþre ne miþe,
> eald æfensceop, eorlum bringe
> blisse in burgum, þonne ic bugendre
> stefne styrme; stille on wicum
> sittað nigende. Saga hwæt ic hatte,
> þe swa scirenige sceawendwisan
> hlude onhyrge, hæleþum bodige
> wilcumena fela woþe minre.

[1–11]

From this survey, we are left to conclude that the phrase *wordum wrixlan* is used in contexts referring to ordinary speech as well as to poetry, song, or entertainment. Accordingly, its use in *Vainglory* might suggest poetry, but again it might not.

What of *soðgied wrecað* (15) then? We have already seen that *gied*, like *wordum wrixlan*, may mean a poem, a song, or a story; as Donald Fry (1974) notes in his gloss of the word, it is "generally applied to oral, traditional knowledge." What then of the compound *soðgied*, literally a true *gied*? The only occurrence of the compound in the poetic corpus is in the opening lines of *The Seafarer*, "Mæg ic be me sylfum soðgied wrecað, siþas secgan," themselves reminiscent of the opening lines of *The Wife's Lament*, "Ic þis giedd wrece bi me ful geomorre, minre sylfre sið." A *soðgied* seems to refer to actual events, not an autobiographical performance (for that would make *be me* redundant), but perhaps a biographical poem or song, one about a person. If it is in fact such, then the drunken men of *Vainglory* could be boasting in poetry, uttering eulogies about themselves or their lineages. This would certainly fit in with the muted heroic and martial suggestions of the poem, and would then be another example of the kind of eulogies uttered by the Germanic people on entry into battle (as in Ammianus Marcellinus) or the eulogies uttered before or during the Battle of Maldon. "Soðgied wrecaþ, wordum wrixlaþ" would then refer to a poetic activity *æt symble*, like the Goths who "scapia matzia ia drincan"; yet, frustratingly, it is possible that the activity referred to consists of ordinary speech (however drunken or belligerent).

We have already seen that *Maxims I* considers the harper happy, the man who has the gift of entertainment which he received from God, "hafað him his gliwes giefe, þe him god sealde," 171. Three poems supply lists of talents that God gives to men. It has been suggested (see Cross; Short) that these passages derive from a sermon of Bishop Haymo of Halbestadt (Migne, *PL*, 118, cols. 781–85), who urges his brothers not to bury the talents God has given them, but to put them to use; Haymo gives some examples: "Et quia alius artem legendi, alius cantandi, alius prædicandi, alius pingendi, alius ea quæ ad orna-mentum ecclesi pertinent fabricandi talentum accepit, alius hoc quod didicit studeat erogare." Whether or not this sermon is the source, the three Old English poems all seem to include in their lists the equivalent of the man who is given *artem cantandi*. In the *Christ* occurs a passage listing the gifts God's son has bestowed on us ("us giefe sealde," 660). To one person he sends wise elo-quence and noble perception residing in his mind and expressed through his mouth; the man to whose spirit the skill of wisdom has been entrusted can declaim ("singan and secgan") on many subjects. Another person knows very well how to stir the harp and greet the joy-wood loudly in the presence of war-riors. Another can correctly express the divine law. . . . And so the son of God distributes his gifts to us on earth; he does not choose to give all wisdom

to any one man in case pride in his skill over and above that of others should
harm him:

> Sumum wordlaþe   wise sendeð
> on his modes gemynd   þurh his muþes gæst,
> æðele ondgiet.   Se mæg eal fela
> singan ond secgan   þam bið snyttru cræft
> bifolen on ferðe.   Sum mæg fingrum wel
> hlude fore hæleþum   hearpan stirgan,
> gleobeam gretan.   Sum mæg godcunde
> reccan ryhte æ. . . .
>   Swa se waldend us,
> godbearn on grundum,   his giefe bryttað.
> Nyle he ængum anum   ealle gesyllan
> gæstes snyttru,   þy læs him gielp sceþþe
> þurh his anes cræft   ofer oþre forð.
>
> [664–71; 681–85]

Clearly the passage lists the talents of individuals. The person who has the God-
given skill of playing the harp is not the person who has the gift of expounding
divine law, and not the person who is given noble understanding in his heart.
It is this last person and not the harper who can "singan and secgan": is he a
poet? Widsith, as we saw, claimed to be able to utter a narrative before the
company in the hall about the gifts he received ("Forþon ic mæg singan ond
secgan spell," 54), and it is reasonable to suppose that he is referring to a performance. In the first poem of Book I of *The Consolation of Philosophy*, Boethius
bemoans his fate and cries out, "Ah why, my friends, why did you boast so
often of my happiness?" ("Quid me felicem totiens iactastis amici?") *Iactare*
in the sense of "to boast" may well have been taken as poetic by an Anglo-
Saxon poet who was familiar with a tradition of autobiographical eulogies, for
the Old English poet translates (*Met*, 2):

> Forhwam wolde ge,   weoruldfrynd mine,
> secgan oððe singan   þæt ic gesællic mon
> Wære on weorulde?
>
> [16–18]

It is possible, therefore, that *Christ* 664–68 refers to a poet, but it is also possible
that it refers to an eloquent orator.

A similar list of God's gifts constitutes the *Gifts of Men*. One man is a bearer of eloquence, "giedda giffæst," another is ready with words:

> Sum biþ woðbora,
> giedda giffæst.   Sum bið gearuwyrdig.
>
> [35–36]

The *woþbora* may well be a poet, as we shall see from the next chapter; he would then be skilful with poems. A *gied*, however, may be a prose tale or a song, as we have seen; however, it is possible, because of the tendency to differentiate in these lists, that the *woðbora* is a poet, the *gearuwyrdig* man is an orator (denying the equation of *gied* with speeches), and yet another man is a singer ("sum leoða gleaw," 52). If *woðbora* is a poet, it is interesting to note his proximity in the list to the nonmusical man who is skilled in words; and if *leoð* are songs, it is interesting to note that the man who knows them is separated from the *woðbora* and the *gearuwyrdig* man, but placed close to (though not identified with) the harper, who knows how to greet the harp with his hands and has the skill of swift movements on the joy-wood:

> Sum mid hondum mæg   hearpan gretan,
> ah he gleobeames   gearobrygda list.
>
> [49–50]

An entertainer and a harper appear together at the end of *The Fortunes of Men*. Once again, God variously bestows gifts. One shall please and entertain a crowd of warriors sitting on benches with their beer; the joy of the drinkers is great. Another person shall sit with his harp at his lord's feet, receive money, and play his harp skilfully; the need for him is great:

> Sum sceal on heape   hælepum cweman,
> blissian æt beore   bencsittendum;
> þær biþ drincendra   dream se micla.
> Sum sceal mid hearpan   æt his hlafordes
> fotum sittan,   feoh þicgan,
> ond a snellice   snere wræstan,
> lætan scralletan   sceacol, se þe hleapeð,
> nægl neomegende;   biþ him neod micel.
>
> [77–84]

Whatever information on the harper's technique this passage may yield, it tells us nothing of the scop. It is generally assumed that the man sitting at his lord's feet (80–84) is a scop, but clearly the text cannot justify this assumption. He is a harper who seems to receive payment for his performance, he seems to have a (permanent) attachment to his lord, and he is a necessary (perhaps "popular") figure in society. He is distinct from the man who ensures *dream* amongst the drinkers in the hall (77–79), though the poet may have implied by the juxtaposition that the harper also contributed to the *dream*, as in *Beowulf*, for example; even this last assumption, however reasonable, rests on a consideration of related passages in the extant corpus rather than on the text of *The Fortunes of Men* itself.

Finally, one may consider the extant poetry for the evidence it provides of the memorisation of the texts. We have noted that a proverb in metrical form dating from the time of Saint Boniface was transmitted in a fixed form. Alan Jabbour has studied those Old English texts that are extant in more than one version—poems like *Cædmon's Hymn, Bede's Death Song,* or sections of *The Dream of the Rood*—and has argued convincingly that variant readings are the product of memorial transmission. Poetic versions of the Gloria, the Creed, and the Lord's Prayer (*ASPR*, VI) were probably designed for memorisation as well; metrical charms and genealogies may also have been learnt. Explicitly, the author of the didactic *Order of the World* instructs his audience to learn the lesson contained in the poem ("Leorna þas lare," 23), to listen to the message of praise and memorise it ("Gehyr nu þis herespel ond þinne hyge gefæstna," 37). This command issues from the poet, who sees himself as a purveyor of knowledge, a "wis woðbora" (2). Apparently it is necessary for the poet to explain the use of poetry for didactic purposes: the concept should not be difficult for his audience to accept, he suggests, for any thinking man will appreciate that long ago men used to impart the truth in the form of poetry (or song), and their audiences used to understand life's mysteries by repeating and memorising the poems:

> Is þara anra gehwam   orgeate tacen,
> þam þurh wisdom   woruld ealle con
> behabban on hreþre,   hycgende mon,
> þæt geara iu,   gliwes cræfte,
> mid gieddingum   guman oft wrecan,
> rincas rædfæste;   cuþon ryht sprecan,
> þæt a fricgende   fira cynnes

ond secgende   searoruna gespon
a gemyndge mæst   monna wiston.

[8–16]

It is not clear whether the poet is referring to a native tradition here or to Old
Testament times. If he has in mind the Psalms, this would justify the association
of "gliwes cræfte, mid gieddingum" with songs possibly produced to the accompaniment of a harp. We cannot even say whether *The Order of the World* is
a song or a poem. However, the only point that needs to be made on its evidence is that compositions in poetic form were committed to memory; here is
clear evidence that some Anglo-Saxon songs or poems were subject to memorial
transmission.

An examination of the extant poetry has not yielded very much reliable
information. Scenes in *Beowulf* depicting poetic activity outside Heorot are
most helpful; *Deor* and *Widsith* furnish some data about the scop and the
gleoman respectively; the other passages we have considered are useful in
supplying a context of semantic association rather than in depicting the poet or
singer in performance, and are particularly useful for confirming the distinction
between poet and entertaining singer, a distinction that is preserved in lists of
the gifts God bestows on mankind. Part of the problem in trying to exploit the
poetry as evidence for poetic activity rests with the wide range of meanings
certain key words or phrases seem to have, so that it is not always possible to
state with accuracy whether a given passage describes poetry, song, or ordinary
discourse. These Old English words for poets and poetry are the subject of the
next chapter.

9

The Words for Poets and Poetry

Time and again in the preceding discussions of Old English passages, we had to withdraw from a conclusion or arrive at an equivocal interpretation because the precise meanings of certain key words were not evident. Often it was not clear whether the passage dealt with poetry, song, or heightened prose, and at times certain words, like *gied*, seemed to be used for all three forms. Our study of oral poetry in Anglo-Saxon England would accordingly be incomplete if it did not include an examination of the words used to refer to poetic activity. In many cases the investigation may reveal nothing more than what we have already discovered, that some words have a wide range of application, but we may hope for greater clarity on the general relation between the various performers and the function of their performances through a consideration especially of semantic contexts. We are primarily concerned with poetry rather than song, but this study will not be able entirely to exclude discussion of the words for song (see Norman: 1938; Von See; Werlich: 1967; Wissmann).

Certain problems and obstacles immediately present themselves. In the first place, in the 600 years from the middle of the fifth to the middle of the eleventh century, Anglo-Saxon social practices were hardly static. The traditions of poetry and song in particular must have been in a constant state of flux, and the words referring to these activities must also have undergone change. Effectively, we have a period of literacy of only 350 years, and even then ninth century records are relatively rare. The problem of chronology is of major proportion: words relating to social practices subject to alteration in time must themselves have undergone changes of meaning or application, yet we hardly have a continuum of writing representative of the whole Anglo-Saxon period. Even the writing we do have is of limited value for our purposes. If we accept that the pre-Christian Anglo-Saxons supported traditions of poetry and song, then it is clear that the words they used to refer to these practices described purely oral activities. Among the illiterate population at large, even after they became Christian, there is no reason why these words should not have continued to be used with their original meanings as long as the phenomena they described were still current. But none of the extant writing in Old English was penned by this illiterate population at large: it was all written by Christian clerics who had been educated in Latin. These writers often needed English words to translate foreign terms: in this field, as in many others, they borrowed Latin words (*antefn* for antiphon, *cantic*, and *graðul* for gradual), they compounded English words (*æfensang* for vespers, *sealmwyrhta* for psalmist) or they simply used English words in new applications. (Among the Xhosa, *izibongo* originally referred to and still refers to an oral eulogy, but written poetry, whether traditional or Western in form, has come to be called "izibongo" as well: all forms of poetry are izibongo, however far removed the modern publications with European rhyme, metre, and stanzaic structure might be from the oral performances of the imbongi.)

Once the extension has been made, the originally precise words assume more generalised denotations and perhaps lose their connotations. This might especially be so for a Christian cleric who was familiar with the wide range of applications of Latin *cantare*, *canere*, and *dicere*, and *carmen*; to him a distinction between poetry and song might not be as evident as to an illiterate peasant, or even if it were, he might not choose to apply the distinction perhaps preserved in the English vocabulary when translating a Latin text that seemingly appreciates no such distinction. This problem is compounded by the need for synonyms for alliterative purposes when composing in verse form: if the sense called for *leoþ*, say, but the line more easily alliterated on *g*, was it not more convenient to use *gied*, especially if any distinction between the two was blurring? Could the *Beowulf* poet not use *gleomannes gied* loosely for a scop's poem because both scop and gleoman were public performers? How much influenced was the tradition of harp-song—and the words referring to it—among Christian Anglo-Saxons by the dominant figure of David? (see Steger). There may be no answers to these problems and objections, and certainly these reservations must underlie the discussion that follows; nonetheless, it may be profitable to proceed.

I shall consider first the four Old English words for poets or performers and follow the paths along which discussion of these words leads us. I exclude from consideration here the word *þyle*, which has on occasion been linked with the poet-words: all the evidence I have consulted leads to the conclusion that the þyle was an orator and in no way connected in the Anglo-Saxon world with poetry (see Norman: 1938; Hollowell). That leaves *scop, gleoman, woþbora,* and *leoþwyrhta.* I shall pay particular attention to the social function of these performers and to their connection (if any) with musical instruments. The most convincing explanations of the word *scop* connects it with a root meaning "to create": the scop was a shaper, creator, maker. As we have seen, the gleoman is a gleeman, a man associated with joy, fun, and entertainment. The woþbora is a bearer of woþ and the leoþwyrhta a maker of leoþ.

Of these four words, then, *scop* is the only simplex, the other three being self-explaining compounds; as such, the scop may well have been the original poetic figure, a personage operating before the need arose to coin compound words for related functionaries. We have already examined four of the occurrences of the word. In the undated poetry, *scop* occurs three times in *Beowulf*: in Heorot there was the clear song of the scop ("swutol sang scopes," 90) in the happy days before Grendel's first attack; the scop performs in Heorot when the Geats arrive ("Scop hwilum sang hador on Heorote," 496 f.); and Hrothgar's scop had to utter hall-entertainment for those on the mead benches concerning the followers of Finn ("ðonne healgamen Hroþgares scop æfter medobence mænan scolde be Finnes eaferum," 1066 ff.). In the first and third passages, the performance may have been accompanied by a harp, though the difficulties posed by the poetic technique of variation and the absence of our modern system of punctuation in the manuscript render such a conclusion debatable; in the third passage the scop's performance of the Finn episode is subsequently referred to as a "gleomannes gyd" (1160). Deor refers to himself as the scop of the Heodenings ("þæt ic hwile wæs Heodeninga scop," 36); nowhere in the autobiographical section is there any mention of musical accompaniment.

There are three other references to a scop in the extant poetry. *Maxims I* says that a man's sword should have gold, a woman should have fine ornaments taken as booty and treasure, men should have a good scop, they should have battle with spears, and strength to protect homes:

> Gold geriseþ   on guman sweorde,
> sellic sigesceorp,   sinc on cwene,
> god scop gumum,   garniþ werum,
> wig towiþre   wicfreoþa healdan.
>
> [*ASPR*, III, 125–28]

Again there is no mention of music, and we are told nothing explicit about the scop except that a good scop belongs among men. One inference, however, has a strong measure of probability: the scop operates in a context of battle. This is a martial passage referring to armour, booty, and war (*sweorde, sigesceorp, garniþ, wic*, and in this context *healdan*); a good scop could claim a position in this list only if he exhorted the troops in battle (see Taylor). This conclusion receives support from the references to poetry in classical authors, as we have seen, although there is no extant association of the scop with battle in Old English or Anglo-Latin, with the possible exception of Eddius's description of the South Saxon magus high on a barrow encouraging his companions and attempting to rob Wilfrid's party of their strength. In *The Battle of Maldon* Englishmen encourage each other with set speeches that may have taken poetic form, but none of them is called a scop.

We learn even less about the scop from the use of the word in a unique poem that Dobbie connects with the school of Canterbury (see Whitbread: 1976); the poem appears in a manuscript of Aldhelm's prose *De Virginitate* written in the tenth century, and opens with a reference to Aldhelm as learned, a good author and a noble scop:

> Þus me gesette   sanctus et iustus
> beorn boca gleaw,   bonus auctor,
> Ealdhelm, æþele sceop,   etiam fuit
> ipselos on æðele   Angolsexna,
> byscop on Bretene.
>
> [*ASPR*, VI, 1–5]

Aldhelm, of course, was renowned as a Latin poet, so we need not necessarily connect this reference to William of Malmesbury's anecdote about Aldhelm's vernacular performances. All one can safely infer from this passage is that *scop* means poet and that it in no way impugned the reputation of a learned bishop to call him a scop, though we have no way of knowing precisely when the poem was composed.

The final reference to a scop in the extant poetry occurs in the thirtieth *Meter of Boethius*, where Homer is said to have been the most skilled in leoþ among the Greeks, the friend and teacher of Virgil, the best of masters to that renowned poet:

> Omerus wæs   east mid Crecum
> on ðæm leodscipe   leoða cræftgast,
> Firgilies   freond and lareow,
> þæm mæran sceope   magistra betst.
>
> [*ASPR*, V, 1–4]

This is a versification of the Old English (ed. Sedgefield: 1899) "Þeah Omerus se goda sceop, þe mid Crecū selest was: se was Firgilies lareow; se Frigilius wæs mid Lædenwarum selest." The Latin original has nothing on Virgil or anything on Homer apart from the introductory "Homer of the honeyed voice sings" ("Melliflui canit oris Homerus," V, II, 3). The Anglo-Saxon prose translator explained that the good scop Homer was the best of the Greeks and the teacher of Virgil who was the best among the Romans; the Anglo-Saxon poet transferred "se goda sceop" of the prose to Virgil, whom he calls the famous scop. Nothing much can be made of this except to note that scop here is applied to two renowned pagan poets.

The word *scop* is used in three compounds. In the previous chapter we noted that the bird speaking *Riddle 8* refers to itself as an old poet of the evening, "eald æfensceop" (5). We also noted in the eleventh-century *Canons of Edgar*, and the *Laws of the Northumbrian Priests* based on it, that priests were discouraged from being ale-poets: "We læraδ, δæt ænig preost ne beo ealuscop" and "Gif preost oferdruncen lufige oδδe gliman oδδe ealascop wurδe, gebete þæt." In the eleventh-century tract called by Liebermann *Be griδe be munde,* the only other compound with *scop, sealmscop* for psalmist (usually David), occurs in the introductory phrase "as the psalmist truly said" ("eal swa se sealmscop soδlice sæde," 23). None of these compounds necessarily informs us about *scop*. The *æfensceop* is a hapax legomenon, and may be a nonce-compound; one must remember that it occurs in a riddle in which the technique is to supply the audience with accurate though misleading or mystifying clues to the speaker's identity: the jay metaphorically is a poet who performs in the evening. The ale-poet compound may well indicate a low social status (in the eyes of Wulfstan), especially when coupled with the gleoman and a context of drunkenness, but this does not necessarily imply that the scop had a low status: Wulfstan felt constrained to prefix *ealu* to *scop* to clarify his intention, and in any case *scop* was the only simplex for a performer that he could use in a concise compound implying the association with drink. Wulfstan is, as far as we know, the only Anglo-Saxon to have committed the compound to writing, and may himself have coined it. A poet who performs psalms is a psalm-poet, sealmscop: this again is inevitable if *scop* is the only simplex referring to a performer. Admittedly, the psalmist is conventionally a harper; but the man who originally coined the compound need not have been troubled by a knowledge that the Anglo-Saxon scop performed without a harp whereas David, the Old Testament sealmscop, sometimes used a musical instrument. One derives no exact information from a consideration of the compounds.

In the extant prose writings, apart from one occurrence of *scop* in Byrhtferth's Manual (ed. Crawford), the word appears mainly in Alfredian translations: in the Boethius, the Orosius, the Pastoral Care, and the Dialogues. In the
section of his manual dealing with rhetoric, Byrhtferth, echoing a well-known
classical rhetorical distinction in story, has occasion to write:

> There is yet a third species of narrative, which in Latin is called *commune*,
> and in English common, or *mixtum*, that is to say mixed; this the Greek
> grammarians term κοινόν or μικτόν. When the poet introduces other per-
> sons [Þonne se sceop in gebringð oðre hadas] who talk with him as if they
> were answering him, the composition is called κοινόν or μικτόν. Those
> works which are called the Iliad and the Odyssey of Homer and the Aeneid
> of Virgil are written in this way. [170–73]

Clearly the scop here is a pagan poet like Homer or Virgil, as in the passage
already quoted from the Boethius. Two other passages in the Boethius offer
further examples of this usage. Referring to the deception of glory, Boethius
quotes two lines from Euripides introduced by "Unde non iniuria tragicus
exclamat" (III, 6). The Old English translation reads "be ðæm wæs gio singende
sum sceop" (XXX, 1). Later, referring to the form of the divine substance
("divinae forma substantiae"), Boethius quotes a line from Parmenides introduced by "sicut de ea Parmenides ait" (III, 12), which the Anglo-Saxon translator
renders "swa swa gio Parmenides se sciop giddode 7 cwð" (XXX, 6).

The compound *sealmscop* for psalmist occurs frequently. While it tells us
nothing about the Anglo-Saxon scop, its use with certain verbs is sometimes
interesting; for the sake of completeness I cite some examples. The translation
of Gregory's Dialogues (ed. Hecht) has the introductory clauses "forþon is wen,
þæt hit wære gesæd þurh þone sealmscop, þa þa he þus cwæð." The translation
of Gregory's Pastoral Care (ed. Sweet: 1871) has the following instances: "Be
ðæm se salmsceop cwæð" (p. 69); "Ða medomnesse ðære strengio se salmscop
ongeat, ða he cuæð" (p. 85); "Be ðæm gesuince spræc se salmsceop, ða he cuæð"
(p. 239); "Be ðæm ilcan se salmscop cuæð" (p. 253); "For ðæm cuæð se sealmscop" (p. 251); "Be ðæm cwæð se psalmsceop" (p. 273); "Be ðæm suiðe wel
cwæð se psalmsceop" (p. 275); "Ðæt tacnode se salmscop, ða he cwæð"
(p. 279); "To ðæm cwide belimpð eac ðæs psalmscopes sang ða he sang, ða
he cwæð" (p. 335); "Be ðæm cwæð se psalmscop" (p. 339); "geðence se ðone
cwide ðe se psalmscop cuæð, he cwæð" (p. 347); "Bi ðæm spræc Dauid swiðe
cuðlice on psalmum, swa he hit oft acunnad hæfde, he cwæð" (p. 373); "Eft
be ðæm ilcan cuæð se psalmsceop" (p. 389); "Ðæt eac gecyðde se psalmsceop

swiðe openlice, ða he cwæð" (p. 391); "Be ðæm wæs eft gecweden ðurh ðone salmsceop" (p. 391); "Be ðæm is swiðe wel gecweden ðurh ðone psalmsceop on ðæm an 7 ðritigoðan psalme, he cwæð" (p. 419); "Be ðæm ilcan cwæð eac se salmscop on ðæm feower 7 fiftiogoðan psalme, he cwæð" (p. 429); and "Be ðæm wæs gecweden swiðe ryhte ðurh ðone psalmscop" (p. 435). In Alfric's sermons (ed. Thorpe) one finds "Soðlice se sealm-sceop awrat be Criste" (p. 106); "be ðam sang se sealm-scop" (p. 116); "swa swa se sealm-wyrhta cwæð" (p. 112); "He onlihte Dauides heortan, ðaða he on iugoðe hearpan lufode, and worhte hine to psalm-wyrhtan" (p. 322); "Be ðam cwæð se sealm-wyrhta" (p. 348); "swa swa se sealm-sceop be ðam gyddigende sang" (p. 410); "swa swa se sealm-scop be gehwilcum rihtwisum cwæð" (p. 516); "Be þisum cwæð se sealmscop" (p. 520); "Mid þyssere fætnysse wolde se sealm-wyrhta beon gemæst, ðaða he cwæð" (p. 522); "Eft, se sealm-wyrhta be Godes gecorenum cwæð" (p. 536); "hi habbað þæt land þe se sealm-sceop embe spræc" (p. 550); "Ponne mæg he cweðan mid þam sealm-sceope" (p. 552); "Se sealm-scop cwæð" (p. 574); "Be ðisum cwæð se sealm-scop" (p. 584); and "swa swa se sealm-scop cwæð be Godes gecorenum" (p. 692). The word occurs also, as we have seen, in the eleventh-century tract *Be griðe be munde*: "eal swa se sealmscop soðlice sæde, þa ða he þus sang," 23.

Far more interesting examples may be found in the translation of Orosius (ed. Sweet: 1883). Orosius (I, 8) cites Pompeius Trogus as his authority on Joseph's prediction of the famine in Egypt: "the historian Pompeius and his epitomizer Justin tells us of this, and amongst other things Justin says . . ." ("Pompejus historicus ejusque breviator Justinus docet: qui inter caetera sic ait"). The Old English version reads, "From ðæm Iosepe, Sompeius se hæþena scop 7 his cniht Iustinus wæran ðus singende" (p. 32). At the conclusion of his quotation from Justinus, Orosius refers to the expulsion of Moses and his people from Egypt: in the Old English "se scop wæs secgende þæt Egypti adrifen Moyses ut mid hys leodum" (p. 34). When Orosius refers to the Trojan war (I, 17), he declines to recount the events inasmuch as Homer, the renowned poet, has clarified them in his superb poem ("Homerus poeta, in primis clarus, luculentissimo carmine palam fecit"), which the Anglo-Saxon translator (see Bately; Liggins) renders "þæt Omerus se scop sweotelicost sægde" (p. 50). In recounting the war between the Lacedaemonians and the Messenians (I, 21), Orosius says that the Lacedaemonians chose as their leader Tyrtaeus, the Athenian poet ("Tyrtaeum, poetam Atheniensem, ducem praelio legunt"; in Old English, "Ac gecuron him anne scop to cyninge of Atheniensem," p. 56). The

Lacedaemonians were defeated in three battles, and were about to give up the struggle, when Tyrtaeus composed and recited a poem to an assembled crowd which so aroused them that they returned to the battle ("Cum desistendum certamine propter metum periculi arbitrarentur, Tyrtaei ducis composito carmine et pro concione recitato, rursus accensi, mox in certamen ruunt"; "Þa hi him nealæhtan, þa getweode hie hwæðer hie wið him mæhten. Se heora cyning ongan ða singan 7 giddian, 7 mid þæm scopleoðe heora mod swiðe getrymede, to þon þæt hie cwædon þæt hie Mesiana folce wiðstondan mehten," pp. 56 and 58). In recounting widespread unrest not only in Rome but in all the provinces (II, 5), Orosius quotes Virgil's lines (*Aen.* II, 368 ff.) on ubiquitous mourning, fear, and the shadow of death ("Ad hæc non Romae tantum talia gerebantur, sed quaeque provincia suis ignibus aestuabat: et, quod poeta praecipuus in una Urbe descripsit, ego de toto Orbe dixerim: Crudelis ubique/ Luctus, ubique pavor, et plurima mortis imago"; "Næs na on Romanum anum, ac swa hit an scopleoðum sungen is þæt gind ealne middangeard wære caru 7 gewin 7 ege," p. 72).

A crucial passage for our purposes occurs at the start of the third Book. After the Greeks had defeated the Persians on a number of occasions, Artaxerxes ordered the Greeks to observe a peace, which they eagerly accepted. Orosius considers this action shameful and roundly condemns it:

> Surely the Greeks could have disdained him who ordered just as firmly as they often bravely conquered him, but they gladly seized the opportunity offered them from whatever source for the peace which they so eagerly desired, for they showed with what difficulty and how wretchedly they hitherto had carried on those wars which they so easily laid aside on even unworthy terms; for what is so intolerable for free and brave men as to lay aside their arms to the power of one who is far away, often conquered, still an enemy, and still threatening, and to serve his peace? The Greeks would not have acted in this way had not the bitter intention of war melted in the hearts of all at only the very sound of a proclaimed peace, and had not the unexpected quiet of peace relaxed them as they became listless and bewildered after long and laborious vigils, before their desires had been stipulated and had arranged the respite itself. [III, 1, trans. Deferrari, 78]

Orosius attributes the Greeks' acceptance of this shameful peace to a failure of their martial resolve caused by their enjoyment of a noncombative situation.

The Anglo-Saxon translator supplies a different motive in his summary of this passage: the Greek fighting spirit was the product of poetic exhortation. The translator repeats the Persian demand for peace and the Spartans' eager acceptance of the terms. From this, one can readily perceive how great a desire they had for battle only as long as their poets were chanting their poems and their deceptions. Surely, Orosius said, such a battle seems undesirable and the times seem more important than that his enemy should be able to sway him so easily with his words? "On þæm mon mæg sweotole oncnawan hu micelne willan hie to ðæm gewinne hæfdon swa heora scopas on heora leoðum giddiende sindon, 7 on heora leasspellengum. Ne geþyncð þe swelc gewin noht lustbære, cwæð Orosius, ne þa tida þon ma, þætte him his feond mæge swa eaþe his mid wordum gestieran?" (94). Either the translator had some source for his information on the operation of Greek poets, or he assumed that the Greek poets functioned like the Anglo-Saxon scop did and attributed to them activities practised by the scop. The translator may, of course, be thinking of Tyrtaeus's poetic harangue quoted above, but that occurred during a conflict between Greek and Greek, not between Greek and Persian. Book II concerns itself with the battles against the Persians; twice Leonidas exhorts his troops (II, 9 and II, 11), and once the fleeing Athenians are turned back by a speech (II, 17), but the translator does not reproduce the latter passage and demonstrates by his translation that he takes the speeches of Leonidas to be nonpoetic ("he . . . wæs sprecende 7 geomriende," p. 80; "he sprecende wæs," p. 84). It is possible, therefore, since there is no textual justification for the activity of the Greek "scopas," that the translator assumed there were among the Greeks, figures comparable to the Anglo-Saxon scop, and that they were responsible for inciting the Greeks to heroic conduct in battle. If this is so, then it is perhaps of crucial significance that the translator seems to disapprove of their activity. They inspire the Greeks with their "leoþ," but also with "leasspellung," untrue facts. The Anglo-Saxon's value judgement here, unwarranted by Orosius's text, implies that he disapproves of those poets who inspire troops to battle with their (eulogistic) poetry. He may have believed that the scop's poems were inaccurate, or that they exerted too much influence over men, or that they were associated with a pagan past; the Alfredian translator's apparent disapproval may well explain the absence of any reference to vernacular oral poets in Asser's biography of the king.

There are two other occurrences of the word *scop* in the Orosius. After the conclusion of the war with the Carthaginians, Scipio Africanus enters Rome in triumph. Behind him in a chariot rode a noble Carthaginian captive, Terence, who was later to become a comic poet ("Scipio triumphans Urbem ingressus est, quem Terrentius, qui postea comicus, ex nobilibus Carthaginiensium captivis . . . secutus est," IV, 19; "Þa him mon þone triumphan ongean brohte, þa eode þær mid Terrentius, se mæra Cartaina scop," p. 202). Finally, Orosius places Nero high in a tower overlooking the burning Rome, declaiming the *Iliad* ("Quod ipse ex altissima turre prospectans, laetusque flammae pulchritudine, Iliadem decantabat," VII, 7; "7 gestod him self on þæm hiehstan torre þe þærbinnan wæs, 7 ongan wyrcan scopleoð be þæm bryne," 260–62).

Let us pause to consider this material before we pass on to the evidence afforded by the glosses. Overwhelmingly, *scop* is used to refer to a classical poet: Virgil, Homer, Parmenides, and Tyrtaeus are all scops. Homer and Tyrtaeus are specifically called *poetae* in the Latin original, and *scop* may be taken as an acceptable translation of *poeta*, a classical poet. *Tragicus* (Euripides) and *comicus* (Terence) are also translated as *scop*: we are probably to take these instances in the same category as the former, classical poets, making of Euripides a tragic poet and of Terence a comic poet rather than dramatists. The range of meaning is extended, however, by the translation of *historicus* (Pompeius and Justinus) as *scop*. We are reminded of Tacitus's statement that the Germans celebrate Tuisto and Mannus "carminibus antiquis, quod unum apud illos memoraie et annalium genus est" (*Germ.* 2): clearly the scop is poet and historian. What he produces is a "scopleoð," a poetic performance: we are reminded of the compound *scopgereord* in Bede's account of Cædmon, which can taken as "poetic language." One cannot identify the classical poeta, tragicus, comicus, or historicus with the Anglo-Saxon scop, but aspects of the functions of these classical figures must have been common to the functions of the scop in order to make the translation suitable: the poeta, tragicus, and comicus, perhaps, like the scop, produced poetry; the historicus, like the scop, dealt with history. As to the *sealmscop* examples, here again one cannot equate the Old Testament psalmist with the Anglo-Saxon scop, although the translation is feasible since both produced poetry. The word *sealmwyrhta*, maker of psalms, seems to be used as a synonym for *sealmscop*, a psalm-poet.

In the Alfredian translations, the verb most frequently associated with the sealmscop is *cweþan*; so predominant is it, that even when another finite verb is used, *cweþan* still introduces the quotation. Other verbs used in the examples quoted are *sprecan* (twice), and *singan* and *secgan* (once each). *Be griðe be munde* uses *singan* and *secgan*. In the examples quoted from Alfric, *cweþan* is again preponderant, although *sprecan* and *awritan* are used once each, and *singan* twice (once in combination with *giddian* in the phrase *giddigende sang*). Nine of the

examples quoted from the extant prose associate the scop with the act of performing; *singan* occurs four times, *giddian* three times, *secgan* twice, and *wyrcan*
and *cwepan* once each. With regard to *cwepan*, the difference between the *scop*
and the *sealmscop* groups is striking. As descriptions of the scop's performance
in public, *singan* and *giddian* seem to be most apt: Tyrtaeus addressing the dis-
heartened crowd "ongan singan 7 giddian," and the "scopas giddiende sindon."
But the verbs may apparently encompass poetic expression in writing as well:
Euripides "wæs singende" (*exclamat*), Parmenides "giddode 7 cwð" (*ait*), Pompeius (and Justinus) "wæran singende" (*ait*), and Virgil's description "an scopleoðum sungen is" (*descripsit*). In Xhosa the noun *izibongo* and the verb *ukubonga*
referred to a purely oral activity, although they have come to include written
productions by extension of meaning; it seems reasonable that *giddian* and *singan*
were originally associated with the scop's oral performances, although the verbs
were extended to include written activities after the conversion. The translator
spurns a splendid opportunity to provide us with a semantic distinction between
composing and performing when he has Tyrtaeus begin to "singan 7 giddian,"
for the Latin explicitly has *composito* and *recitato*, but Nero's recitation of the
Iliad (*decantabat*) is rendered "wyrcan scopleoð": *wyrcan* cannot mean "compose" here and must accordingly mean "perform."

We turn finally to the occurrences of the word *scop* in the glosses and glossaries. The potential value of the glosses as evidence for semantic change is
limited somewhat by the traditional nature of these works—many of the glosses
depend on earlier glosses (see Marshall)—and by the fact that our earliest glosses
date only from the eighth century, perhaps 150 years after the introduction of
Christianity to England. To give only some examples of the interrelationships
of these works: the four earliest glossaries, Epinal, Erfurt, Corpus, and Leiden
(ed. Hessels; Holthausen; Lindsay; Pheifer; Sweet: 1885; Wright: 1884),
draw on four earlier glossaries (Abstrusa, Abolita, Hermeneumata, and Philoxe-
nus) as well as on glosses found in manuscripts of the works of writers like
Orosius, Rufinus, Jerome, and Phocas. Epinal is probably the earliest, dated to
the eighth century by Ker. Part of Erfurt, which is in a late eighth-century hand,
copies Epinal, and Corpus, of the same date, uses Epinal-Erfurt material. Later
glossaries depend on the earlier compilations: Cotton Cleopatra A III (tenth
century), for example, has material derived from Epinal-Erfurt, and Harley
3376 (late tenth century) uses Corpus.

Unfortunately, none of the earliest glossaries includes the word *scop*, though
Corpus does have "Divinos uuitgan." There are in the early glossaries the entries *vates divini* and *poeta vates*, which suggest a connection (though not necessarily an equation, of course) between *divinus*, a prophet, *vates*, *poeta*, and the

Old English *witega*. Before we leave the earliest glossaries, let us note the Leiden gloss "philocain grece scopon"; Hessels comments: "Neither the lemma nor the gloss *scopon* are clear. The nearest approach to philocain is the Gr. φιλόκαιν-ον, a love of novelty or innovation. Kluge (*A. S. Leseb.*) takes *scopon* as AS. *sceop* (*scop*), a poet . . ." (p. 167). The suggested etymology of *scop* as a creator or maker accords with this interpretation, but the form *scopon* is so problematical that further comment might well be futile.

In the late tenth-century glosses of Alfric's Grammar, *uates* is glossed as "witega oððe sceop." Also in the tenth century, in Cotton Cleopatra A III, "scop" is given for *comicus* and "scopas" for *lyrici*. Late in the tenth century, possibly early in the eleventh, Harley 3376 (ed. Oliphant) connects *scopas* with *comedi uel comici* and has an unusually long gloss for *comicus*: "siue est qui comedia scribit. cantator. uel artifex conticorum seculorum. idem satyricus. .i. scop. ioculator. poeta." From much the same period, MS Bod. Digby 146 glosses *pedibus poeticus. i. metricus* as "mid scoplicum meterlicum fotum." In the eleventh-century, MS BM Add. 32246, the vocabulary and supplement appended to Alfric's Grammar, has a number of glosses dealing with public performers, which we shall examine shortly; those that mention *scop* are *tragedi uel comedi* glossed as "unweorðe scopes"; *liricus* as "scop"; and *tragicus uel comicus* as "unwurð scop"; and we should also note the gloss of *poeta uel vates* as "leoð-wyrhta." This latter gloss casts light on two later glossaries associated with Alfric's Grammar, the twelfth-century Cotton Julius A II and the thirteenth-century Worcester Cathedral F 174, both of which gloss *poeta* as "sceop oððe leoðwyrhta."

There are two, possibly three, strains in these examples: there are those glosses that connect *scop* with *vates*, there are those that connect it with theatrical entertainments, and (perhaps part of the preceding group) those that equate *scop* with *liricus*. In discussing these glosses, one should remember that they were designed to suggest to a reader the meaning of a Latin word; one cannot argue for equivalence, but only for an area of congruence in the denotation. The interrelation of *divinus*, *vates*, and *poeta* in the earliest glosses, and their connection with Old English *witega*, for example, does not mean that the witega was a poet; he is connected with *divinus*, a prophet or seer, and it is probably the aspect of divine inspiration or public utterance that allows the connection of *divinus* to *vates* and *poeta*. The gloss of *uates* as "witega oððe sceop," similarly, does not mean that *witega* and *scop* are equivalent, but only that *vates* and *witega* have something in common, and that *vates* and *sceop* also have something in common that is not necessarily identical to the aspect shared by *vates* and *witega*. *Vates*, of course, has its areas of congruence with both *divinus* and *poeta*, and we are probably justified in assuming that the scop was a poet, like the vates and the poeta, though he may well in addition have been a divinely inspired seer like the vates and the divinus. It is unlikely, from the interconnection between these words, that the scop was a despised member of the glossators' community.

As for the glosses with theatrical connections, one should note the conclusions of Mary Marshall that "probably in the Carolingian period, and certainly by the tenth century, a misconception of the ancient methods of staging plays became rather widely diffused" (16), that "the knowledge of the Roman theatre shown in the Old English and Old High German glossaries and glosses of the eighth to the eleventh centuries is thin and elementary as we should expect" (16), and that in the Old English glossaries "theatrical terms were meagrely glossed as ideas without reality" (12). The connection between *comicus* and *scop* was already made in the Alfredian Orosius's translation of *comicus* (Terence), as we saw, and this or a similar association of ideas may account for the Cotton Cleopatra A III and Harley 3376 glosses of *comicus* as "scop" and *comedi uel comici* as "scopas." The exceptionally long gloss of *comicus*, in Harley 3376, as someone who writes comedies as well as someone who composes secular songs could follow from Isidore's definitions of theatrical terms quoted in an earlier chapter. *Poeta* as well as *comicus* featured in some of those definitions, and the scop may find himself in the company of the vernacular singer, the satirist and the ioculator, not because he is equivalent to any of these figures, but because he has in common with them the public performance, and because he can be connected with both comicus and poeta, both of whom, through Isidore's definitions, can in turn be connected with satyricus and ioculator. The citharoedus also featured in Isidore's definitions, and his association with poeta and comicus may account for the *scop: liricus* glosses. Of course, one must concede that it is just as possible that the scop is associated with the ioculator because the scop was one of the members of the popular troupes of wandering minstrels, and that the scop is associated with the liricus because he played a lyre; if this interpretation is insisted upon, then it remains simply to notice that the earliest extant connection of the scop with figures associated with the Roman theatres comes in the tenth century, a period postdating the postulated alteration in the tradition of the scop as a vatic eulogiser and his possible acceptance of the role of public entertainer. The element of social distinction, however, attaches to the scop through his association with vates and indirectly with divinus, and perhaps comes through most clearly in the eleventh-century gloss of *tragicus uel comicus* as "unwurð scop" and *tragedi uel comedi* as "unweorðe scopes," which seems to imply that the dramatic writers or actors could be equated with a low-class scop, with a social role unworthy of the scop, implying in turn that the scop had a serious function in society.

The evidence of the glosses thus suggests that the scop was not associated with public entertainers until after the tenth century (if he ever was), and that the scop was a serious, respected member of the community whose role was more significant than that of entertainment. These conclusions are in harmony with tentative ones derived from a consideration of the evidence of the extant Old English prose and poetry, as well as the ideas suggested, particularly in chapter 2, by a comparative study of existing eulogistic traditions. The element of serious social function is what sets the scop apart from the gleoman.

The word *gleo* (*gliw*, *glig*), cognate with Old Norse *glý*, means joy, glee, mirth. A gleoman is one who creates joy or mirth, an entertainer. He may entertain by playing a lyre, or by clowning or juggling or acting. The gleoman is not necessarily a harper, though he may be, nor is he any one person. Unlike *scop*, which refers to a distinct personage in society, *gleoman* is a generic term referring to various kinds of public performers. If the scop's function in society shifts so that he is conceived of as an entertainer, he may presumably be called a gleoman too. The scop in Heorot, as we saw, produced performances incidental to the situation confronting him at the time, unlike those who uttered poetry outside the hall; he contributed to the *dream* in Heorot, and as such his performance of the Finn episode might well be termed a *gleomannes gyd* (1160) if its function was to entertain the newly arrived Geats and their Danish hosts. The broad range of activities purveyed by a gleoman—all sharing the function of entertainment—may be appreciated most readily from the glosses for *gleo* and *gleoman*.

Epinal, Erfurt, and Leiden have as a gloss for *in mimo* the unusually long "in gliuuae quod tamen ad mimarios vel mimografos (mimigraphos, mimographus) pertinet." Pheifer suggests as the source Orosius VI, 22, which says that Caesar Augustus disliked the title "lord," for he would interrupt and subsequently rebuke any personal interpretation given to a line such as "a gracious and good lord indeed" which might be uttered in the course of a mime while he was watching a play ("spectante ludos pronuntiatum esset in mimo . . ."). "In the mime, i.e. in the mimic play" is glossed as *in gliuuae,* but this is immediately qualified by the statement "which nevertheless refers to mimic plays or the composer of such plays." Clearly *gleo* had a much wider range of meaning, which the glossator was at pains to limit: "*In mimo* means 'in the entertainment' but refers in particular to dramatic performers and performances." Epinal and Erfurt also gloss *facitiae* as "gliu," perhaps derived from Abstrusa "facetias iocos"; again, *gleo* is entertainment, here humour or jesting. Corpus repeats the "facetia glio" and the "in mimo in gliowe" glosses, and has in addition "cabillatio glio" and "gannatura gliu." Both would seem to refer to public insult, satire, or raillery: Epinal has "cauillatio iocus cum uicio"; and Cleopatra I has "gannature cancettende" and Cleopatra III "gannature bysmires."

The word *gleoman,* like *scop,* does not unfortunately appear in the early glossaries, but its later appearance confirms its connection to the early glosses for *gleo* by association with wandering (theatrical) entertainers: the late tenth-century Bod. Digby 146 has "per gimnosphistas þurh witige pleiman gleawe gligman," "parasitis. i. ministris þenum gligman," "parasitorum spilra gliwera" and "parasitorum gliwra cnihta forspillendra þena"; the eleventh-century Aldhelm Glosses (Bod. 97) have "parasitorum gliwera"; BM Add. 32246 in the eleventh century has "pantomimus gligmann," "orcestra uel pulpitus glig-manna yppe," and "mimus jocista scurra gligmon"; the eleventh-century Prudentius Glosses (Boul. MS 189) have "circulator seductor gligmann" and "scurra spilra gliwera"; the twelfth-century Alfric glosses (Cot. Jul. A 11) has "mimus uel scurra gligman"; and the thirteenth-century Worcester Cathedral F 174 Alfric glosses have "mimus uel scurra gleoman."

Clearly gleomen were entertainers associated with those offshoots of the Roman theatres (pantomimus, mimus, scurra, jocista) who wandered about (parasitus, circulator) and were considered morally undesirable (seductor, gimnosphista, the gymnosophistae being "a sect of hermits who disregarded the decencies of life"). It is also worth noting that, apart from the long Harley 3376 gloss associating *comicus, satyricus, scop, ioculator,* and *poeta, scop* and *gleo-man* are kept quite distinct in the glosses. The scop may be a comicus or tragicus, an author of comedies or tragedies, but he is never a scurrilous performer. The distinction is perhaps most clearly seen in the sequence of glosses in the voca-bulary following Alfric's Grammar ("mimus jocista scurra gligmon," "panto-mimus gligman," "orcestra uel pulpitus gligmanna yppe," "tragedi uel comedi unweorðe scopes") and in the supplement ("liricus scop," "poema leoð," "poesis leoðweorc," "poeta uel uates leoðwyrhta," and "tragicus uel comicus unwurð scop"). The gleoman has no connection in the glosses with poetry or indeed with composition; he is a wandering entertainer of dubious repute. For the sake of completeness, I should add a gloss on the Kansas Leaf (dated about 1000) of MS Harley 3376, though the last word is illegible as a result of a fold; if it is in fact *gliwmen,* it supports the conclusion that is already evident, that the word *gleoman* was applied to the wandering theatrical entertainers: "Istriones sunt gestuosi qui se uertunt, dicarum feminarum exprimebant qui imitantur ominem rem facere i., imitatores gliwmen." The general application of *gleo* is exemplified in a gloss to Gregory's *Dialogues*: "gligcræft ars musica, histrionia, mimica, gesticulatio" (1, 9; Padelford, 77).

The connection of *gleo* with music is seen in Wulfstan's connection of miscellaneous *gleo*-joy with harping and piping: "Hearpe 7 pipe 7 mistlice gliggamen dremað eow on beorsele; 7 ge Godes craefta nan ðing ne gymað" (Bethurum, 217). This association of music with drinking and its polar opposition to the pursuit of the divine may also underlie Wulfstan's proscription in the *Canons of Edgar* (ed. Fowler): "And we læraδ þæt ænig preost ne beo ealascop, ne on ænige wisan gliwige mid him silfum oðrum mannum," 59; in the *Laws of the Northumbrian Priests*: "Gif preost oferdruncen lufige oðδe gliman oðδe ealascop wurðe, gebete þæt"; and Alfric's explicit "Ne ge gligmenn ne beon" (*Third Pastoral Letter*, 188: Fowler, 39). The use of *gleo* for general (frivolous) entertainment is seen also in Wulfstan's admonition, "Bisceopum gebyrep, þæt hi ne beon to gliggeorne, ne hunda ne hafeca hedan to swyðe . . ." (*Incipit de Synodo*, 8; Fowler, 39).

Perhaps the most explicit indication of the connection of the gleoman with frivolous entertainment comes in the translation of Gregory's *Cura Pastoralis* (ed. Sweet: 1871). Gregory writes (ed. Migne, 77; trans. Davis), in Book 3, chapter 10, of the different admonishments to be directed at the kindly and the envious; of the former, he says

> The kindly-disposed must, therefore, be told that if they do not bestir themselves to imitate what they approve and praise, the holiness of virtue pleases them in the same manner that the vain art of public performers pleases foolish spectators [sicut stultis spectatoribus ludicrarum artium vanitas placet]; for these extol with favours the performance of charioteers and actors [Illi namque aurigarum et histrionum gesta favoribus efferunt], yet do not wish to be like those whom they applaud. They admire people for the pleasing exhibition [placita] they give, but decline to please others in like manner.

The Old English version talks of the kindly disposed having as much reward "as we have of our laughter, when we laugh at the vain skill of entertainers [swæ we habbað ðæs hleahtres, ðonne we hlihhað gligmonna unnytes cræftes]. We praise their skills [We heriað hiera cræftes], and yet do not desire to possess them, for we have no glory from them [forðæm we hiera nabbað nan lof, 230].

We admire the' great appreciation of their skill, but do not desire the same appreciation." The translator has naturalised and personalised Gregory's reference to charioteers and actors by substituting just "gligmonna" for "aurigarum et histrionum" and the first person "we" for the foolish spectators of Gregory's Latin. Although this is a translation, we might be justified, therefore, in taking the gligman as an Anglo-Saxon figure whose vain skills elicit Anglo-Saxon laughter.

As for the poetry, we have already discussed the single occurrence of *gleoman* in *Beowulf* (1160); we have noted its use in *Widsith* (136); and the only other occurrence in the extant poetry is in *Maxims I*, which says that wise words are fitting for every man, a "gied" is fitting for an entertainer, and skill for a man:

> Wæra gehwylcum wislicu   word gerisað,
> gleomen gied   ond guman snyttro.
>
> [*ASPR*, III, 165–66]

In this context the gleoman seems to purvey wisdom, though of course this does not mean that his performance could not be diverting.

When we considered the occurrences of *scop* in prose (mainly Alfredian), we noted that the verbs most frequently associated with his oral performances were *singan* and *giddian*, and that what he produced was a "leoð" or "scopleoð"; in considering the glosses involving *scop*, we had occasion to cite the eleventh-century glosses "poema leoð," "poesis leoðweorc," "poeta uel uates leoð-wyrhta," and the gloss of *poeta* as "sceop oððe leoðwyrhta," which occurs in the eleventh-century St. John's, Oxford, 154, the twelfth-century Cotton Julius A 11, and the thirteenth-century Worcester Cathedral F 174. When we pass on to consider the words *leoð* and *leoðwyrhta*, we shall have to pay attention at the same time to *singan* and *song*, to *giddian* and *gied*. Any discussion of these words may well be futile until a complete concordance of Old English is produced, and even then the conclusion may well be nothing more significant than that *gied* or *song* were used to refer to poetry, song, and heightened prose. I cannot claim to have consulted every occurrence of these words in Old English; nonetheless, some random notes and impressions may serve as a temporary statement until such time as we have the tools for a definitive study of the semantic interrelationships with due regard for chronology. On the evidence we have so far adduced, the scop would seem to deal with a leoð, and *leoðwyrhta,* a worker of leoð, would seem to be synonymous with *scop.* Analogous compounds exist, such as *sealmwyrhta* for a psalmist, *mederwyrhta* glossing *metric[i]us* for a metre-worker, and *leðerwyrhta* glossing *byrseus* for a leather-worker. The Old English

Orosius, as we saw, translated *Iliadem decantabat* as "ongan wyrcan scopleoð,"
and since the subject was Nero, this seemed to imply that *wyrcan* must be taken
to mean "perform" and not "compose," that is, "to work with" rather than
"to create." Certainly the byrseus works with leather and the metricius works
with metres, but the sealmwyrhta, David, certainly composed psalms: closer
inspection frees us of the restriction, for the Orosius translator adds that Nero
"ongan wyrcan scopleoð be þæm bryne," clearly referring to the burning
Rome before him, and not to the *Iliad*, unless the translator assumed that the
contents of the *Aeneid* and the *Iliad* were identical and "be þæm bryne" refers
to the burning of Troy. We are justified in taking *leoðwyrhta* as either a composer or a performer of leoð, or both. If a scop composed or performed leoð,
then clearly he was a leoðwyrhta, but were all leoðwyrhtan scopas?

Clearly a leoð was a poem: as we saw, *poesis* is glossed "leoðweorc" in the
eleventh-century BM Add. 32246, which also has "poema leoð"; the tenth-
century Cotton Cleopatra A III has *odas* glossed as "leoð." What of the compounds? There are many: *æfenleoð* (an evening leoð), *bismerleoð* (an insulting
leoð), *dryhtleoð* (a lord's leoð), *fusleoð* (a departure leoð), *fyrdleoð* (an army
leoð), *galdorleoð* (a charm leoð), *giftleoð*, *gryreleoð* (a terrible leoð), *guðleoð*
(a battle leoð), *hearmleoð* (a harmful leoð), *hildeleoð* (a battle leoð), *licleoð* (a
leoð for a corpse), *sæleoð* (a sea leoð), *scopleoð, sealmleoð, sigeleoð* (a victory
leoð), *sorhleoð* (a sorrow leoð), *wigleoð* (a battle leoð), and *wopleoð* (a weeping
leoð). Now many of these occur in poetry or in glosses, where the compounds
may be coined for the sake of alliteration or to explicate a Latin word; nonetheless, a clear pattern emerges. Many refer to battle, marriage, and death, and some
(*galdorleoð*, and probably *bismerleoð* and *hearmleoð*) may be considered to operate
in a magical context. The magical or incantational aspect may even be held to
underlie those leoð associated with rites de passage, and indeed also scopleoð
and dryhtleoð; all could be associated originally with a veneration of the ancestors, who are invoked by the vatic scop to protect the ruler, or for protective
sympathy in moments of crisis like battle, or of transition like marriage and
death, or the departure on a journey. The ritual connotation derives a measure
of support from the air of Christian disapproval that occasionally invests the use
of *leoð* or from its association with the devil: Padelford cites "ðæt man idele
leoð ne singe on ðysum dagum"; "ða deoflican leoð to singanne ðe ic ær on
worulde geleornode"; and "Se wæs ærest sumes kaseres mima, ðæt is leasere,
and sang beforan him scandlicu leoð" (82). Such a connotation, of course, does
not always invest the word: in his translation of Boethius, Alfred once uses
leoðwyrhta in a neutral sense seemingly equivalent to his use of *scop* ("What do

the *leoðwyrhtan* sing about this world apart from its various changes?" "Hwæt
singað þa leoðwyrhtan oðres be ðisse woruld buton mislica hwearfunga þisse
worulde?" VIII, 3, summarising a passage referring to tragedians, "clamor
tragoediarum," and citing Homer, II, 2) and in his proem even referring to
himself as exhibiting the skill of the leoðwyrhta:

> Ðus Ælfred us   ealdspell reahte
> cyning Westsexna,   cræft meldode,
> leoðwyrhta list.

A consideration of the use of verbs with *leoð* suggests that *singan* is the most
appropriate, but a different pattern emerges for the compounds of *leoð*. The
compounds occur eighteen times in the poetic corpus, and only five of these
make use of a verb other than *galan* or *agalan*; four of the exceptions use *singan*.
A survey of the use of *galan* reveals a pattern strikingly similar to the use of
singan: the verb is applied to human utterances (in the case of *singan*, often to the
performance of sacred music), to the utterances of heavenly beings, of birds, and
of musical instruments. The related forms *besingan* and *begalan* are often applied
to charms and might suggest incantation. The noun *song*, like the verb, refers
to the performance of humans, heavenly beings, birds, and musical instruments.

Most of the compounds of song are ecclesiastical (*æfensang, æftersang, ciric-
sang, dægredsang, lanesang, lofsang, mæssesang, middægsang, nihtsang, nonsang,
offringsang, primsang, sealmsang, tidsang, uhtsang, undernsang, ymensang*), but
some of them seem to match the pattern for *leoð* compounds (*bergelsang, birisang,
byrgensang, licsang*, a funeral *song*; and *brydsang*, a marriage *song*). These last, of
course, may well be ecclesiastic. One compound with *song* is strikingly absent
from the *leoð* compounds, *hearpsang*: it calls to mind the fact that *leoð* is nowhere explicitly associated with instrumental accompaniment. The *leoð* is produced by men and women, singly or in chorus, by amateur or by scop; the
song seems to fall within the province of ecclesiastics. The verb most frequently
associated with the compounds of *leoð*, *galan*, is etymologically related to *galdor*,
a charm or incantation; *singan* sometimes forms the predicate of *leoð* and its
compounds, and this seems to be a general term meaning "to sing," "to chant,"
or "to perform." As such, *singan* is suitable for both *leoð* and *song*, but *galan* is
not suitable for *song* in its dominant ecclesiastical usage. The character of the
leoð compounds is placed in relief by a comparison with *gied* compounds. On
the face of it, *gied* would seem to be a possible synonym for *leoð*, except that the
verb most commonly associated with it is *wrecan*, and except that its compounds
reveal a different concept. These constitute two groups, those suggestive of
form or performance and those suggestive of (emotional) content: one en-

counters *cwidegiedd, leoðgidding,* and *wordgidd,* as well as *giomorgid* and *soðgied.* The *leoð* compounds are in the main functional, referring to social events.

As a tentative conclusion, then, *leoð* would seem originally to refer to a ritual or sacral performance. Insofar as the scop produced sacral eulogies (dryhtleoð) or poetry to incite the warriors in battle or elegies in praise of a departed member of the community, he was a leoðwyrhta. However, the leoð was not the exclusive preserve of the scop; choral songs at weddings or funerals or work songs could also be ritual or sacral, and these were undoubtedly produced by everyday men and women; individuals could no doubt also produce a leoð on significant occasions whether or not they were scops. Accordingly, a leoð could be a song or a poem or an incantation; when a scop produced a leoð (scopleoð) it was no doubt a poem, when rowers sang a sæleoð or warriors performed their baritus it was what we would call a song. The essence of the word, though, connects it with ritual or ceremony. Whether it was sung or chanted, the leoð was not accompanied by a musical instrument.

And that leaves, finally, the woþbora. Just as the hornbora is the bearer of a horn, a trumpeter, so too the woþbora is a bearer of woþ. The compound occurs six times in the extant poetry. Woðbora is the prophet Isaiah speaking truth in *Christ*:

> Eac we þæt gefrugnon,   þæt gefyrn bi þe
> soðfæst sægde   sum woðbora
> in ealddagum,   Esaias.
>
> [*ASPR*, III, 301–03]

In *Riddle 31* and in the *Chronicle* poem on *The Death of Edgar,* the word seems to be used merely for alliterative purposes as a wise man. *Riddle 31* ends

> Micel is to hycgenne
> wisum woðboran,   hwæt sio wiht sie
>
> [*ASPR*, III]

and in *The Death of Edgar* (33), *wise woðboran* is a variation of *cræftgleawe men* and *hæleð higegleawe*:

> And þa wearð ætywed   uppe on roderum
> steorra on staðole,   þone stiðferhþe,
> hæleð higegleawe,   hata ð wide
> cometa be naman,   cræftgleawe men,
> wise woðboran.
>
> [*ASPR*, VI, 29–33]

The horn, speaking in *Riddle 80*, says that it often gives a "woðbora" a reward for his "giedd":

> Oft ic woðboran   wordleana sum
> agyfe æfter giedde.
>
> [*ASPR*, III, 9–10]

The author of the didactic poem *The Order of the World* refers to himself as a wise woðbora in the opening lines:

> Wilt þu, fus hæle,   fremdne monnan,
> wisne woðboran   wordum gretan,
>
> [*ASPR*, III]

and one of the talented people mentioned in *The Gifts of Men* is a woðbora skilled in giedda:

> Sum biþ woðbora,
> giedda giffæst.
>
> [*ASPR*, III, 35–36]

In view of the recurrent formula *wis woðbora*, we may conclude that the woþbora was respected for his wisdom, and the identification of Isaiah as a woþbora is explicable on this count. Clearly the author of *The Order of the World* is a poet, but does he call himself a woþbora because he is a poet or because he offers wisdom? The woþbora may require a drink after performing a gied in the hall, he may be "giedda giffæst," but is he an orator, a singer, or a poet? The Epinal Glossary has "facudia eloquentia uel þoot" (Erfurt *puood*), and "lepor subtilitas uel uuoþ" (Erfurt *puod*), and Corpus has "lepor wooð" and "cot[h]urno wodhae"; Cotton Cleopatra A III offers us "rhetoribus woðborum." A meaning such as "bearer of eloquence" seems to be suggested for *woðbora*, the eloquence of reason and order; *woþ* may etymologically be connected with the act of weaving, the ordering of the logos (a suggestion kindly offered to me by Morton Bloomfield: see further Wagner; Werlich: 1967). Clearly, a poet might well be a woðbora, but a woðbora could also be an orator or a singer.

The compound *woðcræft* occurs three times in the poetry, twice in *The Phoenix*. We have already quoted the first passage, which establishes a context of song for the phrase *wrixleð woðcræfte* (127); in the second passage the poet urges men not to think that he assembles his leoð or writes his woðcræft from lying words, and he goes on to quote from Job's compositions (gieddinga):

> Ne wene þæs ænig   ælda cynnes
> þæt ic lygewordum   leoð somnige,
> write woðcræfte.
>
> [ASPR, III, 546-48]

Woðcræft would seem to be poetic skill here, or the art of poetry (ultimately the art of weaving with the larynx), a reasonable translation also for its use in the second line of The Whale: now, the poet says, I also want to speak in words, in woðcræfte, through my mind, about a kind of fish, the mighty whale:

> Nu ic fitte gen   ymb fisca cynn
> wille woðcræfte   wordum cyþan
> þurh modgemynd   bi þam miclan hwale.
>
> [ASPR, III, 1-3]

The first example may suggest song and the second two poetry, though all three may simply have the root meaning of "eloquence." Similarly, the bagpipe of Riddle 31 may produce an attractive sound ("fæger hleoþor"), an attractive gift of music ("wynlicu woðgiefu," 18), but in riddles the words are chosen to be deliberately misleading, and we may have to be content with a translation of "gift of eloquence" for woðgiefu. The last poetic compound is woðsong, which is used of the prophecies of the prophets ("witgena woðsong," 46) in Christ.

Whether the woþbora bears poetry, song, oratory, or simply eloquence, etymologically he derives his eloquence from divine inspiration, for woþ comes from Indo-European *wāt-, the same root which, with stress on the following syllable, produces Old English wod, madness, and the name of the god Wodan. We have already seen that the word is cognate with Latin vates, Irish faith, and Welsh gwawd; there is an Old High German cognate of wod, wuot, but not of woþ; and Old Norse has óðr meaning both poetry, apparently, and madness. In the Old Norse tradition the interconnection between óðr and Óðinn is clear: the god inspires poetry as well as the frenzy of the berserk in battle. Dumézil, for example, comments that:

> even Odin's name, which is not obscure, obliges us to put at the center of his character a spiritual concept from which the most effective action issues. The ON word from which it derives, óðr, and which Adam of Bremen translates excellently with furor, corresponds to German Wut "rage, fury" and to Gothic wōds, "possessed." As a noun it denotes drunkenness, excita-

tion, poetic genius (cf. OE wōð "chant"), as well as the terrifying movement of the sea, of fire, and of the storm. As an adjective, it means sometimes "violent, furious," sometimes "rapid." Outside of Germanic, related
Indo-European words refer to violent poetic and prophetic inspiration:
Latin *vates*, Old Irish *faith*. [Dumezil: 1973, 36 f.]

The interconnection of Óðinn and óðr is perhaps best expressed in The Ynglinga
Saga (*Heimskringla*, trans. Laing). Chapter 7 characterises Óðinn as preeminently
wise, and establishes his skill in the field of magic, charms, and witchcraft. "He
taught all these arts in Runes, and songs which are called incantations." The
preceding chapter tells of Óðinn's eloquence, skill in poetry, and influence in
battle: Óðinn

> conversed so cleverly and smoothly, that all who heard believed him. He
> spoke everything in rhyme, such as now composed, which we call scald-
> craft. He and his temple priests were called song-smiths, for from them
> came that art of song into the northern countries. Odin could make his
> enemies in battle blind, or deaf, or terror-struck, and their weapons so
> blunt that they could no more cut than a willow wand; on the other hand,
> his men rushed forwards without armour, were as mad as dogs or wolves,
> bit their shields, and were strong as bears or wild bulls, and killed people
> at a blow, but neither fire nor iron told upon themselves. This was called
> the Berserk fury. [Laing, 11]

This possessed madness clearly invests the Old English word *wod*: Erfurt glosses
ephilenticus, an epileptic, as "uuoda," Corpus repeats this gloss and has in addition "Inergumenos (ἐνεργούμενος, something which is worked on—or woven)
wodan," "Bac[c]hantes uuoedende," "Limphaticus woedendi," and "Lym-
phatico woedendi." Divinely inspired eloquence may take a number of forms.
The Ynglinga Saga passage allows us to postulate—and this brief study of the
words for poet lends supports to the postulation—that the scop produced vatic
poetry under the inspiration of Wodan which encouraged the troops in battle
to fight beyond their own capacities and robbed their enemies of strength.
Nelson Mabunu, a contemporary Xhosa poet, spoke of the role of the imbongi
in battle:

> An imbongi can incite people, because in the olden days when there's
> going to be a war or a battle between two sides, you would always find an
> imbongi. That is where and when the imbongi was regarded as a very im-

portant man, because he would sing praises so that even those who have got water in their hearts could go out fully and fight. . . . I think it is the same way with the Europeans: say now there is a brass band, you know, there is a war and people do not want to come out, to join the soldiers, but if that band is playing right through town you would find many coming up to sign on. [Opland Collection, item 114]

The woþbora was a bearer of wisdom and eloquence granted him as an agent of Wodan; the leoðwyrhta created and performed ceremonial songs and poems; the gleoman was an entertainer. The scop was a distinct figure in society whose eloquence and vatic, inspirational poetry associated with Wodan could merit his description as a "woþbora," whose production of poems on ceremonial occasions could merit his description as a "leoþwyrhta." He was not originally an entertainer, though he might conceivably be called upon to produce poetry for the entertainment of guests, and though in the altered social conditions after the eighth century he may have turned his hand to entertainment to secure a livelihood; on such occasions and in such conditions he might be considered to be acting as a "gleoman." Neither scop, leoðwyrhta, woþbora, nor gleoman was necessarily associated with musical instruments, though the leoðwyrhta, woþbora, and gleoman might produce songs; the gleoman could be (and sometimes was) a man who entertained his audience with musical instruments as well as or in addition to song. With the passage of time, particularly after the introduction of Christianity, the words for these originally oral performers may have weakened their denotations through extension to include artists who wrote down their compositions, especially where Christianity found itself out of sympathy with the sacral or ceremonial character of the oral performances. It is clear that though there might have been areas of congruence in the denotations of these four words, or (in the case of *scop* and *gleoman*, for example) though areas of congruence might have come into being, there is sufficient reason to consider the four words to be distinct. In particular, the scop was originally distinct from the gleoman, and, before the ninth century at any rate, there is no evidence that compels us to associate the scop with a lyre or any other musical instrument; after the ninth century we have only hypothesis as well as the long Harley 3376 gloss for *comicus*, possibly the glosses of *scop* as "liricus," and perhaps the association of *scop* (like *gleoman*) with some of the theatrical figures, to urge upon us the belief that the scop ever assumed a lyre.

How, then, was poetry performed, and what is the relation of the extant poetical texts to the lyre? Earlier in this chapter we considered the verbs applied to the activity of the scop and the sealmscop and suggested that *giddian* and *singan* seemed best to describe the oral performance of the scop (in the Orosius, Tyrtaeus "ongan singan 7 giddian," the "scopas giddiende sindon") although the sealmscop's composition was most frequently introduced by *cweþan*, even in combination with another verb. The text with the highest incidence of words for poetry is the translation of Boethius: for poetic performance, *giddian, singan*, and *cweþan* occur most frequently. *Singan* occasionally occurs in isolation (8.6, 8.7, 18.28, 33.13, for example), but most frequently the verbs occur in combinations, usually with *cweþan*. Variations of "Þa ongan he eft giddian 7 þus singende cwæð" are legion (9.10, 9.29, 33.20, 39.16, 46.2, 48.22, 51.28, 60.27, 64.24, 71.4, 73.22, 94.26, for example), only rarely is the *cweþan* omitted, as in "Ða ongan se Wisdom singan 7 giddode þus" (21.1) or "Ða ongan se Wisdom gliowian 7 geoddode þus" (26.22). This locution is used also by Byrhtferth, who writes of the prophet Isaiah, "Fægere þis hiw geglengde Isaias se witega, þa he þus giddiende cwæð" (Crawford, 176) or of Sedulius, "Swa se wynsuma Sedulius iu gefyrn giddode, þus cweðende" (178); it might be taken to suggest that poetry was neither sung nor spoken, but uttered in a style that combined both actions. This was the suggestion of L. F. Anderson, who based his hypothetical conclusion on the recurrence of the poetic formula *singan and secgan*, as in *Christ* 665, for example, or *Widsith* 54: "The frequent use of this formula indicates that the distinct communication of the subject-matter was of greater importance than the merely musical element and that the recitation of the *scop* was something intermediate between 'singing' and 'saying,' something similar perhaps to chanting or recitative" (39). One should be wary of citing the Boethius locutions as additional evidence in support of Anderson's theory, however, because an analogous set of locutions is used in the same work for ordinary discourse as distinct from poetry: a common introduction to prose following poetry is "Ða se Wisdom ða ðis leoð asungen hæfde, þa ongan he eft spellian 7 þus cwæð" (as in 34.14, 47.3, 58.4, 61.1, 65.1, 70.1, 82.18, for example). "Ongan he eft giddian 7 þus cwæð" seems to be just as formulaic as "ongan he eft spellian 7 þus cwæð"; since *spellian* clearly does not refer to poetic activity (though note the relaxation of this distinction in the Metrical Proem, 4 "ðæt he ðiossum leodum leoð spellode"), one should not jump to conclusions about the frequent combination of *giddian* (which does refer to poetic activity in this text) and *cweþan*. Nonetheless, the poetic *singan and secgan* formula demands attention, as do the combinations of verbs for poetry and speech elsewhere.

There are only two references to the technique of poetic performance, one of them dubious. If Bede's statement in his *De re metrica* ("Videtur autem rhythmus metris esse consimilis qui est verborum modulata composito non metrica ratione sed numero syllabarum ad judicium aurium examinata, ut sunt carmina vulgarium poetarum," VII, 242) refers to English poetry, we have his testimony that the oral poetry was rhythmical. Apart from this, we have only the biased canon 12 of the Council of Clofeshoh in 747, which lays down that priests should not babble in church like secular poets lest, with tragic noise, they mar and confuse the composition and division of the sacred words ("Ut presbyteri saecularium poetarum modo in ecclesia non garriant, ne tragico sono sacrorum verborum compositionem ac distinctionem corrumpant vel confundant"), which seems to imply that the Anglo-Saxon oral poet tended to run his words together in an excited declamation. Neither of these two texts reveals much, though if the poet were declaiming in an inspired manner with the intention of in turn inspiring his audience, his delivery might well have taken the form of a rhythmical chant.

As I have shown, there is no reason to connect the scop with a lyre or any other instrument, at least before the ninth century; like the Scandinavian skald, the scop was a figure distinct from the entertaining harper. It is likely that the scop performed his poetry on ceremonial occasions, as well as in the context of battle; certainly in the latter situation it is extremely unlikely that he carried a lyre with him. The scop was not the only performer of poetry, of course, and in the most convincing depictions of poetry in the community, such as the scenes outside Heorot in *Beowulf*, it is unlikely too that the lyre accompanied the performances. A heightened chant or recitative accordingly seems to have been the most satisfactory mode for the performance of poetry, although it is satisfactory only because it does not contradict the slender evidence available. Recently, however, arguing from an analysis of metrical profiles, Thomas Cable has suggested that Old English poetry was performed without instrumental accompaniment on a melodic base (Cable: 1974; see further Cable: 1975). In the final chapter of his provocative book *The Meter and Melody of "Beowulf,"* Cable writes:

> I shall argue that neither stress nor quantity alone could make the distinctions necessary in Old English poetry—that the main correlate of metrical ictus was relative pitch, and not simply the pitch of ordinary discourse, but a heightened and stylized pattern. . . . I shall suggest that the metrical basis of Old English poetry was the melodic formula, a contour of pitch drawn from a set of five contours out of a possible set of eight, to which words were fitted according to strict rules. [95 f.; cf. Gough]

This theory, too, could explain the tendency of Anglo-Saxons to refer to the production of poetry in combinations of verbs denoting singing and speaking.

What, then, are we to make of the theories of Old English poetic metre (see, for example, Pope; Creed: 1966a) that assume an instrumental accompaniment? Clearly, they are theories, just as Cable's conclusion is a theory. The examination of the semantic evidence in this chapter has suggested that the scop did not play a lyre, although the professional entertainers, the gleomen, may have done so on occasion. There were harpers in Anglo-Saxon England, as there were in the Scandinavian countries, but they were distinct from scop and skald and did not produce poetry. They may simply have provided instrumental music, or they may have sung songs to their (or someone else's) lyre accompaniment. The assumption of instrumental accompaniment for the extant texts is accordingly reasonable if we are clear that they are the texts of songs; in the case of *The Wife's Lament* or *Wulf and Eadwacer*, for example, this is possible. But I myself do not believe that *Beowulf* or *Andreas* or any of the other long narratives were performed with instrumental accompaniment, although of course I cannot prove this suspicion. These texts must be viewed as extensions of the oral tradition, employing the same metre and diction as the oral poetry perhaps, but produced within a cultural milieu that was open to classical and Christian influences and the revolutionary influence of writing. There is no firm reason to believe that the early Germanic people ever sang epics to the accompaniment of a lyre, and there is certainly no evidence that the Anglo-Saxons did so. The extant texts are largely monastic compositions or the dictated compositions of poets like Cædmon; nowhere in the depiction of his process of composition does Cynewulf mention a lyre, and as far as we can tell from Bede's description, Cædmon never touched a lyre. The onus would seem to rest on those who assume lyre accompaniment apparently for all the extant Old English poetic texts to prove their case; all the evidence I have considered here would seem to suggest that this is unlikely.

10

Conclusion

The Anglo-Saxon oral poet is generally conceived of as a harper who enter-
tained the guests in his lord's hall, a scop who could also be called a gleoman.
The evidence examined in the preceding pages tends to contradict this view.
Consider the references to the harp or lyre.

We first read of the instrument in Sidonius Apollinaris, who complains of
the distracting Burgundian strumming and testifies to Theodoric's fondness
for the entertainment of stringed music during dinner. Cassiodorus preserves
Clovis's request for a harper, and Procopius mentions a similar request from
Gelimer: the Vandal king wishes to accompany a song he had composed lamenting his misfortunes. Jordanes and Venantius Fortunatus write of the use of
a harp to accompany recitals of the glorious deeds of the ancestors. From England itself we have Bede's account of the harp passing from hand to hand at a
drinking party, Cuthbert's letter to Lul asking him to send him a harper, and
two proscriptions of harpers at the Council on English Affairs in Rome in 679
and the Council at Clofeshoh in 747. Alcuin's letter to Hygbald urges a preference for readers over harpers in the monastic refectory. The contemporary
poem describing the coronation feast of Athelstan notes the presence of the
harp, and two late legends concerning Alfred and Olaf Cuaran imply that itinerant professional harpers who provided mealtime entertainment were not
uncommon. In the tenth century, Dunstan exhibits skill with a harp, and later
Wulfstan associates harps and pipes with the various entertainments of the beer-
hall, an impression confirmed by the twelfth-century *Vitae Duorum Offarum*'s
account of a feast at Offa's court. In *Beowulf* a harp is played in Heorot, and
Widsith at least once performs to the accompaniment of a harp. In addition to
these references to specific practices, there is the traditional association of the

harp with joy, seen also in the poetic compounds *gleobeam* and *gomenwudu* for harp; the passages in *The Gifts of Men*, *The Fortunes of Men*, and *Christ* that mention a harp contribute little to this body of information.

The evidence of Jordanes and Venantius might be taken to reinforce that of *Widsith*, that the harp accompanied accounts of the heroic deeds of contemporary and historical figures. *Widsith*, however, is not explicit on this point, and Jordanes (whose credibility as a firsthand informant is in doubt) and Venantius both wrote in the sixth century, at least two generations after the main migration of the Anglo-Saxons across the Channel. Apart from these three sources of information, the overwhelming impression created by the references to the harp is that it was used for entertainment; individuals like Gelimer or Dunstan might amuse themselves with the instrument, and Cuthbert's motives are obscure, but in general the harp appears in the hands of a public performer whose function is to entertain his audience. These performances occasionally elicit a fee (Olaf, *Widsith*, *The Fortunes of Men*), and most frequently they provide entertainment during a meal or feast, whether secular (Cædmon's friends, Athelstan's coronation, Alfred and Olaf, Wulfstan) or monastic (council at Clofeshoh, Alcuin). One is left to conclude that in general the harp was used for entertainment especially at meals or feasts by individuals who were often paid for their performances. Indeed, the harper is on occasion found in the company of professional troupes of itinerant dramatic entertainers, the mimi, scurrae, histriones, and joculatores. This connection probably explains the semantic association of the glosses involving *gleo*, and indicates that the gleoman was just such an entertainer.

Harpers might have been pure instrumentalists, but it is clear at least from Jordanes, Venantius, and *Widsith* that the music could be accompanied by a verbal delivery. The only clear extant indication of the character of such a performance unfortunately occurs in a twelfth-century legend of the tenth century: William of Malmesbury has Olaf disguised as a minstrel singing and touching the strings only now and then ("interdum"). It may well be that poetry could have been recited and punctuated from time to time by a chord or a flourish on the harp produced by the performer or a companion; I am inclined, however, to view accompanied performances as songs. The harper, like the Yugoslavian guslar, might have produced narratives (cantilenae, Heldenlieder), or, like Gelimer or Hrothgar (if he is indeed the harper in *Beowulf* 2105 ff.), he might have produced lyrical songs; either way he is a figure distinct from other singers in the community, and distinct too from the poets.

The Greek and Latin writers testify to the existence of choral singing: Tacitus and Ammianus mention the nonverbal baritus sung by the Germans on entry into battle, and Tacitus mentions warriors singing in their camps at night. Sidonius's reference to a Frankish wedding song clearly implies that it is choral, and Gregory's description of a Lombardic sacrifice includes reference to choral singing. In the seventh century, Wilfrid's companions sing a rowing song in chorus, though they substitute a psalm for the traditional text. Four centuries later another group of sailors take to song: although Cnut is credited with composing his song outside Ely, he asks his companions to sing with him ("secum canere"). They may lay down a traditional refrain on which the king improvises, or they may take up the song from him as he utters it; the song itself passes into tradition, however, and in later times is still sung publicly in chorus ("in choris publice cantantur"). Alfric counsels priests not to participate in the secular singing at funerals. Apart from these explicit references, there is the evidence afforded by the compounds of *leop*, which seem to suggest that songs accompanied the rites de passage such as marriage and death, as well as journeying and other climactic occasions like victory in battle. It is evident that there existed a tradition of memorised songs that were performed in chorus on ceremonial occasions, or as work songs.

I have suggested that this tradition of song was probably distinct from the tradition of poetry. Poetry might have featured on the same ceremonial occasions that called for the production of song, but the poet seems not to have provided the incidental entertainment purveyed by the harper. Although poet and harper might both have been prominent figures, especially in an aristocratic court, they were nevertheless distinct figures. The lists of earthly talents contained in *The Gifts of Men* and *Christ*, for example, separate poets and harpers, and the poem on Athelstan's coronation feast has poet and harper contending with one another ("Ille strepit cithara, decertat plausibus iste"). While the scop seems to have enjoyed some established relationship with chief ("Hropgares scop") or tribe ("Heodeninga scop"), the harper was apparently not an official functionary, and may indeed have been an itinerant; the harper, on the other hand, seems to have been a professional, expecting a reward for his every performance, whereas poets might have earned a reward for a performance but could not always expect to do so. The glosses for *scop* and its occurrence in the extant texts suggest a serious, respected function for the poet, whereas the harper and gleoman are often bracketed with scurrilous professional entertainers. Moreover, a common ambit of poetry, especially that associated with the scop, is the battlefield, where one of the poet's primary functions is incitement (note the context of *Maxims I*, 127; the additions of the Orosius translator concerning the scop; and the actions of the South Saxon *magus* in Eddius, if he is indeed a scop); the harper appears most frequently at meals or feasts, where his function is entertainment, not incitement.

The general character of the poetic tradition was eulogistic; poetry dealt with people living and dead. In content the eulogy would tend to include a location of the subject in a genealogical sequence; an assessment of his moral and physical attributes; and a catalogue of his major achievements, often alluded to elliptically rather than narrated coherently or explicitly. Examples of such performances are the poems produced at the funerals of Attila and Beowulf, or the poems of the *Anglo-Saxon Chronicle* and *The Battle of Brunanburh* in particular; Cædmon's hymn offers an example of a eulogy in praise of God, whether it derives from a Christian or a secular tradition. These eulogies may have been ritual in origin; this would seem to be indicated by the association of *leop* with ritual. The eulogy offers a definition of the subject; in a sense, it *is* the subject. A recitation of the eulogies of the ancestors might ensure their sympathetic attention to the affairs of the living: hence, perhaps, the recitation of the praises of the ancestors in the context of battle, as in Ammianus Marcellinus and, vestigially, in *Maldon*. Eulogies dealt not only with the past, they were very much concerned with the present, one of the main functions of eulogies treating the figures of the past being to conjure their influence over the affairs of the present. In the course of his life a man might compose a eulogy about himself or might have eulogies composed about him by others (an honour accorded to Beowulf by a Danish retainer); these might become attached to him and become his in life and subsequently in death. The recitation of a poem about oneself or about a living contemporary would be similar in effect to that of a poem about one's ancestors, since all such poems constitute a continuous and ongoing tradition that is ritual in effect whether the subject is living or dead. It is likely that autobiographical eulogies as well as eulogies of the ancestors featured in the beot or gylp, just as autobiographical poems, like those in honour of the ancestors, were probably uttered individually on the battlefield: vestigially again, an autobiographical eulogy appears in *Maldon* and *Finnsburh*, and such poems are probably the martial utterances mentioned by Tacitus (*Ann.* IV, 47; Hist. II, 22) and Ammianus. It is possible that women participated in this eulogistic tradition; their ululations and exhortations on the battlefield (Tacitus, *Germ.* 8 and *Hist.* IV, 18) or at funerals (*Beowulf*) may have been poetic.

While everyone participated in this tradition of ritual eulogy, the scop merited a special prominence. An individual could communicate with his ancestors through his recitation of their eulogies, thereby deriving benefit for himself or his kin. The scop uttered eulogies in praise of the chief or king and his ancestors, and in so doing ensured the sympathetic attention of the dynasty to the concerns of the present ruler. Since that ruler was sacral, in whose well-being rested the well-being of the people (in Alcuin's words, "regis bonitas totius est gentis prosperitas, uictoria exercituum, aeris temperies, terre habundantia, filiorum benedictio, sanitas plebis"), the scop was in effect establishing the well-being of the people through his eulogies of the ruler: he was the king's poet as well as the tribal poet. Through a line of Wodan-descended kings, he linked the people to Wodan. Such a function would accord with the status of the scop evident in all the extant references to him. He is associated with a king in *Beowulf* and in *Deor*; he is associated with a tribal unit in *Deor* and with people in general in *Maxims I*. Eulogies in praise of ancestors of rulers may be alluded to in Tacitus, and are mentioned in the anonymous life of Saint Athelbert ("Erant carmina de regis eiusdem regia prosapia"); eulogies are uttered in praise of rulers at their funerals in the case of Attila and Beowulf (cf. the *Chronicle* poems on the deaths of Edgar in 975, Alfred in 1036, and Edward in 1065); and eulogies are uttered in praise of living rulers on ceremonial occasions or occasions of great importance (such as victory in battle) in Priscus's account of the evening spent with Attila, in the Latin poem describing Athelstan's coronation feast (cf. the *Chronicle* poem on the coronation of Edgar in 973), and as evidenced by *The Battle of Brunanburh*.

The scop acted as chronicler and historian, and also as mediator between ruler and ruled, between the living and the dead, between gods and men. The effect of his poetry was often to incite his audience to high emotion, particularly martial resolve. This lends greater credibility to the belief that the "boasting" of warriors before (and during) battle was at least in part poetic. Priscus recalls the effect of the eulogies concerning Attila's "victories and virtues in war" ("eius victorias et bellicas virtutes"): some of the audience "took delight in the verses, some, reminded of wars, were excited in their souls, and others, whose bodies were weakened by time and whose spirits were compelled to rest, gave way to tears." The translator of Orosius, departing from his Latin text, blames poets for inciting the Greeks to resist the Persians ("On þæm mon mæg sweotole oncnawan hu micelne willan hie to ðæm gewinne hæfdon swa heora scopas on heora leoðum giddiende sindon, 7 on heora leasspellengum"). Bede ascribes the same effect of exhortation to the poetry of Cædmon.

One might also argue for a separation of the performance of Anglo-Saxon poetry from harp accompaniment by considering the physical details of certain performances. It is unlikely, for example, that warriors carried harps into battle, or that they plucked them while galloping on horseback. In a lord's hall the poet may have performed with decorum or solemnity: in Priscus the two poets offer their contributions at the start of the evening, and they are followed by buffoons without being party to the buffoonery. If one may use this passage as an analogue, perhaps the awkward clause introducing the Finn episode in *Beowulf* ("ðonne healgamen Hroþgares scop æfter medobence mænan scolde be Finnes eaferum") means that the scop had the official function of performing first at a feast, thereby initiating the entertainment that followed his ceremonial performance. *Beowulf* also testifies to the audibility and clarity of the scop's voice in performance. Away from the hall, there is evidence that the scop was more uninhibited: the recitation of poetry is at times associated with vigorous physical movements. Tacitus says of the Thracians in battle that they customarily caper about with songs (poems?) and dances ("more gentis cum carminibus et tripudiis persultabant"); the warriors at the funerals of Attila and Beowulf utter eulogies while galloping on horseback in a circle (cf. the Lombardic sacrificial song in Gregory's *Dialogues*); the Danish retainer in *Beowulf* also produces his poem on horseback; the magus in Eddius and the warriors in *Maldon* and *Finnsburh* are involved in battle or calling out above the din of battle. If poetry was produced on occasions such as these, often at moments of high emotion, there is reason for the *Beowulf* poet's reference to the clear voice of the scop. It is no doubt from such a tradition of declaiming that the Council of Clofeshoh wishes to discourage its clergy when it urges them not to babble in church in the style of secular poets ("ut presbyteri sæcularium poetarum modo in ecclesia non garriant") but to chant in a simple and modest voice ("simplici voce et modesta").

However much he might dominate, the scop was not the only poet in the community; everyone participated in the tradition of eulogy. Little boys like Alfred learnt the traditional poems and in turn passed them on to their children; warriors praised themselves or their ancestors in battle; retainers could praise the heroic exploits of colleagues or visitors like Beowulf. Nor was eulogy the only form of oral poetry. Gnomic wisdom lore, proverbs, legal phrases, incantations, all on occasion took poetic form; poetry was used for mnemonic purposes. Clearly, popular poems such as (in Christian times) Cædmon's hymn, Bede's Death Song or *The Dream of the Rood* participated in an oral memorial tradition: variations in the extant texts demonstrate this. If further evidence were needed, there are the context of the *Proverb from Winfrid's Time*, the explicit instruction to the reader or hearer in *The Order of the World*, the Harley scribble, and the statement (in the Old English version) that Cædmon's teachers transcribed his narrative compositions and learnt them. Some of the noneulogistic forms of poetry were introduced as a result of the conversion to Christianity; nonetheless, they too could come to participate in an oral memorial tradition such as that which carried some legal formulae and pagan charms.

There is evidence that popular forms of poetry and song persisted throughout the Anglo-Saxon period: incantations, secular songs, and licentious entertainments are consistently proscribed in penitentials, councils, and ecclesiastical correspondence. After the conversion, there is an initial movement towards assimilation and accommodation, but ecclesiastics in general (at least those who committed their opinions to writing) seem to settle into an opposition to secular songs and poems or the occasions that produce them. Accommodation can perhaps be seen in the use of a psalm as the text of a rowing song (in Eddius), or in Aldhelm's performance on the bridge in Malmesbury; opposition can be seen in Bede's expressed aversion to non-Christian poets, Alfric's admonition to priests not to attend funerals or encourage the songs of the laity there or simply not to be entertainers ("gligmenn"), and Wulfstan's similar statements about priests serving as entertainers. Incantations are often proscribed, in the penitentials of Theodore and pseudo-Bede (which talks in an obscure passage of "chanting diviners": McNeill and Gamer, 198). The eighth-century Dialogue of Egbert excludes as candidates for the priesthood "those who worship idols; those who through soothsayers and diviners and enchanters give themselves over as captives to the devil" (Question XV). Such attitudes may explain the tendency to use *galan* as a predicate for *leoþ* and its compounds, and the sometimes diabolical connotation of *leoþ*. Ecclesiastical opposition may have been offered on the grounds that the secular performances were heathen and hence diabolical, or because they were uninhibited. The traditions, however, seem to have died hard, and the consistency of the pronouncements seems to argue for the persistence of these popular traditions of poetry and song.

The conversion introduced a revolution in literary taste largely among the educated classes. New forms of poetry and song influenced or entered the popular oral traditions, as we have seen. Two traditions in particular may have been radically affected by the introduction of Christianity, those of the narrative singer or poet and of the tribal poet or scop. It is not at all clear that among the Anglo-Saxons a tradition of explicitly narrative song existed prior to the conversion. References in Greek and Latin writings could be to narrative or to eulogy. Although much of the extant Old English poetry is narrative, the earliest unambiguous reference to such productions is in Bede's account of Cædmon. Cædmon listens to scriptural stories and turns them into poetic form. The hymn is eulogistic, but the subsequent compositions are narrative by request. Narrative is embryonically present in eulogy; Cædmon is asked to turn his poetic talent to the production of narratives, and he is able to do so with considerable success. He may have been asked to do this by persons familiar with the precedent of narrative or edifying poetry within the classical tradition. The extant Old English narrative poems may have been produced in the monasteries, inspired perhaps by classical example but drawing on secular (eulogistic) tradition for diction, imagery, and metre. It is difficult to know whether the heroic cast of the eighth-century saints' lives derived from a secular tradition current outside the monasteries or whether both the extant saints' lives and the vernacular heroic poetry drew on a Christian tradition for their primary inspiration.

Similarly, the origin of harp-song among the Germanic peoples is obscure. Although the instrument is probably Germanic, the popular performances produced to its accompaniment may have derived from classical practices disseminated initially through the Gothic peoples. The chronology is also obscure, so that we cannot even be sure whether or not the migrating Anglo-Saxons brought with them to England a tradition of harp-song (whether narrative or lyrical). Nor can one say whether or not a tradition of harp-song was necessarily connected with a tradition of narrative.

The conversion did reintroduce England to the society of Roman Christendom. Musicians and entertainers, whether itinerant or associated with a fixed place of public entertainment, were a feature of that society. Such itinerants appear in England after the conversion; they may have been familiar to the continental forebears of the Anglo-Saxons, or they may have been a new feature of society introduced in the wake of the conversion. So, too, a tradition of narrative song may have been native, or may have been one of the consequences of the conversion. Individual amateur harpers like Dunstan existed in Anglo-Saxon England, as did itinerant professional entertainers, whether local or foreign; there is reason to believe that harpers were welcome in the beer-halls, and may well have been a common feature of court life. By the end of the period a tradition of narrative song clearly existed, passing on into the cantilenae often exploited by William of Malmesbury in the twelfth century as sources of information. If one may believe William and pseudo-Ingulf, such a tradition was already current in the ninth century. Its origin, however, and its exact propagation are obscure, as is its relation to the Old English narratives that survive in manuscript.

The scop was attached to a sacral king, and is most likely to have survived the Anglo-Saxon migration in the company of a ruler descended from a well-established dynasty. One would expect to find the scop, therefore, in Mercia serving the Iclingas, and least expect him among the Saxons. There is no reason at all why this tradition of ceremonial eulogy in praise of a sacral king should not have been carried over from the Continent. It was, however, threatened by the conversion, not because the ecclesiastics proscribed poetry as such, but because of altered attitudes among the nobility. The traditional concept of kingship was embraced by the church, which then displaced the tribal poet as the link between the king and his divine source of power; in the seventh and eighth centuries, too, many of the members of the ruling houses of England espoused a monastic ideal of ascetic isolation that sent them on pilgrimages or into a monastery. A tradition of eulogy propagated by a tribal poet in these conditions was at least likely to lose its ritual connotation, if it survived at all; perhaps the scop himself became an embarrassing court appendage and was constrained to evolve into a mercenary mendicant, thereby facilitating a blurring in distinction between vatic scop and entertaining gleoman. *Beowulf* itself and some of the later glosses might reflect such a merging of the two traditions. On the other hand, the scop was not a paid professional like the gleoman: whether or not he uttered his poetry, he would remain a retainer of his lord: if his poetry was no longer desirable in the new climate of opinion, there is no reason why he would have to take to the road or seek employment elsewhere.

Alfred does not seem to have supported a scop; nor did the party accompanying Saint Athelbert on his fatal journey to Offa seem to have included a scop. Yet the Latin poem on Athelstan could be taken to imply that a scop performed at the king's coronation feast. From the time of Athelstan, eulogistic poems such as one would associate with a scop appear in the *Chronicle*. The scop's fortunes may have waxed once again in the tenth century as a result of the example set by visiting Scandinavian skalds; even if the tradition of the scop did not experience a revival, eulogistic poetry in praise of rulers may have come to be produced once again. Alternatively, the scop may have persisted as a feature of court life throughout the Anglo-Saxon period, now waxing now waning in influence, but when in the ascendant drawing on the native tradition of popular eulogy that probably existed at all times.

It is difficult to establish a precise history on the basis of the evidence available. Oral traditions alter as the ideals of the society alter. The Christian conversion must have had a radical effect on the tradition of eulogy in praise of a sacral ruler, weakening and undermining and supplanting its basis. The scop disappeared from certain courts and may well have disappeared altogether by the ninth century. In the wake of the Viking settlement, skalds visited England and performed at the royal courts; some skalds served English kings like Athelstan and Cnut. Explicit references to a scop from this later period are lacking; if practising scops still survived in Anglo-Saxon courts in 1066, it is unlikely that they would continue to practise their craft after the Conquest. While popular native poetic traditions would have persisted, a foreign literary taste was current in the courts of the Norman aristocrats.

Bibliography

ASPR: *The Anglo-Saxon Poetic Records*, 6 vols. (London and New York: Routledge and Kegan Paul and Columbia University Press):

   I *The Junius Manuscript*, ed. George Philip Krapp (1931).

  II *The Vercelli Book*, ed. George Philip Krapp (1932).

 III *The Exeter Book*, ed. George Philip Krapp and Elliott Van Kirk Dobbie (1936).

 IV *Beowulf and Judith*, ed. Elliott Van Kirk Dobbie (1953–54).

  V *The Paris Psalter and the Meters of Boethius*, ed. George Philip Krapp (1933).

 VI *The Anglo-Saxon Minor Poems*, ed. Elliott Van Kirk Dobbie (1942).

E.E.T.S.: Early English Text Society.

Alberti, Ludwig. 1968. *Ludwig Alberti's Account of the Tribal Life and Customs of the Xhosa in 1807*, trans. William Fehr. Cape Town: Balkema.

Albertson, Clinton, S.J., trans. 1967. *Anglo-Saxon Saints and Heroes*. New York: Fordham Univ. Press.

Alfric. See Thorpe.

Ammianus Marcellinus. See Rolfe.

Anderson, Earl R. 1977. "Passing the Harp in Bede's Story of Caedmon: A Twelfth Century Analogue." *English Language Notes* 15: 1–4.

Anderson, George K. 1966 (1949). *The Literature of the Anglo-Saxons*, Rev. ed. Princeton, N.J.: Princeton Univ. Press.

Anderson, J. G. C., ed. 1938. Cornelius Tacitus, *De Origine et Situ Germanorum*. Oxford: Clarendon Press.

Anderson, L. F. 1903. *The Anglo-Saxon Scop*. Toronto: Univ. of Toronto.

Anderson, W. B., ed. and trans. 1936. *Sidonius: Poems and Letters*. Vol. 1. London and Cambridge, Mass.: Heinemann and Harvard Univ. Press.

Andersson, Theodore M. 1970. "The Displacement of the Heroic Ideal in the Family Sagas." *Speculum* 45: 575–93.

———. 1974. "The Caedmon Fiction in the *Heliand* Preface." *PMLA* 89:278–84.

Asser. See Stevenson; Whitelock: 1955.

Axton, Richard. 1974. *European Drama of the Early Middle Ages*. London: Hutchinson.

Baird, Joseph L. 1970. "Unferth the Þyle." *Medium Ævum* 39:1–12.

Ball, C. J. E. 1971. "*Beowulf* 99–101." *Notes and Queries* 18:163.

Bately, Janet M. 1970. "King Alfred and the Old English Translation of Orosius." *Anglia* 88:433–60.

Baugh, Albert C., and Cable, Thomas. 1978 (1935). *A History of the English Language*. 3d ed. Englewood Cliffs, N.J.: Prentice-Hall.

Bede. See Albertson; Colgrave and Mynors; Miller; Sherley-Price; Webb, J. F.

Ben-Amos, Dan. 1971. "Toward a Definition of Folklore in Context." *Journal of American Folklore* 84:3–15.

——. 1975. "Folklore in African Society." *Research in African Literatures* 6: 165–98.

Benson, L. D. 1966. "The Literary Character of Anglo-Saxon Formulaic Poetry." *PMLA* 81:334–41.

Beowulf. See Donaldson; Klaeber: 1950 (1922); Raffel.

Bessinger, J. B., Jr. 1958. "*Beowulf* and the Harp at Sutton Hoo." *University of Toronto Quarterly* 27:148–68.

——. 1967. "The Sutton Hoo Harp Replica and Old English Musical Verse." In *Old English Poetry: Fifteen Essays*, ed. Robert P. Creed, pp. 3–26. Providence: Brown Univ. Press.

——. 1974. "Homage to Caedmon and Others: A Beowulfian Praise Song." In *Old English Studies in Honour of John C. Pope*, ed. Robert B. Burlin and Edward B. Irving, Jr., pp. 91–106. Toronto: Univ. of Toronto Press.

Bethurum, Dorothy, ed. 1957. *The Homilies of Wulfstan*. Oxford: Oxford Univ. Press.

Biebuyck, Daniel, and Mateene, Kahombo C., eds. and trans. 1969. *The Mwindo Epic*. Berkeley and Los Angeles: Univ. of California Press.

Binchy, D. A. 1970. *Celtic and Anglo-Saxon Kingship*. The O'Donnell Lectures for 1967–68 delivered in the University of Oxford on 23 and 24 May 1968. Oxford: Clarendon Press.

Blair, Peter Hunter. 1976. "From Bede to Alcuin." In *Famulus Christi: Essays in Commemoration of the Thirteenth Centenary of the Birth of the Venerable Bede*, ed. Gerald Bonner. London: SPCK, pp. 239–60.

Blake, N. F. 1962. "Caedmon's Hymn." *Notes and Queries* 207:243–64.

Bloomfield, Morton W. 1970 (1968). "Understanding Old English Poetry." *Annuale Mediaevale* 9:5–25. Reprinted in Bloomfield, *Essays and Explorations: Studies in Ideas, Language, and Literature*, pp. 59–83. Cambridge, Mass.: Harvard Univ. Press.

Boethius. See Sedgefield: 1899.

Bokwe, John Knox. 1914. *Ntsikana: The Story of an African Convert*. Lovedale, South Africa: Lovedale Mission Press.

Bolton, W. F. 1977. "Alcuin and Old English Poetry." *The Yearbook of English Studies* 7: 10–22.

——. 1979 (1978). *Alcuin and "Beowulf": An Eighth-Century View*. London: Edward Arnold.

Bonjour, Adrien. 1957. "*Beowulf* and the Beasts of Battle." *PMLA* 72:563–73.

——. 1962. *Twelve "Beowulf" Papers*. Neuchâtel: Faculté des lettres, Université de Neuchâtel.

Bosworth, J. 1921 (1898). *An Anglo-Saxon Dictionary*, rev. T. N. Toller. Oxford: Oxford Univ. Press.

Bowra, C. M. 1952. *Heroic Poetry*. London: Macmillan.

———. 1962. *Primitive Song*. London: Weidenfeld and Nicolson.

Brodeur, A. G. 1959. *The Art of "Beowulf."* Berkeley and Los Angeles: Univ. of California Press.

Brodzky, Anne, ed. 1973–74. "Stones, Bones and Skin: Ritual and Shamanic Art," *Artscanada*, vol. 30, nos. 184–87.

Brooke, Christopher. 1963. *The Saxon and Norman Kings*. London: Batsford.

Brooke, Stopford A. 1892. *The History of Early English Literature*. Vol. 1. London and New York: Macmillan.

Bruce-Mitford, Rupert, and Bruce-Mitford, Myrtle. 1974 (1970). "The Sutton Hoo Lyre, *Beowulf*, and the Origins of the Frame Harp." *Antiquity* 44:7–13. Reprinted in Rupert Bruce-Mitford, *Aspects of Anglo-Saxon Archaeology: Sutton Hoo and Other Discoveries*, pp. 188–97. New York: Harper and Row.

Byrhtferth. See Crawford.

Cable, Thomas. 1974. *The Meter and Melody of "Beowulf."* Illinois Studies in Language and Literature 64. Urbana: Univ. of Illinois Press.

———. 1975. "Parallels to the Melodic Formulas of *Beowulf*." *Modern Philology* 73:1–14.

Callaway, H., ed. and trans. 1970 (1870). *The Religious System of the amaZulu*. Reprinted Cape Town: Struik.

Campbell, Alistair, ed. 1938. *The Battle of Brunanburh*. London: Heinemann.

———. 1962. "The Old English Epic Style." In *English and Medieval Studies Presented to J. R. R. Tolkien on the Occasion of his Seventieth Birthday*, ed. Norman Davis and C. L. Wrenn, pp. 13–26. London: Allen and Unwin.

———. 1971a. *Skaldic Verse and Anglo-Saxon History*. The Dorothea Coke Memorial Lecture in Northern Studies delivered at University College, London, 17 March 1970. London: University College.

———. 1971b. "The Use in *Beowulf* of Earlier Heroic Verse." In *England Before the Conquest: Studies in Primary Sources Presented to Dorothy Whitelock*, ed. Peter Clemoes and Kathleen Hughes, pp. 283–92. Cambridge: Cambridge Univ. Press.

Campbell, Jackson J. 1966. "Learned Rhetoric in Old English Poetry." *Modern Philology* 63:189–201.

———. 1967. "Knowledge of Rhetorical Figures in Anglo-Saxon England." *Journal of English and Germanic Philology* 66:1–20.

Carter, Hazel. 1974. "Poetry and Society: Aspects of Shona, Old English and Old Norse Literature." *Zambezia* 3:11–25.

Cassiodorus. See Hodgkin.

Chadwick, H. Munro. 1926. *The Heroic Age*. Cambridge: Cambridge Univ. Press.

Chadwick, H. Munro, and Chadwick, N. K. 1932–40. *The Growth of Literature*. 3 vols. Cambridge: Cambridge Univ. Press.

Chambers, E. K. 1903. *The Medieval Stage*. 2 vols. Oxford: Oxford Univ. Press.

Chaney, William A. 1970. *The Cult of Kingship in Anglo-Saxon England: The Transition from Paganism to Christianity*. Berkeley and Los Angeles: Univ. of California Press.

Chase, Colin. 1974. "God's Presence through Grace as the Theme of Cynewulf's *Christ II* and the Relationship of this Theme to *Christ I* and *Christ III*." *Anglo-Saxon England* 3: 87–101.

Cherniss, Michael D. 1970. "*Beowulf*: Oral Presentation and the Criterion of Immediate Rhetorical Effect." *Genre* 3:214–28.

Chickering, Howell D., Jr. 1976. "Some Contexts for Bede's *Death Song*." *PMLA* 91: 91–100.

Clark, John Pepper. 1970. "The Communication Line between Poet and Public." In *The Example of Shakespeare*, pp. 61–75. London: Longman.

Cockayne, Oswald, ed. 1864–66. *Leechdoms, Wortcunning, and Starcraft of Early England.* Rolls Series. 3 vols. London: Longman, Green.

Coffey, Jerome E. 1969. "The Evolution of an Oral Formulaic Tradition in Old and Middle English Alliterative Verse." Ph.D. dissertation, State Univ. of New York at Buffalo.

Colgrave, Bertram, ed. 1927. *The Life of Bishop Wilfrid by Eddius Stephanus.* Cambridge: Macmillan.

————. 1958. "The Earliest Saints' Lives Written in England." *Proceedings of the British Academy* 44:35–60.

Colgrave, Bertram, and Mynors, R. A. B., eds. 1969. *Bede's Ecclesiastical History of the English People.* Oxford: Clarendon Press.

Cook, P. A. W. 1931. "History and Izibongo of the Swazi Chiefs." *Bantu Studies* 5:181–201.

Coote, Mary P. 1977. "Women's Songs in Serbo-Croatian." *Journal of American Folklore* 90:331–38.

Cope, Trevor, ed. 1968. *Izibongo: Zulu Praise Poems.* Oxford: Clarendon Press.

Crawford, S. J., ed. 1929. *Byrhtferth's Manual.* E.E.T.S., vol. 177. Oxford: Oxford Univ. Press.

Creed, R. P. 1958. "*Genesis 1316*." *Modern Language Notes* 73:321–25.

————. 1959. "The Making of an Anglo-Saxon Poem." *ELH* 26:445–54.

————. 1966a. "A New Approach to the Rhythm of *Beowulf*." *PMLA* 81:23–33.

————. 1966b. "'. . . Wél-Hwelć Gecwæþ . . .': The Singer as Architect." *Tennessee Studies in Literature* 11:131–43.

Cross, J. E. 1962. "The Old English Poetic Theme of 'The Gifts of Men.' " *Neophilologus* 46:66–70.

Curschmann, M. 1967. "Oral Poetry in Medieval English, French and German Literature: Some Notes on Recent Research." *Speculum* 42:36–52.

Davidson, Clifford. 1975. "Erotic 'Women's Songs' in Anglo-Saxon England." *Neophilologus* 59:451–62.

Davidson, Hilda R. Ellis. 1950. "The Hill of the Dragon: Anglo-Saxon Burial Mounds in Literature and Archaeology." *Folk-Lore* 61:169–84.

————. 1967. *Pagan Scandinavia.* London: Thames and Hudson.

Davis, Henry, S.J., trans. 1950. *St. Gregory the Great: Pastoral Care.* Ancient Christian Writers, vol. 11. Westminster, Maryland: Newman Press.

Deferrari, Roy J., trans. 1964. *Paulus Orosius: The Seven Books of History against the Pagans.* The Fathers of the Church, vol. 50. Washington, D. C.: Catholic Univ. of America Press.

Derolez, René. 1968 (1961). "Anglo-Saxon Literature: 'Attic' or 'Asiatic'? Old English Poetry and its Latin Background." *English Studies Today* 2d ser., 93–105. Reprinted in *Essential Articles for the Study of Old English Poetry*, ed. Jess B. Bessinger, Jr., and Stanley J. Kahrl, pp. 46–62. Hamden, Conn.: Archon.

De Vries, J. 1956. "Das Königtum bei den Germanen." *Saeculum* 7:289–310.

———. 1963 (1959). *Heroic Song and Heroic Legend*, trans. B. J. Timmer. London: Oxford Univ. Press.

Dhlomo, H. I. E. 1939. "African Poetry and Drama." *The South African Outlook* 69:88–90.

———. 1948. "Zulu Folk Poetry." *Native Teachers' Journal* (Jan. 1948) p. 48.

Diamond, A. S. 1971. *Primitive Law, Past and Present*. London: Methuen.

Donaldson, E. Talbot, trans. 1975 (1966). *Beowulf*. New York: Norton. Reprinted in *Beowulf: The Donaldson Translation, Backgrounds and Sources, Criticism*, ed. Joseph F. Tuso. New York: Norton.

Dorson, Richard M. 1968a. *The British Folklorists: A History*. London: Routledge and Kegan Paul.

———, ed. 1968b. *Peasant Customs and Savage Myths: Selections from the British Folklorists*. 2 vols. London: Routledge and Kegan Paul.

Duggan, Joseph J., ed. 1975. *Oral Literature: Seven Essays*. Edinburgh and London: Scottish Academic Press.

Dumézil, Georges. 1943. *Servius et la Fortune*. Paris: Gallimard.

———. 1973 (1959). *Gods of the Ancient Northmen*, ed. and trans. Einar Haugen. Berkeley: Univ. of California Press.

Dumville, David N. 1972. "Liturgical Drama and Panegyric Responsory from the Eighth Century? A Re-examination of the Origin and Contents of the Ninth-Century Section of the Book of Cerne." *Journal of Theological Studies* 23:375–406.

Dundes, Alan. 1964. "Text, Texture, and Context." *Southern Folklore Quarterly* 28:251–65.

Dunstan. See Stubbs: 1874; Whitelock: 1955.

Eddius. See Albertson; Colgrave: 1927.

Egil. See Jones: 1960; Pálsson and Edwards.

Einarsson, Stefán. 1934. "Old English *Beot* and Old Icelandic *Heitstrenging*." *PMLA* 49:975–93.

———. 1963. "Harp Song Heroic Poetry (Chadwicks) Greek and Germanic Alternate Singing." *Budkavlen* 42:13–28.

Einhard. See Turner.

Eliade, Mercia. 1964 (1957). *Shamanism: Archaic Techniques of Ecstasy*. New York: Pantheon.

Eliason, N. E. 1952. "The 'Improvised Lay' in *Beowulf*." *Philological Quarterly* 31:171–79.

———. 1963. "The *Pyle* and *Scop* in *Beowulf*." *Speculum* 38:267–84.

———. 1966. "Two Old English Scop Poems." *PMLA* 81:185–92.

———. 1969. "*Deor*—A Begging Poem?" In *Medieval Literature and Civilization: Studies in Memory of G. N. Garmonsway*, ed. D. A. Pearsall and R. A. Waldron, pp. 55–61. London: Univ. of London Press.

Elliott, Robert C. 1960. *The Power of Satire*. Princeton, N. J.: Princeton Univ. Press.

Ellis, Hilda Roderick. 1943. *The Road to Hel: A Study of the Conception of the Dead in Old Norse Literature*. Cambridge: Cambridge Univ. Press.

Evans, Patricia Morford. 1957. "Oral Interpretation in Anglo-Saxon England." Ph.D. dissertation, Northwestern Univ.

Finnegan, Ruth. 1970. *Oral Literature in Africa*. Oxford: Clarendon Press.

————. 1977. *Oral Poetry, Its Nature, Significance and Social Context.* Cambridge: Cambridge Univ. Press.

Foley, John Miles. 1977. "The Traditional Oral Audience." *Balkan Studies* 18:145–53.

Foote, P. G., ed., and Quirk, R., trans. 1957. *Gunnlaugs Saga Ormstungu: The Saga of Gunnlaug Serpent-Tongue.* Icelandic Texts. London: Nelson.

Fowler, Roger, ed. 1972. *Wulfstan's Canons of Edgar.* E.E.T.S., vol. 266. London: Oxford Univ. Press.

Frank, Roberta. 1978. *Old Norse Court Poetry: The "Dróttkvætt" Stanza.* Islandica, vol. 42. Ithaca and London: Cornell Univ. Press.

French, W. H. 1945. "*Widsith* and the Scop." *PMLA* 60:623–30.

Fritz, Donald W. 1969. "Caedmon: A Traditional Christian Poet." *Mediaeval Studies* 31: 334–37.

————. 1974. "Caedmon: A Monastic Exegete." *American Benedictine Review* 25:351–63.

Fry, Donald K., ed. 1974. *Finnsburh: Fragment and Episode.* London: Methuen.

————. 1975. "Caedmon as a Formulaic Poet." In Duggan (1975), pp. 41–61.

Garrison, James D. 1976. *Dryden and the Tradition of Panegyric.* Berkeley and Los Angeles: Univ. of California Press.

Garrod, H. W., ed. 1912. *The Oxford Book of Latin Verse.* Oxford: Clarendon Press.

Gidley, C. G. B. 1975. "*Roko:* A Hausa Praise Crier's Account of his Craft." *African Language Studies* 16:93–115.

Girvan, Ritchie. 1951. "The Medieval Poet and his Public." In *English Studies Today,* ed. C. L.Wrenn and G. Bullough, pp. 85–97. London: Oxford Univ. Press.

————. 1971 (1935). *Beowulf and the Seventh Century: Language and Content.* London: Methuen.

Godfrey, John. 1962. *The Church in Anglo-Saxon England.* Cambridge: Cambridge Univ. Press.

————. 1974. "The Emergence of the Village Church in Anglo-Saxon England." In *Anglo-Saxon Settlement and Landscape,* ed. Trevor Rowley, pp. 131–38. British Archaeological Reports, vol. 6. Oxford.

Goody, Jack, ed. 1968. *Literacy in Traditional Societies.* Cambridge: Cambridge Univ. Press.

Gordon, C. D. 1960. *The Age of Attila: Fifth-Century Byzantium and the Barbarians.* Ann Arbor: Univ. of Michigan Press.

Gordon, I. L., ed. 1960. *The Seafarer.* London: Methuen.

————. 1961. "Oral Tradition and the Sagas of Poets." In *Studia Centenalia in honorem memoriae Benedikt S. Þórarinsson,* ed. B. S. Benedikz, pp. 69–76. Reykjavík: Isafold.

Gough, C. E. 1938. "The Cadence in Germanic Alliterative Verse." In *German Studies Presented to Professor H. S. Fiedler,* pp. 217–43. Oxford: Clarendon Press.

Grant, E. W. 1927–29. "The *Izibongo* of the Zulu Chiefs." *Bantu Studies* 3:205–44.

Grattan, J. H. G., and Singer, Charles. 1952. *Anglo-Saxon Magic and Medicine.* London: Oxford Univ. Pres.

Greenfield, Stanley B. 1955. "The Formulaic Expression of the Theme of 'Exile' in Anglo-Saxon Poetry." *Speculum* 30: 200–06.

————. 1965. *A Critical History of Old English Literature.* New York: New York Univ. Press.

Gregory. See Davis; Hecht; Sweet: 1871.

Grosz, Oliver J. 1971. "The Structure of Praise in Old English Poetry." Ph.D. dissertation, Univ. of Rochester.

Guma, S. M. 1967. *The Form, Content and Technique of Traditional Literature in Southern Sotho.* Pretoria: J. L. van Schaik.

Gummere, Francis B. 1930. *Founders of England.* New York: G. E. Stechert.

——. 1970 (1901). *The Beginnings of Poetry.* Reprinted Freeport, N.Y.: Books for Libraries Press.

Gunnlaug. See Foote and Quirk.

Haddan, Arthur West, and Stubbs, William, eds. 1871. *Councils and Ecclesiastical Documents Relating to Great Britain and Ireland.* Oxford: Clarendon Press.

Hamer, Richard. 1970. *A Choice of Anglo-Saxon Verse.* London: Faber.

Hamilton, N. E. S. A., ed. 1870. *Willelmi Malmesbiriensis Monachi Gesta Pontificum Anglorum.* Rolls Series. London: Longman.

Hatto, A. T. 1970. *Shamanism and Epic Poetry in Northern Asia.* London: School of Oriental and African Studies, Univ. of London.

——. 1973. "Germanic and Kirgiz Heroic Poetry: Some Comparisons and Contrasts." In *Deutung und Bedeutung: Studies in German and Comparative Literature Presented to Karl-Werner Maurer,* ed. Brigitte Schludermann, et. al, pp. 19–33. The Hague: Mouton.

Hauck, K. 1954. "Herrschaftszeichen eines Wodanistischen Königtums." *Jahrbuch für fränkische Landesforschung* 14:9–66.

Hecht, Hans, ed. 1965. *Dialoge Gregor des Grossen.* Darmstadt: Wissenschaftliche Buchgesellschaft.

Heimskringla. See Laing.

Hessels, J. H., ed. 1906. *A Late Eighth-Century Latin-Anglo-Saxon Glossary.* Cambridge: Cambridge Univ. Press.

Heusler, Andreas. 1911. "Dichtung." In *Reallexikon der Germanischen Altertumskunde,* ed. Johannes Hoops, vol. 1, pp. 439–62. Strassburg: Karl J. Trübner.

——. 1957 (1923). *Die Altgermanische Dichtung.* 2d. ed. Darmstadt: Hermann Gentner Verlag.

——. 1960 (1905). *Lied und Epos in Germanischer Sagendichtung.* Darmstadt: Wissenschaftliche Buchgesellschaft.

Hodgkin, Thomas, trans. 1886. *The Letters of Cassiodorus.* London: Henry Frowde.

Höfler, O. 1952. *Germanisches Sakralkönigtum I.* Münster.

Hofmann, Dietrich. 1963. "Die Frage des musikalischen Vortrags der altgermanischen Stabreimdichtung in philologischer Sicht." *Zeitschrift für deutsches Altertum* 92:83–121.

Hofmann, Dietrich, and Jammers, Ewald. 1965. "Zur Frage des Vortrags der altgermanischen Stabreimdichtung." *Zeitschrift für deutsches Altertum* 94:185–95.

Hollander, Lee M. 1968 (1945). *The Skalds: A Selection of their Poems with Introduction and Notes.* Ann Arbor: Univ. of Michigan.

Hollowell, Ida Masters. 1976. "Unferð the Pyle in *Beowulf.*" *Studies in Philology* 73:239–65.

Holt, Basil. 1954. *Joseph Williams and the Pioneer Mission to South-Eastern Bantu.* The Lovedale Historical Series, no. 1. Lovedale, South Africa: The Lovedale Press.

Holthausen, F. 1916–17. "Die Leidener Glossen." *Englische Studien* 50:327–40.

Hume, Kathryn. 1974. "The Concept of the Hall in Old English Poetry." *Anglo-Saxon England* 3:63–74.

Huppé, Bernard F. 1959. *Doctrine and Poetry: Augustine's Influence on Old English Poetry.* New York: State University of New York.

Hutchinson, Bertram. 1957. "Some Social Consequences of Nineteenth Century Missionary Activity among the South African Bantu." *Africa* 27:160–75.

Isidore of Seville. See Lindsay: 1911.

Jabbour, Alan. 1968. "The Memorial Transmission of Old English Poetry: A Study of the Extant Parallel Texts." Ph.D. dissertation, Duke Univ.

———. 1969. "Memorial Transmission in Old English Poetry." *The Chaucer Review* 3:174–90.

Jackson, Bruce. 1972. *Wake Up Dead Man: Afro-American Worksongs from Texas Prisons.* Cambridge, Mass.: Harvard Univ. Press.

———. 1974. *"Get your Ass in the Water and Swim Like Me": Narrative Poetry from Black Oral Tradition.* Cambridge, Mass.: Harvard Univ. Press.

Jackson, John, ed. and trans. 1937. *Tacitus: The Annals.* Clifford H. Moore, ed. and trans. *The Histories.* 4 vols. London and Cambridge, Mass.: Heinemann and Harvard Univ. Press.

James, M. R. 1917. "Two Lives of St. Ethelbert, King and Martyr." *English Historical Review* 32:214–44.

Jammers, Ewald. 1964. "Der Vortrag des altgermanischen Stabreimverses in musikwissenschaftlicher Sicht." *Zeitschrift für deutsches Altertum* 93:1–13.

John, Eric. 1974. "Beowulf and the Margins of Literacy." *Bulletin of the John Rylands University Library of Manchester* 56:388–422.

Johnson, Aubrey R. 1962 (1944). *The Cultic Prophet in Ancient Israel.* Cardiff: Univ. of Wales Press.

———. 1979. *The Cultic Prophet and Israel's Psalmody.* Cardiff: Univ. of Wales Press.

Jones, Gwyn. 1952. "Egill Skallagrímsson in England." *Proceedings of the British Academy* 38:127–44.

———, trans. 1960. *Egil's Saga.* Syracuse: Syracuse Univ. Press.

Jónsson, Finnur. 1907–08. "Das Harfenspiel des Nordens in der Alten Zeit." *Sammelbände der internationalen Musikgesellschaft* 9:530–37.

Jordan, A. C. 1973a. *Tales from Southern Africa.* Berkeley and Los Angeles: Univ. of California Press.

———. 1973b (1957–59). *Towards an African Literature: The Emergence of Literary Form in Xhosa.* Reprinted Berkeley and Los Angeles: Univ. of California Press.

Jordanes. See Mierow.

Kaske, R. E. 1959. "The Sigemund-Heremod and Hama-Hygelac Passages in *Beowulf.*" *PMLA* 74:489–94.

Kellogg, Robert L. 1965. "The South Germanic Oral Tradition." In *Franciplegius: Medieval and Linguistic Studies in Honor of Francis Peabody Magoun, Jr.*, ed. Jess B. Bessinger, Jr. and Robert P. Creed, pp. 66–74. New York: New York Univ. Press.

Kelly, Mary Quella. 1969. "An Approach to an Old English Poetics." Ph.D. dissertation, Univ. of Tennessee.

Keppel-Jones, Arthur, ed. 1960. *Philipps, 1820 Settler.* Pietermaritzburg: Shuter and Shooter

Ker, N. R. 1957. *Catalogue of Manuscripts Containing Anglo-Saxon.* Oxford: Clarendon Press.

Kesteloot, Lylian. 1966. "The West African Epics." *Présence Africaine* 30:197–202.

Kiparsky, Paul. 1976. "Oral Poetry: Some Linguistic and Typological Considerations." In *Oral Literature and the Formula,* ed. Benjamin A. Stolz and Richard S. Shannon, pp. 73–106. Ann Arbor: Center for the Coördination of Ancient and Modern Studies, Univ. of Michigan.

Kirby, Percival R. 1937. "The Musical Practices of the Native Races of South Africa." In Schapera (1937), pp. 271–89.

Klaeber, Fr. 1927. "Attila's and Beowulf's Funeral." *PMLA* 42:255–67.

———, ed. 1950 (1922). *Beowulf and The Fight at Finnsburg.* 3d ed. Boston: D. C. Heath.

Kohler, M. 1941. *The Izangoma Diviners,* ed. and trans. N. J. van Warmelo. Ethnological Publications, no. 9. Pretoria: Dept. of Native Affairs.

Kunene, Daniel P. 1967. "A Historical Study." In Daniel P. Kunene and Randal A. Kirsch, *The Beginning of South African Vernacular Literature.* Los Angeles: African Studies Association.

———. 1971. *Heroic Poetry of the Basotho.* Oxford: Clarendon Press.

Kuse, Wandile F. 1973. "The Traditional Praise Poetry of Xhosa: Iziduko and Izibongo." M.A. thesis, Univ. of Wisconsin.

Lactantius. See Garrod.

Laing, Samuel, trans. 1961 (1930). Snorri Sturluson, *Heimskringla Part Two: Sagas of the Norse Kings,* rev. Peter Foote. London: Dent.

Lattimore, Richmond, trans. 1947. *The Odes of Pindar.* Chicago: Univ. of Chicago Press.

Laydevant, Father F. 1933. "The Praises of the Divining Bones among the Basotho." *Bantu Studies* 7:341–73.

Lester, G. A. 1974. "The Caedmon Story and its Analogues." *Neophilologus* 58:225–37.

Lestrade, G. P. 1935. "Bantu Praise-Poems." *The Critic* 4:1–10.

———. 1937. "Traditional Literature." In Schapera (1937), pp. 291–308.

Liebermann, F., ed. 1960 (1903–16). *Die Gesetze der Angelsächsen.* 3 vols. Reprinted Aalen: Scientia.

Life of Ceolfrith. See Albertson.

Liggins, Elizabeth M. 1970. "The Authorship of the Old English *Orosius.*" *Anglia* 88:289–322.

Lindsay, W. M., ed. 1911. *Isidori Hispalensis Episcopi Etymologiarum sive Originum.* 2 vols. Oxford: Clarendon Press.

———. 1921. *The Corpus Glossary.* Cambridge: Cambridge Univ. Press.

Lönnroth, Lars. 1971. "Hjálmar's Death-song and the Delivery of Eddic Poetry." *Speculum* 46:1–20.

Lord, Albert Bates, ed. and trans. 1954. *Serbocroatian Heroic Songs,* collected by Milman Parry. Cambridge, Mass. and Belgrade: Harvard Univ. Press and The Serbian Academy of Sciences.

———. 1962. "Homer and Other Epic Poetry." In *A Companion to Homer,* ed. A. J. B. Wace and F. H. Stubbings, pp. 179–214. London: Macmillan.

——. 1965 (1960). *The Singer of Tales*. Reprinted New York: Atheneum.

——. 1975 (1974). "Perspectives on Recent Work on Oral Literature." *Forum for Modern Language Studies* 10:187–210. Reprinted in Duggan (1975), pp. 1–24.

McAllister, P. A. 1979. "The Rituals of Labour Migration among the Gcaleka." M.A. thesis, Rhodes Univ.

McNeill, John T., and Gamer, Helena M., eds. 1938. *Medieval Handbooks of Penance*. New York: Columbia Univ. Press.

Mafeje, Archie. 1963. "A Chief Visits Town." *Journal of Local Administration Overseas* 2: 88–99.

——. 1967. "The Role of the Bard in a Contemporary African Community." *Journal of African Languages* 6:193–223.

Magoun, F. P., Jr. 1953. "The Oral-Formulaic Character of Anglo-Saxon Narrative Poetry." *Speculum* 28:446–67.

——. 1955. "Bede's Story of Cædman: The Case History of an Anglo-Saxon Oral Singer." *Speculum* 30:49–63.

Malone, Kemp. 1961. "Cædmon and English Poetry." *Modern Language Notes* 76:193–95.

——, ed. 1962 (1936). *Widsith*. 2d ed. London: Methuen.

——. 1963 (1962). "Two English *Frauenlieder.*" *Comparative Literature* 14:106–17. Reprinted in *Studies in Old English Literature in Honor of Arthur G. Brodeur*, ed. S. B. Greenfield, pp. 106–17. Eugene: Univ. of Oregon Press.

——. 1967 (1948). "The Old English Period (to 1100)." In *A Literary History of England*, ed. Albert C. Baugh. 2d ed. London: Routledge and Kegan Paul.

——. 1971. "A Reading of *Beowulf* 3169–3182." In *Medieval Literature and Folklore Studies: Essays in Honor of Francis Lee Utley*, ed. Jerome Mandel and Bruce A. Rosenberg, pp. 35–38. New Brunswick, N. J.: Rutgers Univ. Press.

Marshall, Mary H. 1950. "Theatre in the Middle Ages: Evidence from Dictionaries and Glosses." *Symposium* 4:1–39, 366–89.

Maryon, Herbert. 1947. "The Sutton Hoo Helmet." *Antiquity* 21:137–44.

Matonis, A. T. E. 1978. "Traditions of Panegyric in Welsh Poetry: The Heroic and the Chivalric." *Speculum* 53:667–87.

Mattingly, H., trans. 1970 (1948). *Tacitus: The Agricola and the Germania*, rev. S. A. Handford. Harmondsworth: Penguin.

Mayr-Harting, Henry. 1972. *The Coming of Christianity to Anglo-Saxon England*. London: Batsford.

Meyvaert, Paul. 1971. "Bede's Text of the *Libellus Responsionum* of Gregory the Great to Augustine of Canterbury." In *England before the Conquest: Studies in Primary Sources Presented to Dorothy Whitelock*, ed. Peter Clemoes and Kathleen Hughes, pp. 15–33. Cambridge: Cambridge Univ. Press.

Mierow, Charles Christopher, trans. 1915. *The Gothic History of Jordanes*. 2d ed. Cambridge, Mass. and New York: Barnes and Noble.

Migne, J.-P., ed. 1844–80. *Patrologiae cursus completus*. Patrologia Latina. Paris.

Miletich, John S. "The Quest for the 'Formula': A Comparative Reappraisal." *Modern Philology* 74:111–23.

Miller, Thomas, ed. 1890. *The Old English Version of Bede's Ecclesiastical History of the English People*. 2 vols. E.E.T.S., vols. 95 and 96. London: Trübner.

Moore, Clifford H., ed. and trans. 1937. *Tacitus: The Histories.* John Jackson, ed. and trans. *The Annals.* 4 vols. London and Cambridge, Mass.: Heinemann and Harvard Univ. Press.

Morris, John. 1973. *The Age of Arthur: A History of the British Isles from 350/650.* London: Weidenfeld and Nicolson.

Mustanoja, Tauno F. 1959. "The Presentation of Ancient Germanic Poetry: Looking for Parallels." *Neuphilologische Mitteilungen* 60:1–11.

———. 1967. "The Unnamed Woman's Song of Mourning over Beowulf and the Tradition of Ritual Lamentation." *Neuphilologische Mitteilungen* 68:1–27.

Myres, J. N. L. 1970. "The Angles, the Saxons, and the Jutes." *Proceedings of the British Academy* 56:145–74.

Mzolo, Douglas. 1978. "Zulu Clan Praises." In *Social System and Tradition in Southern Africa: Essays in Honour of Eileen Krige,* ed. John Argyle and Eleanor Preston-Whyte, pp. 206–21. Cape Town: Oxford Univ. Press.

Nagy, Gregory. 1976. "Iambos: Typologies of Invective and Praise." *Arethusa* 9:191–205.

Napier, A. S., ed. 1883. *Wulfstan: Sammlung der ihm zugeschriebenen Homilien nebst Untersuchungen über ihre Echtheit.* Berlin.

Naumann, Hans. 1931. *Frühgermanisches Dichterbuch.* Berlin and Leipzig: Walter de Gruyter.

Ndabanda. 1966. "Die Bantoe Pryslied." *Bantu* 13:196–98.

Nicoll, Allardyce. 1963 (1931). *Masks, Mimes and Miracles: Studies in the Popular Theatre.* Reprinted New York: Cooper Square Publishers.

Norman, Frederick. 1938. "The Germanic Heroic Poet and His Art." In *German Studies Presented to Professor H. G. Fiedler, M. V. O. by Pupils, Colleagues, and Friends on His Seventy-fifth Birthday 28 April 1937,* pp. 293–322. Oxford: Clarendon Press.

———. 1969. "The Early Germanic Background of Old English Verse." In *Medieval Literature and Civilization: Studies in Memory of G. N. Garmonsway,* ed. D. A. Pearsall and R. A. Waldron, pp. 3–27. London: Univ. of London Press.

Ntantala, Phyllis P. 1971. "The Writer and his Social Responsibility: The Xhosa Writer." Paper read at 14th Annual Meeting of the African Studies Association, 3–6 November 1971, Denver, Colo.

Nyembezi, C. L. Sibusiso. 1948. "The Historical Background to the Izibongo of the Zulu Military Age." *African Studies* 7:110–25, 157–74.

———, ed. 1958. *Izibongo zamaKhosi.* Pietermaritzburg: Shuter and Shooter.

Obiechina, E. N. 1967. "Transition from Oral to Literary Tradition." *Présence Africaine* 63:140–61.

Ogilvy, J. D. A. 1963. "*Mimi, Scurrae, Histriones*: Entertainers of the Early Middle Ages." *Speculum* 38:603–19.

Okpewho, Isidore. 1977. "Does the Epic Exist in Africa?: Some Formal Considerations." *Research in African Literatures* 8:171–200.

Oliphant, R. T., ed. 1966. *The Harley Latin-Old English Glossary.* The Hague: Mouton.

Ong, Walter J. 1975. "The Writer's Audience Is Always a Fiction." *PMLA* 90:9–21.

Opland Collection. *The Opland Collection of Xhosa Oral Poetry,* housed in the Center for the

Study of Oral Literature at Harvard Univ. and in the Speech Archives Unit of the Cory Library for Historical Research at Rhodes Univ.

Opland, Jeff. 1969. "On the Necessity for Research into the Bantu Oral Tradition." *Papers in African Languages 1969*, pp. 79–84. Cape Town: School of African Studies, Univ. of Cape Town.

———. 1970. "Two Xhosa Oral Poems." *Papers in African Languages 1970*, pp. 86–98. Cape Town: School of African Studies, Univ. of Cape Town.

———. 1971. "*Scop* and *Imbongi*: Anglo-Saxon and Bantu Oral Poets." *English Studies in Africa* 14:161–78.

———. 1973. "African Phenomena Relevant to a Study of the European Middle Ages: Oral Tradition." *English Studies in Africa* 16:87–90.

———. 1974. "Praise Poems as Historical Sources." In *Beyond the Cape Frontier: Studies in the History of the Transkei and Ciskei*, ed. Christopher Saunders and Robin Derricourt, pp. 1–38. London: Longman.

———. 1975. "*Imbongi Nezibongo*: The Xhosa Tribal Poet and the Contemporary Poetic Tradition." *PMLA* 90:185–208.

———. 1976a. "*Beowulf* on the Poet." *Mediaeval Studies* 38:442–67.

———. 1976b. "Huso and Mqhayi: Notes on the Southslavic and Xhosa Traditions of Oral Poetry." In *Oral Literature and the Formula*, ed. Benjamin A. Stoltz and Richard S. Shannon, pp. 120–24. Ann Arbor: Center for the Coördination of Ancient and Modern Studies, Univ. of Michigan.

———. 1977a. "Two Unpublished Poems by S. E. K. Mqhayi." *Research in African Literatures* 8:27–53.

———. 1977b. "On Anglo-Saxon Poetry and the Comparative Study of Oral Poetic Traditions." *Acta Germanica* 10:49–62.

———. 1980. "From Horseback to Monastic Cell: The Impact on English Literature of the Introduction of Writing." In *Old English Literature in Context: Ten Essays*, ed. J. D. Niles, London: Boydell and Brewer, forthcoming.

Orosius. See Deferrari; Sweet: 1871.

Osborn, Marijane. 1978. "*Reote* and *Ridend* as Musical Terms in *Beowulf*: Another Kind of Harp?" *Neophilologus* 62:442–46.

Padelford, Frederick Morgan. 1899. *Old English Musical Terms*. Bonner Beiträge zur Anglistik, vol. 4. Bonn: P. Hanstein's Verlag.

Pálsson, Hermann, and Edwards, Paul, trans. 1976. *Egil's Saga*. Harmondsworth: Penguin.

Panum, Hortense. n. d. (1915–31). *The Stringed Instruments of the Middle Ages: Their Evolution and Development*, rev. and trans. Jeffrey Pulver. London: William Reeves.

Parkes, M. B. 1972. "The Manuscript of the Leiden Riddle." *Anglo-Saxon England* 1:207–17.

Parry, Adam, ed. 1971. *The Making of Homeric Verse: The Collected Papers of Milman Parry*. Oxford: Clarendon Press.

Pauw, B. A. 1965. "Patterns of Christianization among the Tswana and the Xhosa-speaking Peoples." In *African Systems of Thought*, ed. M. Fortes and G. Dieterlen, pp. 240–53. London: Oxford Univ. Press.

———. 1975. *Christianity and Xhosa Tradition*. Cape Town: Oxford Univ. Press.

Pettersson, Olof. 1953. *Chiefs and Gods: Religious and Social Elements in the South Eastern Bantu Kingship*. Studia Theologica Lundensia, vol. 3. Lund, Sweden.

Pheifer, J. D., ed. 1974. *Old English Glosses in the Épinal-Erfurt Glossary*. Oxford: Clarendon Press.

Pindar. See Lattimore.

Poole, Russell Gilbert. 1975. "Skaldic Poetry in the Sagas: The Origins, Authorship, Genre, and Style of Some Saga *Lausavísur*." Dissertation, Univ. of Toronto.

Pope, J. C. 1966 (1942). *The Rhythm of "Beowulf."* Rev. ed. New Haven: Yale Univ. Press.

Prinz, Otto, and Schneider, Johannes, eds. 1970. *Mittellateinisches Wörterbuch*. Munich: C.H. Beck'sche Verlagsbuchhandlung.

Priscus. See Gordon, C. D.

Raby, F. J. E. 1934. *A History of Secular Latin Poetry in the Middle Ages*. Vol. 1. Oxford: Clarendon Press.

Raffel, Burton, trans. 1963. *Beowulf*. New York: New American Library.

Raw, Barbara C. 1978. *The Art and Background of Old English Poetry*. London: Edward Arnold.

Rensch, Roslyn. 1969. *The Harp: Its History, Technique and Repertoire*. London: Duckworth.

Rich, George W. 1977. "Icelandic *Rímur*." *Journal of American Folklore* 90:496–97.

Riggio, Milla B. 1972. "Genesis and Exodus: Structure and Narrative Style in Medieval Latin and Old English Poetry." Ph.D. dissertation, Harvard Univ.

Robinson, Fred C. 1970. "Lexicography and Literary Criticism: A Caveat." In *Philological Essays in Honour of Herbert Dean Meritt*, ed. James L. Rosier, pp. 99–110. The Hague: Mouton.

———. 1971. "Review of *Continuations and Beginnings: Studies in Old English Literature*, ed. Eric Gerald Stanley." *English Studies* 52:252–55.

Rolfe, John C., ed. and trans. 1935. *Ammianus Marcellinus*. 3 vols. London and Cambridge, Mass.: Heinemann and Harvard Univ. Press.

Rycroft, David. 1960. "Melodic Features in Zulu Eulogistic Recitation." *African Language Studies* 1:60–78.

———. 1962. "Zulu and Xhosa Praise Poetry and Song." *African Music* 3: 79–85.

———. 1976. "Southern Bantu Clan-Praises." *Bulletin of the School of Oriental and African Studies* 39:155–59.

Sachs, Curt. 1940. *The History of Musical Instruments*. New York: Norton.

Schapera, I., ed. 1937. *The Bantu-speaking Tribes of South Africa*. Cape Town: Maskew Miller.

Scheub, Harold. 1971. "Translation of African Oral Narrative-Performances to the Written Word." *Yearbook of Comparative and General Literature* 20:28–36.

———. 1975. *The Xhosa "Ntsomi."* Oxford: Clarendon Press.

Schlauch, Margaret. 1931. "Wīdsīth, Víthförull, and Some Other Analogues." *PMLA* 46:969–87.

———. 1956. *English Medieval Literature and Its Social Foundations*. London: Oxford Univ. Press.

Schrader, Richard J. 1972. "Beowulf's Obsequies and the Roman Epic." *Comparative Literature* 24:237–59.

Sedgefield, Walter John, ed. 1899. *King Alfred's Old English Version of Boethius De Consolatione Philosophiae.* Oxford: Clarendon Press.

———, ed. 1904. *The Battle of Maldon and Short Poems from the Saxon Chronicle.* New York: D. C. Heath.

Sherley-Price, Leo, trans. 1955. *Bede: A History of the English Church and People.* Harmondsworth: Penguin.

Shippey, T. A. 1972. *Old English Verse.* London: Hutchinson.

Short, Douglas D. 1976. "The Old English *Gifts of Men* and the Pedagogic Theory of the *Pastoral Care.*" *English Studies* 57:497–501.

Sidonius. See Anderson, W. B.

Sisam, Kenneth. 1953a. "Anglo-Saxon Royal Genealogies." *Proceedings of the British Academy* 39:287–348.

———. 1953b. *Studies in the History of Old English Literature.* Oxford: Clarendon Press.

Sklar, Elizabeth S. 1975. "*The Battle of Maldon* and the Popular Tradition: Some Rhymed Formulas." *Philological Quarterly* 54:409–18.

Smith, A. H., ed. 1933. *Three Northumbrian Poems.* London: Methuen.

Smith, M. G. 1957. "The Social Functions and Meaning of Hausa Praise-singing." *Africa* 27:26–43.

Snorri. See Laing.

Steger, Hugo. 1961. *David Rex et Propheta.* Nuremberg.

Stevenson, William Henry, ed. 1959 (1904). *Asser's Life of King Alfred.* Oxford: Clarendon Press.

Storms, G. 1974. "The Author of *Beowulf.*" *Neuphilologische Mitteilungen* 75:11–39.

Stubbs, William, ed. 1874. *The Memorials of St. Dunstan.* Rolls Series. London: Eyre and Spottiswoode.

———, ed. 1887–89. *Willelmi Malmesbiriensis Monachi De Gestis Regum Anglorum.* Rolls Series. 2 vols. London: Eyre and Spottiswoode.

Sweet, Henry, ed. 1871. *King Alfred's West-Saxon Version of Gregory's Pastoral Care.* 2 vols. E.E.T.S., vols. 45 and 50. London: Oxford Univ. Press.

———, ed. 1883. *King Alfred's Orosius.* Part I. E.E.T.S., vol. 79. London: Oxford Univ. Press.

———, ed. 1885. *The Oldest English Texts.* E.E.T.S., vol. 83. London: Trübner.

Tacitus. See Anderson, J. G. C.; Jackson, John; Mattingly; Moore.

Taylor, P. B. 1969. "Heroic Ritual in the Old English Maxims." *Neuphilologische Mitteilungen* 70:387–407.

Terry, Patricia, trans. 1969. *Poems of the Vikings.* New York: Bobbs-Merrill.

Theal, George McCall. 1882. *Kaffir Folk-lore; or, A Selection from the Traditional Tales Current among the People Living on the Eastern Border of the Cape Colony with Copious Explanatory Notes.* London: W. Swan Sonnenschein.

Theodore. See McNeill and Gamer.

Thorpe, Benjamin, ed. 1844. *The Homilies of the Anglo-Saxon Church: The First Part Containing the Sermones Catholici or Homilies of Aelfric.* London: Aelfric Society.

Tierney, J. J. 1958–59. "The Celtic Ethnography of Posidonius." *Proceedings of the Royal Irish Academy* 60:189–275.

Turner, Samuel Epes, trans. 1960. *The Life of Charlemagne by Einhard.* Ann Arbor: Univ. of Michigan Press.

Turville-Petre, E. O. G. 1968. *Haraldr the Hard-Ruler and his Poets.* The Dorothea Coke Memorial Lecture in Northern Studies delivered at University College, London, 1 December 1966. London: University College.

Vansina, Jan. 1973 (1961). *Oral Tradition: A Study in Historical Methodology,* trans. H. M. Wright. Harmondsworth: Penguin.

Van Warmelo, N. J., ed. 1938. *History of Matiwane and the amaNgwane Tribe.* Ethnological Publications, vol. 7. Pretoria: Dept. of Native Affairs.

Vilakazi, B.W. 1938. "The Conception and Development of Poetry in Zulu." *Bantu Studies* 12:105–34.

———. 1945. "The Oral and Written Literature in Nguni." Ph.D. dissertation, Univ. of the Witwatersrand.

Vitae Duorum Offarum. See Wright, C. E.

Von See, Klaus. 1964. "Skop und Sklad: Zur Auffassung des Dichters bei den Germanen." *Germanisch-Romanische Monatsschrift* 45, n.s. 14:1–14.

Wagner, H. 1970. "Studies in the Origins of Early Celtic Civilisation II: Irish *fáth*, Welsh *gwawd,* Old Icelandic *óðr* 'poetry' and the Germanic god *Wotan/Óðinn.*" *Zeitschrift für Celtische Philologie* 31:46–58.

Wallace-Hadrill, J. M. 1971. *Early Germanic Kingship in England and on the Continent.* Oxford: Clarendon Press.

Ward, D. 1973. "On the Poets and Poetry of the Indo-Europeans." *Journal of Indo-European Studies* 1:127–44.

Watkins, Calvert. 1963. "Indo-European Metrics and Archaic Irish Verse." *Celtica* 6:194–249.

———. 1970. "Language of Gods and Language of Men: Remarks on Some Indo-European Metalinguistic Traditions." In *Myth and Law among the Indo-Europeans: Studies in Indo-European Comparative Mythology,* ed. Jaan Puhvel, pp. 1–17. Berkeley and Los Angeles: Univ. of California Press.

Watts, Ann Chalmers. 1969. *The Lyre and the Harp: A Comparative Reconsideration of Oral Tradition in Homer and Old English Epic Poetry.* New Haven: Yale Univ. Press.

Webb, C. de B., and Wright, J. B., eds. and trans. 1976. *The James Stuart Archive of Recorded Oral Evidence Relating to the History of the Zulu and Neighbouring Peoples.* Vol. 1. Pietermaritzburg and Durban: Univ. of Natal Press and Killie Campbell Africana Library.

Webb, J. F., trans. 1965. *Lives of the Saints.* Harmondsworth: Penguin.

Welsford, Enid. 1935. *The Fool: His Social and Literary History.* London: Faber.

Werlich, Egon. 1964. "Der Westgermanische Skop: Der Aufbau seiner Dichtung und sein Vortrag." Dissertation (photocopy), Univ. of Münster.

———. 1967. "Der Westgermanische Skop: Der Ursprung des Sängerstandes in semasiologischer und etymologischer Sicht." *Zeitschrift für deutsche Philologie* 86:352–75.

Whallon, William. 1965. "The Idea of God in *Beowulf.*" *PMLA* 80:19–23.

Whitbread, L. 1976. "The Old English Poem *Aldhelm.*" *English Studies* 57:193–97.

Whitelock, Dorothy. 1948. "Anglo-Saxon Poetry and the Historian." *Transactions of the Royal Historical Society*, 4th ser. 31:75–94.

———. 1951. *The Audience of "Beowulf."* Oxford: Clarendon Press.

———, trans. 1955. *English Historical Documents c. 500–1042.* Vol. 1. London: Eyre and Spottiswoode.

———. 1962. "The Old English Bede." *Proceedings of the British Academy* 48: 57–90.

———. 1969. "William of Malmesbury on the Works of King Alfred." In *Medieval Literature and Civilization: Studies in Memory of G. N. Garmonsway*, ed. D. A. Pearsall and R. A. Waldron, pp. 78–93. London: Univ. of London Press.

Whitman, F. H. 1975. "The Meaning of 'Formulaic' in Old English Verse Composition." *Neuphilologische Mitteilungen* 76:529–37.

William of Malmesbury. See Hamilton; Stubbs: 1887–89; Whitelock: 1955.

Williams, J. E. Caerwyn. 1971. "The Court Poet in Medieval Ireland." *Proceedings of the British Academy* 57:85–135.

Willibald. See Albertson.

Wilson, R. M. 1970 (1952). *The Lost Literature of Medieval England.* 2d ed. London: Methuen.

Wissmann, Wilhelm. 1955. *Skop.* Sitzungsberichte der Deutschen Akademie der Wissenschaften zu Berlin: Klasse für Sprachen, Literatur und Kunst Jahrgang 1954 Nr. 2. Berlin: Akademie-Verlag.

Woolley, Leonard. 1937. *Digging Up the Past.* Harmondsworth: Penguin.

Wormald, C. P. 1977. "The Uses of Literacy in Anglo-Saxon England and Its Neighbours." *Transactions of the Royal Historical Society*, 5th ser. 27:95–114.

Wormald, Patrick. 1978. "Bede, Beowulf and the Conversion of the Anglo-Saxon Aristocracy." In *Bede and Anglo-Saxon England*, ed. Robert T. Farrell. *British Archaeological Reports* 46:32–95.

Wrenn, C. L. 1962. "Two Anglo-Saxon Harps." *Comparative Literature* 14:118–28.

———. 1967. *A Study of Old English Literature.* London: Harrap.

Wright, C. E. 1939. *The Cultivation of Saga in Anglo-Saxon England.* Edinburgh and London: Oliver and Boyd.

Wright, T., ed. 1884 (1882). *Anglo-Saxon and Old English Vocabularies*, rev. R. P. Wülcker. London.

Wulfstan. See Bethurum; Fowler; Napier.

Index

Index of Sources